"At a time when more and more family th
accepting the seemingly inevitable instanti
diagnoses and individualistic models of er
Dr. Tomm and his talented, sophisticated .... offer a clear and
compelling alternative (or complementary) perspective. I am heartened
by the authors' invitation to make sense of client, supervisory, and societal conundrums and transformations in terms of the patterns of interaction unfolding between people. When innovators like these produce fresh and challenging work such as this, our field is renewed and enlivened, and our relationships are provided with a template for moving toward patterns of wellness."
—*Douglas Flemons, PhD, LMFT, co-author of* Relational
Suicide Assessment, *Professor of Family Therapy and Clinical Professor of Family Medicine, Nova Southeastern University, USA*

"At last! A social constructionist approach that focuses squarely on interpersonal patterns, never loses sight of larger societal processes, and can measure and track change! In a world that demands accountability, this will help my students integrate the foundations of family therapy with the relational ideals of postmodern practice."
—*Carmen Knudson-Martin, PhD, Professor and Director of the PhD program in Marriage and Family Therapy, Loma Linda University, USA*

"This book is one of the most powerful demonstrations of relational patterns and their significance in our personal lives that I have ever encountered. With passion, focus, logic, and imagination, Karl Tomm and his colleagues demonstrate why it is so important to move beyond the individual in both our everyday understanding and our therapeutic practices. The present volume overcomes the limits of diagnostic categories by offering them as grounds for dialogue. The book is overflowing with good ideas, both inspiring and practical."
—*Kenneth Gergen, President, The Taos Institute, USA*

"This book makes a critical contribution to the related fields of therapy, counselling, and psychological services. We have been poised, waiting for the next big idea, and the IPscope fills this void. This will undoubtedly become a preferred practice approach solidly built on theoretical foundations that provides a clear framework for inquiring, understanding, deconstructing, intervening, and reflecting on patterns of interaction. It should be included in all therapy and counselling training programs."
—*Barbara McKay, Director of the Institute of Family Therapy, London, UK*

"This volume is a welcomed voice in an ever-increasing world of pathologizing discourse. What we frequently define as a destructive, crazy, or 'bad' person is unhinged by the palpable power of IPscope (i.e., the scope of interpersonal patterns). Extending this approach to explore broader issues of conflict and human challenge reminds us how significant our relational engagements are with others—at all levels—from the dyadic to the global; this is a powerful reminder of how important our relational lives are to our wellbeing and the wellbeing of the planet."
—*Sheila McNamee, PhD, Professor of Communication,*
University of New Hampshire, Co-Founder and Vice President,
The Taos Institute, USA

"Here in Europe, I have been hearing rumors about HIPs and PIPs for years. Finally now, here's the book that explains the IPscope model, and helps me to understand why these rumors sounded so unbelievably enthusiastic. The IPscope is a fascinating relational diagnostic system for distinguishing interpersonal patterns. The different chapters in the book tell the story of the IPscope and how it can be applied in therapy, training, supervision, and in many other domains of life. I warmly recommend this book."
—*Peter Rober, PhD, Professor of Marital and Family Therapy,*
Leuven University, Belgium

"Karl Tomm and his colleagues at the Calgary Family Therapy Centre have been steadily building on his influential conceptual framework of Interpersonal Patterns. This book offers 25 years of development in an exciting and accessible form. Richly illustrated with clinical and training material and integrated with current thinking over many areas it will be of enormous value to trainers, researchers and therapists."
—*Peter Stratton, Emeritus Professor of Family Therapy,*
Leeds Family Therapy and Research Centre, UK

PATTERNS IN INTERPERSONAL INTERACTIONS

In this book we present a comprehensive view of a systemic approach to working with families that was initiated by Karl Tomm more than two decades ago at the Calgary Family Therapy Centre in Canada. The contributors of this edited book articulate the IPscope framework as it was originally designed and its evolution over time. We invite you, experienced professionals and new family therapists, to join with us to explore some of the mysteries of human relationships. While the focus of our explorations revolves around clinical mental health problems and initiatives toward solutions, the concepts are applicable in many domains of daily life. They highlight the ways in which we, as persons, invite each other into recurrent patterns of interaction that generate and maintain some stability in our continuously changing relationships. The stabilities arise when our invitations become coupled and can be characterized as mutual, yet they always remain transient. What is of major significance is that these transient relational stabilities can have major positive or negative effects in our lives. Consequently, we could all potentially benefit from greater awareness of the nature of these patterns, how particular patterns arise, and how we might be able to influence them.

Karl Tomm, MD, FRCPC; **Sally St. George**, PhD; **Dan Wulff**, PhD; and **Tom Strong**, PhD, are all affiliated with the University of Calgary and the Calgary Family Therapy Centre in Alberta, Canada.

THE FAMILY THERAPY AND COUNSELING SERIES

Series Editor
Jon Carlson, PsyD, EdD

Adam Zagelbaum and Jon Carlson
Working with Immigrant Families: A Practical Guide for Counselors

Shea M. Dunham, Shannon B. Dermer, and Jon Carlson
Poisonous Parenting: Toxic Relationships Between Parents and Their Adult Children

David K. Carson and Montserrat Casado-Kehoe
Case Studies in Couples Therapy: Theory-Based Approaches

Bret A. Moore
Handbook of Counseling Military Couples

Len Sperry
Family Assessment: Contemporary and Cutting-Edge Strategies, 2nd ed.

Patricia A. Robey, Robert E. Wubbolding, and Jon Carlson
Contemporary Issues in Couples Counseling: A Choice Theory and Reality Therapy Approach

Paul R. Peluso, Richard E. Watts, and Mindy Parsons
Changing Aging, Changing Family Therapy: Practicing With 21st Century Realities

Dennis A. Bagarozzi
Couples in Collusion: Short-Term, Assessment-Based Strategies for Helping Couples Disarm Their Defenses

Katherine M. Helm and Jon Carlson
Love, Intimacy, and the African American Couple

Judith V. Jordan and Jon Carlson
Creating Connection: A Relational-Cultural Approach with Couples

Len Sperry
Behavioral Health: Integrating Individual and Family Interventions in the Treatment of Medical Conditions

Karl Tomm, Sally St. George, Dan Wulff, and Tom Strong
Patterns in Interpersonal Interactions: Inviting Relational Understandings for Therapeutic Change

PATTERNS IN INTERPERSONAL INTERACTIONS

Inviting Relational Understandings
for Therapeutic Change

Edited by
Karl Tomm, Sally St. George,
Dan Wulff, and Tom Strong

NEW YORK AND LONDON

First published 2014
by Routledge
711 Third Avenue, New York, NY 10017

and by Routledge
27 Church Road, Hove, East Sussex BN3 2FA

Routledge is an imprint of the Taylor & Francis Group, an informa business

© 2014 Taylor & Francis

The rights of the editors to be identified as the authors of the editorial material, and of the authors for their individual chapters, have been asserted in accordance with sections 77 and 78 of the Copyright, Designs and Patents Act 1988.

All rights reserved. No part of this book may be reprinted or reproduced or utilized in any form or by any electronic, mechanical, or other means, now known or hereafter invented, including photocopying and recording, or in any information storage or retrieval system, without permission in writing from the publishers.

Trademark notice: Product or corporate names may be trademarks or registered trademarks, and are used only for identification and explanation without intent to infringe.

Library of Congress Cataloging-in-Publication Data

Tomm, Karl.
Patterns in interpersonal interactions : inviting relational understandings for therapeutic change / Karl Tomm, Sally St. George, Dan Wulff, Tom Strong. — 1 Edition.
    pages cm
  Includes bibliographical references and index.
 1. Family psychotherapy. 2. Families. 3. Interpersonal relations. I. Title.
RC488.5.T66 2014
616.89'156—dc23   2013047899

ISBN: 978-0-415-70284-3 (hbk)
ISBN: 978-0-415-70283-6 (pbk)
ISBN: 978-0-203-79525-5 (ebk)

Typeset in Sabon
by Apex CoVantage, LLC

Cover design: "Wheels of Memories" quilt by Marian Lane, based on the traditional "Drunkard's Path" pattern, with additional inspiration from *Quilt Lovers Favorites*, by designers Wendy Hagar and Shirlene Fennema.

Photograph by Ian Ainslie.

In gratitude for the insights of two magnificent teachers:
Gianfranco Cecchin and Michael White.

CONTENTS

List of Figures   xi
List of Contributors   xiii
Series Editor's Foreword   xvii
Foreword   xix
Acknowledgments   xxiii

Introduction: Origins of the PIPs and HIPs Framework   1
KARL TOMM

1. Introducing the IPscope: A Systemic Assessment Tool for Distinguishing Interpersonal Patterns   13
KARL TOMM

2. Conceptualizing Interactional Patterns: Theoretical Threads to Facilitate Recognizing and Responding to IPs   36
TOM STRONG

3. Teaching and Learning Relational Practice   57
SHARI COUTURE AND KARL TOMM

4. A Life History of a PIP: Snapshots in Time   82
TANYA MUDRY, TOM STRONG, AND JEFF CHANG

5. Can I Give You a TIP? Inviting Healing Conversations in Practice   103
JOAQUÍN GAETE, INÉS SAMETBAND, AND OLGA SUTHERLAND

6. Braiding Socio-Cultural Interpersonal Patterns Into Therapy   124
SALLY ST. GEORGE AND DAN WULFF

CONTENTS

7   His Cave and Her Kitchen: Gendered PIPs and HIPs
    and Societal Discourses   143
    JOANNE SCHULTZ HALL AND INÉS SAMETBAND

8   Sensing, Understanding, and Moving Beyond
    Intercultural PIPs   168
    INÉS SAMETBAND, TAMARA WILSON, AND CHEE-PING TSAI

9   IPs Supervision as Relationally Responsive Practice   187
    JEFF CHANG AND JOAQUÍN GAETE

10 Researching Interpersonal Patterns   210
    SALLY ST. GEORGE, DAN WULFF, AND TOM STRONG

11 Continuing the Journey   229
    KARL TOMM

    *Appendix A: IPs component of the Brief Interview
        Record (BIR)*   249
    *Appendix B: Severity Scales for Pathologizing Interpersonal
        Patterns (PIPS)*   250
    *Appendix C: Strength Scales for Healing Interpersonal
        Patterns (HIPs)*   252

    Index   255

FIGURES

1.1	Acronyms of the IPscope	18
1.2	Sample PIPs	20
1.3	Sample HIPs	24
1.4	Sample TIPs	25
1.5	Sample WIPs	26
1.6	Sample DIPs	27
1.7	Movement among different interaction patterns within an ongoing interpersonal relationship	28
1.8	Linking depressogenic PIPs with antidepressant HIPs	31
1.9	Adopting a second-order perspective to distinguish the orienting effects of one's own distinctions	33
3.1	Figure-ground gestalt shift from faces to relationship	59
3.2	A heuristic sequence in the development of knowledge and/or intuitive skills	62
3.3	Steps to construct a PIP	67
3.4	Steps to bring forth a HIP	69
3.5	Possible movements from PIP to HIP	69
3.6	Typical sequence for the reflecting team process	72
4.1	A major PIP	89
4.2	Several DIPs feeding the major PIP	90
4.3	A TIP to enable movement from the PIP to a HIP or WIP	95
4.4	A HIP to replace the PIP	98
4.5	Possible stabilizing WIPs	100
5.1	Possible IPs for mother in Extract V	117
5.2	Possible IPs for mother and children in Extract VI	120
6.1	Braiding illustration	129
6.2	SCIPs in society and family living	132
7.1	A shift from horizontal to vertical drawing to highlight power differential	150
7.2	Equality through symmetry	152
7.3	Equality through balanced reciprocity	152
7.4	Generic triadic interactions	155

FIGURES

7.5	Specific example of triadic interaction	155
7.6	Discourses related to the socialization of boys and girls	157
7.7	Gender discourses related to adult relationships	158
7.8	Problematic silencing strategies	160
7.9	Excerpt of clinical interview	162
8.1	Moving from PIPs to a TIP and potential HIPs in Scenario 1	176
8.2	Moving from injustice to a HIP in Scenario 3	181
9.1	Describing supervisee's experience as an interpersonal response	191
9.2	Inviting a preferred supervisory pattern	192
9.3	Conceptualizing problematic interaction patterns	192
9.4	Inviting a HIP and a WIP	194
9.5	Initiating a WIP	195
9.6	Participating in a DIP and drifting into a PIP	196
9.7	Two WIPs for "gatekeeping"	197
9.8	A possible DIP slipping into a PIP	198
9.9	Conceptualizing empowering supervisory conversations	200
9.10	Theoretical integration as a WIP	202
9.11	Co-Constructing preferred ways of practice through a WIP	203
9.12	Incorporating evaluation in a WIP	205
10.1	PIP between research and practice	213
10.2	WIP between research and practice	214
11.1	Problematic versus complementary diagnosing	232
11.2	Bernini sculpture suggesting transformation of interpersonal pattern into individual distillate	233
11.3	Possible internalized PIP and HIP	238
11.4	Societal PIPs producing cycles of violence	240
11.5	Societal HIPs promoting reconciliation	241
11.6	Recurrent cycles of injustice and violence	242

CONTRIBUTORS

Jeff Chang, PhD Jeff Chang is associate professor in the Graduate Centre for Applied Psychology at Athabasca University, director of the Family Psychology Centre, and a therapist and supervisor at the Calgary Family Therapy Centre. He has been a registered psychologist in the Province of Alberta for over 25 years and is a clinical fellow and approved supervisor in the American Association for Marriage and Family Therapy. He has worked in children's mental health, employee assistance programs, and private practice and has taught in five graduate programs. Jeff is interested in four key areas in which he combines practice and scholarship: social constructionist therapies, school-based/children's mental health, clinical supervision, and applications of psychology to family law matters. He is co-author (with Philip Barker) of *Basic Family Therapy* (6th ed.) and editor of *Creative Interventions for Children: A Transtheoretical Approach.*

Shari Couture, PhD Shari Couture is a therapist and clinical supervisor at the Calgary Family Therapy Centre. She is a registered psychologist in the Province of Alberta, a member of the American Family Therapy Academy, and an associate member of the American Association for Marriage and Family Therapy. She has worked with children and their families in a variety of residential and outpatient programs and currently, in addition to her work at the Calgary Family Therapy Centre, practices privately in Calgary. In her research she uses a discursive approach to study processes and outcomes in family therapy.

Joaquín Gaete, MA Joaquín Gaete is a Chilean registered psychologist and an associate professor of the School of Psychology at Universidad Adolfo Ibáñez in Santiago. His doctoral studies in counselling psychology at the University of Calgary include extensive training at the Calgary Family Therapy Centre. His research has been related to change processes, focused particularly on how conversational practices can foster human change in therapy, health organizations, and clinical supervision. In his doctoral dissertation he focuses on how professional development is negotiated within clinical supervision conversations.

Tanya Mudry, MSc Tanya Mudry is a PhD student in counselling psychology at the University of Calgary. She has an MSc in both health promotion studies and counselling psychology. Her study interests include family therapy, systemic thinking, social constructionism, discourse analysis, social practice theory, and excessive/addictive behaviors. She completed her doctoral practicum at the Calgary Family Therapy Centre using the HIPs and PIPs approach in her work with families.

Sally St. George, PhD Sally St. George is an associate professor in the Faculty of Social Work at the University of Calgary and a family therapist and clinical supervisor at the Calgary Family Therapy Centre. She conducts workshops on family therapy and qualitative inquiry. Sally serves on the boards of directors for the Taos Institute, an organization dedicated to developing social constructionist practices world-wide, and the Global Partnership for Transformative Social Work, which involves co-developing transformative practices in social work education. For the last 20 years, Sally has worked on *The Qualitative Report* and is currently senior editor for this online journal. In her spare time she enjoys ballroom dancing with her husband, Dan Wulff.

Inés Sametband, MSc Inés Sametband is a registered marriage and family therapist in Calgary, Alberta. She studied psychology at the University of Buenos Aires and practiced as a psychologist in Argentina before moving to Canada. As part of her training in family therapy, she completed a post-graduate internship at the Calgary Family Therapy Centre. Inés is interested in exploring intercultural issues in family therapy from a relational stance, which is the focus of her doctoral studies in counselling psychology at the University of Calgary. Her current research is on the ways in which immigrant family members negotiate cultural identities in family therapy conversations.

Joanne Schultz Hall, MEd Joanne Schultz Hall has a master's degree in education counseling and is an adjunct assistant professor in the Department of Psychiatry, Faculty of Medicine, at the University of Calgary. Joanne has over 37 years of experience working with families at the Family Therapy Program/Calgary Family Therapy Centre where she has provided supervision, training, and consultation. Her special interests include a curiosity about the impact of spiritual beliefs and family/individual values on individuals and their relationships, and the impact of gendered ideas on the family.

Tom Strong, PhD Tom Strong is a professor and counsellor-educator at the University of Calgary who researches and writes on the collaborative, critically informed, and practical potentials of discursive approaches to psychotherapy. A therapist and supervisor at the Calgary Family Therapy Centre, Tom is co-author (with Andy Lock) of *Discursive Perspectives on Therapeutic Practice* (Oxford University Press) and *Social Constructionism: Sources and Stirrings in Theory and Practice* (Cambridge University Press), as well as *Furthering Talk* (with David Paré; Kluwer/Academic). Tom's current research focuses on "Medicalizing Tensions in Counsellor Education" and "Customs, Cravings and Compulsions: Discourses of Addiction and Recovery." For more details on Tom and his research please consult www.ucalgary.ca/strongt.

Olga Sutherland, PhD Olga Sutherland is an associate professor in couple and family therapy at the University of Guelph and a clinical/counselling psychologist in private practice. Olga uses discursive approaches to research (discourse and conversation analysis) to study psychotherapy interaction and social interaction more broadly. Her doctoral dissertation examined the topic of client–therapist collaboration using conversation analysis.

Karl Tomm, MD Karl Tomm is a professor in the Department of Psychiatry at the University of Calgary where he founded the Family Therapy Program in 1973. He is well known in the field of family therapy for his work in clarifying and elaborating new developments in systems theory and clinical practice. For many years he was at the forefront of a new approach to therapy that emerged from systemic, constructivist, narrative, bringforthist, and social constructionist ideas. This approach is collaborative rather than hierarchical and emphasizes therapeutic conversations to deconstruct problems and to coconstruct healing and wellness.

Chee-Ping Tsai, PhD Chee-Ping Tsai is a registered psychologist in Alberta working for over 20 years. She has held an adjunct assistant professor position with the Department of Psychiatry at the University of Calgary and has been an oral examiner with the College of Alberta Psychologists. Her extensive clinical background includes working with children, adolescents, adults, couples, and families. Currently, Chee-Ping is working with cancer patients and their families. Her major areas of professional interests are narrative therapy, systemic family therapy, application of play therapy techniques in family therapy, cultural diversity, multi-cultural counseling, health psychology, and psychosocial issues in cancer care.

Tamara Wilson, MC Tamara Wilson is a registered psychologist in Alberta and provides family therapy for children/adolescents at the Calgary Family Therapy Centre. She completed her bachelor of arts degree at the University of Alberta and her master's degree in counseling psychology at

Yorkville University. Tamara has worked with children and families for the past 13 years within a residential treatment setting and provided in-home family support for children ages 7–11. She has also led both children and parent psycho-educational groups and provided family therapy for adolescents with drug/alcohol addictions. Tamara's professional interests include systemic marriage and family therapy, multi-cultural counseling, and therapy within a spiritual context.

Dan Wulff, PhD Dan Wulff is an associate professor in the Faculty of Social Work at the University of Calgary and has served as a family therapist and clinical supervisor at the Calgary Family Therapy Centre for the past 6 years. Dan also serves on the boards of directors for the Taos Institute and the Global Partnership for Transformative Social Work, as well as serving as a co-editor of *The Qualitative Report*. Dan teaches graduate level social work practice and research courses and has taught post-structural family therapy at Blue Quills College and Grande Prairie Regional College, both in northern Alberta.

SERIES EDITOR'S FOREWORD

"It is the theory that decides what can be observed."
—Albert Einstein

This is a valuable book about a unique systemic approach to family therapy developed over several decades by Karl Tomm and his colleagues at the University of Calgary. It takes some effort to understand their important messages as we are invited to stretch our perceptual abilities to understand their vision of ever-changing relationships. The authors are asking us to utilize a different way of understanding the therapist's task and use a different language to communicate this perspective as well as the importance of language in psychotherapy.

Their framework has become known as the HIPs and PIPs approach (or the Healing Interpersonal Patterns and Pathologizing Interpersonal Patterns approach) to assessment and therapy and uses the IPscope as the basic instrument. It is a constructionist and collaborative approach to working relationally with families. The therapists invite families to proactively choose wellness over pathology.

Their ideas have roots in general systems theory where a change in any one part affects every other part and every system is nested in and influenced by larger systems. However, they have moved far beyond these roots to embrace and integrate social constructionist and bringforthist contributions about language systems that take into account culture and promote all aspects of social justice.

Get ready to learn this method and begin using their brilliant insights to increase your therapeutic effectiveness with families, groups, and organizations.

Jon Carlson, PsyD, EdD
Series Editor

FOREWORD

In reading *Patterns of Interpersonal Interactions* I was reminded of a lamentation once offered by physician, novelist, and language essayist, Walker Percy (1954–1987) on the state of psychiatrists' abilities to articulate their work with patients:

> It is a matter for astonishment, when one comes to think of it, how little use linguistics and other sciences of language are to psychiatrists. When one considers that the psychiatrist spends most of his [or her] time listening and talking to patients, one might suppose that there would be such a thing as a basic science of listening-and-talking, as indispensable to psychiatrists as anatomy to surgeons. (p. 159)

He went on to say that "Surgeons traffic in body structures. Psychiatrists traffic in words" (p. 159). What Percy observed back in the 1950s for psychiatrists now holds more for contemporary therapists such as psychologists, counselors, social workers, psychiatric nurses, family therapists, and other clinicians. Unfortunately most psychiatrists nowadays traffic predominantly in psychotropic drugs. Yet those of us who continue to "traffic in words" and in discourse really do need a sound basic science of listening and speaking to better orient ourselves within our relationships with our clients.

Perhaps one of the reasons that such a basic science has eluded us, is that we have focused far too much on separate individuals, rather than on relationships per se. Could it be that family therapists who strive to *traffic in relationships*, and not just words, might provide guidance to build such a science? The clinical language in which many contemporary psychotherapists traffic (including many of us conducting marital and family therapy) seems to be dominated not so much by a relational orientation, but more by an individual focus. In doing so clinicians are still assigning problems a location inside a person, rather than describing a problematic relational pattern between persons. No one person needs to be assigned as a problem for marital and family therapy to be conceived and practiced effectively and ethically, yet the challenge remains in creating an assessment and treatment system that will help therapists to traffic in more relationally-oriented thoughts, words, and actions.

Of course there have been a number of remarkable efforts over the last 50 plus years to create some wonderful ways of drawing distinctions relationally in psychotherapy. The work of gifted observers of life such as Gregory Bateson, Heinz von Forester, Humberto Maturana, Francisco Varela, and Kenneth Gergen has found its way into our relational knowledge-base helping systemic therapists like Gianfranco Cecchin, Bradford Keeney, Steve de Shazer, Insoo Kim Berg, Michael White, and Karl Tomm to produce some of the key distinction-drawing ways of knowing and doing we need to work in ethically-sound relational patterns with our clients, colleagues, and communities. With the publication of *Patterns of Interpersonal Interactions: Inviting Relational Understandings for Therapeutic Change* I see an effort to provide a basic science of listening-and-talking **relationally**. It is as indispensable to psychotherapists as anatomy is to surgeons, and takes a great leap forward. I say this for a number of reasons.

First, the IPscope approach is the most comprehensive system I know for drawing clear distinctions about relational patterns. Like G. Spencer-Brown's (1973) simple edict, "Draw a distinction," (p. 3), Tomm and his colleagues ask us to "construct interpersonal patterns 'in one's mind's eye' that are ordinarily hard to see" (p. 18, this volume). As Tomm did in his series of break-through papers on systemic questions in the 1980s (e.g., 1984, 1988), he and his colleagues now have made it easier for us as clinicians to appreciate the patterns we draw, about the patterns we observe, in our interactions with others.

Second, the IPscope system helps therapists to embrace important values of relational healing and wellness when making these distinctions. Rather than merely noting repetitive or recurring patterns, the IPscope approach asks us as therapists to consider how we can work with others to create healthier lives while providing us with a simple notational system for noting positive, transformative, cognitive, behavioral, attitudinal, and emotional couplings. Combining these values with a rigorous distinction drawing system as seen through the IPscope helps to keep our humanity in our clinical practice.

Third, the IPscope approach embraces practice-based evidence by which these authors recursively use the IPscope framework as the lens they use to study IPscope process and outcome. There is a pleasing aesthetic for employing such a practice-sensitive reflective stance in their systematic inquiries, but this choice is also ethically pragmatic because all too often the research system for studying the therapy system disregards the clinical values producing results not respectful or useful for the clinician.

Fourth, the IPscope agenda helps relationally-focused therapists to engage in culturally-sensitive interpersonal practices challenging unfair privilege and encouraging social justice. All too often, the systems we use to understand systemic practice seem to ignore larger contexts outside of the local context of our clinics and therapy rooms. Like Foucault (1973), Tomm and his colleagues ask us to conduct a rigorous archeology of the talk we create with our clients and to consider what possible artifacts from previous marginalizing conversations continue to persist in these everyday interactions and what ways we can work together to not only change deteriorating familial patterns, but to also help transform larger, community systems of discourse.

Fifth, the IPscope approach is offered in a tentative, hedging manner reminding us that we are the ones drawing these distinctions. So no matter how useful we find this system of Pathologizing Interpersonal Patterns (PIPs), Healing Interpersonal Patterns (HIPs), Wellness Interpersonal Patterns (WIPs), Transforming Interpersonal Patterns (TIPs), Deteriorating Interpersonal Patterns (DIPs), and Socio-Cultural Interpersonal Patterns (SCIPs), we cannot forget that these are merely helpful guides we are constructing to help us traffic in complex relationships. These "transient relational stabilities" (p. 1, this volume) are just what they are—momentary distinctions made about particular changing human relationships made at certain times and places by certain people within particular cultural sensitivities. Remembering these assumptions helps to make the IPscope a valuable if momentary system depending mightily on therapists who value their relationships with others dearly; and one I think Walker Percy would have loved to see and practice.

Ronald J. Chenail

References

Foucault, M. (1973). *The birth of the clinic: An archaeology of medical perception* (A. M. Sheridan, Trans.). London, UK: Routledge.

Percy, W. (1987). *The message in the bottle: How queer man is, how queer language is, and what one has to do with the other*. New York, NY: Farrar, Strauss and Giroux. (Original work published 1954)

Spencer-Brown, G. (1973). *Laws of form*. New York, NY: Bantam.

Tomm, K. (1984). One perspective on the Milan Systemic Approach: Part II. Description of session format, interviewing style and interventions. *Journal of Marital and Family Therapy, 10*(3), 253–271.

Tomm, K. (1988). Interventive interviewing: Part III. Intending to ask lineal, circular, strategic or reflexive questions? *Family Process, 27*, 1–15.

ACKNOWLEDGMENTS

This book would never have been conceived and written if it were not for the 40 years of ongoing financial support of Alberta Health Services and Alberta Mental Health for the Family Therapy Program (FTP), which eventually became the Calgary Family Therapy Centre (CFTC). In addition, the University of Calgary Department of Psychiatry in the Faculty of Medicine provided direct administrative support, while the Faculties of Social Work, Education, and Nursing provided indirect academic support.

The authors of this book would also like to express appreciation to a large number of individuals who contributed in various ways to provide administrative support: Myrna Fraser, Robin Aurel, and Hazel Hiebert; to develop the ideas: Cindy Beck, Elly Neumann, Ottar Ness, and Monica Sesma; to refine the writing: Lynda Snyder, Emily Doyle, and Beth Lennard; and to bring the book to fruition: Marta Moldvai and Renata Corbani.

INTRODUCTION
Origins of the PIPs and HIPs Framework

Karl Tomm

I invite you, as a reader, to join with my colleagues and me to explore some of the mysteries of human relationships. While the focus of our explorations in this book will revolve around clinical mental health problems and initiatives toward solutions, the concepts are applicable in many domains of daily life. They highlight ways in which we, as persons, invite each other into recurrent patterns of interaction that generate and maintain some stability in our continuously changing relationships. The stabilities arise when our invitations become coupled and can be characterized as mutual; yet, they always remain transient. What is of major significance is that these transient relational stabilities can have major positive or negative effects in our lives. Consequently, we could all potentially benefit from greater awareness of the nature of these patterns, how particular patterns arise, and how we might be able to influence them.

Although I played a central role in developing the approach to relationship assessment described in this volume, it is probably more coherent to say that the framework is the product of unique circumstances at a particular time and place. The Pathologizing Interpersonal Patterns (PIPs) and Healing Interpersonal Patterns (HIPs) model took shape about 25 years ago within the Family Therapy Program at the University of Calgary. I was a relatively young psychiatrist at the time and all of my staff members were involved in its development, including Myrna Fraser, Joanne Schultz Hall, Gary Sanders, Alan Parry, Karine Reitjens, and Carol Liske. I had already been exposed to several family assessment models, including the McMaster family categories schema (Steinhauer, Santa-Barbara, & Skinner, 1984), Minuchin's structural model (1974), Bowen's self-differentiation model (1978), the MRI interactional model (Watzlawick, Bavelas, & Jackson, 1967), Beavers' dimensional model (Beavers, Hampson, & Hulgus, 1985), and Olson's Circumplex model (Olson, Russell, & Sprenkle, 1989). In addition, there were indirect contributions from other outside colleagues, graduate students, family members, friends, mentors, theoreticians, professional networks, and the culture-at-large.

Thus, I find it extremely difficult to trace the myriad of influences that have culminated in the model.

Given the initiative I took in generating and guiding the development of the framework, I will present myself as a mediating "node" at the confluence of these many influences. Whenever I encounter another person and try to connect with his/her experience and perspective, I find it helpful to develop a sense of the context out of which that person arose. Assuming that you, as a reader, might feel similarly, what follows is a brief outline of my personal background, along with a description of a few specific events that contributed in major ways to the formulation of the concepts presented here.

A Personal Journey

I am a White heterosexual male who has lived many middle-class privileges. My parents were of German origin, and migrated independently from eastern Poland to western Canada between World War I and World War II. They met at a German Baptist church in Vancouver, the city where my three siblings and I were born. I was identified as German as I grew up during and after World War II, with the result that I was sometimes bullied at school because the Canadians had been fighting the Germans overseas. Needless to say, I was almost always on the losing end of the "war games" among the children in our neighborhood. Consequently, I learned to conceal my cultural heritage. These early formative experiences sensitized me to social injustice, a sensitivity that continues to serve me well, especially when I listen to it!

My mother experienced a prolonged illness and died of cancer when I was 8 years old. This left me with a deep personal commitment to try to help those who were suffering. While she was ill, I had tried desperately to help her in any way that I could, but I failed to save her. My father remarried and together with my stepmother (also of German origin from Poland) had three more children. Interestingly, all seven of us kids went into medically related fields even though the livelihoods of prior generations had revolved exclusively around farming and business. The desire to help others who were suffering had become our passion. Our father, being caught in the upheaval of World War I during his childhood, obtained only 2 years of schooling and barely knew how to read or write. Yet all three of his sons went to medical school, and his four daughters studied medical biochemistry, nursing, family therapy, and audiology. In retrospect, sexist presuppositions of male privilege may have contributed to these gendered pathways. Nevertheless we discovered that higher education opened doors and provided opportunities to move beyond being defined as immigrants or displaced persons; we had found our way to inclusion and acceptance within the mainstream of our local communities.

Moving on to postgraduate studies, I decided to specialize in internal medicine because I found the invisible mysteries of what was happening in a patient's physiology more fascinating than surgery where the choices seemed so black and white (cut or do not cut). However, while doing residency training in medicine at Ottawa, I had a pivotal experience that sent me in a different direction. I was caring for a young man in the hospital who was dying of malignant melanoma that had spread throughout his body. Because the metastases in his abdomen caused fluid accumulation that pushed up his diaphragm and compromised his breathing, I had to insert a trocar into his abdomen from time to time to drain off the extra fluid so he could breathe more freely and then replace his electrolytes intravenously each time. It was a delicate physiological/biochemical problem and I thought I was doing a good job in keeping him alive. On a particular Friday morning he asked me for a weekend pass to spend some time at home with his family, and I readily agreed. However, when I returned to work on Monday I discovered that he had tried to kill himself over the weekend! I was totally bewildered. Here I was trying to keep him alive, yet he wanted to die. I realized that I had come up against one of my blind spots; I was clearly out of touch with his emotional experience and what was most meaningful in his life. In the interests of filling in that blind spot, I decided to take a year of training in psychiatry. Once I began working with psychiatric patients, however, I found that their suffering was even more mysterious than the patients in internal medicine. I became intrigued and decided to continue studying psychiatry instead.

A Vicarious "Natural Experiment"

A particular series of events during my psychiatry training had a profound impact on my eventual career and the relational assessment model to be described in this book. They revolved around a specific female patient in her late 30s. I was a resident in psychiatry at McMaster University at the time (1969–1972) and was working at the Hamilton Psychiatric Hospital.

The woman had been admitted to the hospital after a suicide attempt. While she was officially under the care of one of my colleagues, I was fully aware of her course from the clinical rounds with the nursing staff that took place daily on the ward. She was diagnosed with depression and was placed in a comprehensive treatment program of antidepressant medication, individual therapy, group therapy, and milieu therapy. Despite these multiple therapies, she remained chronically depressed and suicidal for months. Her husband visited her regularly and was regarded as a major support; he had taken over full care of their three children, maintained a meticulous household, and continued at his full-time job as well.

While she was still an in-patient, a major event occurred outside of her direct care that significantly influenced her condition. Her husband was involved in a terrible car accident and although he was not seriously injured, two people in the other vehicle were killed. The police charged him with manslaughter. The trauma of the accident and the burden of this legal threat overwhelmed him and over the ensuing days he began to flounder. He could no longer cope with his prior workload. Consequently, his wife tried to help out with the children whenever she could get home on a pass from the hospital. As he struggled to manage his responsibilities, she took over more and more of the child-care and some household chores as well. He began doing less and less. She, on the other hand, became progressively more productive, and started to feel better about herself in doing so—to such an extent that after a few weeks the hospital staff felt that she could be safely discharged. Over the next few months she became fully functional as a mother, a homemaker, and a supportive partner. Indeed, during a follow-up appointment, she reported that she felt "completely well for the first time in years." It seemed as if the anti-depressant medication was "finally working." The husband in the meantime felt worse and worse, not only because of the impending trial, but also because he was no longer able to function as well as he had previously.

About 18 months after the tragic collision, the court hearings came to a conclusion. The husband was found not guilty of neglect or any wrongdoing and the charge of manslaughter was dropped. Needless-to-say he was enormously relieved. As a result, he became energized, and began taking over more responsibilities in the home. The more he did, the less his wife did. As he took on more and more of the chores and childcare, she contributed less and less and she began slipping into depression again. Within a few weeks he had taken over almost everything as before. Despite her compliance in continuing the antidepressant medication, the depression re-established itself. Before she could be re-hospitalized, she made another suicide attempt and this time she succeeded in killing herself.

When I heard of her death, I was shocked and deeply shaken. What had happened? This outcome was totally unexpected, especially after she appeared to have made such a complete recovery. I was studying Ludwig von Bertalanffy's (1968) systems theory at the time and the systems aphorism, "a change in any one part affects every other part," seemed to apply in this family system; the changes in the husband's state of mind and abilities affected the wife's activities and mental well-being. In addition, I learned from general systems theory that all systems are nested in, and influenced by, larger systems. In this case the family system was certainly profoundly influenced by the legal system. Finally, the notion of "the whole is greater than the sum of the parts" seemed relevant as well. But just exactly how a whole family system was more than the collection of all its individual members did not become crystal clear to me until much later when I began to explore Gregory Bateson's (1972) ecology of mind and Maturana and Varela's (1980) theory of knowledge.

What became apparent in retrospect was that the husband and wife appeared to be caught in a relationship pattern of "over-adequate/under-adequate reciprocity." Upon reflection, it appeared as if only one member of the couple could be functioning well at any one time. Before the wife was admitted to the hospital, she presented as under-adequate in her functioning, while the husband could be described as over-adequate. After the criminal charges were laid, the husband became under-adequate while the wife gradually shifted to become over-adequate. A second reversal occurred after the court proceedings were concluded: he became over-adequate again and she was relegated to the under-adequate position. The suicide occurred when the wife found herself back in the demoralizing under-functioning role within the relationship; presumably she felt hopelessly trapped and was desperate to get out. From a relationship perspective, both members of the couple could be seen as being caught in a pattern of over-adequate/under-adequate reciprocity, and both suffered deeply, albeit in very different ways.

This "natural experiment" of an outside observer distinguishing the ramifications of a significant unplanned event (the accident), revealed how the power in the systemic dynamics of a couple's relationship could over-ride the effects of the wife's psychotropic medication and other therapies. When I came to see the situation in this way, I resolved in myself to avoid becoming the kind of psychiatrist who might overlook these kinds of relationship influences on the well-being of my patients. Indeed, these reflections resulted in another strong personal commitment—namely, to try to understand families as relational systems and to work with individual patients within their relationship contexts. The end result was a lifelong career in family psychiatry, couple therapy, and family therapy to try to help liberate persons from the suffering created by such problematic interpersonal entanglements.

A Crisis of a Different Sort

It was another major event that catapulted me into clarifying some of the potential implications of my growing awareness of the significance of interpersonal relationships on individual well-being. I had established a specialized Family Therapy Program (FTP) in the Department of Psychiatry at the University of Calgary about a year after I accepted my first academic appointment in 1972. The FTP provided clinical services to families who had children or adolescents with mental problems. The original philosophical and theoretical orientation guiding our work revolved around understanding families as relationship systems and conceiving a child's mental difficulties as a reflection of the functioning of the family system. The program was also designed to provide training in clinical skills for professionals working with such families.

After the FTP had been operating successfully for several years, a new academic department head decided that our data collection should be consistent with that of the other clinics in the Department of Psychiatry. He wanted my staff and me to employ the Diagnostic and Statistical Manual (DSM) of the American Psychiatric Association (1980), which defines individual diagnoses. He insisted that our program should require a DSM diagnosis of at least one family member as an intake criterion for a family to be accepted for treatment. As director of the program, I was opposed to the imposition of the DSM framework for a number of reasons (Tomm, 1990). I wanted my staff to remain free to give priority to understanding problems within a relational systems perspective and not be burdened with diagnosing individuals. I also had a concern about the potential pathologizing effects of psychiatric labeling on children and adolescents. The social stigma associated with a psychiatric diagnosis can add a significant burden to the person labeled and can make recovery more difficult. The labeling effects may be subtle but they tend to become increasingly pervasive and malignant as growing acceptance of the label spreads through the professional and social networks of the child. The label eventually becomes internalized as part of the child's identity where it can have permanent negative effects. I was not willing to accept a diagnostic means that contradicted the therapeutic ends of the FTP.

After several heated exchanges with my department head, I appealed to higher authorities at the university and claimed academic freedom to explore systems theory as an alternative paradigm to the traditional psychiatric nosology promoted by the DSM. This appeal worked temporarily and he relinquished his demands for about a year. However, he subsequently formed a coalition with my funding source, Alberta Mental Health Services (AMHS). Then my department head and the regional director of AMHS confronted me jointly and threatened to withdraw grant support for the FTP if I did not apply the DSM in our clinical work in family therapy. My staff members were now at risk of losing their jobs! This felt like a major injustice. The pressure to submit was formidable. I eventually offered to resign my directorship of the FTP rather than give up my personal priority of focusing on understanding the relationship dynamics that contributed to my clients' suffering.

Fortunately, my department head and the regional director respected my work enough to ask me to stay and we began some genuine negotiations.

I accepted their concerns that we needed to be socially responsible in the allocation of publicly funded resources; our therapy services were limited and we should not be providing costly therapy for "the worried well." Their administrative argument was that if there was a DSM diagnosable mental disorder in at least one family member, then the use of publicly funded treatment resources for that family was justified. My position was that a more therapeutic means to determine eligibility for public services could be developed by drawing upon the systemic understanding of mental problems that was emerging in the field of family therapy. I felt that severely problematic *patterns of interaction* within the family were justification enough because those patterns were actively producing individual pathology in the here-and-now that might become manifest as a chronic mental illness at some point in the future. In other words, by interrupting these patterns early on in the life cycle of a family, we could potentially prevent, or at least ameliorate, subsequent entrapment in individual pathology. I offered to begin developing an alternative diagnostic approach based on family systems understanding that eventually could be used to justify the allocation of limited resources. Given that the field of psychiatry had already evolved over 100 years to develop a classification of mental disorders, while family therapy was barely 30 years old at the time (and there was not yet any consensus regarding nosology in the family field), I asked for some time to develop a systems-oriented framework. I am extremely grateful that the administrators involved eventually accepted my request.

Subsequent Developments

I immediately embarked upon a project in collaboration with my staff at the FTP to modify an earlier conceptual model of Circular Pattern Diagramming (Tomm, 1980) and elaborate a typology of different kinds of interaction patterns among family members. We began by labeling problematic patterns that appeared to have negative effects on the persons who were interacting as "Pathologizing Interpersonal Patterns" or "PIPs." For instance, the pattern of over-adequate/under-adequate reciprocity described previously was conceived of as existing *between* the two members of the couple and not necessarily as a disorder *within* either one of them. We then identified a contrasting type of pattern that appeared to have positive effects on the persons involved and named these "Healing Interpersonal Patterns" or "HIPs." A generic example of a HIP entails *apologizing coupled with forgiving*. This pattern also is enacted in the interpersonal space between the persons involved and potentially has significant positive effects upon both parties. The overall framework came to be known as "the HIPs and PIPs approach" to psychiatric assessment (Tomm, 1991) and the perceptual/conceptual "instrument" used to distinguish these patterns came to be known as the "IPscope" (see Chapter 1).

As a second step toward responding to the administrative concern about eligibility for publicly funded treatment, we devised a six-point "Severity Scale" to rate the intensity and pervasiveness of the PIPs identified in a family assessment (see Chapter 3). The scale is divided into two components, an "experienced severity" rating and a "reported severity" rating. The experienced scale focuses on interactions experienced by the clinician in the here-and-now patterns during an actual clinical interview. The reported scale focuses on the interactions or events that are reported by the family (or by collateral informants) as having occurred prior to the interview.

A small statistical study using the PIPs Severity Scale was carried out shortly after the scale was devised. I asked all the therapists and trainees in the FTP to rate the severity of the most obvious PIP in the family after each clinical interview. We then correlated the average severity of the PIPs in a particular family with the total number of sessions of therapy that family actually received. The analysis indicated that those families with the more severe PIPs were given proportionately more therapeutic interviews than families with less intense PIPs, in a clear linear manner. These findings were then presented to my department head and the regional director. Both felt that the issue of being socially responsible in allocating publicly funded resources to families with more serious problems had been adequately addressed. As a result, the administrative pressure to adopt the DSM fell away and we have maintained a systemic focus and continuous funding for more than 24 years since.

My staff and I went on to differentiate Wellness Interpersonal Patterns (WIPs), Transforming Interpersonal Patterns (TIPs), and Deteriorating Interpersonal Patterns (DIPs) as well. These will all be described in Chapter 1 within the overall framework as originally conceived. We also developed a six-point "Strength Scale" for the HIPs and WIPs, as an effort toward quantifying resilience (see Chapter 3). While the components of the overall PIPs and HIPs framework have continued to evolve, the core concepts have remained intact. Indeed, they have shown to be pragmatic and robust, even though the interpersonal patterns described are almost always elusive and remain mysterious.

It turned out that the perceptual/conceptual activities involved in formulating and describing PIPs and HIPs actually helped new trainees think more systemically. The students were better able to focus on and clarify the systemic process within the families they were working with in therapy. As a result we decided to incorporate descriptions of PIPs and HIPs as part of our routine record-keeping (see Chapter 3). We found that by conceiving of PIPs as existing in the interpersonal space, rather than within the persons who enact the patterns, it was easier to enable change and help liberate those persons from the suffering generated by PIPs.

The Most Recent Developments

Having experienced so many positive effects in applying this approach over the ensuing years, my current colleagues and I recently decided it was time to share these ideas and practices with a wider audience. We began collaborating as a group to collectively prepare this book, even though specific individuals or subgroups took responsibility to write particular chapters. We met regularly over a year and a half to clarify and elaborate relevant concepts, to give each other feedback on our writing, and to link themes across the chapters. Indeed, it has been a very generative, incredibly enjoyable, and heady time. In the process of our collaboration, the ideas have evolved further and have been significantly enriched.

In Chapter 1, I provide an overall explication of the basic model, its applicability, and its general use. In Chapter 2, Tom Strong offers a wide-ranging theoretical overview that supports the systemic and social constructionist perspective out of which the approach emerges. He describes two contrasting forms of knowledge and introduces the fascinating notion of "discursive capture" as we traverse the modern/postmodern divide. In Chapter 3, Shari Couture and I describe a multiplicity of domains in which we engage with students in the process of teaching/learning relational practice through the IPscope. We emphasize the gestalt shift required to work relationally, and highlight the importance of fostering a wellness culture of reflective openness and collegiality to optimize learning. In Chapter 4, Tanya Mudry, Tom Strong, and Jeff Chang apply the PIPs and HIPs concepts in a description of the ebb and flow of daily living and in a course of therapy. They explore the tantalizing question "How is it that objectionable patterns of interaction become so familiar?" In Chapter 5, Joaquín Gaete, Inés Sametband, and Olga Sutherland push the frontier further in distinguishing different kinds of TIPs: the kinds of interaction patterns that we as therapists like to get into with our clients during our clinical work. They not only clarify deconstructive TIPs, as opposed to constructive TIPs, but also distinguish TIP attempts from TIP accomplishments. In Chapter 6, Sally St. George and Dan Wulff extend the concept of interaction patterns into the socio-cultural domain and propose adding Socio-Cultural Interpersonal Patterns (SCIPs) to the framework. They point to the benefits of therapist initiatives in taking SCIPs into the therapy room to open space for families to consciously embrace or reject the influences of societal discourses within their relationships. In Chapter 7, Joanne Schultz Hall and Inés Sametband explore the delicate topics of gender identity, sexual orientation, and power differentials in relationships. How have you tried to navigate these sensitive issues? Joanne and Inés share their insights into some of the complex constraints in the interplay between gendered SCIPs, gendered interactions, and gender identities.

Have you ever found yourself worrying about the possibility of offending someone from another culture? In Chapter 8, Inés Sametband, Tamara Wilson, and Chee-Ping Tsai explore interpersonal patterns in situations of social injustice and multicultural counseling. In particular, they explain how "playing the culture card" does not have to become a conversation stopper but instead, could become an opportunity for new and generative therapeutic conversation. In Chapter 9, Jeff Chang and Joaquín Gaete attend to the oft-overlooked relational dynamics between supervisor and supervisee during clinical supervision and describe collaborative opportunities to expand learning through "covision." In Chapter 10, Sally St. George, Dan Wulff, and Tom Strong present *research as daily practice* and review some research into interpersonal patterns. We hope that you are a practitioner who is also interested in research, but if you are not, please take extra note of this chapter because the authors talk plainly about a new criterion for what could be seen as "good clinical research"—that is, opening space for the consumer of the research to do things in therapy that they previously were unable to do. And finally in Chapter 11, I look at some future prospects of the IPscope in a world of widespread individualism. I suggest further applications of the IPscope by *zooming in* to explore an internalized community in the intrapsychic space and *zooming out* to explore a multiplicity of healing opportunities in the larger socio-cultural space. For those readers who are not already familiar with this framework, Chapter 1 is the place to start. All the remaining chapters are self-sufficient and could be read in any order.

In presenting our focus on interpersonal interaction patterns as influencing mental well-being, we are not claiming that other factors are not also involved. We accept the need for healthy biological functioning and sufficient plasticity in the human brain to enable us to enter into interaction patterns in the first place. We accept the importance of individual temperaments and personality styles in predisposing persons to engage in certain patterns of interaction. We also accept the importance of many cultural factors, such as traditions, values, beliefs, poverty, social discourses, and injustices (see Chapters 6, 7, and 8). What we do claim is that specific relational stabilities constitute extremely significant, albeit temporary, influences that contribute to determining a person's momentary experience and his/her well-being in the here-and-now.

A Comment About Terminology

In this book we use a variety of terms to characterize the perspective we are trying to describe and encourage. As human beings, all of us are active participants in the use of language and co-orient with one another in using certain words and phrases, sometimes in idiosyncratic ways. Rather than striving to become rigorously consistent or doctrinaire, we have decided to accept flexibility and use different terms at various points in the text to convey variations in nuances of meaning and implication, despite the confusions that might arise. Indeed, we acknowledge, and want to preserve, an ongoing tension between the extremes of a relatively objective diagnostic system of relationship dynamics and an elusive constructionist heuristic that is offered as a "serviceable fiction." We imagine a continuum from hardness to softness in our use of different words when pointing to PIPs, HIPs, and other interpersonal patterns. Terms like "diagnostic model," "framework," "typology," "instrument," "device," and "tool" tend to lean toward the harder objective pole; terms like "relational distinctions," "constructions," "concepts," "imaginings," and "heuristic" lean toward the softer constructionist pole; and terms like "perspective," "orientation," "approach," "resource," and "lens" probably lie somewhere in between. We would like to honor your freedom as a reader to make sense of these terms and meanings in whatever way that works for you and your understandings. Our hope is that you might come to appreciate the value of holding and working with these tensions rather than trying to resolve them.

We would also like to acknowledge that this model draws heavily upon medical metaphors by using terms like "pathologizing" and "healing" to describe contrasting types of interpersonal interaction patterns. This is obviously a result of the medical context within which the model was first developed. Other metaphors could have been equally useful, and we have no reservations whatsoever about you as a reader adapting the language to fit your particular context.

Finally, we wish you well in your own unique journey among these relational complexities!

References

American Psychiatric Association. (1980). *Diagnostic and statistical manual of mental disorders* (3rd ed.). Washington, DC: American Psychiatric Association.

Bateson, G. (1972). *Steps to an ecology of mind.* San Francisco, CA: Chandler.

Beavers, R., Hampson, R., & Hulgus, Y. (1985). Commentary: The Beavers Systems Approach to family assessment. *Family Process,* 24(3), 398–405.

Bowen, M. (1978). *Family therapy in clinical practice.* New York, NY: Jason Aronson.

Maturana, H., & Varela, F. (1980). *Autopoiesis and cognition: The realization of the living.* Boston, MA: Reidel.

Minuchin, S. (1974). *Families and family therapy.* Cambridge, MA: Harvard University Press.

Olson, D., Russell, C., & Sprenkle, D. (1989). *Circumplex model: Systemic assessment and treatment of families.* New York, NY: Haworth Press.

Steinhauer, P.D., Santa-Barbara, J., & Skinner, H. (1984). The process model of family functioning. *Canadian Journal of Psychiatry, 29*(2), 77–88.

Tomm, K. (1980). Towards a cybernetic-systems approach to family therapy at the University of Calgary. In D.S. Freeman (Ed.), *Perspectives on family therapy* (pp. 3–18). Toronto, ON: Butterworths Press.

Tomm, K. (1990). A critique of the DSM. *Dulwich Centre Newsletter*, no. 3, pp. 5–8.

Tomm, K. (1991). Beginnings of a "HIPs and PIPs" approach to psychiatric assessment. *Calgary Participator, 1*(2), 21–22, 24.

von Bertalanffy, L. (1968). *General systems theory: Foundations, development, applications*. New York, NY: Braziller.

Watzlawick, P., Bavelas, J.B., & Jackson, D.D. (1967). *Pragmatics of human communication: A study of interactional patterns, pathologies, and paradoxes.* New York, NY: Norton.

1

INTRODUCING THE IPSCOPE

A Systemic Assessment Tool for Distinguishing Interpersonal Patterns

Karl Tomm

"Mutual Forgiveness of each Vice, Such are the Gates of Paradise"
—William Blake, 1793

As noted in the introduction, it was quite early in my career that I developed an interest in understanding family systems as a way to position myself to work more effectively with individual patients who presented with mental suffering. Over the subsequent 40 years this interest has grown and encompassed a wide variety of theories and clinical practices. With respect to theory, it led to a series of explorations including the study of von Bertalanffy's systems theory (1968), Bateson's ecology of mind (1972, 1979), Maturana's bringforthism (Maturana & Varela, 1980, 1992), and Gergen's social constructionism (Gergen & Gergen, 2004). With respect to practices, it led to experimentation with methods in McMaster family therapy (Epstein & Bishop, 1981; Epstein, Bishop, & Levin, 1978), structural family therapy (Minuchin, 1974), strategic therapy (Watzlawick, Bavelas, & Jackson, 1967), Bowenian family therapy (Bowen, 1978), systemic therapy (Selvini Palazzoli, Boscolo, Cecchin, & Prata, 1978, 1980), solution-focused therapy (de Shazer, 1985), and narrative therapy (White, 2007; White & Epston, 1990). In this chapter I will try to pull together several threads from these multiple domains of understanding and practice to present an assessment framework that has enabled my clinical work with families as interpersonal systems.

I will begin with a general systems theory thread. When I first encountered the familiar systems aphorism "the whole is more than the sum of the parts," it made sense to me intuitively. Yet, at the time, I did not comprehend how a whole system entailed more than a collection of all its component parts, nor was I aware that I did not fully understand what was implied. Indeed, it took me a couple of years to generate an adequate understanding. I eventually came to the realization that the way in which a whole system is more than the sum of its parts is that the whole system includes not only all the parts but also all the unique relationships among those parts. Indeed, it is these unique relationships between the component parts that constitute the system as a "whole" system. This insight clarified the core of systems thinking for me and is extremely helpful for anyone trying to understand any kind of system.

However, applying this insight to understand families as systems is complicated by the fact that the parts of a family system (i.e., the individual family members) are easily observable as skin-bounded physical entities who can be seen, heard, and touched, whereas the unique relationships among family members cannot be readily seen and certainly cannot be touched. As the well-known psychiatrist and family therapist Carl Whitaker was fond of saying, "You can kiss a person, but you cannot kiss a family system." Yet it is precisely these family relationships that are so crucial to focus on when generating a family systems understanding. My first systematic attempt to do so was to try to integrate what I had learned about human beings in psychodynamic theory, behavior theory, and cognitive theory to understand relationships among family members. I used the cybernetic metaphor of feedback loops to link various elements of these theoretical contributions to create a model of Circular Pattern Diagramming (CPD; Tomm, 1980) to map out sequences of interpersonal interaction. CPD initially seemed to serve me well in organizing my work with families in therapy. Gradually, however, I became aware of how I was still mostly thinking in terms of multiple individual family members rather than in terms of the interactions between and among them. In other words, I found myself slipping back to old habits of looking at individual persons rather than at the relationships among them. I needed something more substantive to help me sustain a focus on systemic relationships. Eventually I came to realize that if I conceived of interaction patterns as separate "entities" in themselves, existing entirely in the interpersonal space, it became easier to hold to my systemic stance. While such a conception might not appear tenable from an objective point-of-view, it became a "serviceable fiction" that was extremely useful in the practice of systemic therapy.

Prioritizing a Focus on Patterns of Interpersonal Interaction

It seems reasonable to assume that the complexities of human relationships and experiences are endless, and that it is probably impossible to ever fully comprehend and explain human behavior. Consequently, it also seems reasonable to become selective in our efforts to understand, using our specific purpose of enabling therapeutic change as a guiding light or focus. In this book we selectively cast a light on patterns of interpersonal interaction as a basis for making sense of human behavior and experience. We have found that becoming more aware of particular kinds of interpersonal patterns has helped us in orienting our clients toward the kinds of change they prefer. There are several reasons why selective attention to interpersonal patterns can be beneficial.

First, the specific patterns of human interaction in which we are embedded in our daily living have a major influence on our experiences and on our mental well-being. Anyone who has reflected upon his/her experience is aware of how different kinds of interactions have differential effects on one's sense of self. For instance, when we argue with others, we typically feel irritation, frustration, and anger. When we are appreciated by others, we feel pride and gratitude. When we are rejected, we feel deprived, lonely, and sad. When we are acknowledged, we feel affirmed and legitimated. When we are offended, we feel disgust, contempt, or even rage. These differences in our experiences are obvious. What is less apparent is exactly how these experiences are generated, how they are maintained, how they change, how we sometimes get stuck in them, and how we might be able to move out of unwanted experiences. Shining a light on specific interaction patterns helps elucidate the vicissitudes of these experiences.

A second benefit of focusing on interpersonal patterns is that doing so simplifies overwhelming complexity. The connections in a salient pattern capture a great deal of potentially confusing detail. While we readily acknowledge that relying on too much simplicity has a significant downside in obscuring other possible distinctions that might be more useful, a clear systemic focus serves to reduce distractions and allows us to redirect more mental energy toward purposeful cognitive operations to facilitate therapeutic change.

Third, attending to interpersonal interaction patterns amplifies the relevance of specific behaviors. Events that occur again and again, in a recurrent pattern that is enduring and/or persistent, carry a disproportionate amount of weight in generating certain experiences and guiding subsequent actions. In contrast, when a particular event or behavior occurs only once and does not happen again, it becomes virtually insignificant. The singular event just falls away and carries little or no meaning as time unfolds and can usually be safely ignored.

One crucial exception to the latter occurs when the singular event is taken into memory and is re-enacted again and again in a person's imagination; in this case it becomes recurrent and patterned after all. It is the repetition and persistence within a pattern that contributes to the behavior's significance. For instance, if in the course of some family conflict a young child briefly shakes a fist at a parent, and everyone overlooks the action, and it does not happen again, the behavior carries little or no significance. On the other hand, if the child shakes a fist at the parent again and again, one would seek to identify the circumstances within which such behavior arises (e.g., a parent's insults and/or demands for obedience). However, if a parent shakes a fist at the child only once and it never happens again, but the child remembers, and re-imagines the parent's threatening behavior during future episodes of conflict, the child might manifest a recurrent pattern of fearful cowering.

The latter example points to a fourth benefit in attending to patterns. Only part of a pattern needs to be witnessed for other parts of the pattern to be inferred. If one person is cowering, someone else must have done something that is/was inviting such behavior. This points to the "added value" of pattern recognition. Certain categories of behavior predict other complementary behaviors that are often coordinated or "coupled" within an ongoing dance of common interaction patterns. These inferences add to further selective attention to notice, to unearth, and/or to bring forth some of the less obvious, yet extremely significant, components of the interaction that maintain the pattern. Frequently, it is these obscure elements that need to be proactively explicated for focused attention to facilitate enduring therapeutic change. Indeed, the parent may have long forgotten the original incident that the child is still reacting to in memory. Yet the parent's intermittent threatening, or even subtle hints thereof, need to be disclosed and challenged to open space for gradual change in the child's recurrent fear and pattern of cowering.

Coupled Invitations and Relational Stabilities

Several aspects of our unique focus on interpersonal patterns deserve explication. While it is probably more coherent to assume that human relationships are always in flux and are continually changing, we choose to use the notion of recurrent patterns to construct "relational stabilities" in our understandings. The pattern is deliberately imagined as more stable and continuous than it actually is. One reason for doing so has to do with the pragmatic value in having something more "concrete" to work with in our therapeutic efforts with clients. We create stable patterns in our distinctions and conceptualizations as "virtual entities" in our imagination to navigate among therapeutic possibilities. Yet these entities are not arbitrary imaginings; our selective systemic constructions are grounded in what clients do and say, in how they say it, in how others react or respond, and in observable transactions during interviews. The patterns distinguished yield greater clarity, help establish a heuristic focus, and orient our therapeutic initiatives. We actively bring forth and create these stabilities in our understanding of the interactions among family members, and between clients and ourselves, so we can work with them.

A central aspect in this cognitive constructive process is to distinguish the "coupling" of key behaviors of two or more persons as occurring in the interpersonal space.[1] When the behavior of one person becomes coordinated or coupled with a behavior of another person in a recurrent manner, a pattern arises. For instance, the behavior of pursuing may become coupled with a complementary behavior of distancing. The pursuing begets distancing while the distancing begets further pursuing, and the pattern goes on and on in a cyclical or circular fashion. It is tempting to see the complementary coupling as a connection between two persons (i.e., a pursuer and a distancer), but this construal sets the stage for a possible slip back toward individualistic thinking. Our conception of coupling deliberately gives priority to seeing the connection as existing *between the behaviors* in the interpersonal space, and not within either person's character. There is a heuristic reason for this; it helps therapists (and ultimately clients) to externalize pathology, to diminish entanglement in shame and blame, and to open space for therapeutic change. Furthermore, in many situations, the persons interacting can readily exchange their respective behavioral activities/reactivity while the basic interpersonal pattern remains exactly the same. In other words, the original "pursuer" can begin distancing while the original "distancer" engages in pursuing, yet the nature of the coupling in the relationship remains unchanged and "stable."

A second aspect of our construction is to construe the nature of the behavioral coupling as one of "mutual invitations." This theoretical thread comes from Maturana and Varela's (1980) assumption of structure determinism and the notion of structural coupling. Distancing invites pursuing and pursuing invites distancing. Each behavior invites the other in an ongoing dance of interaction. The use of the term "invites" is significant here because it inherently implies the possibility of change. Invitations are never deterministic in a linear manner; invitations can be accepted, or they can be declined. An invitation for a specific reaction or response in a recurrent pattern is usually quite compelling and typically is taken up, which is why the pattern becomes a relational stability. However, potentially it can be rejected, or respectfully turned down. The latter possibilities open space for personal agency toward change. A person previously participating in the pattern could decide to respond differently from what is predicted by the coupling in the pattern. Such agency increases with awareness and may be enhanced when a therapist proactively suggests different kinds of invitations (e.g., for behaviors that counter the usual behavior in the pattern). This possibility will become a recurrent theme throughout this book.

Ordinarily, it is quite difficult when sitting down with a family (or any subsystem of a family, like a parent and child, or two parents as a couple) to actually "see" the structure of their relationship. As implied earlier, our basic biological perceptual apparatus of vision and hearing inherently biases us to see and hear individual persons, rather than distinguishing the unique interaction patterns between them. Yet, it is precisely the latter that we are trying to privilege in developing a systems understanding. To draw upon an analogy of the familiar gestalt image of seeing two faces or seeing a vase (see Figure 3.1 in Chapter 3), we are trying to enable a figure-ground gestalt shift of deliberately moving away from seeing the shapes of the individual faces to seeing the shape of the vase in between. We are encouraging a proactive shift from seeing the characteristics of individual family members (the separate faces) to seeing the nature of the relationship patterns among family members (the shape of the vase) that activate their individual potentialities. This represents a conceptual paradigm shift, which is not easy for some people to achieve. To enable this shift, we have come to define our way of seeing as "looking through the IPscope." For the convenience of the reader, Figure 1.1 provides a complete list of acronyms associated with the IPscope, each of which will be defined next.

Defining the IPscope

The prefix "IP" in the IPscope refers to *Interpersonal Patterns* while the suffix "scope" is intended to draw a parallel with other human-made instruments like the microscope and the telescope that have been invented to help people see that which is difficult to see with the naked eye alone. Thus, by definition the IPscope is a cognitive instrument for distinguishing and describing Interpersonal Patterns (IPs) for systemic assessment. It includes both perceptual and conceptual elements and is intended to help construct interpersonal patterns "in one's mind's eye" that are ordinarily hard to see. When considering the softer versions of our IPscopic distinctions, an analogy with a kaleidoscope might be more apt than a microscope or telescope. As social constructionist

```
IPs    = Interpersonal Patterns

PIPs   = Pathologizing Interpersonal Patterns
WIPs   = Wellness Interpersonal Patterns
HIPs   = Healing Interpersonal Patterns

DIPs   = Deteriorating Interpersonal Patterns
TIPs   = Transforming Interpersonal Patterns

SCIPs  = Socio-Cultural Interpersonal Patterns
```

Figure 1.1 Acronyms of the IPscope

observers, we create multiple colorful shades among the patterns that we distinguish while co-constructing change together with families in therapy.

The component behaviors of a pattern are usually quite easy to see; what is much more difficult is to see the coupling between particular behaviors—that is, "the pattern which connects." What we are looking for are recurrent contingencies. What type of behavior elicits or begets what other type of behavior in a repetitive reciprocal manner? Immediate behavioral reactions in the here-and-now can be more readily recognized as couplings than delayed reactions that occur more remotely in time. Indeed, one of the important conceptual skills required in learning to use the IPscope effectively is to be able to "collapse time" onto a flat surface so that contingent couplings between intermittent or remotely recurring behaviors can become more visible. Difficulties in distinguishing couplings become much greater when the contingencies are irregular and/or when there are significant time intervals between one category of behavior and the contingent reaction or response.

Interpersonal Patterns, or IPs, are formally defined as repetitive or recurrent interactions between two or more persons distinguished by an observer (often a systemic therapist) that highlight the coupling between two classes of behaviors, attitudes, feelings, ideas, or beliefs and that tend to be mutually reinforcing. In this book, we give priority to describing behavioral couplings because they are more observable and generally more accessible in therapy. One's understanding of interaction patterns can be "thickened" when cognitive, attitudinal, and emotional couplings are added, but these couplings require greater inferences that inevitably are less well grounded. The interpersonal patterns maintain themselves as relatively stable components of the overall relationship between the persons interacting. The patterns exist in the interpersonal space and when internalized, predispose either person to re-engage in similar interaction patterns with the same person and with other persons.

In order to simplify and concretize the complexity of interaction in family systems, we developed a standard practice for drawing these interpersonal patterns. Our convention is to use a concrete structure of two arching arrows linking two categories of behavior that are separated by a backward slash (see Figures 1.2a, 1.2b, 1.2c). The slash is a "complementarity marker," a thread taken from George Spencer-Brown (1969) that implies the coupling of complementary behaviors. Whenever possible we use the gerund form of language to describe the behaviors (e.g., the verb "criticizing" rather than the noun "criticism") because the gerund implies the dynamic nature of the interaction. The arching arrows, taken together, imply the circularity or recurrent nature of systemic interaction as we collapse time onto a flat surface. The arrows, taken separately, are to be read as invitations. Two behavioral invitations are selected that

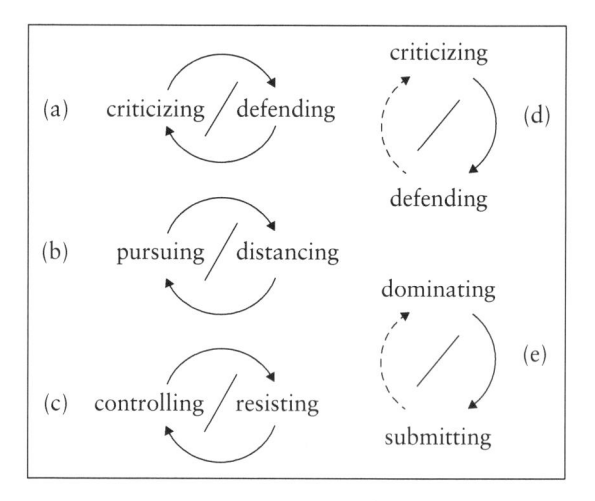

Figure 1.2 Sample PIPs

are mutually reinforcing. It is the coupled mutuality of the invitations that generates the apparent stability of the pattern. Behavior A invites Behavior B, while Behavior B in turn invites Behavior A, and so on, round and round. When there appears to be a significant power differential, we draw the pattern vertically rather than horizontally and place the stronger component in a hierarchical position above the weaker component of the pattern (see Figures 1.2d, 1.2e). The left upward arrow is also broken to imply less influence. This hierarchical positioning of one component becomes very useful in therapy by suggesting a safer starting point for therapeutic initiatives (i.e., to orient toward deconstructing the more powerful component first; more on this in Chapter 7). The simplicity of the diagram generates clarity, which is especially helpful in the face of the complexity of relationship dynamics.

As originally conceived (Tomm, 1991), the IPscope entails a pragmatic typology of five categories of patterns, two with predominantly negative effects and three with predominantly positive effects. The dichotomy of negative versus positive is intended to provide the therapist (and clients) with clear directionality regarding initiatives for preferred change—that is, always act to enable movement from negative to positive patterns. The two negative patterns include "Pathologizing Interpersonal Patterns" (PIPs) and "Deteriorating Interpersonal Patterns" (DIPs). The three positive patterns include "Wellness Interpersonal Patterns" (WIPs), "Healing Interpersonal Patterns" (HIPs), and "Transforming Interpersonal Patterns" (TIPs). Specific examples of each category will be offered in the next section. First, let me provide some definitions.

A **PIP** or *Pathologizing Interpersonal Pattern* is defined as a recurrent interpersonal interaction that invites or increases negativity, pain, and/or suffering in one or both persons interacting or results in significant stress within the relationship. Usually both parties participating in the pattern suffer, but in certain PIPs one party may realize some personal advantages in the pattern while the other party suffers disproportionately, as for instance in the PIP of *dominating coupled with submitting* (see Figure 1.2e). A **DIP** or *Deteriorating Interpersonal Pattern* is a sub-category of a PIP, which creates conditions for a possible or probable slip from a positive pattern (i.e., from a WIP, HIP, or TIP) toward a PIP. Typically DIPs are fleeting, whereas PIPs tend to persist or recur frequently.

A **WIP** or *Wellness Interpersonal Pattern* is defined as a recurrent interpersonal interaction that enables positivity, competence, and/or effectiveness of one or both participants and/or sustains or enhances health in the relationship. Like PIPs, WIPs also tend to be relatively stable and persistent, but in contrast to PIPs, WIPs nurture and/or sustain mental well-being. Fortunately, most of us live in WIPs in our close relationships most of the time. A **HIP** or *Healing Interpersonal Pattern* is a sub-category of a WIP that constitutes a specific "antidote" to a particular PIP by bringing forth positive behaviors and/or experiences (in one or both of the participants) that specifically preclude or contradict some component of the PIP. Distinguishing HIPs during the course of therapy provides more specific directionality for constructive change. A particular HIP can serve as a compass of sorts to help clients escape from a particular PIP. A **TIP** or *Transforming Interpersonal Pattern* is also a sub-category of a WIP, which enables movement from a PIP toward a HIP or WIP. Like DIPs, TIPs are also more fleeting. They typically enable therapists to help clients move out of PIPs and into HIPs and WIPs. TIPs are the kinds of interaction patterns we try to enter into with our clients during the actual doing of therapy and will be described in detail in Chapter 5.

Other types of patterns could also be distinguished. For instance, in Chapter 6 of this book, St. George and Wulff propose distinguishing SCIPs or "Socio-Cultural Interpersonal Patterns" as an extension of the framework to disclose aspects of the larger social domain that become manifest within families. SCIPs are defined as "the behavioral performances that occur when families act in alignment with their ideas or interpretations of the societal discourses within which they live [and] re-inscribe . . . those same societal discourses" (Chapter 6, p. 132). In contrast to the other IPs, SCIPs can have either positive or negative effects, depending on which socio-cultural discourses are taken up and how they are enacted in family living (see Chapter 6). The addition of SCIPs to the framework is extremely useful in that it significantly enlarges the scope of useful therapeutic conversation. In actual clinical practice, the main focus tends to be primarily on two kinds of patterns, PIPs and HIPs, which together provide a useful map to guide therapists and clients away from pathology and toward healing.

It is an observer, usually a systemic therapist, who distinguishes the pattern in the first place and who decides what type of pattern is being described and whether the effects of the pattern are negative or positive. This decision-making has to do with the way in which the cognitive act of drawing a distinction entails attributing properties to that which has been distinguished (Maturana & Varela, 1980). The positive or negative valence of the pattern distinguished is determined on the basis of the observer's intuition about the experiences of the participants engaged in the pattern at any particular moment. That is, PIPs by definition are interpersonal patterns that are having "pathologizing" effects on the persons involved, while HIPs and WIPs by definition are patterns that are having "healing" or "wellness" effects respectively. Sometimes precisely the same behavioral pattern could be seen as having positive effects on one occasion and as having negative effects on another. The specific effect depends on the nature of the behaviors enacted in the pattern and the meanings attributed to those behaviors by the persons involved in the interaction at any particular point in time. Once a particular PIP or WIP becomes established within a relationship system, third, fourth, fifth, and sixth persons are easily recruited into participating in the same pattern with similar activity; thus, they add to its effects. In other words, the mental health effects of a particular pattern may not just be recurrent and repetitive; they could be cumulative and occasionally become exponential.

Examples of the Five Categories of Patterns

Figure 1.2a describes an extremely common PIP occurring between two or more persons when criticism becomes coupled with defensiveness: *criticizing invites defending while defending invites further criticizing.*[2] As each person in the interaction enacts his/her respective criticizing and defending, the behaviors become coupled in a cyclical or circular interaction pattern. Increased criticism invites increased defensiveness and vice-versa. From a systemic perspective, the coupling in the pattern appears to take on a life of its own and induces the participants to continue in it. Over time, the pattern could become stabilized as a major component of an ongoing interpersonal relationship. If the relationship is an important one and the pattern persists for an extended period of time, it tends to promote psychopathological phenomena within the individual participants: for instance, righteous indignation, chronic frustration, aggressiveness, and even hatred in the person criticizing, and oppositional behavior, rebelliousness, paranoia, avoidance, isolation, and/or depression in the person defending. These individual effects then tend to be regarded as reflecting pathology within those persons. Yet, from a systemic perspective, the primary pathology lies in the interpersonal interaction pattern. The individual psychopathology, if it still can be coherently described as individual, is only secondary. Nevertheless, the effects of the pattern of *criticizing coupled with defending* can become extremely destructive in relation to persons and could escalate to precipitate violence, even murder or suicide if an escalation continues without restraint. It is because of these problematic negative effects that the pattern is labelled as pathologizing.

The ubiquitous PIP of *criticizing coupled with defending* is very interesting for a number of reasons. First, the participants in the pattern can readily exchange positions while the pattern remains exactly the same. For instance, the person initially defending could go on the offensive and start criticizing the other person for being so critical; this then becomes an invitation for the other to defend. The participants in the interaction then suddenly change roles but the nature of the interaction pattern remains virtually unchanged. Indeed, the interactants often flip-flop back and forth very easily within the pattern because both parties are so familiar with the overall pattern. Second, this pattern has a strong propensity to recruit additional parties, like other family members, to join in the pattern as well. For instance, if a father begins criticizing a son, the mother could be tempted to join the pattern as well. She could enter the pattern on either side: defend the son against the father's criticism, or join the father in criticizing the son. It does not matter which side she takes, the pattern remains the same except that it becomes more pervasive and intense. Third, given that this particular pattern is so common and most of us are intimately familiar with it, we as therapists are also at risk of being recruited into the pattern. As with the mother, we could enter at either end, by defending the son against the father's unreasonable criticism and in so doing implicitly criticize the father for being critical, or we could affirm the father's authority and criticize the son for being uncooperative or disrespectful. Either way we simply "pour gasoline on the fire" and add to the pathologizing process, which would of course be counter-therapeutic.

A HIP that could serve as a specific antidote to this PIP of *criticizing coupled with defending* might be *selective noticing and acknowledging competence that invites performing more acts of competence*, which in turn, invites more noticing of competence (see Figure 1.3a). Practice threads of drawing out exceptions in solution-focused work (de Shazer, 1985) and noticing unique outcomes in narrative work (White, 2007) are clearly implied in this healing pattern. The reason we consider this HIP a specific antidote to the criticizing coupled with defending PIP (see Figure 1.2a or 1.2d), is that "criticizing" and "acknowledging competence" are mutually exclusive activities, and it is impossible to enact contradictory behaviors at the same moment in time. So, if one person proactively acknowledges competence during an enactment of this PIP, the criticism of the prior interaction is momentarily eclipsed and

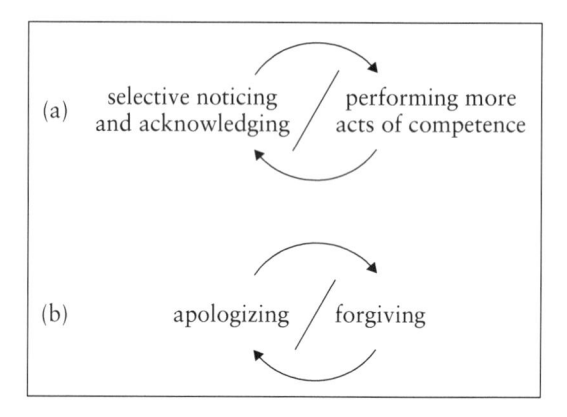

Figure 1.3 Sample HIPs

the other person is invited into a very different response. This yields a high probability that the whole nature of the interaction might suddenly transform into the HIP.

In the *acknowledging coupled with performing competence* (HIP) pattern, the complementary behaviors clearly have positive effects on the participants (e.g., respect arises in the first person for the competence manifested by the other, and greater self-confidence and appreciation arises in the second person because of the acknowledgment). Most human beings have the potential for enacting this healing pattern simply by virtue of having experienced it in their own growth and development. Parents often spend hours and days watching their young children for signs of achievement—for instance, in beginning to walk or talk—and heap praise upon the child when he/she makes progress, which of course supports the child's efforts to continue to perform competently. This healing pattern may, however, be quite difficult to bring forth and maintain when the *criticizing coupled with defending* pattern is very intense and dominates the relationship. A few acknowledgments of competence in such circumstances might not be heard and may not be enough. In this case, therapeutic enactment of a TIP (see Chapter 5) may be required to facilitate a shift from the PIP to a HIP. A more powerful healing antidote might need to be brought forth like *apologizing coupled with forgiving* (see Figure 1.3b), which could be more effective in disrupting an entrenched problematic process.

One of the reasons that a PIP may be so difficult to interrupt and replace is that the participants in the pattern are usually unaware of the fact that their actions are actually perpetuating the pattern. Indeed, while one is immersed in a particular pattern, one tends to narrowly attend to one's own intentions, words, and actions (or the words and actions of the other) rather than to the *coupled interaction* pattern of both parties in which those behaviors are embedded. Furthermore, many individual reactions become habitual and the reactive aspect usually remains non-conscious. A conversation that invites the participants to reflect and become aware and recognize that they are, in fact, immersed in a PIP is often a first step in interrupting it. Such a clarifying conversation of *asking about experiences coupled with disclosing experiences* (see Figure 1.4a) would be an example of a TIP that could invite a shift out of the PIP. Additional generative conversation of *asking reflexive questions coupled with distinguishing new possibilities* (see Figure 1.4b) to proactively identify components of healing or wellness patterns that could be initiated would be another TIP. The former TIP could be regarded as deconstructive, whereas the latter TIP could be seen to be constructive. My co-authors Gaete, Sametband, and Sutherland will provide further clarification of these kinds of TIPs in Chapter 5.

A WIP that would be relevant to the patterns in Figure 1.2a and Figure 1.3a could entail *giving constructive feedback coupled with recognizing and correcting one's mistakes* shown in Figure 1.5a. New learning probably occurs most efficiently when persons are embedded in such interactions. This WIP typically emerges when people ask for help and are given help, or in coaching and teaching situations where explicit guidance is offered, and is accepted as such by the other. Most of us live in various wellness patterns most of the time as we interact with family members, friends, and colleagues. A generic WIP of *showing affection and respect coupled with appreciating affection and respect*, illustrated in Figure 1.5b, is very common in relationships that are satisfying. Other common wellness patterns include *giving service coupled with giving gratitude, providing care coupled with accepting care*, and *acknowledging the other coupled with acknowledging the acknowledgment*.

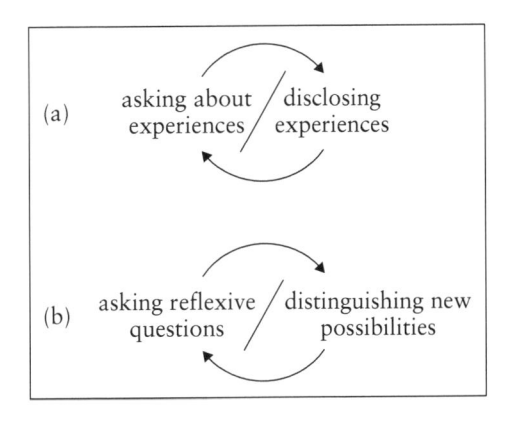

Figure 1.4 Sample TIPs

(a) giving constructive feedback / recognizing and correcting mistakes

(b) showing affection and respect / appreciating affection and respect

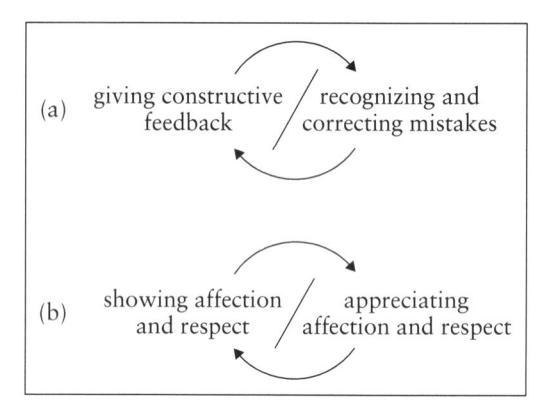

Figure 1.5 Sample WIPs

The efficacy of problem-solving is stronger within the WIP of *giving feedback coupled with learning from mistakes* (see Figure 1.5a) than in the HIP of *acknowledging competence coupled with performing competence* (see Figure 1.3a). But for this WIP to be actualized after a PIP of *criticizing inviting defending* has emerged, there needs to be considerable interpersonal trust and a conviction that the other person has good intentions. If there is insufficient trust, that which may be intended as constructive feedback by one person may be heard by the other as criticism, in which case the other is liable to respond with defensiveness. The result could be that the first person then starts criticizing the second for not taking the feedback as it was intended. In so doing both parties slip back into the PIP of *criticizing coupled with defending*. Because of this risk, it is usually more effective in therapy to first try, in the therapeutic conversation, to bring forth a HIP (see Figure 1.3a) rather than encourage a WIP (see Figure 1.5a) since the HIP is more likely to be successful in avoiding a slip back to the habitual PIP (see Figure 1.2a).

Paying too much attention to another person's possible errors or mistakes in order to give feedback could invite self-conscious awkwardness in the other, and a DIP of *scrutinizing the other coupled with awkward performing* could arise (see Figure 1.6a). The scrutiny in this DIP tends to drift toward *evaluating coupled with evading* that eventually could reactivate the PIP of *criticizing coupled with defending*. Other generic DIPs include *misinterpreting good intentions coupled with expressing disappointment, reducing expectations coupled with reducing performance, distorting feedback coupled with over-reacting,* and *withholding information coupled with failing to learn* (see Figure 1.6b).

Different emotions and their relationships are very significant in generating and supporting different types of interpersonal behavior patterns.

INTRODUCING THE IPSCOPE

(a) scrutinizing performance / self-conscious and awkward performing

(b) withholding information / failing to learn

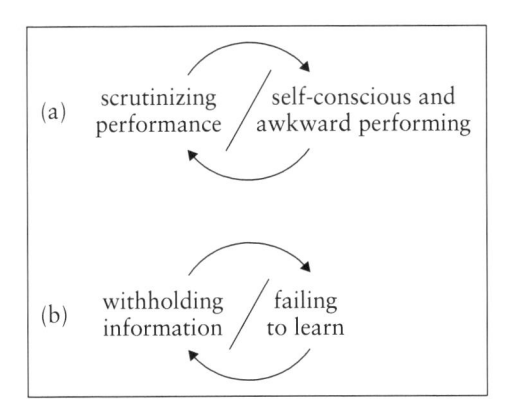

Figure 1.6 Sample DIPs

For example, anger and fear often become coupled in a pattern of interpersonal "emotioning" of *anger coupled with fear* to energize the behavioral coupling of *criticizing coupled with defending*. Analogously, love and pride can become stabilized as an emotioning WIP of *love coupled with pride* to enable the behavioral HIP of *selective affirming coupled with performing competence*. When therapists attend to these underlying emotions and their potential coupling, they are usually more effective in distinguishing the kinds of behavioral couplings that are most relevant in the process of therapy. The strong emotions aroused by any major event in life could be negative or positive and for the most part depend on cultural values and beliefs that have been internalized to give meaning to such events. This is where therapeutic exploration of SCIPs is especially useful. Negative feelings of fear, anger, disgust, and sadness would probably activate DIPs and PIPs. Positive feelings of caring, compassion, and empathy usually activate HIPs or WIPs. In the course of an interview, a therapist might invoke a deconstructive TIP of *asking about restraining SCIPs coupled with disclosing and distancing from these SCIPs* or a constructive TIP of *asking about enabling SCIPs coupled with drawing from and enacting preferred SCIPs*. To maximize wellness, it is incumbent upon family members to develop resilience to move freely among their values, beliefs, emotions, and behavior patterns, always giving priority to HIPs and WIPs. A schematic outline of possible movements among the five categories of interpersonal patterns within an ongoing relationship, or in the process of therapy, is illustrated in Figure 1.7. PIPs could yield to TIPs and enable movement into HIPs and WIPs, where we always remain vulnerable to DIPs that might take us back to PIPs. Obviously, most of us would prefer to live out most of our relationships by interacting on the right side of the diagram.

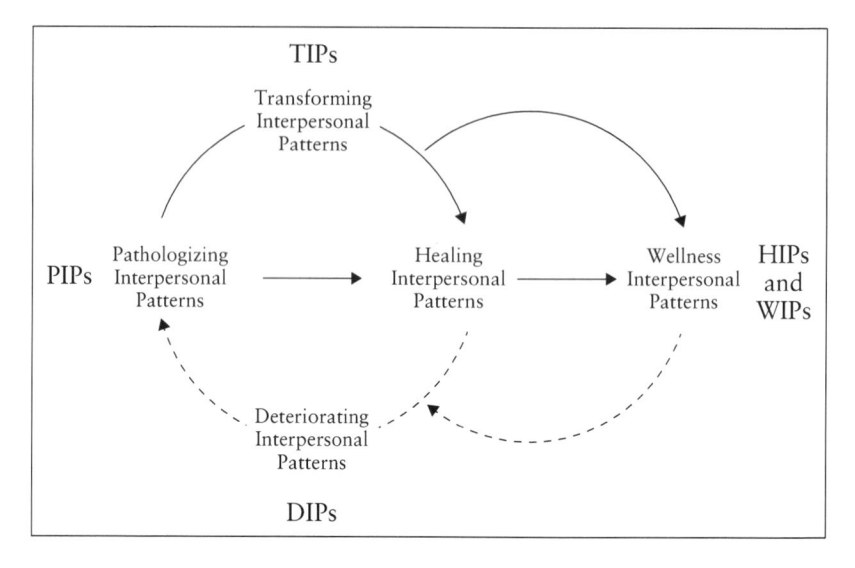

Figure 1.7 Movement among different interaction patterns within an ongoing interpersonal relationship

Similarities and Differences Among Families

We assume that all families will generate a variety of interaction patterns within their relationships, some of which could be characterized as PIPs and others as WIPs. Furthermore, we also assume that over time any major ongoing relationship (between family members, friends, workmates, and/or professionals) will probably evolve to include the full repertoire of all five categories of interaction patterns, even though the specific characteristics of particular patterns are always unique. Inevitably, certain patterns become more fully elaborated and deeply established in one relationship compared to another relationship.

What makes the difference between clinical families (i.e., families who present for therapy) and so-called healthy families is not that the former enact PIPs while the latter enact WIPs. Both sets of families enact both kinds of patterns. Clinical families simply live in PIPs more of the time and have much more difficulty getting out of them. Healthy families also slip into PIPs from time to time, when personal differences come up between family members and conflict arises, but these families tend to recover quickly and easily re-establish HIPs and WIPs in their ongoing living together. The positive experience of living in such families is aptly captured by William Blake's poem cited at the beginning of this chapter: "Mutual Forgiveness of each Vice, Such are the Gates of Paradise" (1793, republished 1982). In contrast, clinical families often languish in their "Hell" of intense PIPs for extended periods of time and are not able to escape them as readily. Yet both sets of families remain similar in that all five categories of patterns are available in their relationship repertoire.

It is very important for therapists to assume that all clinical families do have HIPs and WIPs as part of their relationship system. When we do so, we are inclined to search for them and selectively open space for their re-emergence in the course of therapy. Whether a family fosters pathology, healing, or wellness among its members depends on which patterns dominate their daily activities and experiences. Obviously, a predominance of PIPs is extremely undesirable. However, as noted earlier, active participation in pathologizing patterns is typically outside one's awareness at the time, and the negative effects are usually inadvertent and unintended. For instance, an initiative to obtain cooperation may be intended as constructive, but it could be experienced as controlling (see Figure 1.2c). The resultant reactive resistance is probably intended as self-protective rather than as rejection, denial, or disqualification of the original initiative. Yet when these behaviors become coupled and patterned into a recurrent interpersonal process of *controlling coupled with resisting*, the discrepancy between intentions and effects is overlooked and/or misinterpreted. A straightforward clarifying conversation of *asking about intentions coupled with disclosing intentions* (see Figure 1.4a) can sometimes open space for enormous relief and occasionally create conditions for a spontaneous healing pattern of *apologizing coupled with forgiving* to emerge (see Figure 1.3b). Further questions about SCIPs might disclose assumptions that feed the PIPs, as well as alternative assumptions that might stabilize HIPs.

Because HIPs and PIPs influence the mental health of the persons participating in them so significantly, and do so in opposite directions, we consider a focus on these patterns as extremely relevant to psychiatric and psychological assessment and treatment. It is important to note that our shift in focus from the personal to the interpersonal is not the same as a simple shift in focus from the individual level to the family level. The qualitative mental health differences between families lie in which interpersonal patterns predominate, not with the characteristics of whole families themselves. We focus on identifying or "diagnosing" the PIPs, not the families in which they are enacted. There is no need to diagnose whole families. Indeed, I am opposed to classifying and labelling families as "dysfunctional," "enmeshed," "psychosomatic," "depressogenic," or "schizophrenogenic." Insofar as one identifies with a particular family, the pejorative labels attached to that family also become attached to the self. Diagnosing whole families simply pathologizes more people.

The process of clinicians assessing a person's mental health and determining if he/she has a mental illness is, in itself, a culturally sanctioned pattern of interaction of *diagnosing persons coupled with identifying with a disorder* (a SCIP; see Chapters 6 and 11) that could have either pathologizing or healing effects. For instance, diagnosing could be experienced as healing when a person or family is relieved to discover that something definable is wrong and can be medically treated. However, as noted in the introduction, when this process becomes one of primarily sticking unwanted psychiatric labels onto persons, it could become profoundly pathologizing regarding their identities. Our alternative is for clinicians to distinguish, assess, label, and diagnose selected *interpersonal patterns of interaction* as pathological rather than the individuals or families participating in those patterns. This implies a fundamental shift in focus from the personal to the interpersonal. The negative stigmatizing effect of labelling is thereby applied to the pathologizing pattern itself rather than to the persons enacting it. In other words, labelling PIPs pathologizes the externalized pathology, not the persons or the family immersed in the problematic process. A further effect of labelling an *interaction pattern* is that doing so opens space for the persons involved to more easily disassociate from the pattern, which could be the beginning of healing. Finally, the distinction of a specific PIP implies the possibility of logically conceiving of a specific HIP as an antidote (more on this in Chapter 3). These are all potentially constructive influences on the mental health of the persons involved in the patterns. Thus, the HIPs and PIPs "means" to assessment does not contradict the therapeutic "ends" of our clinical program—it contributes to them.

What becomes increasingly important in one's lived experience and to one's mental health is not only which patterns predominate but also the intensity of those patterns and the flexibility in movement among them. We feel that it is socially responsible to allocate limited treatment resources to interrupt intense PIPs that are actively producing pathology, regardless of whether one distinguishes an individual mental disorder or not. Indeed, if a diagnosable disorder is not yet evident, but severe PIPs are allowed to continue, a mental disorder may be expected to emerge later. Thus, PIPs that are intense and persistent should be given a high priority for treatment. This would be in keeping with a basic principle of triage: treat the most treatable first. In other words, it seems more justified to apply limited professional resources to interrupt intense PIPs that are occurring in the present than to treat an easily diagnosable but less treatable patient, who may be the victim or "end product" of ongoing PIPs that persisted over extended periods of time in the past (see Chapter 11).

Deconstructing Individual Diagnoses Into PIPs

The approximately 200 PIPs alluded to in the original paper (Tomm, 1991) about this framework were sorted into a relatively small number of common PIPs that could be associated with specific diagnoses or certain kinds of clinical presentations. As an initial step to develop an alternative to DSM categories, my colleagues and I at the family therapy program began differentiating specific PIPs that appeared to generate or aggravate particular individual mental problems.

For instance, an individual client presenting with depression could often be seen as embedded in general relationship patterns of *dominating with oppressive practices coupled with submitting with depressive practices* (see Figure 1.8a). The dominating feeds the submitting which feeds the depression, which in turn feeds further dominating and so on. Another common, but more specific, pattern associated with depression is one of *blaming or diminishing the other coupled with blaming and diminishing the self* (see Figure 1.8b). The pervasive tendency to criticize oneself when feeling depressed elicits corrective feedback from others which is often experienced as criticism and may serve to deepen the depression, even when the feedback arises from good intentions. Healing antidotes to these two depressogenic patterns might entail *acknowledging and relinquishing oppressive practices coupled with protesting oppression and assuming more personal agency* and *affirming and crediting the other coupled with affirming and crediting the self* respectively.

Clients presenting with psychotic symptoms are often deeply embedded in a general pattern of *ostracizing and excluding coupled with manifesting bizarre thoughts and behavior* or a specific pattern of *invalidating and/or disqualifying coupled with showing confusion and/or incoherence*. Paranoia sometimes emerges from persistent patterns of *withholding information coupled with reacting with suspicion*. Lying and stealing are commonly associated with living in patterns of *judgmental condemning*

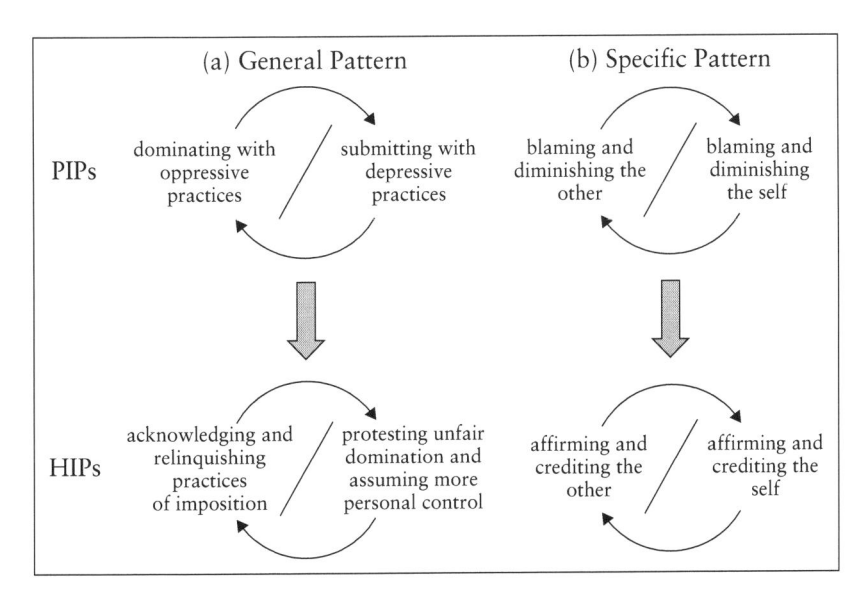

Figure 1.8 Linking depressogenic PIPs with antidepressant HIPs

coupled with deceptive evading and/or *demanding honest disclosure and threatening punishment coupled with withholding the truth and/or telling alibis or misleading truths*. If there is sibling rivalry it can be aggravated by *parents claiming to treat siblings exactly the same coupled with siblings searching for differences in treatment and complaining about unfairness*. Adolescent rebelliousness is often associated with *parents imposing outer controls coupled with adolescents protesting and rejecting outer controls*.

Specific healing antidotes to each of these kinds of PIPs have been formulated to provide guidance for therapeutic initiatives. In other words, we describe both problems and solutions in terms of interpersonal interaction. Conceiving of a possible HIP to counter a particular PIP provides a map that orients both therapists and families in their efforts to move toward wellness. However, it is almost always more useful therapeutically to co-construct together with clients the specific IPs that apply in their particular relationship, in their particular situation, at a particular point in time, rather than apply previously defined exemplar PIPs and their formulaic antidotes. The further we move along in therapy, the more likely we are to explicitly draw specific patterns on a blackboard or pad of paper together with the family. Being co-creative fosters an "experience-near" process that is grounded in local relevance and is more liable to yield realistic possibilities for change. Attention to the nuances involved in clarifying these different interaction patterns has also led to explorations with different kinds of questions that therapists ask to enable therapeutic movement (Tomm, 1987, 1988) and to differing styles of clinical interviewing which are commented on in subsequent chapters of this book.

Students who join our program are now routinely introduced to our PIPs and HIPs framework for understanding interpersonal process. They are invited to look into our IPscope together with us to learn how to see in their developing mind's eye the kinds of relationship patterns that our experienced staff members have come to see quite readily by virtue of their experience in understanding systemic process. My hope is that this book will provide opportunities for a wider audience to join in this constructionist and/or bringforthist orientation and realize the potential benefits of a systemic perspective in their clinical work.

Our focus on interactional assessment has not been limited to family systems. It has been extended to social networks (e.g., friendships, families of origin, neighborhoods), larger social systems (e.g., workplace, education, health care, the law) and cultural patterns (e.g., sexism, heterosexism, racism, classism, ethnocentricity). Some of these extensions will be elaborated in the following chapters in this book, especially Chapters 6, 7, 8, and 11. Indeed, the ubiquitous PIP of *dominating coupled with submitting* can be seen as contributing to pathology in human relations in a wide range of domains beyond families, including large groups or communities, and even whole nations.

INTRODUCING THE IPSCOPE

An Unresolved Conundrum

While the simplicity of the PIPs and HIPs diagrams helps clarify and summarize a great deal of complexity, the drawings can easily be mistaken for first-order descriptions of objective realities. It is easy to drift into assuming that "the patterns are really there." We are definitely not trying to imply objectivity in drawing patterns that illustrate the recurrent nature of interpersonal interaction. We regard ourselves as systemically oriented observers who selectively draw out perceptual distinctions of recurrent behaviors that are then conceptually coupled and placed in the drawing for focused attention. In other words, it is the therapist-as-participant-observer who actually creates and names the pattern in his/her distinctions for the pragmatic purpose of orienting the process of therapy. An ongoing awareness of the creative activity of the observer in generating the distinctions and the couplings incorporated in the diagram is sometimes hard to maintain, yet it is this second-order perspective of "looking at our looking to see what we are seeing, and see how our seeing guides our therapeutic initiatives" that we are hoping to convey. For instance, the coupling of the same behaviors could be distinguished by a therapist as a PIP in one situation and a HIP in another. For instance, a PIP of *reducing expectations coupled with reducing performance* in a situation of underachieving may call for a HIP of *increasing expectations coupled with increasing performance* (see Figure 1.9a). However, in a situation of burnout the latter "HIP" could be more coherently distinguished as a

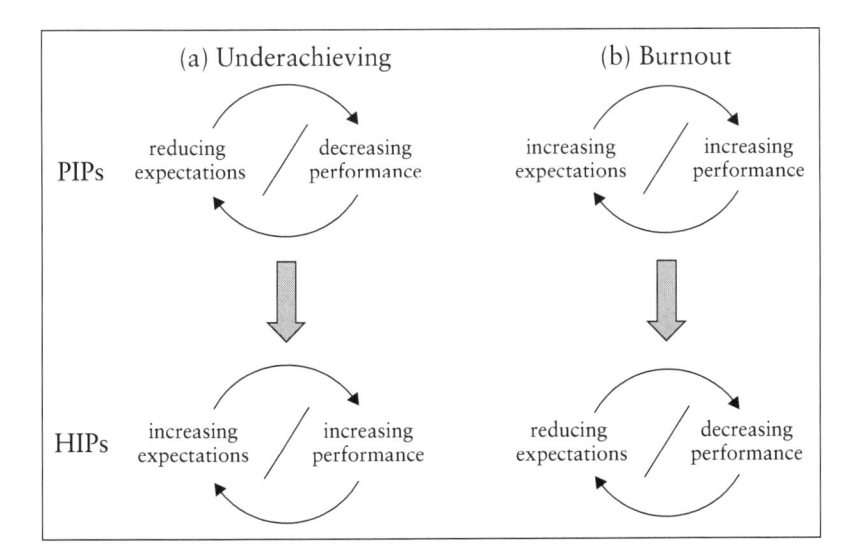

Figure 1.9 Adopting a second-order perspective to distinguish the orienting effects of one's own distinctions

PIP, in which case the previous "PIP" could be distinguished as a HIP (see Figure 1.9b). In actual practice, the elusiveness of the patterns themselves serves to remind us of our own activity in bringing them forth in our understandings. But sometimes this is not enough, especially when we labor under a strong desire to know "what's really going on" in difficult clinical situations.

The unresolved issue continues: how can we highlight this creative process within the diagrams to remind ourselves of our activity in distinguishing these patterns? It would be helpful in maintaining a second-order constructionist stance if we could incorporate an Escher-like depiction of our own activities in drawing these distinctions as part of the diagram itself. If only we could draw ourselves drawing the conceptual distinctions that we draw cognitively as we work with our clients, we would undoubtedly maintain a clearer mindfulness of our bringforthist responsibilities during the conduct of therapy. This could help reduce the chances of an overt or covert slip back toward a rigid objectivist view. Needless-to-say, we have not yet found an easy way to do so. We have experimented with placing Maturana's "eye" alongside the diagram, to remind us that the pattern is a result of our "IPscopic way of seeing," but this convention has not been taken up by our group. You, as a reader, are invited to join us on this journey to find simple yet heuristic ways to reflect on the complexities of family life, and of family therapy, in ways that help us help the families we serve.

Notes

1. In keeping with our desire for simplicity, most of our interpersonal patterns are presented as two-person (dyadic) coordinations of recurrent behaviors, as a way to emphasize the complementary nature of the pattern. In three-person or more complex systems, subgroups often join in on either side of the complementarity. Alternatively, third parties may remain outside of the interaction temporarily.
2. Verbal descriptions of coupled invitations that reflect specific interpersonal interaction patterns are italicized throughout the book to highlight them as transient relational stabilities in the interpersonal space.

References

Bateson, G. (1972). *Steps to an ecology of mind*. San Francisco, CA: Chandler.
Bateson, G. (1979). *Mind and nature: A necessary unity*. New York, NY: E.P. Dutton.
Blake, W. (1982). *The complete poetry and prose of William Blake* (D.V. Erdman, Ed.). New York, NY: Anchor Books.
Bowen, M. (1978). *Family therapy in clinical practice*. New York, NY: Jason Aronson.
de Shazer, S. (1985). *Keys to solution in brief therapy*. New York, NY: Norton.

Epstein, N., & Bishop, D. (1981). Problem-centered systems therapy of the family. In A. Gurman & D. Kniskern (Eds.), *Handbook of family therapy* (pp. 444–482). New York, NY: Brunner/Mazel.

Epstein, N., Bishop, D., & Levin, S. (1978). The McMaster model of family functioning. *Journal of Marriage and Family Counseling, 4*(4), 19–31.

Gergen, K. J., & Gergen, M. (2004). *Social construction: Entering the dialogue.* Chagrin Falls, OH: Taos Institute.

Maturana, H., & Varela, F. (1980). *Autopoiesis and cognition: The realization of the living.* Boston, MA: Reidel.

Maturana, H., & Varela, F. (1992). *The tree of knowledge.* Boston, MA: Shambhala.

Minuchin, S. (1974). *Families and family therapy.* Cambridge, MA: Harvard University Press.

Selvini Palazzoli, M., Boscolo, L., Cecchin, G., & Prata, G. (1978). *Paradox and counterparadox: A new model in the therapy of the family in schizophrenic transaction.* New York, NY: Jason Aronson.

Selvini Palazzoli, M., Boscolo, L., Cecchin, G., & Prata, G. (1980). Hypothesizing-circularity-neutrality: Guidelines for the conductor of the session. *Family Process, 19*(1), 3–12.

Spencer-Brown, G. (1969). *Laws of form.* New York, NY: Dutton.

Tomm, K. (1980). Towards a cybernetic-systems approach to family therapy at the University of Calgary. In D. S. Freeman (Ed.), *Perspectives on family therapy* (pp. 3–18). Toronto, ON: Butterworths Press.

Tomm, K. (1987). Interventive interviewing: Part II. Reflexive questioning as a means to enable self-healing. *Family Process, 26*(2), 167–183.

Tomm, K. (1988). Interventive interviewing: Part III. Intending to ask lineal, circular, reflexive and strategic questions? *Family Process, 27*(1), 1–15.

Tomm, K. (1991). Beginnings of a "HIPs and PIPs" approach to psychiatric assessment. *Calgary Participator, 1*(2), 21–22, 24.

von Bertalanffy, L. (1968). *General systems theory: Foundations, development, applications.* New York, NY: Braziller.

Watzlawick, P., Bavelas, J. B., & Jackson, D. D. (1967). *Pragmatics of human communication: A study of interactional patterns, pathologies, and paradoxes.* New York, NY: Norton.

White, M. (2007). *Maps of narrative practice.* New York, NY: Norton.

White, M., & Epston, D. (1990). *Narrative means to therapeutic ends.* New York, NY: Norton.

2

CONCEPTUALIZING INTERACTIONAL PATTERNS

Theoretical Threads to Facilitate Recognizing and Responding to IPs

Tom Strong

> "The nature of pattern is not something you can fool around with."
> —Gregory Bateson (1982, p. 353)
>
> "All distinctions are mind, by mind, in mind, of mind. No distinctions, no mind to distinguish."
> —R. D. Laing (1970, p. 82)

Family therapists join families' problem conversations and interactions in ways they hope make a beneficial difference. How they make sense of such conversations and interactions involves particular kinds of noticing and dialogue. Part of Gregory Bateson's (1972) research-derived legacy to family therapy has been a focus on patterns of communication and interaction. On the clinical initiative of Karl Tomm, family therapists at the Calgary Family Therapy Centre (CFTC) have been developing and using a unique, pattern-oriented approach to relational sense-making for some time (Tomm, 1991). Using this approach orients us to how we join the families in therapy's conversational work of making things better. It even focuses part of our clinical record-keeping (see Chapter 3). In this chapter, I will conceptually orient readers to how we notice and join communication or interactive patterns that inform our work with clients. CFTC's Interpersonal Patterns (IPs) inform how we assess, intervene, and track therapeutic concerns and progress made in addressing them in our conversations with families.

Some Personal and Historical Context

Delving into the rich ideas that inform therapeutic practice (e.g., Lock & Strong, 2010, 2012) was my response to a personal sense of conceptual inadequacy. Armed with a BA in Political Science, my first "real job" involved working with kids on probation on the streets of Prince Rupert, a small city on British Columbia's northwest coast. I then got my teaching qualifications, returned to set up an alternative high school for these kids, and was later recruited into a junior high school counseling role because I "could talk to kids." I chose to go to graduate school where I thought I could learn about counseling "correctly and effectively." In learning to counsel in collaborative, generative, and strength-focused ways, I came to increasingly reflect upon what clients and I may problematically take-for-granted. In the ideas of relational, narrative, solution-focused, and collaborative practitioner-authors, I found both conceptual and practical ways of being helpful. In narrative therapy terms, however, references to the ideas of these approaches seemed "thin," so I kept reading and learning to better integrate social constructionist and relational ideas of practice. The ideas keep evolving with me as I teach, research, supervise, and practice in critically reflective, generative, and collaborative ways.

As I moved on to academic life, I became fascinated with how family therapists regard their communications with families (and those family members have with each other). What was it about therapists' communications that promoted change or "helped" to sustain sameness? How were families who came to the CFTC problem organized through their communicating and interacting? If families did not function or appear as "structures," I wondered how I, as someone who had practiced on both sides of the poststructural divide (more on this divide later), should regard patterns like the Pathologizing Interpersonal Patterns (PIPs) I collaboratively identified and worked on with families. However, it became apparent that my communications with families, and family members' communications with each other, could not represent in words experiences and relationships "as they actually were." Social constructionist and poststructuralist therapists had abandoned such structural efforts to name experience "correctly" and instead invited families to join them in reflective and generative searches for preferred language by which they could better interact. These searches, however, are as much about new words, stories, and discourses as they are about new ways of interacting. Meaningful interaction within families and in family therapy can be challenging to grasp, so I offer this chapter to synthesize diverse ideas, research, and clinical experience into my account of IPs.

Recognizing Family Members' Patterned Interactions

Family therapy emerged, in part, from recognizing that individual clients' concerns could often be best understood and addressed in the relationships in which they occurred. Accordingly, concerns about a child's misbehavior were not seen as occurring independently from those social contexts. Contexts, however, can seem like circumstances in which one finds oneself and not circumstances one can do much about. Close examinations of family therapy helped to highlight how concerns occurring in such social contexts may be understood and *performed* in and through family members' patterned ways of responding to each other (e.g., Bateson, Jackson, Haley, & Weakland, 1956). Family contexts, in other words, were shaped by family member interactions. While individually-oriented therapists had focused on clients' thoughts, feelings, or behaviors, many family therapists suggested noticing and engaging with family members' ways of interacting (Nichols & Schwartz, 2008). To return to Bateson's (1980) language, family therapists' focus needed to be on "the pattern which connects" (p. 8) concerns to the people enacting them. He developed his views as an anthropologist studying how cultures interacted, views he adapted to studying therapeutic conversation (Bateson et al., 1956; Reusch & Bateson, 1951).

Bateson was also an early contributor to the cybernetic movement. Cyberneticians focused on predictable, rule-governed behavior in self-directing systems—human systems included. The cybernetic metaphor attracted many family therapists who saw in it more causal and instrumental potentials than did Bateson. Family systems, by such a causal view, included structures to be identified and acted upon by neutral observers, such as strategic family therapists.

This purportedly gender and power neutral understanding of families, along with a mechanistic view of family members and family therapy interactions, attracted considerable criticism. A feminist critique (e.g., Goldner, 1988) focused on obscured power differentials and essentialized gender roles in families (e.g., women *by nature* must stay at home to cook and clean), for how these roles could be perpetuated in the views and practices of family therapists (see Chapter 7). A second-order cybernetics critique (e.g., Hoffman, 1985) grew out of recognizing that therapists were *subjectively* engaged in the conversations within which first-order cyberneticians thought they could objectively diagnose family members' conversational patterns. Said differently, second-order cyberneticians view objective diagnostics as impossible; therapists had to factor their own engagement with families into any understandings and patterns they might assess. Further, the cultural and linguistic insights of social constructionists like Gergen (1985) found their way into family therapy, calling into question objective and essentialist diagnoses when value-bound uses of language were at stake. While family therapy began from a view that family problems had a patterned and interactional organization to them, by the end of the 1980s, many family therapists had moved away from first-order cybernetic metaphors to conversational or linguistic metaphors for family problems (e.g., Anderson & Goolishian, 1988). Of primary concern to both feminists and constructionists were potential non-collaborative practices of family therapists who applied the first-order cybernetic metaphor of practice in presumed expert and objective ways. The structural, or essentialized, view of families had positioned therapists to be diagnosticians of "what was really going on," and with such diagnoses they could treat families.

Interest in the diagnostic potentials of the first-order cybernetic metaphor for many family therapists waned as interest in the conversational and poststructural approaches (e.g., narrative, solution-focused, and collaborative) grew. However, with this move came concern that family interactions were obscured as stories, strengths, and exceptions to problems became the therapeutic focus, with some critics bemoaning the disappearance of families in these approaches (e.g., Minuchin, 1998). A conversational or discursive (people responsively using language) metaphor replaced a cybernetic focus on how people in relationships predictably interacted. This development, however, occurred while much of the mental health field moved toward a medicalized focus on diagnoses and evidence-based treatment as the basis for funding and administering therapy (Conrad, 2007; Rapley, Moncrieff, & Dillon, 2011; Sharfstein, 1987; Wylie, 1995). Such an individualized and medicalized direction conflicts with how most family therapists, particularly those embracing poststructural and systemic ways of practice, conceptualize families' relational concerns (e.g., Strong, 1993). Administrative and other implications of this individualistic, psychiatric direction affected family therapists practicing from a relational or systemic approach (Tomm, 1991; see the Introduction). Such concerns prompted some family therapists to propose relational diagnostic schemes (e.g., Kaslow, 1996) while other constructionist practitioner-authors responded to such proposals with alarm (Andersen, 1996; Gergen, Hoffman, & Anderson, 1996).

For social constructionists or poststructuralists, there is no ultimate discourse to take us beyond discourse to things as they really are. Any discourse offers ways to understand and communicate, but each does so in ways that constrain possibilities as much as they are enabled (e.g., Fairclough, 1989) for those who take up the discourse. Family therapy discourse is no different, and seeing clients' concerns as relational patterns of communication or interaction both enables and constrains how therapists might interact with families. Therapists may identify clients' concerns as being enacted in recurring and distinguishable patterns of family members' interactions. Such distinctions enable family therapists to speak to colleagues and administrators about what they see and address in helping families. However, such distinctions, made in diagnostic discourse, have the potential to constrain therapeutic possibilities and sometimes, in Massumi's (2011) words, they "discursively capture" the people involved in their use. Such discursive capture occurs when families, family members, or therapists lock themselves into a *singular* discourse of understanding and act accordingly. Treating bereavement, for example, solely as a spiritual or medical issue (as bereavement symptoms needing treatment) can preclude conversations about legal or other relevant matters. Being captured, in this sense, means having fewer ways to understand and respond. Stated differently, families and therapists can become *used by* language instead of being discerning *users of* the language by which they live. The flip side of discursive capture is to be enabled or even released by our uses of language, to live and interact in ways our uses of language facilitate. Our therapeutic interest is with joining families in finding discourses that help them escape discursive capture, to find preferred possibilities for interacting, and to go on together in acceptable ways.

From one perspective any diagnostic scheme is a "disaster" (Gergen et al., 1996), while others see diagnostic discourse as a means to bring administrative and clinical order to what would otherwise be a circumstance of linguistic anarchy when making clinical or administrative reference to disorders (cf. American Psychiatric Association [APA], 1994). Historically speaking, family therapists have oscillated between these two perspectives in making sense of clients' concerns, but the following digression will help to clarify the aims and concerns that can seem at stake. The IPs system differs from typical diagnostic schemes in that the patterns we associate with family concerns and well-being are not pre-defined in standardized descriptions. We prefer to descriptively name IPs in contextualized and changing ways that fit for us and the families consulting us.

Family Therapy and the Modern/Postmodern Debate

A longstanding anti-diagnostic tradition persists in mental health (e.g., Szasz, 1961), and some of that history relates to how client concerns have been culturally and scientifically represented in ways that now seem laughable, unjust, and even dangerous (Cushman, 1995; Foucault, 2009; Grob, 1991). While debates continue about what should or should not be included in psychiatry's diagnostic system (e.g., Frances, 2012), it can help to revisit the modern big picture aims that animate efforts to get diagnosis, in psychiatry and family therapy, "right."

Modern enlightenment science grew out of a convergence of desperate human concerns mapped onto an investment in knowledge that could address those concerns. Aristotle had earlier referred to the kind of knowledge sought as "techne" (Bernstein, 1983). Techne is the kind of knowledge one associates with applied science or engineering. It is the kind of technical knowing people can point to with confidence. From an era of bubonic plagues, fires, and corrupt priests twisting truth in self- or institution-serving ways, modern science grew to promise a knowable universe, one which could be understood with certainty and controlled like "clockwork" (Dolnick, 2012). The names most associated with this era and its promises of techne were Descartes and Newton. Spectacular *techn*ological developments followed from this scientifically-derived knowledge in physics, biology, and chemistry. However, the social sciences yielded much less certain knowledge and people could not be studied, understood, and technologically controlled in the same way as rocks or trees (Winch, 1958). The human sciences seemed capable of showing how humans, differently and somewhat predictably, interpret their experience in interpersonal and intercultural processes of understanding (Gadamer, 1988). Such processes of understanding do not offer the same modern scientific knowledge commonly associated with techne and technology.

Seen in modern scientific terms, diagnostic classification, such as that pursued in publishing the DSM-5 (APA, 2013), appears to promise the same kinds of technologically certain knowledge as one associates with moon landings or cracking the atom. For many, the modern scientific dream promised a universe that could be brought under human control. Encompassing human interaction, ultimately attainable scientific knowledge could thus be used to correctly understand and direct human behavior (Toulmin, 1990). To those taking up hermeneutic (Bernstein, 1983) or social constructionist (e.g., Gergen, 2009) views of human science, such pursuits are exercises in unattainable techne. Human social concerns cannot be scientifically discovered and addressed through rational-technological means in the same application of science and engineering that enables increasingly sophisticated forms of air travel.

Postmodernists and poststructuralists have struggled with these scientific and technological views of the mental health field, seeing in them "regimes of truth" for legislating or managing human affairs, extending to self-management (e.g., House, 2005; Rose, 1990). One postmodern impulse has been to resist such forms of potential discursive capture (Deleuze & Guattari, 1988; Massumi, 2011), or to at least see applied forms of human knowledge (e.g., those used in family therapy) not as techne, but as a different kind of Aristotelian knowledge: phronesis. Phronesis is pragmatic and procedural wisdom, the situated kind that is adaptable and interactional—the kind that Schön (1983) referred to as knowing-in-action. Phronesis is a humbler kind of wisdom when contrasted with techne. Techne refers to universally correct knowledge according to which immediate experience, such as experience of family interactions, can be "matched" and addressed. Phronesis instead refers to contextualized knowledge (i.e., knowledge "fitting" the context as opposed to matching it in some universally correct way) produced in and from human interactions, such as the changing interactions of family members with family therapists. Some postmodernists and poststructuralists are suspicious about knowing of any kind, for what such knowing might reify or constrain (e.g., Newman & Holzman, 1997). In the wake of postmodern critiques, particularly about psychiatric diagnoses, considering problematic patterns of interaction in families as potentially "fitting" PIPs offers, in my view, a still helpful form of phronesis.

Inside family therapy, there has recently been considerable debate over knowledge claims of any kind, particularly those that lead to systematizing or warranting therapist expertise or authority over clients (e.g., Anderson & Goolishian, 1992). The postmodern era partly arose out of what Paul Ricoeur (1976) referred to as a hermeneutics of suspicion (i.e., skeptical ways of understanding) for scientific and other forms of received wisdom. There has been a Derridean impulse to "deconstruct," if not subordinate, such claims of techne so as to collaboratively engage clients' ways of knowing (e.g., Larner, 1999). Seeing therapy itself as a site for constructing knowledge from the interactions of therapists and clients, many postmodern family therapists turned away from how those interactions could construct problems to collaborations focused on client-preferred relationships, outcomes, and meanings (e.g., Madsen, 1999). It is also in this regard that many postmodern family therapists critically respond to diagnostics of any kind in working with clients. Returning to Ricoeur (1976), alongside any hermeneutics of suspicion (skeptical deconstruction), there needs to be a hermeneutics of affirmation (ways of committing to valued and trusted understandings) or a willingness to stake a wager on some forms of knowledge over others. Whether they bring unacknowledged implicit ideas about the concerns clients present or they embrace explicit views of client concerns according to diagnostic systems, therapists do not practice without some sense of what client concerns are about or what needs to be done about them. Modern or postmodern family therapists are guided by some ideas and ways of distinction-making over others when helping families. IPs offer family therapists generative ways of distinction-making that are consistent with a poststructural view of patterned human interaction.

Conceptual Context

Seeing human interaction in terms of patterns is not new to thinkers outside of family therapy and mental health. In this next section, I want to relate ideas from sociology, anthropology, and linguistic philosophy to a pattern view of human interaction and meaning, linking these ideas to the IPs ideas and practices used at the CFTC. The dominant view in most approaches to therapy has been that problems are internal to individuals, in terms of psychological, biological, knowledge, or skill pathologies or deficit. Although systems (von Bertalanffy, 1968), biopsychosocial (Engel, 1980), socio-contextual (Adler, 1979), and ecological (Bronfenbrenner, 1981) ideas have informed therapeutic approaches for some time, psychotherapy's dominant contemporary metaphors come from cognitive neuroscience and artificial intelligence (Cushman, 1995; Teo, 2005). Family therapy approaches have cycled through many different metaphors as well (cf. Rosenblatt, 1994).

In approaching the ideas and metaphors of family therapy, it can be helpful to bear in mind a particular insight from Edmund Husserl (1970). Husserl, a phenomenologist, sought to re-insert subjectivity back into science, to consider how our sense-making relates to experience. In his original efforts, he saw his phenomenology as a way of reconciling subjectivity with objectivity, of getting back to the sensory bedrock of experience, the essential and transcendental *lived experience* of how things actually are. While most social scientists have offered third-person, objective accounts of human experience, people live and experience life (and each other) on the basis of first-person experience. Probing further, and responding to critics such as Heidegger, Husserl came to question the notion that the essence of elements of experience could be understood as they actually were in some universal or transcendental way. His profound insight was what is now referred to as the "natural attitude"; it refers to people's ways of living by unquestioned forms of understanding or sense-making.

What has confounded philosophers and social scientists until relatively recently is that people, particularly cultures and groups of people, could live successfully by very different ways of understanding or making sense of experience. Might successful and unsuccessful living need to be differently understood across diverse human contexts of understanding and interaction? Might Husserl's natural attitude translate across these diverse human contexts differently, extending to how cultures and families "do" life together, and to the very metaphors family therapists use in unquestioned ways in working with families?

This segue through Husserl's concept of the natural attitude sets a stage for considering therapists' distinction-making in family therapy, and for considering how family members may live and respond to each other by their own natural attitudes. When tempted by the certainties (Amundson, Stewart, & Valentine, 1993) of our natural attitudes in responding to each other, humans can negate or even do violence to each other. This applies to therapists as much as it does to family members (Strong & Sutherland, 2007). Integrating awareness of Husserl's natural attitude with a contemporary social constructionist view of practice (Lock &

Strong, 2010), a remarkably different (and more humble) stance from which to practice family therapy can emerge. Instead of aiming for universally correct diagnostic understanding, constructionist family therapists (e.g., Madsen, 1999) aim to make distinctions *with* clients about the concerns they present. Discerning patterns of interaction from *what* clients in family therapy talk with each other about that matters to them, particularly for *how* they talk about what matters, can help therapists describe clients' concerns in experience-near ways amenable to the practice of family therapy. Attending to families' patterned *hows* and *whats* is a particular kind of noticing worth elaborating.

As interpretive beings, humans selectively attend to what is in their circumstances. How they interpret such phenomena shapes human meanings for those phenomena, and correspondingly, how such phenomena come to be experienced (Barad, 2007). Thus, the distinctions we make in social and other circumstances typically owe something to prior experiences (including forms of training) attuning us to what seems specifically relevant (or "natural") to us in such circumstances (Merleau-Ponty, 1962). It is in this sense that narrative therapists selectively listen for problem-saturated stories or solution-focused therapists attend to solution-oriented client talk instead of other ways they could attune their listening and responding. Distinction-making is an interpretive act as Scheflen (1978) highlighted in his article, "Susan Smiled," in which a client's smile during a session came to mean various things for therapists given their varied approaches to practice. Diagnostic schemes—IPs included—are typically developed to diminish such variability. At the CFTC, IPs are used in both softer (i.e., tentative and transitory) and firmer ways (i.e., when used for diagnostic and administrative purposes).

We encourage using the IPscope to enable diverse kinds of distinction-making—the kinds that fit for therapists and families in their work together. In the developmental stages of what we now call the IPscope, efforts were made to identify and classify common PIPs. This kind of a priori naming, however, can be constraining for therapists who prefer that descriptive language for patterned interactions come from interactions with family members over what concerns or suits them. So, a frequent conversation among contributors to this book has revolved around concerns about reifying any IPs description (see Chapter 11). One such concern has been that therapists might engage families with pre-made names for the PIPs, much as they might interview for the diagnoses of the DSM-5 (APA, 2013). Thus, a key distinction informing the IPscope as we present it is that relations are stabilized in and by patterns of interaction, for better or worse. Families oscillate between patterned stabilities (PIPs and WIPs) and more transient disruptions to those stabilities—Deteriorating Interpersonal Patterns (DIPs, the non-preferred kind) and Transforming Interpersonal Patterns (TIPs, the preferred kind).

Back to patterns in family therapy, one could ask, "Why focus our therapeutic distinction-making on them?" Sociologically speaking, here it can help to revisit some differences between ethnomethodologist Harold Garfinkel (e.g., 1967) and other theorists (e.g., Parsons, 1951) who accounted for social behavior by pointing to more nebulous features of contexts. For Garfinkel, social behavior becomes predictable through how those sharing a social context come to anticipate each other's responses, such as through how family members develop familiar ways of interacting. His departure from other contextual explanations of shared behavior is that he looks at how the familiarity of such contexts is recognizable in the responses of family members to each other. Garfinkel focuses on how social (i.e., family) members show each other how they are making sense of each other, through the ways they observably attend to and respond to each other. Family life, in this sense, is *done* or relationally coordinated through family members' responses to each other. New developments or responses tend to take families or other social groupings out of what is familiar and coordinated, so being creatures of habit, the tendency is to stay in familiar responding and not in endless unfamiliar improvisation.

Where language fits in this view of coordinated human responses or interactions rests with how it is *used* to make new distinctions, or keep things familiar, even if that means (often unintentionally) keeping it problematically familiar (Garfinkel, 1967; Maturana & Varela, 1988). A coupling of how people interact and the meanings they derive through sustaining their interactions can stabilize both objectionable meanings and objectionable interactions (Strong & Tomm, 2007). Therefore, it is important to keep in mind a distinction pointed out by former members of Bateson's research team at the Mental Research Institute (Watzlawick, Bavelas, & Jackson, 1967)—namely, that beyond the semantic meanings attributable to the words of people's responses, *how* their words get used with each other can be seen to indicate how they relate to each other (see Chapter 4).

Language use pertains as much or more to the quality of communicative response, in what Watzlawick and others (1967) described as the command feature of communicating, as it does to any purported semantic or symbolic information (i.e., word) exchange. From an outsider's perspective, the quality of one family member's language use can be understood in terms of how other family members respond to it. Whether well or poorly received and responded to, what can emerge is a coordination of family members' responses to each other in specific kinds of language use (Maturana & Varela, 1988). Regardless of one partner's intentions in communicating, the other can respond in ways the partner finds objectionable, with both partners becoming reactive to each other in unwanted but still coordinated ways of responding (Strong & Tomm, 2007).

As outsiders aiming to join and make a difference in the kinds of coordinated forms of language use I have been describing, it can help to adopt an ethnomethodological (Garfinkel, 1967) stance on how partners are making sense of each other, through how they respond to each other. To focus on speakers' intended meanings can distract from an awareness of the interaction; what matters is how their communications are coordinated in recurring ways of responding.

Social practice theorist Theodore Schatzki (2002) speaks of these recurring ways of human responsiveness (positive or negative) as a "mesh" of entangled interactions that choreographs a particular (and typically unchosen) form of social order. For Schatzki, who draws on ethnomethodology, this is how social reality is constructed and maintained in and through people's interactions. Social practices are people's recurring "sayings and doings," and it is through these sayings and doings that particular meanings and identities arise for the people so engaged with each other. These social practices, or what I have been referring to as patterns, take on a life beyond what individual partners want, forming what John Shotter (1993) referred to as the "joint actions" of our conversational realities. Such communications between people involve more than mere transmissions and receptions of information. Instead, such communications can become habitual and complementary (cf. Kelso & Engstrom, 2008) as linguistic or relational coordinations encompassing and thereby shaping each partner's communications. "Complementarity" is a familiar term for many family therapists (e.g., Watzlawick et al., 1967), yet it can be challenging to grasp if one has been focused on individual behavior. For me, it speaks to the kinds of unintended consequences that follow from acting from individual intentions, while failing to recognize their relational consequences (Ness & Strong, 2014). This can occur in reactive ways despite either person's good intentions. When persons go a next step and find a cultural discourse to justify their position in the recurring reactivity, a stable and complementary social practice often follows (Nicolini, 2013). Family therapists can view family interactions as social practices, joint actions, or structural couplings—as meaning arising in and from what family members do through interacting in recurring ways with each other.

Often what family therapists do in their interactions with families involves hearing differing accounts or stories (Scott & Lyman, 1968) from family members. In this differential accounting for the concerns that motivated the family to come to therapy, therapists can quickly lose a sense of patterned interactions and become seduced by the accounts they hear. In aiming to reconcile the details of family members' accounts, therapists can miss how these accounts are continually re-enacted among family members back into what become normal family interactions. A family therapist adopting a social practice perspective, Dreier (2008) describes family therapists as being responded to as strangers in families' ongoing conversations. What matters for Dreier is that family members come to do their problem conversations and interactions differently as a result of therapy. In other words, changes in how family members talk with each other, more than their semantic meanings in communicating with each other, focus a social practice or IPs view of therapy. As strangers in families' conversations, therapists can let members' accounts guide them when what is more therapeutically relevant is how family members have come to coordinate those accounts in unwanted, patterned communications.

Therapists seduced by family members' accounts (and a perceived need to reconcile or judge them for correctness) may be afflicted by a well-ingrained Cartesian view that thought precedes and is separate from action. With words seen as the primary vehicle of thought and purported meaning, it is difficult to not feel pulled into *what* clients have to say about each other as a therapeutic focus. But returning briefly to Schatzki (2002), "Meaning is not a matter of difference, abstract schema, or attributional relativity, but a reality laid down in the regimes of activity and intelligibility called 'practices'" (p. 58). The sayings and doings coordinated in and by family social practices, or patterns of interaction, are compelling conversational realities (Shotter, 1993), quite apart from any intentions and personal meanings family members may bring to or take away from those realities.

Ethnomethodologists and discourse analysts informed by ethnomethodology and social constructionism (e.g., Edwards & Potter, 1992; Wooffitt, 2005) also take up a social practice view applied to how particular kinds of interactions occur in communications. Their view is that humans prefer a socially ordered life over a constantly improvised one, and being creatures of habit, we tend to drift into recurring patterns or coordinations of interactions. They focus on what is taken-for-granted in social interactions: the tacit interactions escaping notice by those engaged in enacting them in patterned ways (e.g., Pollner, 1987). Their focus is on making such tacit and micro-social interactions evident through particular ways of noticing, and by naming such interactions in ways recognizable once identified and named. Their focus is also dialogic and procedural, on distinguishing how such things are socially accomplished through how people respond to each other over sequences or patterns of communicative interaction. By contrast, a monologic view of greeting would focus only on the utterances of individuals. A dialogic view instead would focus on how greetings are completed over a sequence of interactions (often in taken-for-granted ways) between individuals. In my own discursively-oriented research, I have similarly looked at how therapists and clients complete question and answer sequences in ways that highlight the sayings and doings of their communicating (e.g., Strong, 2008).

The point I am building to is that a social practice approach, with an ethnomethodologist's orientation to micro-interactions as these are enacted in recurring relations, offers a way of seeing and responding to how family members' concerns are enacted among them. While therapists cannot understand meanings exactly as they have arisen for family members in problem and other patterned interactions, they can observe a choreography, or patterned interactions, that anchor such meanings for them.

IPs

Interpersonal patterns (IPs) are similar to the kinds of social practices or coordinations of interactions I have been describing. At the CFTC, patterns are our diagnostic focus (Tomm, 1991), whether these be unwanted and hurtful patterns (Pathologizing Interpersonal Patterns, PIPs), changing patterns (Transformative Interpersonal Patterns, TIPs), emerging patterns of wanted behavior (Healing Interpersonal Patterns, HIPs), deteriorating patterns of unwanted behavior (Deteriorating Interpersonal Patterns, DIPs) or established patterns of well-being (Wellness Interpersonal Patterns, WIPs). An IPs-assessment focus is deliberately interpersonal, and while individual concerns are not overlooked, these are seen as occurring within these kinds of interpersonal patterns mentioned. Therapy, accordingly, is about identifying unwanted or objectionable patterns of interaction and finding new ways of interacting and conversing so that the family can move on to more preferred patterns of interacting together (Strong & Tomm, 2007).

Later in the book, I join with colleagues Tanya Mudry and Jeff Chang (see Chapter 4) to reflect on how the IPscope encompasses transitions and patterns between DIPs, through PIPs, to TIPs and HIPs, and finally WIPs. These different, transitory IPs can become, in Wittgenstein's (1953) words, "language games" that come to stabilize in familiar interactions. Staying with Wittgenstein, new language games, or what we have been calling IPs, begin in new reactions. Life is such that unfamiliar or unexpected developments cannot be always addressed by our existing language games or IPs. How such developments bring forth preferred (TIPs) or non-preferred (DIPs) reactions and how such reactions stabilize into either HIPs or PIPs can be important clinically. By this reasoning, what matters is not so much how a family responds to an individual development (say, a visit from a teen's first boyfriend, or a parent's sudden illness); it is how a pattern can emerge from preferred or non-preferred reactions.

One of the more unique things associated with the formulation of a PIP is not just the unwanted pattern, but how family members inside PIPs come to negatively characterize each other. Failing to coordinate an acceptable interaction on something important, family members often come to relate to each other in pathologizing ways, justifying their continued participation in the PIP accordingly. However, patterns do not fully account for personalities or motivations, despite how convincing a negative view of one's PIP's partner can develop inside a PIP. A social practices (Dreier, 2008; Schatzki, 2002) and narrative view (e.g., Gubrium & Holstein, 2009; White & Epston, 1990) of identity is that identity varies according to different meshes of recurring conversational interactions, or what we have been referring to as IPs. Said another way, our sense of our conversational partner (i.e., his/her identity as we understand it) is anchored in the kinds of social interaction we develop over time with him/her. IPs, as a diagnostic scheme for identifying family concerns and wellness, promote a curiosity for not only the recurring unwanted patterns of interaction but also a mindfulness for how identities can be anchored in certain IPs (see Chapter 11). A kind of double whammy occurs in a PIP: family members are often caught up in a pattern of interaction they do not recognize as a pattern, and inside the PIP they come to understand each other in ways that result from the PIP. For those inside them, PIPs develop their own internal logic and behaviors based on that logic. They have an inertia that is embedded in each partner's ways of reacting and their perpetuation owes something to staying stuck inside that mutual reactivity.

A distinction, alongside PIPs, that we make at the CFTC is to distinguish responding from reacting. PIPs occur between family remembers in reactive or "natural" ways. Responding involves conscious reflection, whereas reacting lacks this kind of consciousness. While therapists' comments can serve as a resource or "conversational reminder" (J. Gaete, personal communication, May 25, 2012) for clients to respond to one's partner differently, they seldom are enough to initiate, let alone anchor a more preferred IP. Ultimately, a new, preferred pattern needs to be performed without such reminders, though these can be useful in initiating a TIP (see Chapter 5). TIPs are destabilizing interactions for families, though these occur and point to a preferred or accepted direction. We are as clinically interested in how families enabled these TIPs themselves, as we are with any TIPs that might have come out of our work with them in family therapy. For a TIP to become a HIP, or even a more enduring WIP, family members need to take up new and preferred ways of responding they find possible in the TIP and stabilize these new ways of responding into HIPs or WIPs.

As Dreier (2008) pointed out in his research of families when they were not in therapy, new ideas or actions developed in therapy are up against how families are accustomed to doing family life together outside of therapy. So, while responding differently in therapy—with therapist coaching and helpful reminders—can be achieved, the true test of a HIP is the family's ability to perform it spontaneously on their own. While family members may verbally indicate that such HIPs are emerging, and that they can consciously and deliberately initiate and maintain these HIPs on their own, a truer test of the HIP is its spontaneous (or taken-for-granted) occurrence in and beyond therapy.

The IPs approach can, of course, be applied to broader cultural, even national, interactions in which polarizing positions, for example, have created unhealthy relations, such as those that occur between enemy countries, or in how people of different political parties interact with each other. Inside such PIPs people come to pathologize or demonize each other based on their reactivity in what are predictable and identifiable interactions. However, the same can be said for the customs people develop in their healthy and transformative interactions. Meaning is coordinated through many levels of interaction according to Pearce and Cronen (1980), with each level shaping the interactions occurring above or below. How people learn to pathologize (i.e., treat as medically pathological) and reactively interact inside their families is not unique to families; in other words, such forms of interacting go on around them, and are even shaping the possibilities they draw on to get beyond any PIP.

WIPs are those ongoing yet usually tacit ways of interacting that can easily be overlooked. PIPs often occur in one aspect of family life, while the family continues, in other aspects of its functioning, to sustain enduring WIPs. Narrative therapists (e.g., White & Epston, 1990) speak of how problems sometimes eclipse resources, and PIPs can focus both family members and family therapists on problems while obscuring enduring healthy interactions, like those of WIPs. Competence-focused therapists (e.g., Waters & Lawrence, 1993) suggest we extend our therapeutic curiosities to those places where families do family life well in ways that escape notice. For us, this means joining families in recognizing and sometimes foregrounding WIPs.

It can help to revisit the earlier mentioned notion of discursive capture (Deleuze & Guattari, 1988; Massumi, 2011) to clinically reflect on how family members can be entangled in meanings (and actions associated with them) that are beyond their intentions. Cultural discourses offer particular ways of enabling or constraining reality. They are the distinct ways of understanding and evaluating experience and phenomena one can identify in cultures (like differences between how a naturalist, a forester, and a lumberjack would relate to a grove of trees). When a parent's cultural discourse of having to teach an adolescent responsibility runs up against a teen's discourse of needing independence, a conversational deadlock can develop into what we have been calling a PIP. People, however, are neither the discourses they draw on in a PIP nor the personalities the PIP (or their PIP antagonist, so to speak) would prescribe for them. Equating one's language, and the beliefs enabled by that language, with who one is, or can be, is highly problematic. There is always more that can be said, and more discourses to be used for understanding and speaking.

Thus people can take up different positions in other discourses—the parent could understand and talk from the teen's discourse of independence, for example. Positioning theorists (e.g., Harré & van Langenhove, 1999) take the view that people can be more discerning of the discourses they use in responding to each other (see Chapter 10). Since a discourse is a partial way to understand and relate to phenomena and each other, it can be extremely important to listen for and engage with what has not found articulation in clients' discourses (e.g., Shotter & Katz, 1998). PIPs require sameness and predictability in meaning and how partners react to each other. For TIPs or HIPs to occur involves new ways of interacting and conversing not entangled in the sameness of PIPs. As outsiders or strangers to families' PIPs, how we recognize they *do* PIPs through their responses to each other can help us differently respond to how they respond to each other in our work with them. It is in this way that IPs can be seen as social practices given how family members engage each other in their varied relational ways of living together.

IPs as a Conversational Resource

For Russian socio-cultural psychologist Lev Vygotsky (e.g., 1986), language is both a tool and a result in dialogues of any kind. For those of us at the CFTC, IPs offer a linguistic tool, a resourceful way of making sense of family interactions that produce particular results for therapists interacting with families and their members. Similarly, IPs, for us, "frame" (Goffman, 1974) how to make sense of concerns and well-being in families. However, to frame or be framed comes close to what I was describing earlier as discursive capture (Massumi, 2011), an influence or result of how one might use IPs. So, it can be one thing to orient oneself to listen for and respond to a PIP but quite another to be open to recognize and respond to a HIP (i.e., one that is welcomed once recognized as such) that spontaneously emerges in the course of therapy. It can also be the case that families coming to understand their concerns as plausible PIPs can be empowered to interact differently.

An important aspect of the IPscope is the way it helps us generatively, discerningly, and transiently use language to put apt names to clinically relevant family patterns of interaction. The transitory use of IPs helps us to avoid discursively capturing families with the names we give to their IPs. IPs as a conversational or therapeutic resource, like any way of sensemaking a therapist might take up or propose, opens some possibilities for understanding and action while constraining other possibilities. If used as the basis for engaging with families, or describing their concerns, potential issues can arise as to how therapists can use IPs in ethical and collaborative ways (Strong & Sutherland, 2007). Understandings or ways of interacting based on IPs may not be taken up by families, or the utility of any particular IP may wane over time for a therapist or family. PIPs offer hopefully fluid or changeable descriptions of family members' interactions, while any HIP, like any new way of responding to one another, can, if it is unchanging, grow stale and become problematic over time, such as continual apologizing. If taken up as a tool by families, IPs offer members ways of connecting preferred and non-preferred interactions to how they respond to each other—responses they can choose to continue or alter. This is a very different (and more relational) way of making sense of family concerns than the all-too-common way family members can pathologize other members and relate to them accordingly. As a conversational resource, IPs can be helpful to therapists as well, to recognize when their interactions with family members are resulting in ways of being together preferred by both members and the therapist.

Concluding Comments

In this chapter I offered a conceptual grounding for the IPs approach used at the CFTC. These ideas extend those that originally informed Karl's (1991) development of this system, adding views from discourse (Harré & van Langenhove, 1999) and social practices (Nicolini, 2013) theory. Karl was responding to expectations that staff use individually focused Diagnostic and Statistical Manual of Mental Disorders (5th ed.) diagnoses, a discourse quite different from family therapy's discourses of practice. The IPs system enables practice to occur on family therapy's most enduring conceptualization of family life, including family problems: patterned stabilities in family members' interactions. While some postmodern therapists may feel queasy with this kind of assessing, an IPs formulation focuses on concerns as well as areas of well-being. A PIPs formulation offers fluid ways of making distinctions that are focused on relational patterns of interaction, and in ways that are intentionally transitory.

References

Adler, A. (1979). *Superiority and social interest: A collection of later writings* (H. L. Ansbacher & R. R. Ansbacher, Eds.). New York, NY: Norton.

American Psychiatric Association. (1994). *Diagnostic and statistical manual of mental disorders* (4th ed.). Washington, DC: American Psychiatric Association.

American Psychiatric Association. (2013). *Diagnostic and statistical manual of mental disorders* (5th ed.). Washington, DC: American Psychiatric Association.

Amundson, J., Stewart, K., & Valentine, L. (1993). Temptations of certainty. *Journal of Marital & Family Therapy, 19*(1), 111–123.

Andersen, T. (1996). Language is not innocent. In F. Kaslow (Ed.), *The handbook of relational diagnosis and dysfunctional family patterns* (pp. 119–125). New York, NY: John Wiley and Sons.

Anderson, H., & Goolishian, H. (1988). Human systems as linguistic systems. *Family Process, 27*(4), 371–393.

Anderson, H., & Goolishian, H. (1992). The client is the expert. In S. McNamee & K. Gergen (Eds.), *Therapy as social construction* (pp. 25–39). Newbury Park, CA: Sage.

Barad, K. (2007). *Meeting the universe halfway*. Durham, NC: Duke University Press.

Bateson, G. (1972). *Steps to an ecology of mind*. New York, NY: Ballantine.

Bateson, G. (1980). *Mind and nature: A necessary unity*. New York, NY: Bantam Books.

Bateson, G. (1982). Paradigmatic conservatism. In C. Wilder & J. Weakland (Eds.), *Rigor and imagination: Essays from the legacy of Gregory Bateson* (pp. 347–355). New York, NY: Praeger.

Bateson, G., Jackson, D., Haley, J., & Weakland, J. (1956). Toward a theory of schizophrenia. *Behavioral Science, 1*(4), 251–264.

Bernstein, R. J. (1983). *Beyond objectivity and relativism: Science, hermeneutics, and practice*. Philadelphia, PA: University of Pennsylvania Press.

Bronfenbrenner, U. (1981). *The ecology of human development: Experiments by nature and design*. Cambridge, MA: Harvard University Press.

Conrad, P. (2007). *The medicalization of society*. Baltimore, MD: Johns Hopkins University Press.

Cushman, P. (1995). *Constructing the self, constructing America: A cultural history of psychotherapy*. New York, NY: Perseus.

Deleuze, J., & Guattari, F. (1988). *A thousand plateaus: Capitalism and schizophrenia* (B. Massumi, Trans.). Minneapolis, MN: University of Minnesota Press.

Dolnick, E. (2012). *The clockwork universe: Isaac Newton, the Royal Society, and the birth of the modern world*. New York, NY: Harper Perennial.

Dreier, O. (2008). *Psychotherapy in everyday life*. New York, NY: Cambridge University Press.

Edwards, D., & Potter, J. (1992). *Discursive psychology*. London, UK: Sage.

Engel, G. (1980). The clinical application of the biopsychosocial model. *American Journal of Psychiatry, 137*(5), 535–544.

Fairclough, N. (1989). *Language and power*. London, UK: Longman.

Foucault, M. (2009). *History of madness* (J. Khalfa, Ed.; J. Murphy, Trans.). New York, NY: Routledge.

Frances, A. (2012, May 11). Diagnosing the D.S.M. *The New York Times*. Retrieved from www.nytimes.com/2012/05/12/opinion/break-up-the-psychiatric-monopoly.html?ref=us

Gadamer, H. G. (1988). *Truth and method* (2nd ed., H. Weinsheimer & D. G. Marshall, Trans.). New York, NY: Continuum.

Garfinkel, H. (1967). *Studies in ethnomethodology*. Englewood Cliffs, NJ: Prentice Hall.

Gergen, K. (1985). The social constructionist movement in modern psychology. *American Psychologist, 4*(3), 266–275.

Gergen, K. (2009). *Relational being*. New York, NY: Oxford.

Gergen, K., Hoffman, L., & Anderson, H. (1996). Is diagnosis a disaster? A constructionist trialogue. In F. Kaslow (Ed.), *The handbook of relational diagnosis and dysfunctional family patterns* (pp. 102–118). New York, NY: John Wiley and Sons.

Goffman, E. (1974). *Frame analysis: An essay on the organization of experience.* Boston, MA: Northeastern University Press.

Goldner, V. (1988). Generation and gender: Normative and covert hierarchies. *Family Process, 27*(1), 17–31.

Grob, G. N. (1991). Origins of DSM-I: A study in appearance and reality. *American Journal of Psychiatry, 148*(3), 421–431.

Gubrium, J., & Holstein, J. (2009). *Analyzing narrative reality.* Thousand Oaks, CA: Sage.

Harré, R., & van Langenhove, L. (Eds.). (1999). *Positioning theory: Moral contexts of intentional action.* Oxford, UK: Blackwell.

Hoffman, L. (1985). Beyond power and control. *Family Systems Medicine, 3*(3), 381–396.

House, R. (2005). *Therapy beyond modernity: Deconstructing and transcending profession-centred therapy.* London, UK: Karnac.

Husserl, E. (1970). *The crisis of European sciences and transcendental phenomenology.* Evanston, IL: Northwestern University Press.

Kaslow, F. (Ed.). (1996). *The handbook of relational diagnosis and dysfunctional family patterns.* New York, NY: John Wiley and Sons.

Kelso, J. A. S., & Engstrom, D. A. (2008). *The complementary nature.* Cambridge, MA: MIT Press.

Laing, R. D. (1970). *Knots.* London, UK: Penguin.

Larner, G. (1999). Derrida and the deconstruction of power as context and topic in therapy. In I. Parker (Ed.), *Deconstructing psychotherapy* (pp. 39–53). London, UK: Sage.

Lock, A., & Strong, T. (2010). *Social constructionism: Sources and stirrings in theory and practice.* New York, NY: Cambridge University Press.

Lock, A., & Strong, T. (Eds.). (2012). *Discursive perspectives on therapeutic practice.* New York, NY: Oxford University Press.

Madsen, W. (1999). *Collaborative therapy with multi-stressed families.* New York, NY: Guilford.

Massumi, B. (2011). *Semblance and event: Activist philosophy and the occurrent arts.* Cambridge, MA: MIT Press.

Maturana, H., & Varela, F. (1988). *The tree of knowledge.* Boston, MA: Shambhala.

Merleau-Ponty, M. (1962). *The phenomenology of perception* (C. Smith, Trans.). London, UK: Routledge & Kegan Paul.

Minuchin, S. (1998). Where is the family in family therapy? *Journal of Marital and Family Therapy, 24*(3), 397–403.

Ness, O., & Strong, T. (2014). Relational consciousness and the conversational practices of Johnella Bird. *Journal of Family Therapy, 36*(1), 81–102.

Newman, F., & Holzman, L. (1997). *The end of knowing.* New York, NY: Routledge.

Nichols, M., & Schwartz, R. (2008). *Family therapy: Concepts and methods* (8th ed.). Boston, MA: Allyn & Bacon.

Nicolini, D. (2013). *Practice theory, work, and organization: An introduction.* New York, NY: Oxford University Press.

Parsons, T. (1951). *The structure of social action.* New York, NY: Free Press.

Pearce, B., & Cronen, V. (1980). *Communication, action and meaning: The creation of social realities.* New York, NY: Praeger.

Pollner, M. (1987). *Mundane reasoning.* New York, NY: Cambridge University Press.

Rapley, M., Moncrieff, J., & Dillon, J. (Eds.). (2011). *De-medicalizing misery: Psychiatry, psychology and the human condition.* New York, NY: Palgrave Macmillan.

Reusch, J., & Bateson, G. (1951). *Communication: The social matrix of psychiatry.* New York, NY: Norton.

Ricoeur, P. (1976). *Interpretation theory: Discourse and the surplus of meaning.* Fort Worth, TX: Texas Christian University Press.

Rose, N. (1990). *Governing the soul.* New York, NY: Routledge.

Rosenblatt, P. (1994). *Metaphors of family therapy: Toward new constructions.* New York, NY: Guilford.

Schatzki, T. (2002). *The site of the social: A philosophical account of the constitution of social life and change.* Pittsburgh, PA: University of Pennsylvania Press.

Scheflen, A. E. (1978). Susan smiled: On explanation in family therapy. *Family Process, 17*(1), 59–68.

Schön, D. (1983). *The reflective practitioner: How professionals think in action.* New York, NY: Basic Books.

Scott, M. B., & Lyman, S. (1968). Accounts. *American Sociological Review, 33*(1), 46–62.

Sharfstein, S. S. (1987). Third-party payments, cost containment, and DSM-III. In G. L. Tischler (Ed.), *Diagnosis and classification in psychiatry: A critical appraisal of DSM-III* (pp. 530–538). New York, NY: Cambridge University Press.

Shotter, J. (1993). *Conversational realities.* Newbury Park, CA: Sage.

Shotter, J., & Katz, A. (1998). "Living moments" in dialogical exchanges. *Human Systems, 9*(2), 81–94.

Strong, T. (1993). DSM-IV and describing problems in family therapy. *Family Process, 32*(2), 249–253.

Strong, T. (2008). Externalizing questions: A micro-analytic look at their use in narrative therapy. *International Journal of Narrative Therapy and Community Work, 3*(1), 59–71.

Strong, T., & Sutherland, O. A. (2007). Conversational ethics in psychological dialogues: Discursive and collaborative considerations. *Canadian Psychology, 48*(1), 94–105.

Strong, T., & Tomm, K. (2007). Family therapy as re-coordinating and moving on together. *Journal of Systemic Therapies, 26*(2), 42–54.

Szasz, T. S., (1961). *The myth of mental illness.* New York, NY: Harper & Row.

Teo, T. (2005). *The critique of psychology: From Kant to postcolonial theory.* New York, NY: Springer.

Tomm, K. (1991, Spring). Beginnings of a "HIPs and PIPs" approach to psychiatric assessment. *Calgary Participator, 1*(2), 21–22, 24. Retrieved from www.familytherapy.org/documents/HIPsPIPs.PDF

Toulmin, S. (1990). *Cosmopolis: The hidden agenda of modernity.* Chicago, IL: University of Chicago Press.

von Bertalanffy, L. (1968). *General system theory: Foundations, development, applications.* New York, NY: George Braziller.

Vygotsky, L. (1986). *Thought and language* (Rev. ed., A. Kozulin, Ed.). Cambridge, MA: MIT Press.

Waters, D. B., & Lawrence, E. L. (1993). *Competence, courage, and change: An approach to family therapy.* New York, NY: W. W. Norton.

Watzlawick, P., Bavelas, J. B., & Jackson, D. (1967). *Pragmatics of human communication: A study of interactional patterns, pathologies, and paradoxes.* New York, NY: Norton.

White, M., & Epston, D. (1990). *Narrative means to therapeutic ends.* New York, NY: Norton.

Winch, P. (1958). *The idea of a social science and its relation to philosophy.* London, UK: Routledge & Kegan Paul.

Wittgenstein, L. (1953). *Philosophical investigations* (G. E. M. Anscombe., Trans.). New York, NY: Macmillan.

Wooffitt, R. (2005). *Conversation analysis and discourse analysis.* London, UK: Sage.

Wylie, M. S. (1995, May/June). The power of DSM-IV: Diagnosing for dollars. *Family Therapy Networker,* pp. 22–32.

3

TEACHING AND LEARNING RELATIONAL PRACTICE

Shari Couture and Karl Tomm

"Instructive interaction is impossible. All we can do is create contexts for learning."
—H. Maturana (personal communication, June 22, 1983)

"Knowledge is not handed over but co-constructed through mutual talk."
—D. Paré and M. Tarragona (2006, p. 3)

Educators teaching relational practice encourage students to move away from skin-bounded individualistic understandings and focus on behavioral couplings in the interpersonal space. The IPscope (see Introduction and Chapter 1) is a pragmatic tool that helps both teachers and students conceptualize this interpersonal space. At the Calgary Family Therapy Centre (CFTC) we utilize this lens to invite our students into rich conversations that give priority to expand their relational understanding of both problems and solutions.

Most of us are socialized into habits of perceiving and understanding other persons as separate individuals. For the most part, these habits are non-conscious. They are also quite pervasive and strong. As a result, it is usually difficult to enter into, to hold onto, and to work within *a relational perspective*. We do not expect our students, or ourselves, to ever completely escape individualistic habits of thought. However, by using the IPscope we can cultivate perceptual and conceptual counter-habits to challenge our strong individualistic tendencies. This helps us become more flexible and think relationally, as well as individually.

In this chapter we will expand on what we mean by shifting from the individual to the relational and describe how educators can invite learners to use the IPscope lens when moving toward more systemic understandings and practices. We discuss a variety of teaching/learning activities, heuristically conceptualized within seven domains. In our description of each domain we highlight Wellness Interpersonal Patterns (WIPs) that teachers and students engage in with each other to cultivate a generative learning process. A key element of this teacher/student WIP is our commitment to co-create a collegial environment that invites genuine teamwork. Our student interns are all at the graduate level and most of them bring a great deal of knowledge and many rich life experiences with them when they first arrive at the CFTC. We acknowledge their pre-existing knowledge and endeavor to extend our skills together. Throughout this chapter we also offer both a learner's and a teacher's perspective in using the IPscope and end with a discussion of implications for both educators and students.

A Gestalt Shift

Although my colleagues and I (Karl) originally developed the IPscope framework for use by experienced therapists, we created it within a teaching program, so it also became a learning tool for new practitioners. We eventually used the IPscope as a perceptual/conceptual instrument to guide students to make a shift from seeing problems and solutions as located within individuals, to understanding them as relational patterns in the interpersonal space. Both of us (Shari and Karl) see this change in seeing and understanding as a figure/ground gestalt shift.

The distinction between figure and ground relates to the fact that perception is relative rather than absolute. Simply expressed, something can be considered soft or hard only when compared to something else. A boiled egg is soft in comparison to a walnut or rock, but hard in comparison to a raw egg or warm butter. Perception results from the contrast of a figure from a background. What ends up being the figure—that is, what we give priority to and focus on—depends on how we perceive, and construct, the world around us at any particular moment. Indeed, the process of focusing itself "hardens" the figure while the background simultaneously "melts" further away. This is not a new concept in psychology (Koffka, 1935). Most readers will be familiar with the well-known gestalt image of two facial silhouettes versus a black chalice or vase in between (see Figure 3.1).

Depending on a person's focus, the faces can become the figure as the black chalice drifts into the background, or the shape of the vase can become the figure while the faces dissolve into the background. Most observers can deliberately "will" themselves to see one or the other and can move back and forth between the two perceptions with relative ease. However, the same ease is not usually forthcoming with respect to perceptual movement between an individualistic perspective and a relational perspective when doing therapy. If the two faces are taken to represent the individual perspective of seeing the characteristics of two separate individuals, and the shape of the black vase is taken to represent the nature of the relationship between those persons, most observers tend to

Figure 3.1 Figure-ground gestalt shift from faces to relationship

get stuck in seeing the individual faces and have difficulty seeing the shape of the vase—the relationship between them.

It is not only our Western socialization to think in individual terms but also our perceptual senses of vision and hearing that bias us to primarily see separate persons and to remain relatively fixed in an individualistic perspective. Thus there is a need for proactive tools and learning experiences to enable practitioners to "see and hear" what a relational perspective might yield (i.e., to see the "shape of the vase" in a specific relationship). It will always remain relatively easy to return to an individual perspective from time to time and see the shape of the individuals. However, once the capacity to see a relationship has been well established, it becomes possible to work from either stance in a complementary manner (i.e., attending to both individuals and relationships in the ongoing course of therapy). We believe that students can accomplish this gestalt shift more easily when they work together with instructors using the IPscope lens as a teaching/learning tool.

Our Collaboration

In keeping with this figure/ground conceptualization, we have intentionally paired two authors in this chapter who see through two lenses of a different sort. The first author, Shari Couture, will speak from a position of someone who has relatively recently been introduced to this conceptual orientation and who continues to find this gestalt shift central in her work with families and in supervising students. The second author, Karl Tomm, will offer his insights as an experienced practitioner and teacher using the IPscope framework for 25 years. In this chapter we will periodically interject our personal experiences and perspectives through an improvised conversation. We hope that our embedded interactions might provide a way for you as a reader to access some of the thinking behind our writing and at another level allow us to perform what we see as a major part of the teaching/learning at the CFTC: the generative interaction between educator and student.

Early Conceptual Developments: Creating a Framework to "See Systemically"

As a young academic psychiatrist, I (Karl) tried to integrate my existing knowledge of psychodynamic mechanisms, cognitive processing, and behavior theory using a cybernetic metaphor of feedback loops. I was trying to simplify and clarify my understanding of the importance of relationships in an individual patient's experience and mental well-being for my own work, and for the purposes of teaching medical students and residents in psychiatry. The first result was a model of Circular Pattern Diagramming (CPD) for relationship assessment (Tomm, 1980). Even though CPD served me well for several years, I eventually abandoned that model for a number of reasons. One had to do with its implicit grounding in objectivist assumptions. If something is taken to be objectively true, then we are stuck with it as a "reality," and the degrees of freedom for alternative realities and potential change are reduced. Another reason had to do with insufficient focus on the interpersonal aspects of the process that could provide adequate resistance to counter my persistent non-conscious drift toward individualistic thinking. It was only when I learned to focus more rigorously on the complementary coupling of reactive behaviors of two or more persons that I was able to dissolve the background of skin-bounded individuals and distinguish "the pattern that connects" (Bateson, 1972, p. 8) more clearly. The creation of the IPscope made it easier for me to "see" the systemic process, in terms of making interpersonal rather than person-based distinctions. When I was able to bring the interpersonal patterns (IPs) into the foreground of my own work with families, it became easier for me to help my students see them as well.

Making the Conceptual Shift

I (Shari) was an intern at the CFTC over 13 years ago, yet my learning experiences remain surprisingly vivid in my mind. Since my training, I have been practicing as a family therapist and I currently am a therapist and supervisor at the CFTC. I am in a novel position to comment on the experiences of learning at the CFTC as both learner and teacher. My own gestalt shift has changed my practice and ultimately my ability to help others make these changes in understanding.

I would like to offer an example to illustrate how I found myself re-conceptualizing client problems in new ways at the CFTC. I was studying a video of a family interview that took place after the son was released from the hospital where he had been admitted because he was cutting his arms. The therapist (Karl) asked questions that highlighted a Pathologizing Interpersonal Pattern (PIP), which I conceptualized as *the son communicating feelings of doubt that he could keep himself safe coupled with the father communicating certainty that the son must keep himself safe* (i.e., follow a safety contract). Karl's use of circular questions clarified the interactive PIP of *paternal demanding coupled with adolescent withdrawing* that invited more of the same stuck interactions. He also used reflexive questions to bring forth a Healing Interpersonal Pattern (HIP) in which the father could downgrade his stance of certainty and move from demanding his son's safety to understanding his son taking small steps (with some help from dad) to keeping himself safe. The more the father replaced demands for his son's safety with tentatively asking about his experience, the more the son replaced withdrawing behaviors with a willingness to take some small steps forward in dialogue with his dad.[1]

Before coming to the CFTC, I had worked in an agency with adolescents who had been removed from their homes. Our focus in working with these youths was intrapersonal, to the point that even when the family was involved, I was more of an advocate for the adolescent, working to help clarify his or her individual experience for the family to accept. Initially, when I worked with families at the CFTC I felt the usual strong pull to work intrapersonally, especially when (as in the previous example) the adolescent's safety was at risk. As with many professionals, this is what I had previously been trained to do. The pull to concentrate on the adolescent's individual experience left me with a blind spot regarding how interpersonal patterns between family members fueled this young person's feelings of doubt and his impulse to self-harm, and how a focus on relational patterns could enable something different. Even worse than simply remaining in the dark, a solely intrapersonal focus left me at risk of unintentionally joining the father's pattern of demanding too much from the adolescent. With the IPscope lens I was able to fill in the blind spot—that is, see the shape of the vase—and re-conceptualize the son's behaviors and feelings as part of an interactional pattern with the father (or the therapist). I could then orient to the possibility of joining forward-moving Transformative Interpersonal Patterns (TIPs; see Chapter 5), rather than add to the repetitive pathologizing pattern.

Karl: This is a good example of the conceptual shift we are talking about (i.e., to notice interpersonal patterns rather than focus on intrapersonal, skin-bounded qualities and characteristics). From what you recall, Shari, what stands out the most about your experience in making this shift?

Shari: One memory that remains very clear in my mind was an instance in which you were offering us, as students, a framework to understand our learning process. You described a series of steps in learning from non-conscious incompetence, to conscious incompetence, to conscious competence, and finally to non-conscious competence (see Figure 3.2). I vividly recall identifying with a feeling of conscious incompetence when working within systemic understandings and frantically trying to cultivate movement to the next two stages. To help us move forward despite the unsettling experience of incompetence, you offered these steps within a conversation in which we discussed this as a typical, almost inevitable, part of the learning process. As such you invited us to join you in exploring how we could begin to try on our new IPscope lens to move toward greater competence.

Karl: Other students have described a transient experience of feeling de-skilled after they have been at the CFTC for a few weeks trying to use the IPscope. Not only were they striving to implement not-yet-developed systemic interviewing skills, they felt they had actually lost their prior individually oriented interviewing skills. Did you experience anything like this?

Shari: Yes, absolutely. I had already been working in the mental health field for a number of years. I started my internship at the CFTC feeling as though I was at least consciously competent as a clinician and perhaps felt as though I periodically even practiced in the realm of non-conscious competence. At the CFTC, however, I definitely felt the growing pains of feeling consciously

Nonconscious lack of competence
⬇
Conscious lack of competence
⬇
Conscious competence
⬇
Nonconscious competence

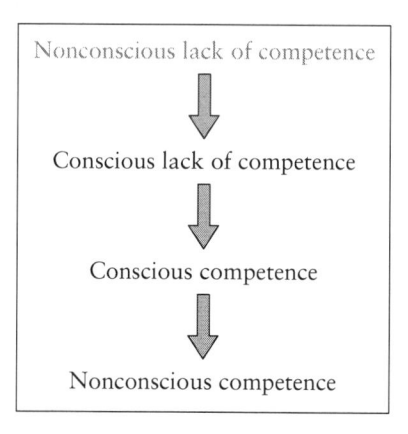

Figure 3.2 A heuristic sequence in the development of knowledge and/or intuitive skills

incompetent as I made the difficult stretch to identify relational patterns through the IPscope. This is an experience I hear current students consistently describe during supervision. In my role as a teacher now, my past experience as a learner at the CFTC helps me empathize with them as they negotiate this difficult gestalt shift.

Karl: Is there some way that the striving for interpersonal competence could actually undermine prior individually oriented skills?

Shari: Interesting question, Karl. This is exactly how some students often experience it. For example, as students attempt a shift to an interpersonal focus they often forget or stop using useful questions coming from narrative therapy to externalize problems from individuals (White & Epston, 1990) or from solution-focused therapy to notice exceptions (de Shazer, 1994). Because of the challenges in making the shift to the interpersonal most of the students' energies are directed at seeing the interactional patterns. But once the students start seeing the shape of the vase and begin to move easily between the intrapersonal and interpersonal, they seem to remember those forgotten skills again. The previous intrapersonally oriented skills become interpersonal skills as they are integrated within the IPscope framework. For instance, students start using externalizing questions to separate PIPs from family members and solution-focused questions to bring forth HIPs.

Creating Optimal Conditions for Learning

At the CFTC we have carefully designed our physical space to maximize observation and reflection of our practice with two-way mirrors and videotaping capabilities in every interviewing room. Within this architectural space we have cultivated a culture of openness and collegiality. Staff clinicians continually create opportunities for students to utilize this design to observe other therapists practice, invite them to work as a part of a team in their own and other's work with families, and offer many opportunities for students to immerse themselves in ongoing conversations about systemic theory and practice.

In order to provide more detail about how staff and students accomplish this at the CFTC, we will describe our training activities in seven interrelated domains: situating, lecturing/listening, demonstrating/observing, involving/doing, supervising/reflecting, documenting, and searching/researching. We are not suggesting that these domains function separately or in a stepwise sequence but rather as dynamically interrelated aspects of our teaching and learning activities. We conceptualize these domains as coupled IPs because each one consists of WIP-like couplings between students and instructors. In doing so, we are emphasizing a central aspect of the training at the CFTC in fostering generative WIPs between students and teachers: recurrent learning interactions between educator and learner. In the following sections, we will describe these domains and give examples of how teachers and students negotiate learning in their own interaction patterns.

1. Situating (Seeking Preferred Influences Invites Responding With Valued Influences)

Shari: I would like to ask you, Karl, to comment on how you came to situate yourself at a place like the CFTC in the first place.

Karl: As a learner myself, I came to realize that the single most significant action I could take to influence the direction of my own learning was to place myself in a situation in which the context of that situation would have the kinds of ongoing influences upon me that I wanted. For instance, when I first joined the Department of Psychiatry at the University of Calgary in 1972, I felt an enormous amount of pressure to "fall in line" and enter into a traditional pattern of hospital-based psychiatric practice and work with individual patients. However, I knew that I wanted to evolve in a different direction—namely, to learn more about families as systems, and about family therapy. So I consciously and deliberately set about collecting a group of like-minded family oriented colleagues around me, locally, nationally, and internationally. I started a clinical family therapy program and hired colleagues from various disciplines who shared my passion for systemic understanding. I designed a physical space with several two-way screens and video cameras to maximize opportunities for team members to observe each other's work. In addition, I actively encouraged openness by exposing my own clinical work, by welcoming feedback, by explicitly acknowledging my interviewing mistakes, and by sharing the learning that I derived from them. These initiatives contributed to the conditions for my own continuing development as a systemic therapist. Unwittingly, I was fostering a WIP of *seeking and welcoming feedback coupled with giving feedback for new learning*, which is a pattern that continues to benefit all of us and especially our students. What about you, Shari? Did you, and the students you know of, make deliberate decisions to situate yourselves here?

Shari: Like myself, most current students describe initially choosing the CFTC for its systemic focus. One student recently described the CFTC as "offering an intense immersion in systemic ideas where students are surrounded with like-minded people whose theories and practice hang together congruently." At the same time, students also come to highly value the enactment of WIPs (like the example Karl just mentioned about *welcoming and appreciating feedback coupled with offering feedback*) and the people at the program who cultivate an open, team-oriented environment. Practitioners and students at the CFTC describe the program as having "a culture of openness that seems to just come with the place." One recent student drew an analogy with the saying, "it takes a community to raise a child," and her experience at the CFTC where she felt like she was "part of a community that raised a therapist." Another recent graduate described valuing our open-door policy; if she felt stuck, confused, or a need to debrief, she could consult any staff member. Karl, you mentioned how the architectural design of the physical space at the CFTC enables practitioners to work collaboratively. You designed the space to encourage seeing through many different eyes. However, could you comment on how locating oneself in such a physical space does not guarantee that the people within this space will experience the intended benefits?

Karl: I am glad you are highlighting this, Shari. I have visited some programs that are designed with two-way screens but seldom actually use them. Within our context, both student practices and instructor practices are regularly observed, reflected upon, and enhanced through live supervision, reflecting team process, and the review of recorded sessions. All the students and staff are recognized as full members of the team and collectively support one another in the work we do in trying to help families.

Shari: Yes, Karl, and this comes back to how the people at the CFTC co-create this collegial environment by engaging in a student/learner WIP inviting teamwork. Although there always is a certain amount of hierarchy within a training program, speaking as a person who has experience as both a teacher and learner at the CFTC, I think there is a continual effort to enact WIPs to balance this hierarchy with contestability. For example, students are asked to give feedback to staff members in relation to our clinical work, in reflecting teams, observations, research projects (see Chapter 10) and this feedback is valued and utilized. Eventually, within this interactional pattern, students offer their feedback in a collegial manner and this is coupled with acceptance and serious reflection on the feedback. Ultimately, mutual participation in this WIP invites supervisor versus student lines to soften and helps the team move toward what Chang and Gaete call "co-vision" (see Chapter 9).

2. Lecturing/Listening

Parallel to our practicum or internship style of learning, we provide a formal theory course with a series of lectures to offer an intellectual understanding of systemic interaction and of systemic therapy. All interns at the CFTC are expected to take this course. Lecturing may seem incongruous with our acceptance of Maturana's theoretical insight into the impossibility of direct teaching, or passing knowledge from one person to the next through the one-way delivery of instruction. However, while lecturing may appear like a one-way process, it can also be conceived of as a series of WIPs in the classroom, such as *talking coupled with listening, leading coupled with following, modeling coupled with copying,* and *asking coupled with answering.* From a systemic perspective, it is not just an instructor offering knowledge and skills; the students bring forth the instructor as knowledgeable through their attention, interest, questions, and responses (Bavelas, Coates, & Johnson, 2000).

Because of the high degree of consensual coordination that is possible through language, lecturing can be helpful in providing conceptual structures or what Shotter (2008) called *conceptual prosthetics* to stabilize and hold the experiential learning: prostheses through which "like telescopes or microscopes in other sciences, we can 'see' influences at work which would remain otherwise rationally-invisible to us" (p. 60). This is especially true when, while lecturing, we regularly describe clinical situations to provide clarifying examples of the applicability of the concepts and the PIPs framework. The instructor's orientation to continually apply systemic concepts is eventually passed to the students who are asked to integrate what they have learned in a written assignment of a clinical study at the end of the course.

Karl: One of the students' questions that inevitably comes up in my lectures is "how do you identify a PIP when you are working with a family?" In my clinical experience nowadays, PIPs and HIPs usually just "pop" into my mind as I sit with a family and watch the process.
Shari: Yes, that may be your experience now, after looking through the IPscope for so many years. Students, however, need more direction than waiting for PIPs to pop into their heads. Can you offer the reader more information on how you teach students to notice these interaction patterns?
Karl: When a student asks, "Where do I start to identify a PIP?" I suggest that a good place to begin is with one's intuition about the most intense negative emotion among the participants of the interaction. Once this emotion has been identified, one looks to

selectively identify various behaviors that manifest that negative emotion. The next step is to search among these manifesting behaviors to identify those that evoke high levels of reactivity among other participants in the interaction. Then, one looks for specific complementary behaviors among those reactive behaviors that are most liable to reinforce the evocative behaviors. One keeps searching for specific evocative behaviors and specific reactive behaviors that appear to be mutually reinforcing until such interconnected behaviors come clearly into focus. Finally, one imagines a coupling of exemplars of the two types of behavior in the form of gerunds into a recurrent interpersonal pattern and a PIP "pops up," like magic, as a relational stability (see Figure 3.3).

Shari: Could you give the reader an example?

Karl: Sure. Similar to the case you discussed earlier, a family comes in with concerns about an adolescent son. The parents begin complaining about the boy's lack of application at home with chores and at school with homework. Meanwhile the son looks down at the floor. The father barks out, "Pay attention!" and comes across as extremely frustrated. I intuit that he is very angry. I notice his raised voice and his pervasive criticism of the boy. These behaviors express his anger and evoke occasional scowling by the boy. The father demands a clarifying response when the boy scowls, and the boy reacts by turning away. His scowling and withdrawal behavior appear to reinforce the father's harassment and criticism and feed the intensity of the anger. I note that the father's incessant pressuring reinforces the boy's resisting and the resisting in turn reinforces the pressuring. So in my mind's eye the pressuring and resisting become coupled, and the pattern pops up as a PIP for me to work with.

- Intuit the strongest negative emotions that seem to be active in the main participants of the interaction.
- Identify observable behaviors that reflect these negative emotions.
- Selectively focus on those behaviors that trigger a high level of reactivity from the other participant, and name a key behavior from each participant, that appears to reinforce the negative behavior of the other.
- Bring forth and highlight the coupling of exemplar behaviors that produce a recurrent pattern of interaction (using gerund descriptors whenever possible).
- Ask a series of circular or triadic questions to confirm or revise one's emerging understanding of the PIP.

Figure 3.3 Steps to construct a PIP

Another more conversational means to identify a PIP entails asking a series of circular questions. The interviewer takes note of a problematic behavior X and asks the person enacting X, "When you do X, what do other people typically do?" This is a proactive behavioral effect question, which could then be followed by a reactive behavioral effect question like, "And when he/she reacts with Y, what do you typically do?" to track sequences of interaction that come full circle. Alternatively, the interviewer could engage in triadic questioning where he/she could ask third parties about the interaction between two other parties to disclose the PIP, "When (Person A) does X, what does (Person B) do?" and "When B reacts with Y, what does A do?"

Shari: And what do you tell the students about how to formulate HIPs?

Karl: If we sincerely believe that all families already have healing patterns as part of their repertoire (see Chapter 1), we will search for and identify those pre-existing competencies within the family. We selectively look for and attend to spontaneous positive transactions in the session, or notice events that could be framed, or reframed, as positive. For instance, we ask questions about how they typically recover from their problems, and selectively talk their own HIPs back into action. Grounding ourselves in our genuine passion for helping clients in distress, positions us to accomplish this more easily.

Shari: Noticing or asking about the accomplishment of the family's unique HIPs coupled with family members sharing or enacting these HIPs is a very common TIP we engage in at the CFTC. The circular questions (i.e., behavioral effects questions, triadic questions, see also Chapter 4) we previously discussed as useful to identify PIPs can also be instrumental in conversationally bringing forth HIPs. They help students initiate systemically focused conversations that coax awareness of both pathologizing and healing patterns of interaction. The work you present on reflexive questions gives additional concrete guidance for students to initiate transforming conversations with families (Tomm, 1987a, 1987b, 1988). Karl, we have discussed attending to the HIPs families are currently enacting, but what if the therapist can't see sufficient evidence of the family's own HIPs?

Karl: There is a sequence of concrete cognitive steps (see Figure 3.4) that a therapist could take to try to construct a HIP on behalf of the family. The first step is to imagine a behavior that contradicts or is incompatible with one of the behaviors in the PIP, and which could potentially serve as an "antidote" by squeezing out or precluding the performance of the PIPish behavior. The next step is to find a complementary behavior that could couple with the antidote to stabilize it as a recurrent preferred behavior. Going back to the earlier example, parental "giving space" for more autonomy or "gentle inquiring" about the son's experience could probably qualify as antidotes because they would be incompatible with the father's pressuring. And "taking initiative" or "responding" could be antidotes for the boy because they are incompatible with his resisting. These antidotes are then connected invitationally to generate a HIP of inquiring coupled with responding (see Figure 3.5). This imagined HIP then gives me guidance in formulating my questions to possibly bring the pattern forth in the family interaction.

Teachers providing lectures in which they describe central concepts help students become co-oriented with the instructor in the basic theory. Questions from the students are extremely important in this lecturing-listening process

- Search for evidence of the family's own healing behaviors and draw them out (by noticing positive initiatives and asking a series of circular questions).
- If the family's healing behaviors are not readily identifiable, imagine a possible behavior that would contradict or preclude one of the behaviors in the PIP.
- Search for a complementary behavior that is also inconsistent with the PIP behaviors and that could reinforce and stabilize the imagined healing behavior.
- Couple the healing and complementary behaviors in an imagined interaction pattern (using gerund descriptors whenever possible).
- Exploit opportunities to ask reflexive questions to bring forth the component behaviors of the imagined HIP.

Figure 3.4 Steps to bring forth a HIP

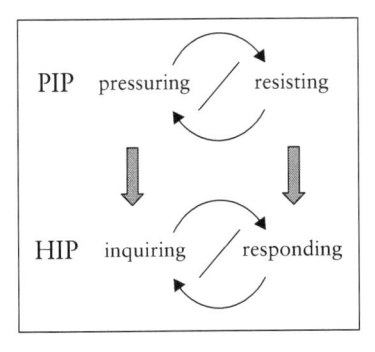

Figure 3.5 Possible movements from PIP to HIP

because they give the instructor an opportunity to listen to the listening of the student and get a sense of what is being heard, what is being misunderstood, and what is being missed. Providing ample opportunities for students to ask questions is, of course, essential to allow the interactive learning (WIP) of *asking coupled with answering* to emerge.

3. Demonstrating/Observing

As soon as the new interns arrive at the CFTC, they are invited to sit in the therapy room with a therapist or observe through a two-way screen. In this way, they are able to watch interaction patterns among family members and between families and therapists that have been discussed in class and see what they look like in actual practice. We encourage the interns to observe each of the therapists on staff and eventually other students, to witness different interviewing styles, yet see how we all hold a systemic perspective in common. Sometimes a senior therapist or supervisor will sit behind the mirror with a group of students and comment on the process in the session as it is unfolding, thereby providing an opportunity for students to see through the eyes of the supervisor moment-by-moment. In addition to the obvious invitation to observe clinical process and clinical practice in these situations, supervisors simultaneously extend other covert invitations for students to observe and learn through their acts of supervision, teaching, and reflection.

An extremely important ritual at the CFTC is the weekly "screening" interview. Therapists (and eventually students) are asked to identify a therapy process with one of their families that seems to have become stuck and invite that family in for a consultation by a senior therapist while the whole team, including the students, observes behind the two-way screen. The therapist and consultant describe and demonstrate their work and at some point during the interview the team offers an open and spontaneous "team reflection" for the family (Andersen, 1987), which will be described next. The weekly regularity of these meetings provides continued opportunities for demonstration and observation that helps us learn from each other and extend our skills in seeing through the eyes of others. While students may appear most attentive to, and conscious of, the content of the consultation they are listening to, they are actually more like sponges, continuously absorbing many details of the ongoing therapeutic process. Learning through watching occurs at many levels, and much of it occurs outside of conscious awareness, (e.g., noticing body posture; head, hand, and leg movements; facial expressions; eye movements; tone and rate of speech; coordinations among family members; therapist timing and interruptions).

4. Involving/Doing

For students at the CFTC, the first active involvement with actual families occurs indirectly through participation on reflecting teams, which is a valuable transitional step between observation and actually conducting therapeutic interviews. Reflecting team activity occurs not only during official screening interviews but also on an ad hoc basis when there are two or more persons observing a session. All of the interview-room-plus-observation-room couplets have reversible mirror and sound systems, so a therapist could call upon the observing group[2] at any time to switch the lights and sound and offer their comments about the family's situation.

In our typical procedure of utilizing a reflecting team, we begin by introducing ourselves to the family through the screen and then deliberately turn inward toward one another to discuss our impressions of the family's situation within a closed circle of the team. This places the family in a more obvious observer position, which allows more of their mental energy to flow into deeper listening (instead of simultaneously devoting energy toward preparing responses while listening, which occurs in an ordinary face-to-face conversation). For the reflection itself, we start with selective acknowledging and affirming responses that are grounded in actual events during the session, taking care to comment on every family member present. This helps provide a positive base upon which subsequent and perhaps rather challenging comments could more readily be accepted. Beginning deliberately with positive comments also serves to help reflecting team members overcome their own problem-focused noticing habits.

We then give team members full freedom to comment on whatever resonated for them during the session and encourage them to do so in a conversational manner with one another. For instance, if the family's situation re-activates memories of a personal life experience of a team member, that person is encouraged to briefly comment on the salient personal connection. In this way, family members see team members as human beings in a common journey of living, rather than as professionals passing judgment, which often comes as a significant relief for families. Team comments about the family are offered in a subjunctive mode of tentative expressions like "it seemed to me . . ." and "I wonder whether . . ." rather than objective certainties, to allow more space for observing family members to "take it or leave it."

When the emergence of new ideas begins to wane (usually after 5–10 minutes), any team member could ask, "Should we give it back to the family now?" as a signal to invite any final comments. Then by reversing the lights and sound again, the reflecting team gives back the initiative to the therapeutic system. Typically, the therapist then asks each family member (usually from the youngest to the oldest) about his or her

- Therapist inquires about the family's interest in a reflection.
- If interested, reverse the lights and sound system.
- Team members introduce themselves through the mirror.
- Close the team circle, placing family in observing position.
- Begin with affirming comments based on observed events in a conversational mode, mentioning every family member.
- Offer personally resonating impressions of intuitively important relationship issues in a subjunctive mode.
- Signal impending conclusion "Should we give it back . . . ?"
- Reverse the light and sound systems again.
- Therapist inquires about each family member's take on the team's comments (from youngest to eldest).

Figure 3.6 Typical sequence for the reflecting team process

reactions to the team's comments (see Figure 3.6). In this way we learn what family members found salient, and the students on the team often get immediate feedback on their contributions.

Shari: Karl, you describe several functions of these reflecting teams in advancing the learning of our students. They offer an opportunity to see another's seeing, a transition from observing to doing, and a way to take up or embody a less problem-focused, objectivist stance. I find that involvement in reflecting also invites us to focus on the team process and not just the content of the conversation. In my opinion, one of the important outcomes of our participation in these reflections is their integral role in engaging students in WIPs that accomplish teamwork. It is obvious that student contributions are not peripheral in the reflecting process. From the very first screening they share their opinions, and their contributions are coupled with genuine integration and/or reflection on their useful ideas (a WIP of *doing coupled with learning*).

Karl: I concur, Shari. The trust communicated to the students in this WIP of *contributing coupled with integrating* constitutes a strong invitation for them to take up their roles as mutual partners on the team. Our trust in the students' pre-existing knowledge and competence to participate in this way derives from our realization that they have lived in relationships themselves for many years and already have an enormous amount of intuitive understanding about relationships. Our job as teachers is mainly to help them hone and apply that prior knowledge to become increasingly therapeutic for families.

After students have observed experienced therapists work and have participated in reflecting teams, they are expected to begin conducting their own therapy sessions under supervision. We require students to arrange for live supervision of the first five sessions as they begin to provide therapy, so that if necessary, the supervisor can readily be called into the session to help out if a problematic process escalates. Later, when supervisors and students have developed confidence in the student's ability to conduct clinical interviews, students are encouraged to proceed to see families on their own, with continuing intermittent verbal and live supervision.

We believe that this aspect of our training, the learning by doing, is the most significant of anything we have to offer in the program. We are extremely grateful to the many families who collaborate with us in providing this invaluable learning opportunity by allowing our interns to work with them clinically.[3] As the therapy process proceeds, a WIP typically emerges between the family and the intern with *the family progressively opening up to work with the student coupled with the student stepping further into the role of practitioner*. There are inevitable beginner struggles of how to best formulate questions, how to sequence questions, how to attend to several family members at the same time, how to balance talk time, and how to get children to talk that create an enormous amount of anxiety for students. However, we try to harness this anxiety to serve as a resource to mobilize motivation to learn. When this domain of learning is combined with the others, most notably what we discuss next, knowledge about the doing of therapy gradually becomes embodied in the student.

5. Supervising/Reflecting

The supervisory offerings at the CFTC are extremely rich. While we utilize various forms of supervision, we give priority to live clinical supervision (over written, verbal, or video supervision), because with the live process both student and teacher are grounded in immediate common experiences of witnessing the family situation and the therapy. Live supervision usually occurs from behind a two-way screen, but occasionally the supervisor sits in the same room with the therapist and family. A telephone call-in system is available but is used sparingly to avoid inadvertently undermining the student therapist. A bug-in-the-ear system[4] is also available. It allows supervisors to embed potentially useful questions in the immediacy of the ongoing session, which the intern can introduce seamlessly (or is free to ignore). Given that the process of supervision will be elaborated in greater detail in Chapter 9, we will shift here to focus on reflecting processes in our learning activities.

We encourage the activity of reflection in every aspect of our work. We always reflect on our own, of course, but what is so special about the CFTC is how much of the reflection takes place conjointly in team conversation. Discussions take place, before and after regular sessions and screenings, behind the mirrors in observation, in staff and student offices, and in the videotaping suite. Many students comment that without this opportunity for reflection they would feel lost in their learning.

Karl: These continual conversations between students and staff are so central to our teaching/learning. When students first arrive, it is usually hard for them to make sense of the complexity of therapeutic initiatives taking place in the therapy room. They often ask, "How did she or he know to ask that?" If I was behind the mirror with them, I might respond by asking, "Did you happen to notice that action/reaction (part of a PIP) earlier? And how it got them stuck? And how the therapist's question to invite a difference (HIP) got them moving forward?"

Shari: Would you also say that we often address the question of "why this over that" in these conversations? Ultimately we are inviting students to make choices in how they will contribute to a specific direction in their therapeutic conversations. Could you talk more about how this is taught in the WIPs of teaching/learning?

Karl: When I talk about four alternative ethical postures (Strong, Sutherland, Couture, Godard, & Hope, 2008) that we as therapists can adopt in our decision-making about how to intervene therapeutically, I try to open space for students to become more aware of the differential effects of initiatives we could take during interviews. I make a heuristic assumption that in every clinical situation there are always multiple ways we could intervene therapeutically, all of which could be helpful. This assumption keeps us looking for alternative options and wondering about their possible effects. Thus, we actively create opportunities for making more choices. While I acknowledge my own preference for adopting an ethical posture of empowerment, I also try to open space for students to make their own choices about what posture suits them best in their own personal style of interviewing. Perhaps this could be conceived of as a WIP of *empowering students to decide coupled with students taking more responsibility for deciding (how to intervene)*, which helps them grow and mature as competent clinicians.

Given that our program also has excellent videotaping facilities with remote controlled cameras in every therapy room, we encourage students to record their interviews and review them later, on their own, with other students, or with their supervisors. There is an enormous learning advantage in being able to start and stop a recording to reflect upon and/or discuss a specific sequence of events in a session and consider alternative possible responses or questions by an interviewer. It is during these reflections that the second-order perspective of how we are actively constructing therapeutic possibilities becomes clearly evident. Sometimes we arrange special seminars for reviewing recordings together to take full advantage of this kind of learning.

Shari: As a student, I remember the palpable experience of witnessing and understanding a second-order perspective as I watched recordings of sessions. As we slowed the talk down it became easier to challenge the notion that therapists could objectively identify interaction patterns between family members (first-order) and then intervene through one-way directives. I began to notice how both clients and therapists co-construct change through collaborative interactive patterns (second-order).

Karl: The therapist's initiative to foster change will be described later (in Chapter 5) as a TIP: a two-way (emergent) conversational accomplishment. But how did observing tapes help you see these interaction patterns differently, Shari?

Shari: As I slowed down the talk while viewing the recording and engaged in parallel conversations with my supervisor, I increasingly understood the IPscope as an instrument to enable the dialogic process in therapy. Early on I remember the pull to understand the IPscope framework solely as a diagnostic tool. Initially, a clear diagnostic tool was very attractive to me as a PhD student who had been influenced by modernist notions of therapeutic evaluation, academically and in practice. However, while I observed recorded sessions I was better able to see the coupling between the client and therapist as the therapist "talked to listen" (Hoffman, 2002, p. 247) and, for example, took a stand (asking a reflexive question or offering an opinion) in a way that invited clients to contribute to it as a developing proposition. I noticed how the therapist listened generously rather than formed a rebuttal, and formulated a new intervention as the speaking partners took conversational turns (Shawver, 2000). As I was repeatedly encouraged to understand my interactions as coupled with members of the families that I worked with, I made another shift from my previous modernist, diagnostic notions of therapy to a more collaborative conversational understanding (e.g., Anderson & Goolishian, 1988). Currently, in my role as a teacher, it is gratifying to see students using the IPscope as a tool to gradually orient themselves to join families in shared conversational work rather than solely for identifying interactional patterns.

Karl: Students benefit from continual reflective conversation as it helps them see first- and second-order IPs and move from delivering one-way interventions to joining two-way conversational developments. However, sometimes students like to be told how to give the "right" intervention because joining conversational developments seems too complex or mysterious for new therapists. How did you experience this?

Shari: Looking back now, as a student I think the notion of conversational developments actually took some of the pressure off. If my question did not get the intended or hoped-for response, it was not a failure but another avenue to explore with the client. The pressure remained to join these conversations in forward-moving ways. However, I felt decreased need to be the expert with the magical question and more at home as a conversational partner utilizing an IPscope lens that helped me orient to problematic patterns and solution patterns. This reminds me of the WIP you described earlier of *empowering students to decide how they will interview coupled with students taking more responsibility for their interviews*. Precisely because there is no right answer students are invited to make these conversational decisions and develop into confident yet curious practitioners.

Students are also given a scheduled opportunity to continue reflective conversations about their experiences separate from supervision of live sessions or recorded sessions. A regular bi-weekly meeting is devoted to "group process learning" for all the interns in the program during a particular semester. At these meetings students are invited to identify and share their current conceptual challenges and personal "growing edges" in new understandings and skill development to extend the ongoing learning interactions between students and staff.

The repeated opportunities to join developing patterns or watch others join these interactions at the CFTC invites critique and reflection "which parallels the reflexivity that is the hallmark of postmodern practice" (Paré & Tarragona, 2006, p. 3). In this teaching process knowledge is not necessarily handed over but generated through continual reflective conversations. As Strong mentioned in Chapter 2, *techne* is a term to describe knowledge as pre-given and meant to be delivered (i.e., manualized interventions in evidence-based practice) and *phronesis* as pragmatic and procedural wisdom, the kind that is adaptable and interactional. In the teaching/learning processes we describe here, we endeavor to bring forth the IPscope as phronesis or a type of "knowing-in-action" (Schön, 1983).

6. Documenting (Requiring IP Formulations/ Conceptualizing and Writing IPs)

Staff at the CFTC devised a clinical record system to deliberately document PIPs and HIPs in relational patterns. Therapists complete a Brief Interview Record, or BIR (see Appendix A), after each interview. Among other things, therapists record specific behavioral couplings within interaction patterns of the family system and/or in the therapeutic system on the BIR. Students are expected to describe and rate the most salient PIP in each session and to conceive of a corresponding HIP brought forth in session, and/or for possible use in subsequent interviews. The tasks of rating the PIPs on the "Reported Severity" and "Experienced Severity" scales (see Appendix B), and rating the HIPs on the "Reported Strength" and "Experienced Strength" scales (see Appendix C), require the student to reflect more deeply on the interpersonal process in both the family system and the therapeutic system. Indeed, these recording tasks actually serve to sharpen the relational focus when using the IPscope lens. Students work hard to clarify the PIPs and HIPs in their personal reflections upon their interviews and then to summarize their work with a particular family in the final closing summary. Supervisors are available to review both the students' brief interview records and their closing summaries to clarify their emerging understandings of the patterns they have heard about, witnessed, and/or experienced during the sessions.

Shari: Describing this documenting process reminds me to comment on the tension evident throughout this book between what we have called "relational stabilities" (see Chapter 1) or "discursive captures" (see Chapter 2) and more loose, elusive, or dynamic ways of understanding relational patterns. Balancing this tension can be confusing for students especially initially when they feel de-skilled as they shift toward more systemic practice, and find themselves drawn toward more concrete formulations where they feel compelled to "nail down the PIP and HIP." In this book, we maintain that the relational patterns we see through the lens of the IPscope are but one way of understanding our work with families—a way in which we as observers are actively implicated.

Karl: Yes, as noted in Chapter 1, by deliberately bringing forth these IPscope patterns we are drawing distinctions upon distinctions rather than uncovering any underlying "real" structure of relationships.

Shari: At the same time, however, we encourage students to ground or momentarily stabilize their understanding of interactional patterns through the coursework and in the clinical record system. We give students the task of capturing these patterns through written descriptions and patterned diagrams. The opportunity to momentarily halt elusive IPs in this way is valuable for students as they begin to grasp and conceptualize possible relational stabilities.

7. Searching/Researching

As well as cultivating a culture of openness within the CFTC, we extend the learning WIP of *welcoming feedback and other perspectives coupled with offering feedback and other perspectives* to professionals and agencies outside our program. We actively search for new developments in the field and regularly bring outside scholars and clinicians to the CFTC to share their knowledge and skills with us. As a result, our patterns of practice have actually changed several times over the years. Current students not only witness but also are part of that evolutionary interactional process (i.e., engage in WIPs between staff and outside practitioners) while they are with us. Former students are occasionally shocked and dismayed to discover that we have abandoned certain ideas and practices and moved on to embrace others.

Karl: I remember quite vividly how some former students were very upset when after teaching Milan systemic therapy for several years, I announced at a conference that I had abandoned the Milan approach. What happened was that as I embraced Maturana's theory (which challenged the validity of functionalism) and adopted some of Michael White's narrative practices (White, 2007; White & Epston, 1990), I moved on to a stance of bring-forthism (Maturana & Varela, 1992). Some people have said of me, that I have been "blessed with a good sniffer" to search out new promising developments in the field. Indeed, bringing new ideas home to the CFTC has been a significant part of my work that has been very enjoyable in my career.

Shari: And this has many benefits for those of us who welcome the opportunities made possible by your olfactory talents! In addition to the many visiting practitioners, your extensive travelling to present elsewhere and extend your ideas has had an enormous impact on the CFTC, not only in the more obvious sense of building on our ways of practicing, but also in stimulating our own curiosities and WIPish searching.

As a collective group of staff and students in a clinical program, we engage in regular monthly research meetings to review selected aspects of the literature and/or to present, implement, or discuss various research projects. Indeed, during the 2008–2012 academic years, Drs. St. George and Wulff introduced ongoing qualitative studies of PIPs and HIPs in the program as a whole (see Chapter 10). In doing so they were able to demonstrate to students experientially how research and practice can become intimately intertwined. The rare opportunity to engage in "research as daily practice" invites a novel way of integrating often-overlooked opportunities to advance our work. We believe that the overall atmosphere created by these multiple learning events and processes has been extremely supportive and enabling of the professional development of our students in terms of their own knowledge and skills in therapy and research. In fact, many students choose to continue their conversations at the CFTC after they have completed their internship by using the program as a site for their own research projects (e.g., Couture, 2006).

Concluding Comments

We began this chapter with a quote from Maturana who proposed a distinction between teaching and creating contexts for learning. At the CFTC we clearly give priority to cultivating an open reflective context for interactive learning. Such a context can only be achieved collectively through active collaboration among staff and students. When working alone as a therapist day-after-day, one could inadvertently create conditions for a conservative drift in one's understanding and clinical practices. In isolation, one comes to see fewer alternatives and fewer possible options for therapeutic change. Predictably, this drift tends to take practitioners back toward a more individualistic perspective. Given the potential generativity of interpersonal interaction, students as well as experienced therapists would be well-advised to situate themselves in contexts where, at least occasionally, they can see themselves and their relationships with clients through the eyes of others. This gives them other perspectives to draw upon in their work. If they are also able to choose a context that is proactive in fostering a systemic orientation, the generativity could be further enhanced.

Throughout this chapter there has been an implicit underlying tension between stabilized or captured ways of understanding the IPscope, as opposed to a more conversational or generative tint to this lens. We use both grounding diagnostic-based and dynamic practice-based conceptualizations of the IPscope. We value the objectivist, stabilizing applications when they are employed within a reflective, conversational context. We prompt our students to look through the IPscope to momentarily stabilize problematic interpersonal patterns and then bring into focus possible TIPs that might conversationally transform these patterns. We label relational patterns as if they exist to organize our work while recognizing that we actively construct them as we make distinctions through the relational IPscope lens. We are not trying to erase these tensions. As other authors in this volume suggest, recognizing these tensions in our ongoing dialogues at the CFTC is fundamental to our ethical use of this framework.

The consensus at the CFTC is that staff therapists have, in part, situated themselves within the program because the WIPs of IPscope-oriented teaching are generative for teachers as well as students. Indeed, our collaboration in this writing has extended our own learning and renewed our enthusiasm for participating as educators in teacher/learner relational patterns. The improvised dialogue within this chapter is intended to illustrate some of this process. Our hope is that we may have also offered something potentially generative for our readers who might take up some aspects of this approach in their learning and teaching, to adjust their focus, and bring forth heuristic shapes of a "relational vase" in their own learning activities.

Notes

1 See Couture (2006) for a summary of the doctoral dissertation that describes these conversational developments.
2 The family's consent for observation is always obtained in advance, and although the observing groups consist mainly of staff and students from the program, visiting professionals from multiple disciplines are often invited to join the process, thus offering another avenue to cultivate an open, generative environment.
3 This generous collaboration by families is voluntary and by consent but may reflect some reciprocity in that the clinical services are funded by a grant from the provincial government and there is no cost to the families.
4 We have the technology at the CFTC to give the student the option of wearing a device in his/her ear that allows him/her to hear the supervisor's reflections from behind the screen throughout the session.

References

Andersen, T. (1987). The reflecting team: Dialogue and meta-dialogue. *Family Process, 26*(4), 415–428.
Anderson, H., & Goolishian, H. (1988). Human systems as linguistic systems: Preliminary and evolving ideas about the implications for clinical theory. *Family Process, 27*(4), 371–393.
Bateson, G. (1972). *Steps to an ecology of mind.* San Francisco, CA: Chandler.
Bavelas, J. B., Coates, L., & Johnson, T. (2000). Listeners as co-narrators. *Journal of Personality and Social Psychology, 79*(6), 941–952.
Couture, S. J. (2006). Transcending a differend: Studying therapeutic processes conversationally. *Journal of Contemporary Family Therapy, 28*(3), 285–303.
de Shazer, S. (1994). *When words were originally magic.* New York, NY: Norton.
Hoffman, L. (2002). *Family therapy: An intimate history.* New York, NY: Norton.
Koffka, K. (1935). *Principles of gestalt psychology.* New York, NY: Harcourt, Brace, & World.
Maturana, H., & Varela, F. (1992). *The tree of knowledge.* Boston, MA: Shambhala.
Paré, D., & Tarragona, M. (2006). Generous pedagogy: Teaching and learning postmodern therapies. *Journal of Systemic Therapies, 25*(4), 1–7.
Schön, D. (1983). *The reflective practitioner: How professionals think in action.* New York, NY: Basic Books.
Shawver, L. (2000). Postmodern tools for the clinical impasse. *Journal of the American Academy of Psychoanalysis, 28*(4), 619–639.
Shotter, J. (2008). *Conversational realities revisited: Life, language, body and world.* Chagrin Falls, OH: Taos Institute.

Strong, T., Sutherland, O., Couture, S., Godard, G., & Hope, T. (2008). Karl Tomm's collaborative approaches to counselling. *Canadian Journal of Counselling, 42*(3), 174–191.

Tomm, K. (1980). Towards a cybernetic-systems approach to family therapy at the University of Calgary. In D. S. Freeman (Ed.), *Perspectives on family therapy* (pp. 3–18). Toronto, ON: Butterworths Press.

Tomm, K. (1987a). Interventive interviewing: Part I. Strategizing as a fourth guideline for the therapist. *Family Process, 26*(1), 3–13.

Tomm, K. (1987b). Interventive interviewing: Part II. Reflexive questioning as a means to enable self-healing. *Family Process, 26*(2), 167–183.

Tomm, K. (1988). Interventive interviewing: Part III. Intending to ask lineal, circular, reflexive and strategic questions? *Family Process, 27*(1), 1–15.

White, M. (2007). *Maps of narrative practice.* New York, NY: W. W. Norton.

White, M., & Epston, D. (1990). *Narrative means to therapeutic ends.* New York, NY: Norton.

4

A LIFE HISTORY OF A PIP

Snapshots in Time

Tanya Mudry, Tom Strong, and Jeff Chang

When I (Tanya) was asked to introduce myself and how I became involved in systemic family therapy, I was not entirely sure exactly where to start. Had I always thought systemically? Had I always seen and experienced patterns in families, and in my own family? Had I noticed PIPs and HIPs in my own family-of-origin? I think not, at least not consciously. Similar to noticing PIPs in a relational context, it is not until you notice and reflect on your transitional history that change patterns become identifiable. Prior to my doctoral counseling psychology internship at the Calgary Family Therapy Centre (CFTC) I had been engaged in traditional individual therapy (primarily cognitive behavior therapy, CBT) practicum experiences. I worked with clients to change their distorted thoughts and dysfunctional behaviors toward more functional and healthy ways of being and living. I was often frustrated by a lack of progress outside of the therapy context; it was as though clients reverted back to their dysfunction as soon as they returned to their relational contexts (i.e., with their children or spouse). This was part of my motivation to begin working in family therapy; I thought I could help facilitate more sustained change if family members were involved.

When I began my internship at the CFTC (under the supervision of Jeff and Tom, co-authors of this chapter), I felt that I was prepared in a theoretical sense to begin working with families using a systemic approach. I had read in the area and was intellectually familiar with the Healing Interpersonal Patterns (HIPs) and Pathologizing Interpersonal Patterns (PIPs) framework. It was not until I began trying to put this theoretical orientation into practice in my work with families—guiding my lookings and listenings through a HIPs and PIPs lens—that I realized I was undergoing my own transitional process as a new family therapist. I often found myself slipping back into "serial individual interviewing" and was often "under the influence of CBT" as Jeff would say. There were parallel change processes going on in the therapeutic context of the family and in my own professional development as a family therapist learning the HIPs and PIPs approach. Just as my families were learning to reduce their PIPs and increase their HIPs to construct more preferred ways of being together, I, too, was learning to practice in a different way, reducing old, familiar patterns of individualistic practicing, and relying more on relational practices. I was able to see how conceptualizing family problems through a HIPs and PIPs perspective—that is, noticing HIPs and using Transforming Interpersonal Patterns (TIPs)—was both helping families in my work with them and also helping me become more relational.

The case study used in this chapter is based on one of the first families I saw at the CFTC. Both Jeff and Tom supervised me while I worked with this family. I saw them over 6 months, sometimes as a whole family unit, sometimes as dyads, or as individuals. I was fortunate to see incredible changes occur over the months that I worked with them, and I am grateful for all that they have taught me. The family members have been given pseudonyms, and the dialogue in the examples used in this chapter is a composite of the conversations we had together.

Initially, I (Tom) struggled with conceptualizing family concerns using the interpersonal patterns (IPs) framework, having earlier left behind what I thought were structuralist notions of problem description for a poststructuralist sensitivity to language use in family therapy of any kind (Strong, 1993). However, in adapting to the flexible use of the IPscope at the CFTC, and by valuing Wittgenstein's (1953) notion of "language games," I came to appreciate that families could be stuck in patterned ways that an IPs formulation could help me identify and address. I still think PIPs are an ephemeral kind of relational phenomenon: patterned ways of being families get into and out of either on their own or with our help. It makes sense to me that each identifiable PIP can have a particular life course—each comes into being and dissolves in unique and fleeting ways. The same could be said about HIPs, which similarly wax and wane. Wellness Interpersonal Pattern (WIPs) can be seen as those enduring and resilient ways of interacting that act like the family's interactional immune system. Tracking the life of a PIP, from its earliest stages as a Deteriorating Interpersonal Pattern (DIP), to its replacement by a HIP, and subsumption into the family's WIPs seemed an interesting process-oriented way for us to feature the IPscope across a broader ecology of therapeutic and family interaction.

My (Jeff) earliest paid work in the human services was as a child and youth care worker in residential programs for adolescents. My colleagues and I were helpful to the youth who lived in residence, but the improvements seemed to be spoiled by a visit home. My view of interpersonal aspects of human problems evolved from blaming "bad kids," to blaming "bad parents," to blaming ecosystems (Bronfenbrenner, 1979). Like Tom,

I operated from structuralist approaches to family therapy (Haley, 1987; Minuchin & Fishman, 1981) that focused more on family organization than family process. As an early adopter of solution-focused (de Shazer, 1985) and narrative (White & Epston, 1990) ideas, I learned to focus on times when families acted differently than how they described the problem—what we refer to here as TIPs, HIPs, and WIPs. In the hybrid style I developed (Chang, 1998), sometimes I spent more time inviting families to discuss the patterns and sequences of the problem, so it was not a stretch to notice DIPs and PIPs.

Entering and Exiting PIPs

Social and physical reality could be an ongoing challenge to engage with, were it not for the ways people make such realities acceptably familiar to themselves and each other. For family members, keeping things acceptably familiar enables them to understand, act, and move forward together, in ways they can accept, or at least will not find persistently objectionable. When our experience is not familiar or acceptable, we tend to use our words and actions to make them so. This includes how we conceptualize our interactions with others. While we cannot point to each other's internal thoughts or emotional "pictures" (like those found in the thought bubbles of cartoon characters), we can respond to each other in ways that can make a social or physical reality either acceptably familiar or something worthy of our objection. The ways through which people simultaneously respond to circumstance and each other are at the heart of our views of relational well-being and pathology.

Central to our IPs view is a focus on how family members coordinate, through their interactions, ways of keeping things acceptably familiar. When family members' interactions are experienced by one another as objectionable (Strong & Tomm, 2007) DIPs arise, which if repeated, can stabilize into PIPs. Thus, the therapist's role is to interpret and respond to how family members interpret and respond to each other. This involves a particular kind of therapeutic noticing of what family members notice in each other's responses, whether acceptable or objectionable. TIPs, HIPs, and WIPs are acceptably familiar interpretations and responses—within families and between[1] family members—while DIPs and PIPs refer to interpretations and responses that are unacceptably familiar to family members. In this chapter, we expand on this view, linking an IPs view of relational interaction to how problematic patterns emerge, how they become patterned in objectionable ways, and how differences invited by the therapist can facilitate conversations that foster acceptably familiar ways of relating.

Throughout this book, our team of authors will be referring to clinical problems as arising and being maintained primarily within patterned ways of relating. While much of life can feel improvised in response to the unexpected, we do not usually navigate life as if we are trying to make our way through a foreign country in a foreign language. Instead, we tend to develop relational habits or social practices (Schatzki, 2010; Shove, Pantzar, & Watson, 2012), which enable us to coordinate our lives together in mostly acceptable ways—even if we do not fully understand or agree with each other. Tacit and patterned familiarities by which we "do" or socially practice life with each other (Heidegger, 1962) help us coordinate our lives—unless our efforts at coordination are breached by unanticipated developments. Life is coordinated in some acceptably familiar ways—until it is not.

Unanticipated developments can come from seemingly anywhere: the changing individualities of people in relationships (e.g., in the family life cycle, in individual life span transitions, changes in health status) or unexpected developments in people's work, cultural, or physical circumstances (e.g., economic downturn, natural disaster, relocation). At that point, we are thrown off our previously familiar interactions, challenging us to revise how we coordinate our actions—hopefully in ways that establish new and accepted patterns of living together. If we find new developments objectionable, they can set off DIPs. With some relational repair work or adaptations, families can overcome a DIP and learn to accommodate the unanticipated with new, yet acceptably familiar, interactions. However, when a DIP stabilizes, a PIP develops via the recursive coupling of family members' objectionable interactions. Seen this way, relational life oscillates between accepted familiarities anchored in patterned interactions and destabilizing objectionable developments that can also become objectionable familiarities.

A closed or *discursively captured* system (e.g., couple, family) is one in which participants fail to recognize or escape from objectionably patterned interactions. Such a system is anchored in patterns of understanding and acting that reject new developments (and members' reactions to each other in responding to such developments), much like an immune system rejecting a virus (cf. Esposito, 2011). Instead, such systems are sustained by the patterned, if not expected, sameness of people's reactions to each other. So, the notion that people could develop particular patterned ways of interacting that would incorporate every eventuality they might face defies social or physical worlds, in which constant and unanticipated ways of becoming are inevitable (Deleuze & Guattari, 1988; Massumi, 2011). Instead, in relational life, rather than getting things right without any further need to revise our ways of relating, we oscillate between stabilizing patterns of responding and destabilizing ways of responding to what we deem acceptable or objectionable (e.g., Keeney, 1983).

The primary way people "do" the patterned ways of relating we are describing is through forms of communicative interaction. In such interaction, our uses of language can mislead us, particularly if we focus only on the logocentric nature of communicating (the semantic *what* of our communications, sometimes referred to as the *digital* channel), and overlook *how* we perform our talk with each other (the *how* of our communicating, sometimes referred to as the *analogic* channel; Derrida, 1976; Watzlawick, Bavelas, & Jackson, 1967). Therapists can fall prey to this oversight as well, focusing on differences over *what* family members say to each other, while *how* partners and members speak of these differences with each other can escape notice. Unanticipated developments for partners and families can arise either way, in and over the emerging course of their communication. The *how* comes into clearer focus when one privileges the coupling of the *whats*. These developments can stabilize into clinical concerns, evolving from DIPs to PIPs, out of a relational reactivity anchored in the patterned *hows* and *whats* of their unacceptably familiar interactions. Our therapeutic ways of responding and intervening are designed to re-coordinate interpersonal patterns—to transform PIPs to HIPs and then (hopefully) to WIPs. We welcome and join family members in amplifying the acceptable developments they already experience (*their* HIPs, so to speak)[2] and we *use circular and reflexive questions to clarify PIPs* and *to initiate change* (i.e., *our* TIPs).

As relationally- or systemically-oriented therapists, we are less concerned about how a PIP originated and more concerned about how it becomes *sustained* in patterned interactions that discursively capture partners or family members (Massumi, 2011; Watzlawick, Weakland, & Fisch, 1974). This is not to say that history, as narrated by each family member, is irrelevant. In fact, family members' ways of telling each other onset or origin narratives may be central in maintaining unacceptable patterns. Even two well-intended people can become discursively captured by a PIP if each person reacts objectionably to the other's performed intentions (i.e., their "sayings and doings"; Schatzki, 2010) in ways that eventually become patterned. This said, how might a PIP develop among family members out of an unanticipated and unacceptable development around which they interact?

We do not believe that unacceptable ways of responding to a new circumstance are determined by one person's psychopathology. Instead, we focus on how problems are coordinated by people's ways of responding to each other. This is not to suggest that people do not encounter problems with their circumstances or that some individuals are more or less vulnerable than others. However, as family therapists, we consider how problems can become anchored in familiar yet objectionable ways of relating. An individual's problem (e.g., a health concern) can invite a welcomed and accepted response from family members, or not. A new shared development (e.g., financial challenges) can similarly invite acceptable or unacceptable family interactions (e.g., Strong, Wulff, Mudry, St. George, & Sametband, 2012). PIPs emerge out of objected-to relational responses or reactions that come to persist in patterned ways.

Some suggest that there can be an almost hypnotic element to what we have been referring to as PIPs (e.g., Kershaw, 1991), that family members' objectionable patterned responses are cued, and reacted to reflexively, in ways that sometimes feel outside of their control. With a social practices view of PIPs (e.g., Schatzki, 2010; Shove et al., 2012) such reactions become anchored in objectionable, yet tacitly familiar, patterned interactions for those caught up in them, performing patterned interactions without thinking about them, much like any habit people perform without conscious awareness. Or as White (2007) suggests, the discourses that sponsor PIPs are taken for granted. A problem-saturated story is a filter through which meaning is jointly constructed, which can later capture how family members come to interpret and react to each other's behavior. PIPs, accordingly, require tacit habits of reactivity from those who perpetuate them. When therapists and clients jointly identify PIPs, therapists can ask questions to invite clients to reflect upon their reactivity and initiate TIPs.

One premise of this book is that stabilized relational patterns in couples and families, whether healing or pathologizing, owe much to how family members respond to each other over time, especially in how they respond to unanticipated developments. As therapists focused on client preferences, we attend to the HIPs family members notice—with or without our helping them to notice such HIPs. The challenge for therapists is to learn to recognize, highlight, and help stabilize HIPs that the family may have already performed, in ways that family members take up again. However, we are also interested in co-constructing HIPs as "relational antidotes" to PIPs. HIPs that endure and enhance relationships may become WIPs—the kinds of relationship patterns that enable family members to stay responsive to, and accepting of, each other. We assume that families regularly perform WIPs and HIPs, even when they present themselves in desperate circumstances (Waters & Lawrence, 1993) with PIPs that have discursively captured how family members understand and respond to each other. We are interested in how families and therapists collaborate to escape this discursive captivity, by enacting TIPs, "PIP antidotes" as found in HIPs, and stabilized patterns that eventually become WIPs. It is not uncommon to hear how families who overcome adversity emerge stronger, as their new ways of relating to one another stabilize (Urban Walker, 2006).

In the remainder of this chapter we trace the "life history" of a PIP as it occurred within a client family seen at the CFTC. We then relate therapeutic interventions and family developments we see as related to the PIP's modification and replacement. For us, PIPs depend on a patterned and familiar objectionability that, in order to change, require new conversations that can bring forth and pattern acceptably familiar ways of responding between partners and members. Let us now turn to therapy for the Andrews family and how these ideas about IPs apply.

Evolving IPs in the Andrews Family

The Andrews family consisted of daughter Brianne (16), mother Wanda (41) who described herself as a "full-time mom," stepfather Russell (39) who was working out of town for 2 weeks of the month, and son Tim (12). Brianne's biological father, Kurt, whom Brianne traveled to see during school vacations, lived in a neighboring province. At the start of family therapy, Brianne had just returned to the family home after living in a youth shelter and successfully completing a residential drug treatment program; she was now sober, and was hoping to begin school again. In conversation with me (Tanya), their therapist, the family identified the following problems and desires:

- Wanda and Russell identified Brianne as exhibiting explosive anger, being verbally and physically abusive, and having a history of breaking trust and boundaries with past drug use and sexual acting out.
- Wanda and Russell wanted to strengthen their communication skills and co-parenting strategies.
- All family members identified their desire for respectful interactions.
- Wanda and Russell expressed concern about the deteriorating relationship between Brianne and Tim.
- Russell and Brianne had a tumultuous relationship. Brianne felt judged and controlled by Russell, which led to her rebelling, while Russell felt disrespected by Brianne. [PIP: Correcting & controlling / Protesting & rebelling]
- Brianne and Russell agreed that they regularly got into arguments that seemed to "take on a life of their own." Before the argument even began, both Russell and Brianne were "on edge" and ready to counter one another.

The reader may readily recognize several possible avenues of questioning that could invite the performance, and yield descriptions, of PIPs. Indeed, we noted many potential directions and several PIPs. Therapists who use the IPscope as a lens for their therapeutic noticing tend to see many PIPs pieced together from family members' individualistic, and sometimes blameful, descriptions. However, these distinctions of PIPs are most useful when they orient the initiatives of therapists toward therapeutic change even when the family is not aware of these distinctions or does not take them up. In any given course of therapy, the therapist and family can explore several PIPs, some that dissolve rather quickly and others that persist.

Moreover, the vicissitudes of language invite us to refer to and write about IPs as nouns. Accordingly, if we are not careful, we may reify IPs. Therapists can be tempted to find the "right" one, or become frustrated with families when they do not agree with how we have (brilliantly) distinguished their PIP. In our view, IPs are perhaps best understood as "serviceable fictions" or ways of making sense of family member interactions.

As the Andrews family requested, we attended to the patterns of Wanda and Russell's communication and co-parenting; Brianne's temper and the interactions her expressions of temper engendered; the ways in which family members showed respect for each other, and how at times they missed expressions of respect; and the patterns of conflict between Brianne and Tim. However, the PIP we focused on, that seemed to hold the greatest urgency for the family, occurred mainly between Russell and Brianne. For the purposes of this chapter, we illustrate it in Figure 4.1.

From Acceptably Familiar to Unanticipated and Objectionable Developments

In this section, we describe how DIPs along the way may have unexpectedly contributed to the main PIP we formulated previously. Reflecting about life before the recent troubles with Brianne, Wanda stated that as

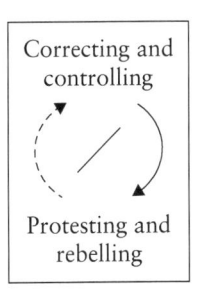

Figure 4.1 A major PIP

a young child, Brianne was often "defiant." Wanda managed Brianne's defiant behavior sometimes by yelling and spanking, and sometimes by removing favored activities or items, maintaining constant attention to her imminent misbehavior. As Wanda stated, "She was good as long as I kept on her." Brianne complied, usually grudgingly. We distinguished the DIP of *Wanda scrutinizing Brianne's behavior coupled with Brianne complying grudgingly* (see Figure 4.2a).

Wanda indicated that once Russell moved in, Brianne (who was 7 years old at the time) began resisting his attempts to set limits. Russell thought that Wanda needed his help to provide Brianne with "a firm hand," and that given his financial and emotional support of the family, Brianne should respect him as a father figure. On the other hand, Brianne gushed about how wonderful her biological father, Kurt, was when she came home from visits. Based on the family's description, we noted the DIP of *Russell giving direction and expecting respect coupled with Brianne resenting Russell and showing disrespect* (see Figure 4.2b).

When Brianne was 12, Wanda got a call from the vice-principal. Brianne had been caught smoking marijuana in a park adjacent to the school. After a consultation with the youth substance abuse treatment agency ("who said she was just fine," said Wanda disdainfully), Brianne continued to use. This eroded Wanda's confidence in counselling services, inviting the DIP of *professionals minimizing problems coupled with avoiding professional help* (see Figure 4.2c).

The three DIPs the family described could all be seen as objectionable developments. Although they were problematic, they did not devolve into PIPs until family members became mutually reactive in a *sustained* way. In other words, a negative development for one member might be accepted or seen as "not worth sweating over," and the family member or relationship moves forward. On the other hand, family members might

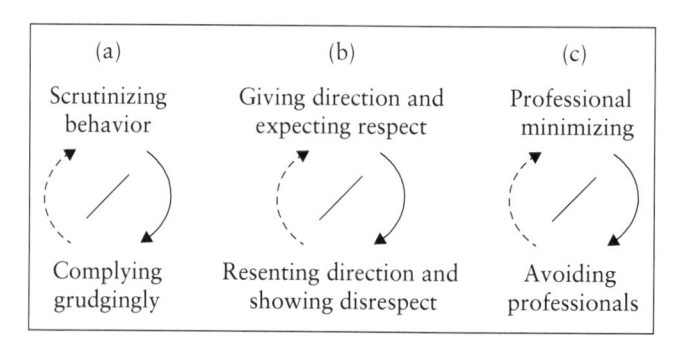

Figure 4.2 Several DIPs feeding the major PIP

respond in a highly reactive way, leading to the emergence of a PIP. As the family continued to engage in sustained patterned interactions with one another, and in relation to various helping professionals (i.e., addiction counsellors), problems worsened until Brianne's substance use prompted placement in a youth shelter and family intervention.

In the next section we outline the therapeutic approach I (Tanya) utilized with this family, using Karl Tomm's interventive interviewing (Tomm, 1987a, 1987b, 1988) with therapeutic questioning. We provide hypothetical questions and responses, explaining the intention and effect of the questions, and we depict a possible life history of a PIP.

Clarifying PIPs Through Circular Questions

Circular questions are exploratory questions that are helpful for a therapist to orient to the client's situation (Tomm, 1988). Circularity is a core feature associated with an IPs approach to practice and relates to the notion that people are interconnected through the recurrent and familiar ways they respond to each other, whether overtly in outer dialogues and interactions, or internally in inner (private) dialogues (Billig, 1996). Therapists can use circular questions, an important conversational intervention of the Milan family therapists (e.g., Boscolo, Cecchin, Hoffman, & Penn, 1987), to bring forth the patterns that connect persons, objects, actions, perceptions, ideas, feelings, events, beliefs, and contexts in recurrent interactions.

I used circular questions to identify and clarify the family's PIPs. It is important to re-emphasize that this is not a matter of finding the one right PIP. We pay selective attention to interpersonal patterns. We "deliberately imagine" (see Introduction) relational phenomena like PIPs. We would not want to suggest that PIPs are somehow real beyond their pragmatic utility to the therapist and family.

The process of therapy is organic and fluid, and as we interview, we may be intervening in more than one PIP simultaneously, and through the interviewing process, we may be inviting clients into an interactional view of family problems without targeting a specific PIP directly. For the purpose of this chapter, we showcase one particular PIP so we can highlight its transformation. In the first session, I asked about a sequence of events, using *distinction-clarifying questions,* or questions used to introduce or clarify a key distinction that may have implications in a system of beliefs (Tomm, 1987b) and *behavioral effects questions* to track familiar sequences.

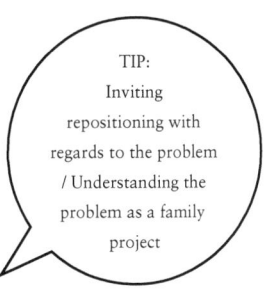

> TIP: Inviting repositioning with regards to the problem / Understanding the problem as a family project

Tanya:	Russell, from your point-of-view, can you predict when Brianne will, as you put it, "Blow up and storm off?"
Russell:	Well, it doesn't have to be for anything, but it's usually when her mother or I tell her to do something.
Tanya:	Brianne, then what happens?
Brianne:	I don't like it. They're so picky. It just pisses me off that they want me to do everything around there. They are always on my back, picking at every little thing I don't do.
Wanda:	That's because if we didn't, you would never do anything.
Tanya:	Let me get back to getting a picture of what everyone actually does. (*To Brianne*) So then you do what?
Brianne:	Well, I take off out of the house.
Wanda:	Not before telling us what assholes we are....
Tanya:	Let me come back to that....
Brianne:	Well you guys are yelling at me, so why shouldn't I? You try to control everything I do.
Tanya:	Tim, what are you doing as all this is happening?
Tim:	I just try to stay out of it.
Tanya:	So, Brianne, when you go out, where do you go? What do you do?
Brianne:	I just go out to my friend's. I used to get high, but I'm really trying hard not to do that anymore.

Annotations:
- Invitation into a DIP: Wanda interrupting Brianne and defending
- Therapist feeling pulled into a PIPish conversation, but redirects conversation.

In one respect, I am simply gathering information. However, asking for a sequence of events may constitute a TIP and initiate a HIP in that family members could come to see that their interactions are patterned. It is also important to listen for the HIPs that family members are already performing. In this case, Brianne refers to "getting high" as what she "used to do." This might provide an opening to attempt to nurture a pre-existing HIP, if the rest of the family sees that as a useful distinction as well. We will return to this, and other possible HIPs, later.

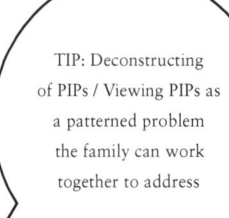

Annotation: TIP: Deconstructing of PIPs / Viewing PIPs as a patterned problem the family can work together to address

After eliciting a description of the sequence of events, I used *interpersonal perception questions* (questions that inquire about what family members think other members might experience) to invite family members to put themselves "in the shoes of" others:

Tanya: Russell, how do you think Brianne feels when you and Wanda tell her what to do?

Russell: I guess she feels frustrated and controlled.

Tanya: Brianne, did he get that right?

Brianne: Yeah, I guess so.

Tanya: Well, how do you think Russell feels when you do the opposite of what he is asking?

Brianne: He is probably upset and angry at me for not listening. I know he cares about me and doesn't want anything to happen to me.

Tanya: Russell, what difference does it make to you that Brianne does have some idea of how you feel and what's motivating your behavior?

Russell: I never thought about it before. I'm glad she knows that, that I care about her, but I think she still feels angry and resentful about any little thing her mother and I ask.

Wanda: And if she knows we care, why can't she just accept our direction? We don't want her to be a druggie. We want her to develop good habits and be a responsible person. We do know a little something, you know. We're not stupid.

Tanya: And Wanda, when Brianne resists your direction, what do you do?

Wanda: I dig in even more. And she just gets madder. I know it doesn't work, but I don't know what to do.

Tanya: Tim, what's your take on what your mom and Russell do?

Tim: Well, I don't think that Brianne should talk to them that way, but I don't think what my parents do helps either. I just wish people wouldn't get so mad all the time.

> TIP: Asking Russell and Brianne to describe how the other feels / Russell and Brianne seeing effects of their interactions

> TIP: Asking Tim how he understands and is affected by the conflict / Family members are able to see the effect of interactions on non-involved others

Here, I used circular questions to generate a contextual understanding of the particular PIP that seemed most troubling to the family and that maintained some aspects of the problem (see Figure 4.1). Our focus on interpersonal patterns is more likely to orient us to focus on how problems are sustained, rather than on the presumed causes (e.g., Watzlawick et al., 1974; White, 1989). Interpersonal perception questions helped family members to understand what others were feeling in relation to their behaviors and responses, thereby co-constructing a greater awareness of these patterns. These questions also enabled the involved members to see how "third parties" were involved and affected by the patterns.

Facilitating Change Through Reflexive Questions

One of the ways therapists collaborate with families to bring about change is to recognize and join a preferred direction that is already occurring but has somehow escaped their notice. Through their questions and responses, narrative therapists and solution-focused family therapists (e.g., Madsen, 1999) invite family members to recognize such change directions as exceptions to, or unique outcomes from, objectionable developments and interactions. From our perspective, it is more useful to notice what families are already doing that is consistent with their preferred directions, which in turn invites more preferred responses from family members as well. We not only invite family members to recognize these preferred directions (HIPs) but also want to see if we can help these preferred directions stabilize into recurrent and acceptable ways of responding and going forward together (WIPs). For example, a conversation might look like this:

Tanya: Are there times when you are getting along at home?
Wanda: Well, we watched a movie together as a family on Friday night.
Tanya: Oh! You watched the movie together? All in the same room? How did you manage that?
Brianne: Yeah, they finally let me choose the movie, so I didn't have to watch a stupid kids' movie for Tim.
Tanya: So, allowing Brianne to choose the movie allowed you guys to watch together. What else helped?
Russell: Wanda was willing to sit down and relax for a bit. She is always busy cleaning and doing things. It was nice for her to join us . . . and Brianne didn't complain at all. She was smiling for once.
Tanya: Okay, so Wanda was relaxing, Brianne chose the movie and she was smiling. That sounds great!

TIP: Asking for exceptions / Narrating and thickening exceptions

Reflexive questions (Tomm, 1988) are a conversational way to invite family members to recognize and build on pre-existing HIPs, or to invite consideration of new HIPs. Such questions can bring forth changes in family members' thinking and behavior by inviting them to reflect on the unwanted implications of their current perceptions and actions (that may be PIPs) and move toward preferred HIPs and WIPs. In the vignettes we described above,

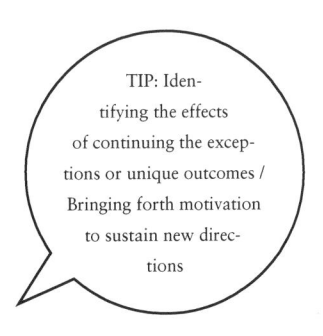

> TIP: Identifying the effects of continuing the exceptions or unique outcomes / Bringing forth motivation to sustain new directions

there were several conversational openings that a therapist could have explored as potential HIPs. For example, Brianne states that she "used to get high, but I'm really trying hard not to do that anymore." Russell infers that Brianne feels "frustrated and controlled" by his and Wanda's actions, which Brianne confirms is accurate. Later Brianne affirms, "I know [Russell] cares about me and doesn't want anything to happen to me." Wanda confirms she knows "it doesn't work" to "dig in" and acknowledges, "I don't know what to do." Tim states, "I just wish people wouldn't get so mad all the time." Any of these comments could provide an opening for the therapist to stimulate a conversation about family members' helpful desires, intentions, and actual behaviors.

In the following passage, we explore one example of using reflexive questions pertaining to a TIP to transform a PIP into a HIP (see Figure 4.3). The focus was on opening space for families to distinguish new possibilities for change. I began the conversation:

Tanya: Brianne, what do you think would happen if you fall back into using drugs and rebelling when people ask you to do things?

> Future-oriented question highlighting potential consequences

Asking reflexive questions / Distinguishing possibilities for change

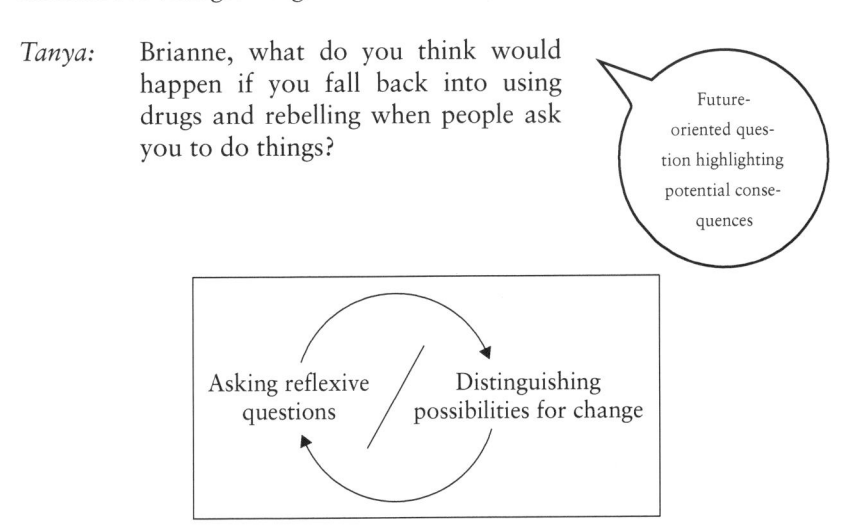

Figure 4.3 A TIP to enable movement from the PIP to a HIP or WIP

Brianne: I would probably become an addict again.

Tanya: Right away? Just like that? Or would there be some kind of downhill slide?

Brianne: Well, so far, I haven't used. I'm afraid that if I had a really bad blow out with Mom or Russ, that I might go that way, and I don't want to.

Tanya: Has it happened so far that you have thought about it, but then stopped yourself?

Brianne: I think about using every day. Most days—not seriously. But last week, I almost texted my old connection.

Tanya: Really? How do you account for the fact that you didn't? How did you stop yourself? *[Wonderment question]*

Brianne: I just thought, "Well if I do that, my life in the family is over."

Tanya: Wanda, what's your reaction to what Brianne just said?

Wanda: Well, I'm scared to death that she will use again. It scares me when she says she thinks about it all the time, but I guess I shouldn't be surprised. I know how hard it was when I quit smoking. But I'm glad that she values her family, and I'm proud of her for trying so hard.

Tanya: Russell, let me ask you, if Brianne continues down this road of blowing up when she is asked to do things at home, what kind of father-daughter relationship would you two have? *[Future-oriented catastrophic expectation question]*

Russell: Well, we wouldn't have a relationship at all. We're starting to see some little changes, so I guess I am a little hopeful.

Tanya: What changes have you noticed?

Russell: Well, we went grocery shopping and didn't kill each other. She actually asked to come and it was kind of fun.

Tanya: Oh, you did! Brianne, did you have fun, too? *[Amplifying constructive change question]*

Brianne: Yeah, it was OK. He was goofing around, juggling the apples.

Tanya: How were you able to go shopping without fighting, when you can't at home?

Brianne: Russell wasn't telling me to do things differently.

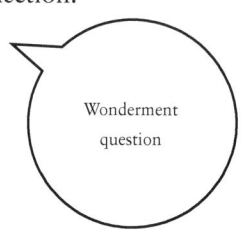

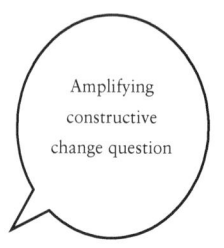

Tanya: He's not telling you what to do. What are you talking about instead?

Brianne: Food, school, life . . . maybe he would want to listen to me about the good decisions I'm making.

Tanya: So rather than fighting about what Brianne should be doing, you might be talking about the good decisions Brianne is making?

Brianne: Yeah, and then I can be proud of my good decisions and it'll be easier to make good decisions.

Tanya: So if Russell supported you and acknowledged you when you made good decisions, it would be easier to make good decisions?

Brianne: Yes, I think so.

> Unexpected context question

> Distinction-clarifying question

> Introducing a hypothesis

Here, the therapist invited the family to open space to new possibilities and connections in the meanings, behaviors, and events surrounding the unacceptable PIP of *correcting coupled with rebelling* that could become acceptably recoordinated. Future-oriented questions (life with or without fighting), unexpected context change questions (shopping), distinction-clarifying questions ("What were you talking about instead?"), and introducing a hypothesis ("So rather than fighting about what Brianne should be doing, you might be talking about the good decisions Brianne is making?") invited family members beyond what had been objectionable between them to consider more acceptable ways of interacting that enabled this new coordination. This introduced the HIP of acknowledging Brianne's good decisions: encouraging and bringing forth Brianne's intention to recognize choices and make good decisions. These questions allowed the family and me to explore additional possibilities to interacting in ways that were not conflictual. The use of these reflexive questions helped us to co-construct a preferred reality in a collaborative way.

> Possible HIP: Acknowledging good decisions / Recognizing choices & making good changes

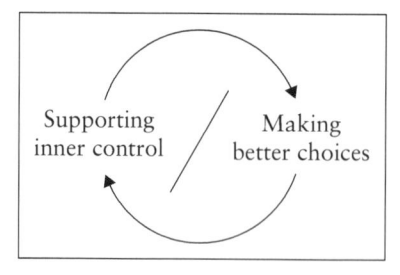

Figure 4.4 A HIP to replace the PIP

Seeing a problem as *correcting and controlling coupled with rebelling and protesting* is preferred over "Brianne is deviant and a drug addict." When the problem was located in the interactional patterns, everyone in the family had a role to play in making changes. Reflexive questions helped the family see the possibility for a different kind of life. They were able to co-construct an alternative way of living, with less fighting, less correcting and controlling, and consequently less rebelling and better choosing. As Russell and Wanda learned to support Brianne in recognizing and making good decisions, and began helping support her inner control, Brianne was able to make better, less harmful decisions, yielding a HIP of *supporting inner control coupled with making better choices* (see Figure 4.4). Consequently, Russell and Wanda began to feel better about Brianne's growth and were better able to express appreciation, ultimately decreasing conflict in the family and opening space for more mutual respect.

Conclusion

Family members typically go about their lives interacting in ways that they interpret and respond to as acceptably familiar. However, a different kind of familiarity can develop in families around objectionable ways of reacting—a familiarity we join family members in recognizing and naming as PIPs. These are patterns that are not acceptable but the family has become used to them; they become stable ways of reacting that they would generally not live by if they could avoid them. Some PIPs are obvious and stabilize conflicts between family members in ways that are very familiar to therapists. The same familiarity pertains to the more acceptable stabilities of HIPs and WIPs as well. However, sometimes the latter escape notice, enabling a PIP to be foregrounded while subordinating the significance of these other preferred IPs. One aspect of our role as IPs-informed therapists is to recognize and invite family members to identify, stabilize, and perhaps build on HIPs they may be overlooking and that PIPs too often obscure. Similarly, we can join families in recognizing and sustaining their WIPs, the enduring patterns of interaction which anchor their well-being. In other words, PIPs can end up dominating families and family therapy when HIPs and WIPs go unrecognized and are not acted upon.

It is important to see all the IPs we have been describing as transitory and as changeable patterns of members' ways of responding within families. That said, humans generally tend to prefer stability in their lives, particularly if it is acceptably familiar. Families sometimes get captured in the PIPish ways we have been describing, particularly when they have not found alternative ways of going forward together. How family members adapt to changing circumstances can be provoked by both a change in shared circumstance and a change in how members relate to each other. Since DIPs can become PIPs stabilizing in the unacceptable familiarity of family member interactions, we see the conversational practices of family therapists as very useful in inviting family members to recognize, co-construct, and collaboratively enact preferred alternative patterns of interaction (HIPs).

In this chapter, we first elaborated on what we meant by the different IPs of the IPscope, and then described work with a family, tracing the pre-therapy development of a particular PIP in therapy. While there are other PIPs that were enacted by the Andrews family, we selected conversations that related to this particular PIP, describing some uses of circular and other forms of questioning to clarify the PIPs, and reflexive questioning to enable the family to re-coordinate their interpersonal patterns. We have also interwoven aspects of theory to account for why we are more attentive to some aspects of family members' relating over others and to support our reasons for the conversational practices we use with families in therapy. There is an element in what we have been saying that suggests that challenging circumstances for families can sometimes be less of an issue for families' collective well-being than the reactivity that can develop and stabilize between family members as a response to those circumstances. Our interest is with moving beyond the stabilities of reactive PIPs toward more responsive HIPs and WIPs and we have used this chapter to show how we conceptualize one family making such a shift with therapeutic assistance. Of course, the same PIPish problems that can overtake families can overtake therapists working with families as well, as therapists can get bogged down with families in familiar yet objectionable ways.

With regard to WIPs, family therapy as mentioned earlier can be a space where enduring patterns fostering family well-being can be identified and embraced more purposefully. We see this occurring through ways our questions invite such WIP identifications (e.g., "what things do you do as family members that are most worth continuing?") but also

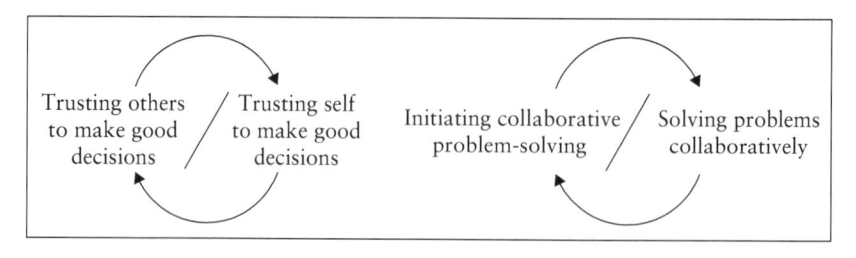

Figure 4.5 Possible stabilizing WIPs

through how therapists join and amplify family members' interactions when WIPs occur. Using our case example, here are possible WIPs that could sustain the family in resilient ways of being:

- *supporting inner control coupled with making healthy choices;*
- *recognizing and celebrating good decisions coupled with making good decisions;*
- *trusting others to make good decisions coupled with trusting self to make good decisions;* and/or
- *initiating collaborative problem-solving coupled with solving problems collaboratively.*

As these WIPs stabilize (see Figure 4.5), they have the potential to be a source of resilience in the family.

Notes

1. Although "among," which should be used when referring to more than two persons, is grammatically correct, in our view it deemphasizes the interactions between members.
2. Noticing and eliciting HIPs and thickening them into WIPs is similar to what narrative therapists do when interviewing about unique outcomes, or what solution-focused therapists do when they elicit exceptions, assuming that the focus is on the interpersonal space.

References

Billig, M. (1996). *Arguing and thinking* (2nd ed.). New York, NY: Cambridge University Press.

Boscolo, L., Cecchin, G., Hoffman, L., & Penn, P. (1987). *Milan systemic family therapy: Conversations in theory and practice.* New York, NY: Basic Books.

Bronfenbrenner, U. (1979). *The ecology of human development: Experiments by nature and design.* Cambridge, MA: Harvard University Press.

Chang, J. (1998). Children's stories, children's solutions: Social constructionist therapy for children and their families. In M. F. Hoyt (Ed.), *Handbook of constructive therapies* (pp. 251–275). San Francisco, CA: Jossey-Bass.

Deleuze, G., & Guattari, F. (1988). *A thousand plateaus: Capitalism and schizophrenia*. Minneapolis, MN: University of Minnesota Press.

Derrida, J. (1976). *Writing and difference* (A. Bass, Trans.). Chicago, IL: University of Chicago Press.

de Shazer, S. (1985). *Keys to solution in brief therapy*. New York, NY: W. W. Norton.

Esposito, R. (2011). *Immunitas: The protection and negation of life* (Z. Hanafi, Trans.). Malden, MA: Polity.

Haley, J. (1987). *Problem-solving therapy* (2nd ed.). San Francisco, CA: Jossey-Bass.

Heidegger, M. (1962). *Being and time* (J. MacQuarrie & E. Robinson, Trans.). New York, NY: Harper Collins.

Keeney, B. (1983). *The aesthetics of change*. New York, NY: Basic Books.

Kershaw, C. (1991). *The couple's hypnotic dance: Creating Ericksonian strategies in marital therapy*. New York, NY: Routledge.

Madsen, W. (1999). *Collaborative therapy for multi-stressed families*. New York, NY: Guilford.

Massumi, B. (2011). *Semblance and event: Activist philosophy and the occurrent arts*. Cambridge, MA: MIT Press.

Minuchin, S., & Fishman, H. C. (1981). *Family therapy techniques*. Cambridge, MA: Harvard University Press.

Schatzki, T. (2010). *The timespace of human activity: On performance, society, and history as indeterminate teleological events*. Lanham, MD: Rowman & Littlefield.

Shove, E., Pantzar, M., & Watson, M. (2012). *The dynamics of social life: Everyday life and how it changes*. London, UK: Sage.

Strong, T. (1993). DSM-IV and describing problems in family therapy. *Family Process 32*, 249–253. doi: 10.1111/j.1545-5300.1993.00249.x

Strong, T., & Tomm, K. (2007). Family therapy as re-coordinating and moving on together. *Journal of Systemic Therapies, 26*(2), 42–54.

Strong, T., Wulff, D., St. George, S., Mudry, T., & Sametband, I. (2012). *Finances and family therapy: A practice guide* (Unpublished manuscript).

Tomm, K. (1987a). Interventive interviewing: Part I. Strategizing as a fourth guideline for the therapist. *Family Process, 26*(1), 2–13.

Tomm, K. (1987b). Interventive interviewing: Part II. Reflexive questioning as a means to enable self-healing. *Family Process, 26*(2), 153–183.

Tomm, K. (1988). Interventive interviewing: Part III. Intending to ask lineal, circular, strategic, or reflexive questions? *Family Process, 27*(1), 1–15.

Urban Walker, M. (2006). *Moral repair: Reconstructing moral relations after wrongdoing*. New York, NY: Cambridge University Press.

Waters, D. B., & Lawrence, E. L. (1993). *Competence, courage, and change: An approach to family therapy*. New York, NY: W. W. Norton.

Watzlawick, P., Bavelas, J. B., & Jackson, D. D. (1967). *Pragmatics of human communication*. New York, NY: W. W. Norton.

Watzlawick, P., Weakland, J., & Fisch, R. (1974). *Change: Principles of problem formulation and problem resolution.* New York, NY: W. W. Norton.

White, M. (1989). Family escape from trouble. In M. White (Ed.), *Selected papers* (pp. 59–63). Adelaide, Australia: Dulwich Centre.

White, M. (2007). *Maps of narrative practice.* New York, NY: W. W. Norton.

White, M., & Epston, D. (1990). *Narrative means to therapeutic ends.* New York, NY: W. W. Norton.

Wittgenstein, L. (1953). *Philosophical investigations* (G. E. M. Anscombe, Trans.). New York, NY: Macmillan.

5

CAN I GIVE YOU A TIP?

Inviting Healing Conversations in Practice

*Joaquín Gaete, Inés Sametband,
and Olga Sutherland*

In this chapter, we explore Transforming Interpersonal Patterns (TIPs): "a sub-category of a WIP [Wellness Interpersonal Pattern], which enables movement from a PIP [Pathologizing Interpersonal Pattern] toward a HIP [Healing Interpersonal Pattern] or WIP [Wellness Interpersonal Pattern]" (see Chapter 1, p. 21). Therapists may engage in TIPs to introduce distinctions that open space for more healing patterns of interaction to occur among family members. We envision TIPs as a process by which therapists and families collaboratively bring forth virtuous (i.e., collectively preferred) articulations of clients' preferred ways of living together. We explore conceptual elements and therapy practices involved in the conversational accomplishment of these patterns. First, we introduce the notion of two-fold characterization of TIPs (constructive and deconstructive) and illustrate how each therapeutic initiative may be accomplished conversationally. Additionally, we introduce the distinction of TIP attempts from TIP accomplishments, to hint at how participating in TIPs may contribute to an empirical realization of a broader collaborative stance to family therapy. Transcripts of recorded family therapy sessions served as a basis for our conceptualization. Rather than providing strict rules on how to navigate the gap between PIPs and HIPs, we offer examples of TIPs. Therapists may find these examples helpful as heuristics to scaffold the construction of therapeutic change in similar situations.

About the Authors

I (Joaquín), as a therapist in Santiago, Chile, was initially trained in the strategic therapy model developed at the Mental Research Institute in Palo Alto, California. Something never felt right about having a strategic stance with clients; I believe that theoretical frameworks shape our very way of being! Since then, I have been trying to nurture a more collaborative stance to practice. Possibly, this chapter will make evident how engaging in TIPs may help embody such a stance. Second, as a researcher, I have been studying human change processes in therapy and other settings. What still intrigues me the most in the field of therapy is this insight: that to change, the "pill" humans take is something called "talk," but how talk brings about human change seems to be a largely unexplored territory in terms of research. It is my hope that this chapter will show why examining TIPs—a particular kind of talk—might shed some light on these issues.

I (Inés) used to work on a family therapy team influenced by the Milan Team's systemic approach. In working with families, our team would come up with complex and provocative interventions, and I often wondered why families came back to see us—even if we had the best intentions to help, we could really "tick people off." Years later, in search of new ideas and ways of working with families, I came across Karl Tomm's work and I started to focus more on clients' responses to my and other therapists' actions. I was amazed to see what I had not seen before; there was so much to work with in how clients and therapists responded to each other. I believe that focusing on TIP accomplishments (TIPs that may be initiated by therapists and taken up by clients) can be very helpful for therapists in training, as well as helping families more effectively. I hope our chapter is an invitation to such a focus.

I (Olga) completed my PhD clinical practicum at the Calgary Family Therapy Centre (CFTC) where I began learning about systemic thinking and systemic approaches to therapy. My interest in co-authoring the chapter on TIPs stems from my fascination with regularities or shared aspects of social relationships and interaction. As a therapist, I have found it valuable to apply generic conceptual knowledge of human subjectivity and relationships, afforded through my exposure to multiple client situations, to understanding interactions among family members in my work with a specific family. As a researcher, I use discursive analyses of social interaction (conversation and discourse analysis) and appreciate the attention within these approaches to the microfeatures of talk and insights they offer concerning the details of how interactional patterns are established and transformed discursively—that is, through social interaction. Preparing this chapter gave us an opportunity to reflect, both conceptually and analytically, on what is involved in changing problematic interpersonal patterns (IPs) through language, in the context of family therapy.

Two Types of TIPs: Constructive and Deconstructive

At least conceptually, any conversation distinguished as being helpful or resulting in therapeutic effects constitutes a part of a TIP. Tomm (1991) defined a TIP as a "conversation to identify a healing alternative that opens the possibility of consciously and deliberately redirecting the interaction in a healing direction" (p. 3). Although he acknowledged that "becoming aware of [being] immersed in a PIP is often a first step in interrupting it" (p. 3), he reserved the term "TIP" for conversations that focus on developing healing alternatives, as opposed to challenging clients' problematic ideas or responses. We propose expanding the concept of TIPs to include both the deconstructive and constructive elements of client-therapist conversations, assuming that clients' awarenesses of being engaged in a PIP may be an important step in their ability and willingness to join in constructing alternative, more preferred conversations. The micro-lens we use to explore actual therapy conversations later in this chapter will empirically demonstrate that each turn can be seen as a therapeutic collaboration. It is our hope that the co-constructive nature of *both* constructive and deconstructive initiatives will become evident through our micro-analysis; otherwise put, that both types of TIPs constitute therapeutic projects jointly accomplished in the immediacies of the therapeutic dialogue. Tomm (see Chapter 1) offered two prototypical TIP descriptions: *clarifying* conversations (i.e., "*asking about experiences coupled with disclosing experiences*," p. 25) and *generative* conversations (i.e., "*asking reflexive questions coupled with distinguishing new possibilities*," p. 25). We propose that these two prototypical TIPs can be used either within deconstructive or constructive initiatives. For example, therapists may invite clients into clarifying conversations to explore non-preferred ways of relating and, therefore, deconstruct PIPs (e.g., "And when he blames you, how is it that you would most likely feel and respond?"). Clarifying conversations may not only identify PIPs but also bring forth HIPs (e.g., "What was it like for you when he supported you in your decision?"). On other occasions, therapists may invite clients into generative conversations with the purpose of moving in a deconstructive manner—for example, by inquiring about the possible connection between a PIP and a non-preferred identity (e.g., "How does yelling relate to how you want to be as a father?"). Finally, therapists may also invite clients into generative constructive conversations to creatively envision alternative ways of relating or dealing with problems that may better fit with their preferences (e.g., "What would you like to see different in being a mother?").

IPs-oriented therapists intentionally pursue TIPs and avoid deteriorating and pathologizing conversations; there is a deliberate sense of directionality (from PIPs to HIPs). Therapists position themselves as unique participants in conversations in adopting this transforming orientation—a compass of sorts to be used within the ongoing therapeutic process. Accordingly, we believe these two means of TIPing (deconstructive and constructive) are most commonly observed in therapists' interactions with families and less in interactions among family members. This is not to negate that families strive to transform their relationships and interactions as well. However, clients may not be fully aware of initiating more healing conversations and may not see these attempts as evidence of change. The therapeutic potential of TIPs in clients' interactions may be realized if therapists notice, highlight, support, or at least do not obstruct these emerging transforming initiations from clients. Let us further explore deconstructive and constructive TIPs and provide an example of each.

Deconstructive TIPs are transforming conversations in which individualistic construals are challenged and a more relational perspective on clients' concerns of living are brought forth and co-constructed. Families engaging in these TIPs may recognize how their individual responses are coupled or linked in a circular fashion, enhancing their abilities to take a meta-perspective on their relationships. As Mudry, Strong, and Chang (see Chapter 4) suggest, family members may not be fully aware of the objectionable assumptions they live by in their conversations with other members; those assumptions are so familiar that people can get "captured" by them. Responding in PIPish ways appears to be the only alternative available for them. Deconstructive TIPs involve "loosening up" such assumptions by implicitly opening space to bring forth preferred ways of relating (WIPs). Note that we are not suggesting that in deconstructive TIPs assumptions are eliminated, but rather dealt with *as* assumptions. In so doing, engaging in deconstructive TIPs opens space for re-evaluating previously held assumptions and identifying alternative, *preferred* assumptions. Thus, engaging in deconstructive TIPs allows family members to consider how their own assumptions that are implicit in their responses may both influence and be influenced by PIPs. Tomm (1991) elucidated:

> One of the reasons that a PIP may be difficult to interrupt and replace is that the participants in the pattern may be unaware of the fact that their behavior is actually perpetuating the pattern. Indeed, while one is immersed in a particular pattern, one tends to attend to the possible meanings of the specific behaviors being enacted (whether it is one's own behaviors or those of the other) rather than to the overall interaction pattern itself. (p. 3)

Tomm further suggested that helping family members recognize that they are immersed in a PIP may not be sufficient for transforming interactions. Through *constructive TIPs* therapists may identify and explore healing alternatives with families. If therapists' invitations are taken up and supplemented, families may start their healing journey enacting HIPs and WIPs. Although we present deconstructive and constructive TIPs as conceptually distinct, in practice they often overlap. A therapist's intent to introduce alternative understandings may enhance family members' recognition of their current problematic contributions to interactions. Likewise, therapists who invite families to consider their concerns and behaviors more systemically may bring about spontaneous changes in their relationships.

We conceive of both deconstructive and constructive TIPs interactionally—that is, as involving matched or coupled contributions of at least two parties (Tomm, 1991). A key distinction here is that of an *attempt* versus *accomplishment*. The therapist's propositions of healing alternatives (attempted TIPs) may be taken up by family members (achieved TIPs), contributing to changes in their interactions (HIPs and WIPs). However, attempted TIPs may also not be accomplished. An attempt to compliment or support someone may or may not result in that person feeling complimented or supported (e.g., a compliment or empathy may be experienced as an offensive remark or as patronizing), generating a misunderstanding from which participants may move forward by further conversational negotiations (Sametband & Strong, 2013). This distinction is similar to Tomm's distinction between the *intent* of an action and the *effect* of this action on the other (Tomm, 1991). Overall, we propose considering therapists' interventions and practices interactionally, to include clients' responses (e.g., uptake, decline, expansion) and subsequent communication (interventions may have delayed effects). As Strong (see Chapter 2) suggests, focusing only on therapists' intended meanings or interventions as one-way accomplishments can be confusing; how therapists' and clients' communications are coordinated in recurring ways of responding is what matters. We further propose reserving the term "patterns" for interactions that recur, as opposed to responses that get coupled occasionally (Tomm, 1991).

Let us offer case studies illustrating deconstructive and constructive patterns followed by the discussion of implications for therapy practice and training. These case studies are taken from screening interviews at the CFTC involving a therapist inviting his or her colleagues to join one of the regularly scheduled sessions with a family (see Chapter 3). The most common reason for initiating a screening session is the therapist feeling stuck and seeking helpful directions or tips (i.e., TIPs) from other therapists. We propose the following analysis as one of many ways of understanding and describing how TIPs are and are not accomplished in therapeutic conversations.

Deconstructive TIPs

Attempting to Deconstruct a PIP

The following session segment (Extract I) involves two parents (a Caucasian, heterosexual couple in their 40s) and two children (males,

C1 age 14, and C2 age 12). The presenting concern is the elder child's aggression directed at the parents. The PIP can be described as *controlling coupled with resisting* (the more the parents expect that the child acts appropriately, the more the child feels constrained or controlled to act in preferred ways, and consequently resists the parents' efforts to influence him and vice versa). Dan (therapist) and Sally (consultant) invite the family to deconstruct their assumptions and interactional responses.

Sally (S) invites the family members to share their ideas and "theories" to explore why they were experiencing no further positive changes in the family (a "plateau") in their therapeutic work with Dan (D). The father (F) attributes minimal progress to his son's (C1) lack of insight into his behavior and its impact on others in the family. Both sons (C1 and C2) are present in the session (the PIP is instantiated here by C1 and F).

Extract I

1	F:	I'm running out of theories, you know. The one is
2		that there seems to be either a problem at the
3		executive level, a disconnect, you know, not having
4		the insight on what is actually happening. So, when
5		you use words like "sorry" it means "I will change,"
6		or if you do this, this is what is going to happen
7		next. In the sense like if I have this kind of social
8		interaction with people, it will (inaudible) in the
9		wrong way, so therefore I won't do it . . . If you
10		don't do your chores, you will lose your money . . .
11		this is probably . . . {gestures a plateau with hands}
12	S:	{Brings her hands to her mouth and slightly sighs}
13	D:	{Scratches his back}
14	F:	{Looks at M} . . . the level we are struggling? I-I-I
15		don't know, is it a containment strategy? Insight
16		seems to be, sometimes
17	S:	OK.
18	C1:	{Stretches his body and looks behind}
19	F:	lacking, or if somebody in his
20		situation they know they are in trouble but they
21		don't know why they are in trouble, you explain
22		why, but still can't figure it out how to stay out of
23		that trouble.
24	S:	OK, so insight might be part of your theoretical
25		explanation for why things are plateaued, anything
26		else that may explain this plateau {looks at M}, at
27		least theoretically . . . Just ideas?

Instead of explicitly identifying and challenging the *controlling coupled with resisting* PIP, in Extract I we notice S and D privileging the "two faces" as opposed to the "vase" (see Chapter 3): S and D seem to avoid taking up the family's familiar explanations, rooted in intrapersonal dynamics, and focus instead on ideas introduced by the clients that take into account interpersonal processes. Interestingly, the therapists do not offer systemic explanations directly to the family (e.g., identify the PIP *for* them). S and D seem to explore the situation from a position of curiosity, avoiding a prototypical Deteriorating Interpersonal Pattern (DIP), such as *scrutinizing the other's behavior coupled with the other's self-conscious awkwardness*. They pursue a certain version of a clarifying conversation, recurring throughout the session—namely, *asking about experiences coupled with disclosing experiences*.

Specifically, in lines 1–16 we see the therapists ignoring multiple opportunities during F's speech to thicken and explore his individually oriented explanation of the problem (C1's lack of insight into his problematic behavior). Non-verbally, S and D (and C1) seem to show minimal uptake of F's PIPish theory (C1's lack of insight). S brings her hands to her mouth and slightly sighs and D scratches his back.[1] After F ends his turn, S explicitly invites alternative and additional understandings of the problem, holding insight as only a partial explanation of the problem ("OK, so insight might be part of your theoretical explanation . . ."). She then redirects the conversation away from the PIP by selecting M as the next speaker (with her gaze).

The next extract illustrates how S's attempt to initiate a TIP was unsuccessful: M does not join in constructing alternative understandings of the problem. Then, S and D persistently and irreverently (Cecchin, Lane, & Ray, 1992) continue performing further TIP attempts: D first asks for other family members' possible competing theories and then shifts to discussing his own experience with the parents' expectations.

Extract II

29	D:	{Looking to M} I think of the time when we first
30		met and I think it was you who said, "We need to
31		do something to find out how far we can go . . .
32		what he seems to understand, what he seems to
33		not understand . . . and maybe it has to do with
34		something like expectations" {looks at S and then
35		back at M}
36	M:	Yes. What I don't understand is that he is kind
37		and friendly towards other people but when he
38		gets home he takes all these bad moods and
39		aggressiveness on us (pause) I don't understand that.

40 S: OK, any other theories? Of the plateau? (silence)
41 OK, so it could be what you have told us about
42 expectations, is that what you were suggesting?
43 That that could be sort of an explanation for the
44 plateau? Insight could be—those two might be
45 related to each other—any other theories on
46 the plateauing?
47 D: C2 would be always thoughtful in our sessions,
48 "this is not working," he is the one who would
49 say initially, "we are not getting anywhere," he
50 was the courageous one to say it out loud. So you
51 guys {looks at C1 and C2} have some ideas about
52 what could get things going in a better way?
53 C2: I have to think about that, at the moment no.
54 D: OK.
55 S: Are there some questions that you wish D had
56 asked? Or topics he might approach that he
57 didn't do but kind of underneath you were
58 hoping that that would have come out?
59 M: No . . . there was enough (inaudible) that we
60 would bring to the table if we felt that there was
61 something else . . .
62 D: One of the things that I was feeling was that, I
63 was too (inaudible) to your frustrations as
64 parents with the behaviors that you were
65 dealing with C1 and C2, and I was feeling kind of,
66 like I really needed to come up with something,
67 that I really wanted to keep finding something to
68 provide the answer, so I kind of feel that plateau
69 too, and that's why maybe having this meeting
70 with all these other folks—maybe they could help
71 producing more ideas. So the plateau for me
72 was more like they have to find something . . .
73 and then you emailed me and said you really
74 wanted to work this out with your family. And
75 that confirmed for me that we had to keep working . . .
76 S: So if things don't change, what are you most
77 worried about?
78 M: The anger from C1. I don't want that. I don't
79 want a family to have this, that he feels we are
80 against him, and we feel he is fighting us.
81 S: C1, is that your feeling too? That your house is
82 kind of a battle zone?[1]
83 C1: Yeah.

---

1 Sally (S) asked us to add here the following note: "Since the time of this session I (S) have been much more cognizant of *not* using violent metaphors in my languaging because I worry that we are contributing to violent behaviors inadvertently by using such language."

In line 29, we see D making a TIP attempt by proposing an alternative understanding of the problem. He cites M's prior speech ("... and I think it was you who said: We need to do something..."), which can be seen as a way to find a relational explanation in M's words, as opposed to alternative understandings coming from the therapist. M, in response, does not endorse D's proposal and presents C1's aggression as a personal disposition or trait in lines 36–39 ("he is kind and friendly towards other people but . . . he takes all these bad moods and aggressiveness on us").

S once again interrupts M ("OK, any other theories?" in line 40) to redirect the conversation and open space for alternative ideas. She acknowledges two ways of understanding the situation: F's "insight" and D's "expectations," while continuing to ask for alternatives (lines 41–46). In the subsequent conversation (lines 55–77), we see S and D as determinedly attempting to generate alternative ideas. For example, D describes his experience of feeling pressured to generate solutions for the family, implicitly proposing that not only the eldest son but also D himself has been the recipient of the parents' expectations (lines 62–75). S builds on D's idea that the parents may feel an urgent need to experience change and explores with the parents the apprehension that may underlie this urgency or expectation of change ("So if things don't change, what are you most worried about?"). We see this question as a TIPish attempt to bring forth some catastrophic expectations. In a deconstructive TIP, this can be a way to mobilize some emotional energy toward moving away from what is problematic. In line 82, S metaphorically introduces a relational perspective to the problem—a conflictual home environment as a "battle zone." Despite the therapists' attempts to initiate TIPs, some family members seem reluctant to join and supplement such invitations to accomplish an actual TIP. However, D and S's attempts can be seen as openings for a different kind of conversation, one in which family members are invited to and respond from a curious and novel stance.

Deconstructing a PIP

"Language enables us to put things in public space . . . no longer just a matter for me [but] for us together."
—C. Taylor (1985, p. 259)

The next extract, taken from the same screening session, illustrates the accomplishment (initiation-completion) of a TIP. S continues to search for relational explanations of aggression (i.e., aggression as a response rather than an inherent personal quality or disposition). This time, we view the conversation as a clarifying TIP. S asks about C1's experiences, which invites C1 not merely to clarify for himself, but for everybody else in the room, what his experience was like. This practice of eliciting the *details* of C1's experience allows S and C1 (and those in the room hearing their conversation) to accomplish an interpersonally-oriented account of his aggression and anger.

Extract III

1	S:	In your ideas of emotions . . . do you think that
2		anger has a place or has a purpose, or is a sign
3		of something? How do you make sense of anger
4		. . . or these kinds of emotional reactions?
5	F:	It is a legitimate, human expression . . . but it is
6		how you deal with it, and how you deal with
7		whatever is triggering that emotion. We talk
8		about it, that's the way you take it out of your
9		system, having a conversation about it.
10	S:	(*inquires in detail about C1's experience of*
11		*anger*)
12	F:	But when you are on the bus, do you feel that
13		anger?
14	C1:	No. It's like I know when I get out of the bus
15		school ends officially, and like I don't know.
16		Why . . . but I just feel . . . Mhm! . . .
17	S:	So it starts when you get off the bus and the
18		official end of school. When this starts,
19		what kinds of pictures enter your mind, or what
20		kinds of words enter your mind, or what are you
21		thinking about, as you are taking those steps
22		out of the bus, and you start to feel this boil?
23		{draws a spiral with her finger in the air}
24	C1:	I'm just thinking: "Oh great, this is gonna happen
25		again, again, again."
26	S:	So what are you anticipating?
27	C1:	Yeah, I'm pretty sure it'll happen again.
28	S:	So you are kind of thinking what's gonna happen
29		when you walk in the door.
30	C1:	Yeah.
31	S:	Are you thinking this in your school day at all?
32	C1:	No.
33	S:	So you are not looking back, you are looking . . .
34	C1:	Forward.
35	S:	Forward. And what are some other pictures you
36		have . . .
37	C1:	The fights.

In line 1, S initiates a TIP by inquiring about C1's experience. Jointly with C1, she explores his experience of family interactions, which he visibly struggles to articulate (". . . I don't know why . . ."; lines 14–16). F replicates this clarifying (as opposed to scrutinizing) way of engaging with his son ("But when you are on the bus, do you feel that anger?"; lines 12–13). C1's final response in line 16 (". . . Mhm!") to S and F's clarifying initiatives struck us as a different kind of (cooperative) response. It was as if C1 was somehow making manifest this recurrent experience as part of the ongoing conversation. From our perspective, S also seems to orient to C1's response as expressing a recurrent, unpleasant experience, which could be treated as a conversational object of sorts ("So 'it' starts . . ."). Further, she uses a series of clarifying questions (". . . what kinds of pictures enter your mind, or what kinds of words . . . what are you thinking about . . ."; lines 17–23) as invitations to "thicken" or "dress up" C1's previous attempt at articulating it (the "Mhm!"). C1's response in lines 24–25 ("I'm just thinking: 'Oh great, this is gonna happen again, again, again'") shows that he is anticipating a familiar experience—one that he may be a participant in, but not necessarily the initiator of (i.e., he could have said "I'm furious and want to kick a stone" or "I'm angry"). Further to S's exploration ("So you are not looking back, you are looking . . ." in line 33, and "Forward. And what are some other pictures you have . . ." in lines 35–36), C1 indicates that he is anticipating "the fights." His description can be seen as a response to S's invitations to explore the situation from a different angle, a relational one.

In this conversation, we see the progression of a different line of understanding: from the assumption of C1's responses as the expression of personal traits ("lack of insight," "aggressiveness"), to the possibility of C1's responses as part of a more complex relational pattern. S and C1's talk brings forth a relational understanding of C1's experience as part of a PIP (*responding to anticipated fights*). In doing so, they enact a TIP consisting of talking the "private into public space," as the quote from Taylor suggests. In the following extract, we see S focusing further on the family members' interactions in an attempt to bring forth alternative understandings to the PIP.

Extract IV

38	S:	What do those things (*arguments on different*
39		*topics*) have in common?
40	M:	We expect him to do certain things that he
41		doesn't like.
42	S:	OK. Is it being told what to do, like? Like parents
43		say you have to do this, this is your job, {looks at

```
44            D} that's what often happens to families, right?
45            Parents tell kids what to do . . . is that where the
46            explosions are anticipated? (pause)
47     F:     {Looking at C1} and then sometimes, like you
48            say, "I wanna do what I wanna do, don't tell me
49            what to do." You, you like saying that.
51            Yeah. When you get mad, the anger builds and
52            builds. You can't really soften it, so yeah.
53     S:     But I wanna get clear, what it is that makes you
54            angry, cause chores are chores, but I have a
55            feeling that it is something you are anticipating,
56            and you are anticipating the fights, and the
57            fights comes from, I'm thinking, being told what
58            to do. Maybe that's not it, but
59     C1:    It's like a little bit of it, but
60     S:     But what else then?
61     C1:    But um it's just basically that. I just remembered
62            it's just basically dealing with what they tell me
63            to . . . so
```

In line 38–39, S describes interactions as *patterned* responses and invites a more refined and abstracted understanding of "fights" that transcends the content of specific arguments ("WHAT do those things . . . have in common?"). In lines 42–46, S clarifies the accuracy of her understanding of conflict as arising out of the parents' expectations and instructions to C1. Possibly to minimize attributions of blame, she "softens" her proposal by offering an impersonal description of telling children what to do as a common parental practice ("like parents say you have to do this, this is your job, {looks to D} that's what often happens to families, right?"; line 42–44). F and C1 join in constructing the description of a PIP by highlighting C1's contributions. In line 47, F states ". . . and then sometimes, like you say, 'I wanna do what I wanna do, don't tell me what to do' . . .," to which C1 responds in the next turn "Like when I'm really mad. Yeah," confirming S's proposition that C1's anger is a response to "being told what to do" (lines 53–58). Further, we see S's openness to being corrected by C1 ("MAYBE that's not it, but" in line 58) as a possible indication of her preference to deconstruct the PIP collaboratively.

In sum, we believe that the extracts of this screening session at the CFTC illustrate how clarifying TIPs can accomplish a deconstruction of PIPs (e.g., *controlling coupled with resisting*). The way that family members are invited to account for a problematic experience can be one way in which the PIP gets clarified. Our interpretation of the extracts help to show how a problematic experience is alternatively accounted for through shifting co-developed meaning: from C1's lack of insight to his reactions being a legitimate response to family pressures and interactions. The conversation can be seen as deconstructive of a PIP, through a recurrent TIP (multiple variations in clarifying conversations), using questions to invite further degrees of articulation leading to mutually acceptable understandings of the problem.

Constructive TIPs

> "It is 'in' words-in-their-speaking that we can find the political and ethical influences of interest to us at work."
> —J. Shotter (1993, p. xv)

A conversational accomplishment of a constructive TIP is evident in the following interactions. We transcribed a segment of another video-recorded family therapy screening session involving Karl (K) as a consultant, an intern therapist (I) and a family composed of a mother (M) and her two young sons (T1 and T2, ages 12 and 10; there are two other children and a grandmother in the family not present in this session). The presenting concern is the boys' consistent refusal to comply with M's requests. A PIP may be discerned from both the family members' *description of their interaction* and their *actual interaction* in the session: M insisting on T1 and T2's compliance by engaging in nagging and yelling (e.g., repeating requests and concerns multiple times, raising her voice), with the children ignoring her requests or refusing to engage or comply. K works with the family to co-construct an alternative interpersonal pattern characterized by M selectively noticing the children's acts of cooperation and the children spontaneously demonstrating compliance. Let us explore the details of this TIP.

Extract V

```
1  M:  It's taken me a long time to learn to be patient
2      with the kids, and sometimes my mom doesn't
3      have that, and she gets mad and she yells and
4      then they yell and it's a big yelling match.
5  K:  So you decided when you became a mother that
6      you wanted to be a different kind of mother
7      than your mother?
8  M:  Yes {laughs}
9  K:  Did you?
10 M:  Well a little bit different. She is very strong, she
11     has amazing roles, she has a beautiful, quiet
```

12		beauty about her and in a lot of ways I do want
13		to be like her.
14	K:	So you are the same in many ways, but you wish
15		you didn't have to depend on yelling as much.
16	M:	Yeah.

Tomm has suggested that therapists may find it more effective to address the "upper" (i.e., most powerful) part of the PIP first, in order to bring forth an eventually more equitable change process (see Chapter 1). Accordingly, we observed that K first engaged (in Extract V) in a TIP with the parent, who is culturally invested with more power. Then (in Extract VI) we observed K participating in a TIP with the children. Thus, this and subsequent extracts show constructive TIPs of bringing forth *being patient* (parent) and *being cooperative* (children) as preferred conversational responses.

In Extract V, we see a TIP going from a PIP of *nagging coupled with ignoring* toward a HIP of *acting patient coupled with responding cooperatively*. First, M expresses that it has taken her a long time to be patient with the kids, that this "big yelling match" is a pattern also enacted at times by her own mother and the children (lines 1–4). These descriptions could be seen as instantiating a PIP *nagging and yelling inviting ignoring and refusing*. In his response, K asks first a clarifying question (TIP attempt) checking his own assumption about M having previously made a decision to become different as a parent than her own mother ("So you decided when you became a mother that you wanted to be a different kind . . ."). M's response shows a partial agreement with this assumption ("Yes {laughs}" in line 8) to which K further inquires, seeking clarification ("did you?"). With this question, K treats his own attempt as being still problematic, facilitating M's possibility to further elaborate her previous response. She engages in appreciating her mother ("SHE is very strong, she has amazing roles, she has a beautiful, quiet beauty about her and in a lot of ways I do want to be like her"), possibly allowing K to propose a slightly different understanding or distinction. In lines 14–15, K offers "not depending on yelling" as M's possible preference in how she understands motherhood. M's response confirming K's utterance ("Yeah" line 16) can be seen as a joint accomplishment of an ongoing generative TIP (*asking questions about preferences coupled with identifying preferred possibilities*).

The way K's response is formulated ("So you are the same in many ways, but you wish you didn't have to depend on yelling as much") has implications for our discussion of constructive TIPs. We contend that the use of the term "depend" is not accidental. It implies that M *had to* rely on yelling despite her desire to abstain from it. We consider that

CAN I GIVE YOU A TIP?

the use of this term serves as a way to manage the issue of blame and accountability for yelling—encouraging M to acknowledge her potentially unhelpful or problematic responses to the children while "saving face." Moreover, the intention to respond to the children differently (HIP) is "found" in M's own words rather than presented as coming from K. Thus, K invites M to consider a different description of her experience (as having had to depend on yelling, rather than choosing to yell), which is novel but familiar enough for M to try it out as an aspect of the experience that she might not have contemplated before. One way to organize the previous extract in terms of the IPscope is shown in Figure 5.1.

Understanding and accounting for the therapeutic process using TIPs can offer therapists and researchers a sense of directionality. Here, K and M engage in a constructive type of TIP (*asking clarifying questions coupled with identifying preferred ways of being*) that may, in turn, translate into a HIP in the mother's interaction with the children. We see this conversation as displaying a jointly accomplished TIP in which the therapist's questions helped bring forth M's amenability to change (declaring wanting to be "patient"), and some of her actual capacity to be an agent of change (not having to "depend on yelling"). We see this conversation oriented to a HIP in which M might actually enact "being patient," which may invite "cooperation" on behalf of the children (which may in turn strengthen M's willingness and capacity to engage in "patient practices").

PIP	TIP	HIP
Nagging	Asking (clarifying) questions	Acting patient
Ignoring	Identifying preferred ways of being ("patient")	Responding cooperatively
(e.g., "yelling match")	(e.g., K: "you wish you didn't have to depend on yelling?/ M:"YEAH")	(Not in transcript; Anticipation of future possibilities of interaction)

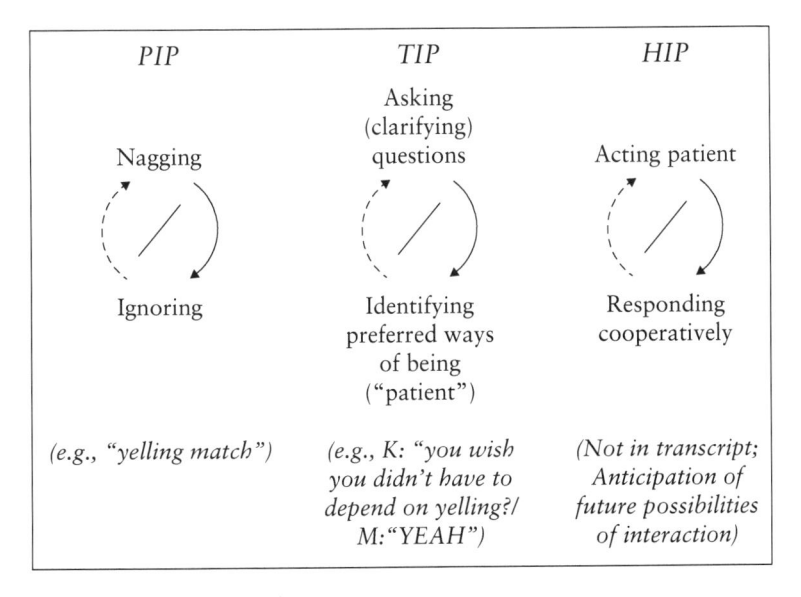

Figure 5.1 Possible IPs for mother in Extract V

Although not in this transcript, we frequently observe therapists at the CFTC explicitly bringing forth these anticipations through reflexive questions (e.g., "If you didn't have to depend on yelling, and somehow you got better at being patient, how do you imagine your kids would respond to that?").

The following two extracts illustrate the enactment of a similar TIP in the therapist-children conversation. In Extract VI, we demonstrate how the therapist later addressed the second, "lower" component of the *nagging invites ignoring* PIP. This extract also shows how a constructive type of TIP helped the children articulate a preferred way of being ("being cooperative").

Extract VI

1	K:	How are the boys in terms of cooperating, like do
2		you find that they are able to follow boundaries
3		and requests?
4	M:	I have to repeat myself at least three times
5		before I get a response. Today is a perfect
6		example. T1 left his goggles downstairs . . . and
7		there is no answer . . . (*describes in detail having*
8		*to repeat the same instruction three times and*
9		*the son's lack of response each time*).
10	K:	What do you think about what your mom just
11		said, T1? (*inaudible*) Does she have to ask three
12		times before it works, or?
13	T1:	Well, when she asks the first time I say yes but I
14		don't say it very loud, and the second time I
15		either won't be able to hear her or I won't
16		respond, and then the third time I have to yell
17		back.
18	K:	Oh OK, so sometimes you don't hear her.
19	T1:	Yeah.
20	K:	Now, what would you say about your ability to
21		cooperate? Would you say that as you are
22		getting older you are getting stronger in
23		cooperating, or?
24	T1:	A little bit
25	K:	A little bit. Do you feel good about that like do
26		you like the idea of being a cooperative person
27		and helping, and so forth?
28	T1:	{*Nods affirmatively*}
29	K:	OK, what kinds of things do you enjoy helping
30		with the most?
31	T1:	Helping my brother play videogames.

```
32  K:   Oh OK, OK but I was thinking of cooperation in a
33       different sense in terms of cooperating with the
34       family to be able to, you know, have a place.
35       Where you can sleep, and eat, and go to school
36       and all that kind of stuff. The things that you
37       have to do in life to keep on living and moving
38       forward?
39  T1:  Helping my mom when she needs something
40       done, helping my grandmother when she needs
41       something, helping cook the food, helping make
42       beds and stuff like that.
43  K:   Oh great! You do all those things?
44  T1:  Yeah, most of the time.
45  K:   Wow! So you are good at cooperating then.
46       Great!
47  M:   Most of the time?
48  T1:  Most of the time. {smiles}
49  M:   OK.
50  K:   Most of the time.
51  M:   Can I disagree?
52  K:   Occasionally? {laughs} Who would you say of all
53       four of you kids is the strongest at cooperating?
54       Do you think you are stronger than your
55       younger brothers and sisters?
56  T1:  {Nods}
57  K:   OK. Who would you say is the second
58       strongest at cooperating?
59  T1:  T2.
60  K:   And who would you say is least able to
61       cooperate?
62  T1:  T3.
```

The therapist's reflexive question in line 1 (e.g., Tomm, 1988) elicits M's account of T1's ability to cooperate. The question implicitly invites a discussion that particular (cooperative) responses from the children are desirable. In other words, rather than proposing a HIP directly (e.g., it may be helpful if the children cooperated more), K embeds an alternative within his question (which is a potential antidote to ignoring and refusing) and invites M to reflect on the extent to which a proposed HIP is enacted by the children (see Figure 5.2).

K proceeds to explore T1's account of his ability to cooperate (lines 20–62). For example, he invites T1 to endorse the idea that cooperation is a valuable skill or strength, evoking a shared cultural understanding that mastery of a skill is desirable (e.g., "Do you feel good about . . . being a

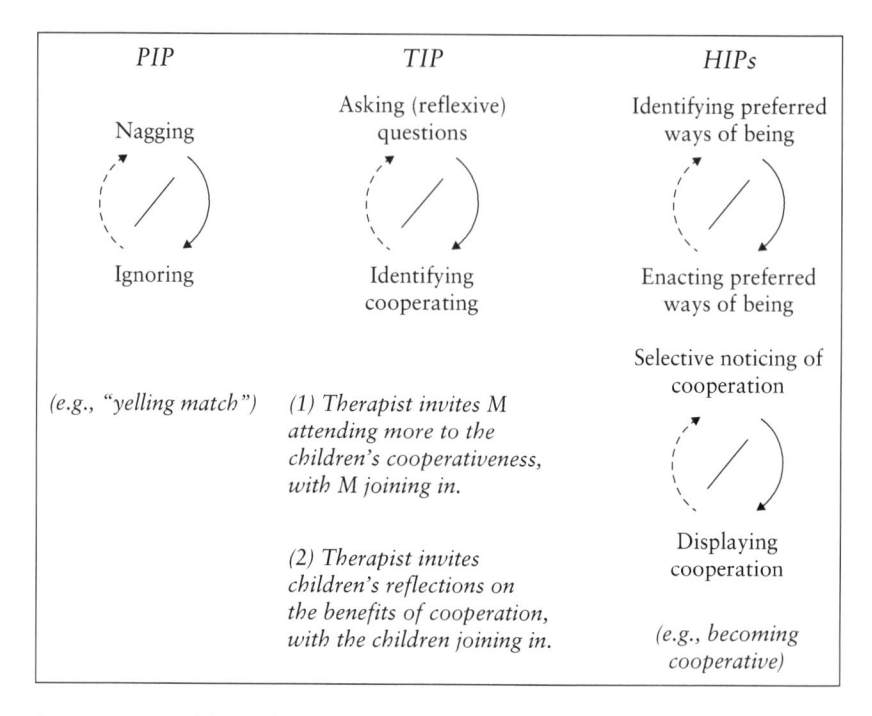

PIP	TIP	HIPs
Nagging	Asking (reflexive) questions	Identifying preferred ways of being
Ignoring	Identifying cooperating	Enacting preferred ways of being
		Selective noticing of cooperation
(e.g., "yelling match")	(1) Therapist invites M attending more to the children's cooperativeness, with M joining in.	
	(2) Therapist invites children's reflections on the benefits of cooperation, with the children joining in.	Displaying cooperation
		(e.g., becoming cooperative)

Figure 5.2 Possible IPs for mother and children in Extract VI

cooperative person . . .?"). K further introduces the idea that cooperation is necessary for survival (lines 32–38). Difference questions ("as you are getting older," "who . . . is strongest at cooperating" lines 21–23 and 52–55) may be a useful way to invite the family members to explore alternative possibilities for meaning and action, by introducing temporal or inter-person comparisons (Tomm, 1987, 1988). The repetitiveness of these difference questions also allows for the distinction of "cooperation" to be talked more deeply into the system. Overall, K encourages T1 to explore his contributions to family interactions that would more closely reflect his preferences and values. When in line 47 M begins distinguishing T1 as non-cooperative or not as cooperative as he claims to be (DIP), K uses humor and proposes a shift back into a more strength-based discussion that recognizes T1's cooperativeness (TIP). In this conversation, we view the TIP conversation as helping the children articulate, through reflection rather than nagging, preferred ways of being and relating to others ("being a cooperative person," "cooperating"). Therapist and children did not identify an explicit HIP in this extract. However, mirroring the conversation between the therapist and the mother in Extract V, here in Extract VI the therapist and children could be seen as orienting to an implicit HIP: the TIP (i.e., bringing forth the children's amenability to be more "cooperative") may facilitate the children actually enacting "being cooperative" at home, which may strengthen M's capacity to engage in "patient practices." Additionally, the TIP displayed in Extract VI may be conducive to a *second HIP* of *selectively noticing cooperative practices coupled with displaying cooperation.*

Extracts V and VI demonstrate how constructive TIPs can be used to orient participants in the conversation toward co-constructing alternative understandings. We see how the therapist works with the family to co-develop new possibilities for understanding family members' actions and identities that may have gone unnoticed before. In doing so, such constructive TIPs may pave a path for developing a different kind of interaction among family members.

Implications for Practice and Training

"The word is correct if it brings the thing to presentation."
—H. G. Gadamer (2004, p. 410)

In this chapter, we explored TIPs—conversations that enable therapeutic shifts in interactions among family members. We proposed that if families join in with the therapist, TIPs may be a stepping stone on the road from PIPs to HIPs and WIPs. We discussed and illustrated two ways in which IPs can be collaboratively brought to presentation through therapeutic talk: deconstructive and constructive TIPs. In the deconstructive type, TIPs offer opportunities for families to step outside of their unacceptably familiar ways of relating (e.g., PIPs) in order to articulate, evaluate, and revise them. In the constructive type, TIPs offer opportunities to bring forth and sustain preferable ways of relating (e.g., HIPs).[2]

Family therapists may find appealing an interactional perspective on TIPs as conversational collaborations or accomplishments, joined in and completed in varying degrees by families. Such a perspective may enhance therapists' awarenesses of how and when their attempts at TIPs are taken up (or not) by the clients. Traditionally, therapists' training emphasizes practitioners' interventions without taking into account how these are received by their clients. By retrospectively focusing on TIP attempts and their completion, training for therapists may become more effective as it provides a tangible example of how therapeutic conversations unfold, step by step. This may help therapists to better orient to clients' preferred relationships and understandings, rather than advancing exclusively their own meanings. Further, identifying and examining TIPs retroactively may be useful for supervisors and therapists-in-training to better understand how to propose changes as collaborative invitations to clients. For example, as suggested in the analysis of Extract II, a particular question (e.g., "So if things don't change, what are you most worried about?") could be identified as particularly helpful within deconstructive TIPs (i.e., to recruit collaborative efforts to move away from PIPs); thus, supervisory dyads may jointly reflect and articulate more clearly the intention of therapeutic questions. In addition, therapists participating in reflecting teams may find it useful to identify TIPs as possible openings for their reflections back to families. From their position as observers behind the mirror, they may be able to orient to alternative understandings that may have not been taken up during the session with the family but that could still be helpful as a reflection offered to families.

We were uncertain about how to best theorize family members' initiations of alternative patterns (as TIPs or HIPs not joined by other family members or incomplete HIPs). In reviewing therapy sessions, we focused on TIPs in client-therapist conversations, as these were more easily discernible to us. We extend the invitation to other researchers who may choose to examine TIPs in within-family conversations. Another area for future research and theory development could be created by exploring when each TIP type may be most helpful. For example, it is possible that a deconstructive TIP may be most fruitful in conversational contexts characterized by clients' strong commitments to certain assumptions and ways of responding. Deconstructive TIPs may invite clients into a critical and reflexive position toward their favored assumptions, beliefs, and values and their impact on their relationships (see Chapter 6). Constructive TIPs may be used when family members are already cognizant of their potentially unhelpful contributions to the relationship and when they experience a shortage of alternative, more helpful understandings or ways of relating.

In sum, we see TIPs as both enactments and articulations of a *therapeutic mind*—of differences that make differences, of a movement with direction (Bateson, 1972). As enactments of this mind, TIPs are components of therapeutic conversations through which, for example, families can clarify their experience, generate possibilities, and extend them through continued dialogue. As articulations, TIPs are ways of talking that may help participants in the therapeutic process to bring forth a healing direction from a PIP that calls for deconstruction and change, or toward a HIP that calls for co-construction and endorsement.

Within this view of a therapeutic mind, our view is that therapists may benefit both by becoming more purposeful in their initiations of TIPs and by acknowledging that their TIP initiations not taken up by clients may serve as a compass for readjusting their approach to the conversation. We see a TIP-informed therapy, then, as a doubly intentional activity. On the one hand, in their TIP *attempts* therapists invite clients to consider what therapists themselves distinguish as being a healing direction. On the other hand, by distinguishing between TIP attempts and accomplishments, we see TIP-informed therapy as an activity in which therapists also intend to readjust their approach to clients' responses—so that the conversation is guided for these collaborations. We believe that a tip worth remembering is that TIPs are most likely to be therapeutic if they are practiced deliberately and collaboratively.

Notes

1 We don't know how S and D experienced F's PIPish theory at that very moment. We noticed and transcribed those non-verbals into the transcript to suggest that S and D's non-verbals *could have been a way to respond* to the PIPish direction in the conversation. We believe that expert/attuned therapists often feel IPs and think *with* those feelings (rather than *about* them) in orienting themselves in TIPish ways. Far from being detached, neutral observers, we see therapists as using those feelings as *action-guiding anticipations* (Shotter, 2011) as to how they might act next in a therapeutic situation.
2 Thus, we see TIPs as quintessentially incarnating an interventive interviewing approach to family therapy. For a detailed presentation of this approach, see Tomm (1987, 1988).

References

Bateson, G. (1972). *Steps to an ecology of mind*. New York, NY: Ballantine Books.
Cecchin, G., Lane, G., & Ray, W. A. (1992). *Irreverence: A strategy for therapists' survival*. London, UK: Karnac.
Gadamer, H. G. (2004). *Truth and method* (J. Weinsheimer & D. G. Marshall, Trans; 2nd rev. ed.). New York, NY: Continuum.
Sametband, I., & Strong, T. (2013). Negotiating cross-cultural misunderstandings in collaborative therapeutic conversations. *International Journal for the Development of Counselling, 35*(2), 88–99. doi: 10.1007/s10447-012-9169-1
Shotter, J. (1993). *Cultural politics of everyday life*. Toronto, ON: University of Toronto Press.
Shotter, J. (2011). *Getting it: Withness-thinking and the dialogical . . . in practice*. Cresskill, NJ: Hampton Press.
Taylor, C. (1985). *Philosophical papers: Volume 1, human agency and language*. Cambridge, MA: Cambridge University Press.
Tomm, K. (1987). Interventive interviewing: Part II. Reflexive questioning as a means to enable self-healing. *Family Process, 26*(2), 167–183.
Tomm, K. (1988). Interventive Interviewing: Part III. Intending to ask lineal, circular, strategic or reflexive questions? *Family Process, 27*(1), 1–15. Retrieved from www.familyprocess.org
Tomm, K. (1991). Beginnings of a "HIPs and PIPs" approach to psychiatric assessment. *Calgary Participator, 1*(2), 21–22, 24.

6

BRAIDING SOCIO-CULTURAL INTERPERSONAL PATTERNS INTO THERAPY

Sally St. George and Dan Wulff

In our chapter we explain how we see family therapists becoming able to contextualize a family's concerns by including talk about societal discourses that play a role in how families enact their everyday lives. Working from Tomm's (1991) heuristic of understanding family interactions by distinguishing Pathologizing Interpersonal Patterns (PIPs), Healing Interpersonal Patterns (HIPs), and Wellness Interpersonal Patterns (WIPs), we have wondered about potential connections between problematic behaviors within families and certain societal discourses (Hare-Mustin, 1994) in which families, and indeed all of us, are immersed. By societal discourses, we are referring to key ideas that societies hold as to what persons in that society should believe and how they should behave (e.g., children belong to their parents, education is required to be successful, marriage is forever). The term "dominant discourses" is often used in narrative therapy (White & Epston, 1990) to refer to those large organizing discourses (often cast as "isms"—racism, sexism, ageism) that exert influence over persons and groups. While we include consideration of those larger discourses, in this chapter we are more focused on the smaller, daily, more local ideas that become influential and are expected within our immediate families and communities (e.g., what counts as success, what should happen in what order, what is considered healthy, what responsibility looks like).

We are not conceptualizing societal discourses as inanimate actors in the lives of people. They do not force people to act in certain ways. Rather, we imagine them as becoming part of relational dynamics in a relatively stable interpersonal space in the life of a family. When these societal discourses are actively being taken up by families and woven into their everyday lives/interactions (oftentimes as WIPs and sometimes as PIPs), we refer to them as Socio-Cultural Interpersonal Patterns (SCIPs). When persons incorporate these ways of living into their lives, they could be referred to as discourses-in-action, or just "SCIPing along."

We nurtured this idea through a series of four practice-based research projects conducted at the Calgary Family Therapy Centre (CFTC) between 2008 and 2012 (see Chapter 10). In the current chapter, we offer specific ways in which practitioners can "talk societal discourses into the therapy room" and examine ways in which family members perform or enact larger societal discourses or expectation sets that may lead toward problematic interactions or wellness patterns of behavior. We also think that talk of societal discourses in the therapy room can contribute to a greater awareness of how discourses are implicated in daily life practices for all families, not just those who come to therapy.

Our experience with "talking discourses into therapy" and including this notion of SCIPs into the IPscope framework has been steady, but it is still relatively new to us (and we think to the field of family therapy as well). There is much to develop and evolve in this arena, and we hope that our chapter can positively contribute to this widening of the therapeutic lens.

Purpose

Our intention in this chapter is to present an additional IP within the IPscope framework that we are calling a SCIP. We use the term SCIP to help us more richly and complexly understand family members' ways of coordinating with each other and their communities as they try to live satisfying and rewarding lives. We plan to do this by making visible that which has typically not been examined or included in the conceptualization of family dilemmas and conversations with families in the therapy room—namely, societal discourses (see Hare-Mustin, 1994).

Background

I (Sally) became interested in incorporating societal discourses into family therapy work when my supervisees and I were having trouble making sense of client decisions and actions. For example, we were struggling with how women in a transitional housing center would "sabotage" the benefits that were offered to them (e.g., finishing their high school equivalency, following through on job training, getting their driver's licenses) by not attending classes or violating their housing contracts and yet become outrageously angry when they were not given free turkeys for their Thanksgiving dinners. Through many discussions in which we charged ourselves with the task of figuring out how this made perfect sense, we came up with explanations that were larger than individual motivations and behavior. We came up with a working idea that these women who had been put down in most of their relationships throughout their lives did not feel entitled to those things most women were entitled to, but they definitely were entitled to a free turkey. The discourses of entitlement and who is worthy and who is not made sense to us and helped us work with the women from a different angle. After working with the IPscope for a year, I just felt there had to be a connection between what I called larger societal discourses and PIPs and HIPs. That is why we went forward with the research projects described in Chapter 10, to meld the IPs with societal discourses.

My (Dan) early educational background in sociology has constantly echoed in my work as a family therapist and as an educator. Conceptualizing my clinical work has steadily progressed from individual thinking, to couples and families, to multiple family groups and communities, to larger societal influences. Each shift was associated with my efforts to find more useful explanations as to how things are and how they could be. Clarity of positions, questions, and answers have always seemed to me to be worthy goals but have remained tantalizingly unobtainable. Informed by social constructionist thinking, I am learning to embrace the tension between trying to simplify and appreciating complexity. The IPscope framework has provided another avenue for me to navigate among various constructions of how things work, all in the service of providing ever-more legitimate help to families.

Theoretical Connections

Historically, systemic family therapy theoreticians and practitioners have added significantly to the understanding of how families' patterns of interaction can impact the behaviors of individuals and how all behavior interrelates with other behaviors (Bateson, 1988; Becvar & Becvar, 2012). We also employ this relational view to conceptualize how family behaviors are interconnected with behaviors and beliefs at extended family, community, and societal levels (Schultz, 1984) by considering societal discourses and stories as appropriate and vital elements within our therapeutic work.

If we conceptualize families' dilemmas/troubles *without* consideration of how families use societal discourses to justify and animate their behaviors, we risk oversimplifying the family's patterns of interaction, and possibly work with the family as if it were a caricature of itself. In contrast, by imagining a family as a system nested within other larger social systems (e.g., extended families, communities, societies) and actively performing societal discourses, we can better understand how the behavioral patterns we discern in therapy make sense in the lives of the families we see and also within the larger social ecology (Waldegrave, Tamasese, Tuhaka, & Campbell, 2003). Thinking that all family patterns of interaction are coherent by simply examining the single level of the nuclear family system ignores the influences from outside, missing many facets of the larger interpersonal space that may be pivotal in developing a more nuanced and appreciative understanding of families' interactions. This braiding of family patterns and influences from the outside is what we are terming SCIPs. SCIPs are not the societal discourses themselves, but rather the ways in which persons weave those discourses into their daily lives and their embodied interactions. For instance, a father may have internalized the societal expectation to be a "good provider" for his family to such an extent that he spends an inordinate amount of time away at work with the result that his family feels ignored and criticizes him for his absence. The resultant PIP of *criticizing coupled with distancing* within the family might yield more easily to therapeutic conversation if the societal discourse of being a good provider is also talked into the therapy as a SCIP.

In this chapter, we will be languaging the family, members of the family, and societal discourses in ways that may seem to accentuate hard differences among them, but these depictions should be read with the understanding that these distinctive terms are not manifestly unique, autonomous, or material. We use words to point to entities, meanings, and phenomena, but it is in the performance that the meanings become manifest and alive. Our language expressions in English are insufficient for us to provide an adequate rendering of this *braiding* of persons, activities, interactions, cultures, and ideas.

By adding SCIPs to the ways we conceptualize families' dilemmas in therapy, we are aiming to link the micro and macro reflexively (Pearce & Cronen, 1980); societal discourses are implicated in family troubles while family troubles re-inscribe those societal discourses. Continuing the previous example, during a neighborhood gathering, there is talk among the adults about earning enough to provide the kids with the latest in technology or clothing, as well as talk about how difficult it is to please everyone inside and outside the family. At the same time, the father in our example is complimented by his peers for his admirable work ethic. There are multiple ongoing complementarities here in which we all participate to sustain or to modify connections and influences, for better or for worse. Just as change in an individual sends ripples of influence through the family system, changes in a family can impact the larger systems within which the family exists, including the larger sets of expectations that societies hold, albeit more slowly. When families fit into larger systems and align themselves with discourses in ways that are expected and traditional, those cultural patterns and practices are reinforced and strengthened. When families drift away from the ways they are "supposed to be," two outcomes may arise. The families may be sanctioned, criticized, or punished in various ways for such noncompliance with expected standards or ways of behaving. Another outcome could be that if enough persons deviate from the expected patterns, those societal expectations/ mandates may lose validation and support and over time changes may occur in those larger expectation systems (Bateson, 1988). Back to our example, the following year, three fathers at the neighborhood gathering were discovered to have become stay-at-home fathers and were enjoying their closer relationships with their children! By including SCIPs in our conceptualizing and therapy talk, families are encouraged to see how the scripting of societal discourses has influenced them and to see possibilities that are available in re-writing their stories not only for themselves but also for the impact on changing those larger scripts.

In moving from the micro to the macro, we realize that we are tending toward understanding families in sociological rather than psychological terms in our efforts to enhance our abilities to help families. In making this move, we anticipate some critique from psychology and psychiatry, especially if we become too doctrinaire. Holding to a sociological stance too firmly could be described within our IPscope lens as a PIP: *asserting disciplinary stances coupled with defensive and criticizing comments from other disciplines*. We prefer to envision the potential of a more comprehensive and complex picture of human behavior by pooling perspectives associated with various disciplines including anthropology, medicine, public health, and economics. A WIP in this instance could be conceived as *distinguishing and addressing larger societal influences (SCIPs) invites relinquishing capture in intrafamilial PIPs and moving forward more freely*. Our focus in this chapter is on the levels of practice and discourse in and around the family that we use to provide the grounding or context for the family's interpersonal life. Including the idea of SCIPs into the IPscope framework adds another vantage point from which to consider the interpersonal space in families.

In conceptualizing SCIPs and their relationship to the IPscope framework, we realized the two-dimensional circular diagram used to portray PIPs, HIPs, WIPs, TIPs, and DIPs does not adequately illustrate the multidimensionality of the notion we were trying to describe through the SCIPs idea. At this point, we do not have a preferred visual representation for SCIPs but we are hoping to perhaps develop a three-dimensional computer graphic. At this stage, we work within the IPscope general framework as a way to further refine our thinking around the SCIPs idea. We think the IPscope helps us do a better job of illustrating this notion, but we anticipate further evolution of this idea.

Considering macro level processes (societal discourses) as operative on the micro level appears intuitively acceptable (and perhaps even attractive), but beyond this, how do these two levels specifically relate? What would this relationship look like if we could actually see it being performed? Back to our example, what ideas and thoughts are being entertained by the father when the father actually decides to go to work when his children are calling for attention? What implications does this pose for the couple/family? We see the societal discourses and their performances within families' lives as forming a patterned relationship that has some stability, but not so much stability so as to specifically allow us to explain or predict behaviors with accuracy. Rather than see the interpersonal patterns as derivative of societal discourses, we see the societal discourses and interpersonal behaviors to be braided in ways that reveal how they are related and intertwined to create a larger picture of family life. It seems that in the braiding (see Figure 6.1), we can see and appreciate mutual or partnered influence.

A braid includes three or four strands or threads that are laced together into a patterned weave—each strand wound into an interconnection with the other strands. One is the strand of experiencing—the direct, material, and embodied interaction with the world through first-hand experience. *The father feels anxious and restless sitting around the house when he could be earning.* Another is the strand of naming—the process by which we select certain experiences and distinguish and name them from the rest of the experiences. "*I am just being lazy at home when I could be working.*" A third is the strand of coupling—the joining of emotioning and interpersonal behaviors into patterned interactions—*feeling relief in leaving for work coupled with feeling abandoned and criticizing absence*. The fourth strand represents collective values, beliefs, and societal discourses. *In our culture, fathers must provide, yet in our neighborhood fathers must be participant parents.* All four strands become intertwined in a braid to symbolize a SCIP—the interplay among our experiences of the world, the distinctions we make, the patterned interactions we develop, and the societal discourses of our community/society.

Figure 6.1 Braiding illustration
Source: Photo courtesy of Jessica Koloen.

Origins of the Notion of SCIPs

SCIPs evolved from a CFTC research project in which we looked at the relationship between parent-child conflicts in family therapy and associated societal discourses (see Chapter 10). The project was in response to a desire to conduct research on Karl Tomm's ideas on interpersonal patterns and our interest in studying societal discourses in therapy. In addition, we are believers that the world of research and inquiry has become too segregated from practice, and we were looking for ways to reduce that gap. Therefore, we were interested in developing practices in which practitioners could conduct research of their own within the context of their work without need of external funding, specialized personnel, or time outside of their practice.

Through the course of this practice-based inquiry, the therapists and interns became more attuned to the societal discourses that they noticed were expressed in their therapy sessions and began recording them next to the PIPs in their session records. Anxious to put theory into practice, and excited about trying some newly developing ideas, the interns started asking about these societal discourses in sessions (not very skillfully at first), but they were introducing them into the therapeutic conversations with their families. This is an example of what we call *research as daily practice*—the designing and conducting of research amidst practice, utilizing systematic ways of understanding and acknowledging places of non-understanding to plan ways of intervening or generating fresh ideas that are increasingly more suitable and effective with clients. We noticed that SCIPs added a layer of abstraction that was less behaviorally grounded than the PIPs or HIPs yet seemed to contribute significantly toward elucidating the more relevant PIPs and HIPs. Over time, we have become more confident in distinguishing connections between societal discourses and the interpersonal space within families and have become more articulate in portraying this relationship.

Clarifying and Defining SCIPs

Our View of Societal Discourses

In his book *Shalimar the Clown,* Salman Rushdie (2005) stated, "Our lives, our stories, flowed into one another's, were no longer our own, individual, discrete" (p. 37). We, like Rushdie, do not regard stories or discourses as creations or possessions of individuals. In addition, we believe that people tell and retell stories and from these multiple and ongoing tellings, behaviors become affected and these stories collectively become part of a society's lexicon. From these stories (and their ongoing enactments), we learn society's truths (or preferred realities) and become so intimately connected with them that our ways of being, understanding, and acting that are influenced by these stories are thought of as just "who we are." Frank (2010) explains the relationship between stories (discourses) and persons this way: "People not only think *about* stories; far more consequentially, people think *with* stories" (p. 47). Thinking and experiencing *with* stories nicely articulates the mutual importance of persons and the stories and discourses of their lives. However, the discourses are impactful only to the degree that they are actually taken up by persons. With SCIPs we attempt to highlight this "taken-up-ness."

We like the way our colleagues (see Chapter 4) talk about "discourses that sponsor PIPs" as a way of understanding how families seamlessly integrate societal stories and discourses into their daily interactions. In addition, we can apply Shotter's (2012) distinction between *aboutness* and *withness* to persons and the social discourses in their lives. When we talk *about* persons and discourses as separate entities, we tend to distance ourselves from the two and see them as alien to each other, emphasizing their differences. *Withness* embraces the relational qualities, the ways in which the strands are inextricably braided.

Because of the taken-for-granted presence, pervasiveness, and influence of these stories and discourses, it often takes a crisis or interactions with members from another community of stories and discourses for us to become aware of the stories and discourses that support and justify the behaviors that become so central to us. As we more directly and deliberately reflect upon these stories and discourses and the ways in which we "take them up" in our behaviors and interactions (Heritage, 1991), we have the possibility of seeing how they constrain us as well as open alternatives for paths not (yet) taken.

All societies have stories about what constitutes "the good" or the good life from which members of that society learn the expected ways of successful living and relating. We refer to those scripts for living as the *invisible and unwritten rules* that are accepted and shared as a community for living—as societal discourses. Each of our attempts to live up to these stories and discourses serves to re-inscribe them and each of our enactments perpetuates them.

Families may attempt to live up to these stories and discourses by acting them out in a variety of ways. Such differences may actually rewrite or redefine discourses, thereby collectively having some impact on how those discourses are understood and embraced differently. Remembering that discourses are social constructions (Gergen & Gergen, 2004), there are numerous opportunities for families to enact the discourses in a variety of ways, some to their advantage or others to their detriment. Given that we regard knowledge to be effective action, a review of how societal discourses and their subscribed behaviors well-served the persons using them can add significantly to the understandings of our lives and how to enact change.

Socio-Cultural Interpersonal Patterns (SCIPs)

We define SCIPs as the behavioral performances that occur when families act in alignment with their ideas or interpretations of the societal discourses within which they live. In addition, the performances usually reinscribe and build confidence in those same societal discourses (Wetherell, 1998). In other words, persons are "caught up" in discourses (Heritage, 1991) by enacting the behaviors resonant with those discourses, and those behaviors then become the ongoing validation for the discourses to remain viable. The patterning of a SCIP can be graphically displayed as in Figure 6.2.

Visualized in this way, one can see that a SCIP could introduce a therapeutic conceptualization that highlights a belief/action interaction that can be either unhelpful and limiting (PIP) or helpful and healthful (HIP). Therefore, SCIPs can be considered part of the interpersonal environment in which intrafamily PIPs and HIPs grow.

Subscribing to a preferred assumption or belief oftentimes is laced or braided with behaviors consistent with those assumptions or beliefs such that those behaviors appear to be automatic, inevitable, or a matter of individual or personal choice. As long as the behaviors work within our families' lives, all is well. But when those behaviors fail to achieve what families most want, we as therapists can examine the supportive ideas braided into them and perhaps open a window to envision alternative ideas and behavioral interactions.

Therefore, we believe that the behaviors that become patterned in families arise from understandings about the world in which we live. These accepted understandings become braided with behaviors that in some ways reflect those understandings (see Chapter 4). It may be the

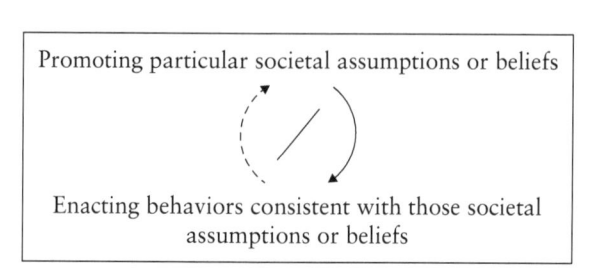

Figure 6.2 SCIPs in society and family living

understandings of the societal discourses that become entrenched in persons, even moreso than the overt behaviors we see—the behaviors are just examples of enactments of the discourses or scripts within which we operate. By conceptualizing with SCIPs, we can talk with our families in ways that develop a wider array of behavioral possibilities that could be more satisfying.

Seeing and Hearing SCIPs

An interesting re-visioning of the therapeutic relationship becomes possible by looking at SCIPs. Clients are in positions to speak back to the discourses of their lives by questioning them, endorsing them, challenging them, altering them, or rejecting them. Engaging in this sort of therapeutic conversation, clients not only come to therapy to simply receive help. By examining the limiting or harmful effects of societal discourses as they manifest in their behavior patterns, as well as the creative potentials of societal discourses, they are simultaneously contributing to their larger community by working to reshape or re-imagine societal discourses and/or validate the usefulness of some societal discourses in animating certain preferred behaviors.

From our perspective, families in family therapy experience difficulties in part as a result of living consistently within some of these societal discourses. Success within a given society may be contingent upon moving effectively among these discourses and trouble can result when one steps out of publically sanctioned discourses and practices. We believe that simple adherence to the preferred and/or expected behaviors of one's community or society does not ensure safe passage in life. Some of the societal discourses that have "grown up" within a given community or society may contain seeds of trouble for those who use them as standards for their behavior. For example, in the West, the pursuit of material wealth that is so evident in our media may be seen and taken up by persons in that society as a guiding principle, superseding other activities such as building interpersonal relationships or improving one's community. The unrestricted and single-minded pursuit of money may create many difficulties for a person or family even though the agenda of attaining material wealth is strongly advocated in the messages pervasive in our society.

Another example of a societal discourse that commonly emerges in family therapy is that of a child's place and voice within a family. Some families come to therapy subscribing to discourses of the importance of children being obedient and submissive, while others come in under the influence of discourses of parents giving their children maximal voice and choice. We think of these as more *local* discourses; they are not discourses that originate from the larger social "isms" such as racism, ageism, ableism, and so on. For us, these family and therapy discourses are derived from shared societal viewpoints and preferences; we must bear in mind that therapists are also socially inducted into most of these discourses. As members of the community and society of our clients, these societal discourses influence us as well. We also need to remember and keep in mind that multiple SCIPs can be active simultaneously, whether viewed in a collective package of support or conflict.

SCIPs are complementary constructions to the IPscope heuristic for conceptualizing family troubles and options for change, helpful in seeing relational patterns that may be less visible by using only micro binary behavioral systems of relating. As with PIPs and HIPs, rather than being seen as real or true phenomena, SCIPs may be considered to be lenses through which to look at human behavior, providing a tint or shading that brings certain ideas into view or into sharper relief.

Patterned interpersonal behaviors can be seen as supported and validated by received, and largely unquestioned, societal expectations and discourses. Using a SCIPs lens, therapists are invited to look at the scripts or discourses that we have literally grown up in within society. The process of socialization is so fundamental to our growing up and living within a society that we may have adopted certain practices without recognizing that we have learned these practices; we may actually think these ways of thinking and behaving are innate to all humans or the result of individual choice. Extending the logic that therapists are never exempt from discursive capture as we have just noted, we need to also pay attention to how we can be discursively captured by our workplace discourses and professional discourses (Fairclough, n.d.). The years of training, professional preparation, disciplinary alignment, agency/organizational procedures, and ethical/legal mandates all play a significant role in helping us shape professional selves. It is tempting to see ourselves as free agents in performing our roles as therapists, but a closer look reveals the many influences (deliberate and unplanned) that are braided into our professional performances and identities.

There are usually certain words and phrases that people use that could potentially alert us to the insertion or inclusion of some societal discourses in our conversations. Sometimes we hear ideas introduced with the phrase, "The reality is . . .," or "The only choice is . . .," or we hear a conclusive statement: "That is the way it has always been done." These phrases represent truth claims that mark only certain behavioral patterns as legitimate and tacitly establish an intolerance of the knowledges other people may hold that are different from our own. Thus adding SCIPs to a conceptualization of therapeutic practice is our way of naming societal discourses and inviting them into our therapeutic conversation. They are lived out in families' interpersonal spaces in ways that are sometimes harmful (inviting various PIPs) *and* sometimes healing (inviting various HIPs), as well as in the formation of certain kinds of therapeutic relationships we establish with families in the therapy room (we may also be recruited into SCIPs that support PIPs).

Highlighting societal discourses in the therapy room can be approached from different vantage points. We may see them in everything we do—we are literally awash in these discourses constantly with no conscious awareness required. By distinguishing them in our talk, we may be able to raise an awareness of daily activities in a way that allows more critical reflection including an examination of their effects on us. The process of figuratively "stepping out of them" can create a discursive opening to offer new directions as to how to act—in a sense creating a TIP to help people make the discourses more visible and manageable in new ways. The discursive openings available in therapy allow the macro influences on one's life to be widened or loosened, perhaps reshaping the social discourses into new forms and possibilities.

We provide some examples of SCIPs (societal discourses and associated PIPs) and questions that could be posed to "talk" these societal discourses into consciousness during therapy:

- Discourses of certainty support the PIP of *demanding coupled with defending*. Discourses of certainty are often marked by conversations in which there is one right answer and alternative answers are wrong. For example, this may be seen in the tension or conflict between the generations (parent-child or parent-grandparent) that *invite* parental rigidity. Sample questions that might be asked include "When you listen to your ideas and then listen to your daughter's ideas, how do they compare?" "Do you explain your ideas from a position of knowing that you are right?" "If both of you explain your ideas from a position of knowing that you are right, how do you decide what to do?" "If you were able to genuinely listen to your daughter's ideas as legitimate and possibly even better than your own, what would your relationship be like with her?" These questions can invite conversation about the perspective that feeds a tendency of approaching relationships from a position of individual or personal certainty. Absolute confidence in the rightness of a position fuels the PIP of *demanding coupled with defending*. Each participant in such a PIP operates with surety that disallows any consideration of another legitimate point-of-view.
- Discourses of privilege support the PIP of *intruding coupled with retreating*. From many societal discourses, we can derive the idea that some in society are privileged and deserve special treatment while others do not—this could be associated with educational level, wealth, religious affiliation, race, or gender. Assumptions of privilege create

conditions rife for bullying. Imagine how being bullied due to speaking English with an accent and the ability to speak another ("foreign") language *invites* withdrawing and becoming solitary. Some questions that might be asked include "If someone behaves outside of the norm for your community, neighborhood, or family, what kind of pressures are exerted on them to conform?" "How does following the norm or behaving the way others say you should behave turn out to limit relationships?" "Have you ever defended someone who was being bullied? How did you decide to do that? Would you do it again?" By asking these questions we place the spotlight on the limitations of privilege for both the privileged and the not-so-privileged.

- Discourses of justifiable violence support the PIP of *attacking coupled with counterattacking*. We see this frequently in parenting, for instance, when mothers and daughters threatening one another *invites* a standoff. Some possible questions that could be asked are "Are there times when you believe that doing violence to another person is okay?" "What is your stance on the idea that more violence can stop violence?" "Where do these ideas come from?" "If you refuse to attack or counterattack within a relationship, what would others think?" "What are the rules or conditions when using violence on another person is permitted or required?"
- Discourses of acceptability/unacceptability support the PIP of *challenging coupled with defending*. For example, a desire to re-inscribe or re-affirm one's home country's cultural practices may *invite* a defense of the new country's cultural practices that vary from the home country. Some possible questions to ask could include "To what degree do you think it is possible to accept one set of cultural or societal beliefs/behaviors while appreciating another set from a different cultural or societal tradition?" "How do you compare the cultural standards of your upbringing with the standards of your local community?" "When you see your preferred societal or cultural standards from another's eyes, what do you notice?"

SCIPs in a Clinical Example

Let us present a clinical situation. A three-generation immigrant family from Romania who moved to Canada 10 years ago came to family therapy. The parents were upset with their 17-year-old daughter, Luminata, who refused to help out at home, rejected parental expectations, skipped school, was believed to be sexually active, and was suspected of drinking on weekends. Luminata threatened suicide whenever she was pressured by her parents to comply with their wishes or expectations. The paternal grandparents, whose English speaking ability was very limited, lived in a basement suite in the family home. The parents tried "everything" (mostly threats and punishment) and were exhausted, felt hopeless, blamed their daughter's behavior on being in a Canadian high school with children of local families who also showed limited parental respect, and experienced constant criticism from the grandparents regarding their inadequate parenting of Luminata. The daughter saw her family as rigid, not in tune with Canadian society, overbearing, and inept at understanding her, and as a consequence, she occasionally voiced a desire to commit suicide.

Based in the intergenerational interactions described by this family, one could view the situation as a clash between societal or cultural discourses (see Chapter 8)—the grandparents, and to a certain extent the parents, were attempting to construct and operate a family based upon the idea that parents are in a hierarchically superior position to the daughter while Luminata was pressing for another form of family whereby children are allowed greater freedoms, and perhaps even more significantly, a rearrangement of the family structure and roles that give the children more voice and greater ability to openly contradict their parents (and grandparents). These two family arrangements were being contested in this family, and the family therapist was invited to join in this contest.

The therapist must decide *how* to relate to the family in their current situation. A therapist could align with the parents and work to reinforce their authority within the family system—in effect, joining the parents against Luminata. Alternatively he/she could advocate for the child's position and try to make a space for her voice and ideas to receive more attention and credence—in effect, siding with Luminata against her parents. Each of these options would re-inscribe the PIP (see Chapter 8)—simply adding the therapist as another participant on one side or the other of the PIP of *pressuring for compliance coupled with resisting that pressure*. He/she could serve as a mediator or broker and try to negotiate a peace agreement of sorts between these two sides. This mediator approach conceives of the trouble as occurring between two incongruent positions, effectively bypassing consideration of alternatives other than either of the two poles (and perhaps polarized) positions. Each of these therapeutic choices is grounded in ideas about what therapy could/should be that connect with certain professional, disciplinary, or institutional discourses regarding preferred practices and outcomes.

Alternatively this family situation could be viewed through a SCIPs lens to navigate family relationships—this situation invites a conversation about larger competing frames or discourses. The family members could be seen as standard bearers for different preferred ways of striving for the good and desirable. For example, conversations could directly engage the differences/challenges in living within different cultures/traditions, discussing the experiences of being representatives of different generations, or discussing parent-child arrangements from different times and places (and how the parents and children experience those alternative arrangements). Our proposition in this chapter is that bringing in this form of conversation provides a broader therapeutic conversation that connects the family's troubles to the larger societal discourses in which we all find ourselves immersed. By opening this type of conversation, therapists may come to some unique opportunities to discuss the interpersonal space within a family that interrupts the PIP coupling of *personally attacking invites defending* along with some additional ways of stimulating HIPs (in fact, this different type of conversation may itself be a Transforming Interpersonal Pattern [TIP] or perhaps even a HIP by inviting a disruption in the PIP).

Because our presuppositions are usually unquestioned or unexamined, *talking these ideas into* family therapy to make this conversation listenable is sometimes challenging. A key issue in including SCIPs is how to introduce this idea in a way that opens the possibility for the clients to see the relevance of discussing the societal discourses. The automatic or practiced quality of our interpersonal behaviors often renders the supportive discourses invisible. Just experiencing dominating discourses as a choice among several (rather than the only one) can diminish the authority of the dominant discourse.

Here we are reminded of two of Michael White's notions. The first is the "absent but implicit" (White, 2011), specifically referring to guiding ideas that are not usually seen or discussed, but upon reflection, one can see the impact such ideas can have in people's attempts to create preferred relationships. The second is "exoticizing the domestic" (White, 1993), in which we take the routine, the daily, and hold it up for special examination and consideration—to see it as something special, unusual, or distinctive. Bringing societal discourses into the therapeutic conversation reconnects the behaviors with their supportive cast of ideas, explicating more threads of influence. The decontextualization of behavior by excluding the braided ideas that strengthen and justify those behaviors can limit our understanding of our behaviors, especially when we want to modify them.

SCIPs and PIPs: SCIPs and HIPs

Returning to our case example, conceptualizing Luminata and her parents and grandparents as engaged in a battle of individual wills with each other invites a personalization that blinds us to the influence of larger discourses. We could describe the PIP as *challenging invites defending* and the HIP as *compromising invites cooperating*. However, if we include discourses into our conceptualization by noticing the role that tradition plays and adding that to the conversation, we may be able to entertain different therapeutic conversations that could be more facilitative of improved relationships. For example, we could ask any of the following questions regarding the discourses of tradition:

- What traditions are you already aware of that might be feeding the positions you and/or your family member hold in this interaction? Who could shed a different light on these traditions?
- What is important, traditionally speaking, and worth protecting when your family is engaged in arguing through challenging one another and defending one's own position?
- What are some other ways of trying to make your points-of-view known and respected that would be true to the traditions you want to uphold?
- What would you be honoring if you were to lessen the challenging?

Perhaps by asking these questions, the parents and grandparents could better own their relationships with the discourse of tradition and they might be able to critically examine the pros and cons of their approach to parenting Luminata, while Luminata could look at the pros and cons and meanings in her life with respect to living within and outside of her parents' traditions. Luminata could be following a path of a local Canadian adolescent approach to establishing an adolescent's identity and value apart from her family-of-origin. This local adolescent tradition also can be strongly held.

We could also notice a discourse of acceptability as part of the situation described. To address that discourse we could ask the following questions:

- To what degree would others approve if you changed your ways of getting along? Who would approve and who would disapprove?
- To what extent do challenging and defending positions affect the ways in which you belong to or are being set apart from your community?

By posing such questions, Luminata might be able to claim her relationship with the notion of being acceptable within her peer group. She might be able to take a more clear-eyed view of how this position is useful and how it is not, and the adults in her life could also look at the merits of what has been taken-for-granted in terms of acceptability through the lens of a new culture. If all family members could discuss the ideas they embrace as ideas rather than as personal referendums of self-worth, the therapeutic talk would take a different tack.

Therapists also embrace certain societal discourses that may impact the process of doing therapy with families in positive or negative ways. The discourse of expertism encourages therapists to adopt positions of authority over families such that a lack of therapeutic progress may be perceived by the therapist as an affront to his/her skill or ability as a therapist. Attending to the pull of this discourse may allow the therapist to be wary of how this discourse may encourage certain practices that steal initiative from families in therapy, in effect involving the therapist in a PIP of *attempting to assert one's position over another and thereby inviting a defensive posture in return* (see Chapter 8). To address this discourse, we could ask some of the following questions:

- How does expert knowledge, like the advice of professionals, contribute to your not getting along as well as you would like?
- To what extent have I (as the therapist) enacted a role of being the expert in your family? Have I refused that role in your opinion?
- What is the role of your own expertise in getting along or not getting along?

Closing

We are invested in helping therapists more richly conceptualize the dilemmas and troubles that families bring to therapy and in helping families make changes that are meaningful. To that end, we are interested in noticing and influencing the societal discourses that are embedded in our society's institutional mental health discourses that often limit the therapists' and family members' discursive flexibility. Many taken-for-granted practices in providing services to families (e.g., financial arrangements, physical plant, policies of inclusion/exclusion, clinic hours) exert pressures and limitations that may restrict the helpful potentials of therapy.

It may be a formidable task, but we believe that our daily interactions with our families and their daily interactions with others may stimulate small social change and difference with respect to the societal discourses that prevail in our lives. Sustaining daily efforts to contribute to making visible the usually unexamined influences in our lives can become part of grassroots efforts to change our worlds for the better.

A short story can serve as an illustration. A family of grandmother, mother, and three daughters came to therapy with complaints of arguing and constant upset in their household. The PIP seemed clear—*criticizing coupled with resisting*—and each family member could readily occupy either the criticizing position or the resisting position. I (Sally), the therapist, asked the family what thoughts the women in this family had about strong women, about feminism, and about gender influences on strong women. This sparked a lively discussion across the generations with committed opinions that (a) women had to be strong for themselves and for others, and (b) relationships needed to be strong to support strong women. I then asked about the influences that invited them to fight and argue with each other, given they held fierce beliefs about the strength of women. They answered, "We see what you mean!" However, I was not sure what meanings they were holding, so the family explained. They believed they were influenced to fight and argue to show strength as did many of the people they associated with at work or at school. They realized that they were subscribing to a SCIP that supported arguing as an indication of strength. They explained how they preferred a version of a strong woman as one who was confident, articulate, lived in peace, harmony, and interdependence. But the story continues. They returned to therapy explaining that being seduced by the perceived connection between arguing and trying to be strong led all of them to reconsider and take action regarding their use of arguing at work and school with their female peers and co-workers.

Taking these understandings into one's larger life-world and engaging with others around these issues constitutes a talking back to the discourses in ways that either challenges them or leads to preferred behaviors. The discourses become fertile ground from which to examine one's behaviors and find potentials in alternatives. In particular, the spreading of these examinations into one's communities affords the possibility of social action on a grassroots level. We hope that you can see this as one way of contributing to not only more family harmony but also to a more socially just world.

References

Bateson, G. (1988). *Mind and nature: A necessary unity*. New York, NY: Ballantine.

Becvar, D. S., & Becvar, R. J. (2012). *Family therapy: A systemic integration* (8th ed.). Boston, MA: Pearson.

Fairclough, N. (n.d.). *The dialectics of discourse*. Retrieved from www.sfu.ca/cmns/courses/2012/801/1-Readings/Fairclough%20Dialectics%20of%20Discourse%20Analysis.pdf

Frank, A. W. (2010). *Letting stories breathe: A socio-narratology*. Chicago, IL: University of Chicago Press.

Gergen, K. J., & Gergen, M. M. (2004). *Social construction: Entering the dialogue*. Chagrin Falls, OH: Taos Institute.

Hare-Mustin, R. T. (1994). Discourses in the mirrored room: A postmodern analysis of therapy. *Family Process, 33*(1), 19–35.

Heritage, J. (1991). *Garfinkel and ethnomethodology*. Cambridge, MA: Polity.

Pearce, W. B., & Cronen, V. E. (1980). *Communication, action and meaning: The creation of social realities*. New York, NY: Praeger.

Rushdie, S. (2005). *Shalimar the clown*. Toronto, ON: Random House of Canada.

Schultz, S. K. (1984). *Family systems thinking*. Northvale, NJ: Jason Aronson.

Shotter, J. (2012). More than cool reason: "Withness-thinking" or "systemic thinking" and "thinking *about* systems." *International Journal of Collaborative Practices, 3*(1), 1–13. Retrieved from http://ijcp.files.wordpress.com/2012/06/shotter_final_english-cool-reason_new.pdf

Tomm, K. (1991). Beginnings of a "HIPs and PIPs" approach to psychiatric assessment. *Calgary Participator, 1*(2), 21–22, 24.

Waldegrave, C., Tamasese, K., Tuhaka, F., & Campbell, W. (2003). *Just Therapy—A journey: A collection of papers from the Just Therapy Team, New Zealand*. Adelaide, Australia: Dulwich Centre.

Wetherell, M. (1998). Positioning and interpretive repertoires: Conversation analysis and post-structuralism in dialogue. *Discourse & Society, 9*(3), 387–412. doi: 10.1177/0957926598009003005

White, M. (1993). Deconstruction in therapy. In S. Gilligan & R. Price (Eds.), *Therapeutic conversations* (pp. 22–61). New York, NY: W. W. Norton.

White, M. (2011). *Narrative practice: Continuing the conversations*. New York, NY: W. W. Norton.

White, M., & Epston, D. (1990). *Narrative means to therapeutic ends*. New York, NY: W. W. Norton.

7

HIS CAVE AND HER KITCHEN
Gendered PIPs and HIPs and Societal Discourses

Joanne Schultz Hall and Inés Sametband

In this chapter, we invite practitioners to consider therapeutic conversations as opportunities to explore cultural discourses on gender and address ways they are enacted in family relationships and in the development of individuals' identities. We propose that utilizing the IPscope framework may help therapists better orient to these conversational opportunities. Together, therapists and family members can identify Pathologizing Interpersonal Patterns (PIPs) that are promoted by constraining gendered discourses and collaborate in generating and negotiating preferred gender identities and relationships within Healing Interpersonal Patterns (HIPs) and Wellness Interpersonal Patterns (WIPs).[1]

Locating Ourselves

I (Joanne) was born and raised in California and immigrated to Canada after graduate school. Although both my parents were also born and raised in the United States, they had European roots and provided a fairly traditionally organized, middle class household. They valued education and encouraged females to excel academically. My graduate training, interestingly, did not include any course work on gender despite the second wave of feminist thinking in the 1960s. However, after accepting employment at a child treatment center in Calgary in 1974, I became interested in exploring women's experiences related to mental health and mental health services from a feminist perspective. That interest expanded to exploring the feminist critique of family therapy, of mental health practices generally, and extending to the critique of the feminist critique by women of color. For over 33 years I have been employed at the University of Calgary Family Therapy Program, which became the Calgary Family Therapy Centre (CFTC).

My first exposure to systems theory and to a consciously experienced PIP was during my coursework while I was in graduate school getting a master's degree in education counseling. An undergraduate course offered by the faculty of home economics caught my eye because I was interested in working with families and I understood that the systems theory content might be relevant to my career aspirations. What is of greater interest, however, was my embodied experience of the effects of pathologizing patterns related to gender. Our professor made it clear that she was going to grade on the bell curve so that a certain portion of the class would fail the course and only a few would get A grades. I felt an inordinate pressure to get an A in the course, and as the course progressed I became more and more anxious, eventually breaking out in a case of weeping eczema on my fingers, which required medication and heat lamp treatments. Of particular note in this situation was the political and contextual underpinning for my professor's use of the bell curve to mark the students, given that this was unusual within the university. At the time, the Home Economics Department seemed to be undervalued and considered less academic or scholarly.[2] I believed that the professor was trying to legitimize the course and garner respect for the department by utilizing what would be regarded as a rigorous marking system. Thus, the lower status of the department likely played a significant role in creating conditions for a PIP of *professorial pressuring to perform inviting students' worrying and pressuring selves to perform*.

I (Inés) was born and grew up in Buenos Aires, Argentina, and moved to Canada as an adult (see Chapter 8). My interest in cultural discourses on gender is fueled by a curiosity (and a bit of frustration) on how these discourses and ideas seem to influence our relationships. In my experience, the discourses on womanhood I have been immersed in have felt quite limiting and constraining. I have had to push back and protest many assumptions made about my way of interacting with others based on rigid ideas about women. When these gender discourses take over, I find myself having to justify the time I spent on my career, when or whether I will become a mother, or even that I can move furniture because I am strong. I feel frustrated when these narrow descriptions are used as the only way to make sense of who I am in my relationships with others—as if all the rest did not matter. However, this frustration also feeds my curiosity of what else is out there—what are other ways in which people understand and perform gendered relationships that fit for them? As a family therapist, I find it useful to focus on gender from a relational stance that opens possibilities for people to find ways of being gendered that fit for them.

Gender Through an Interactional Lens

Although there is a welcome trend toward gender equality in relationships (Illouz, 2012; Rankin Mahoney & Knudson-Martin, 2009), essentialist views on gendered relationships (i.e., heterosexism, homophobia) still remain highly prevalent in our society. Those who continue to believe and enact these ideas exclude and shadow any gendered relationship that does not fit into these prevailing views, contributing to the isolation and derogation of non-dominant gendered relationships. For us, these rigid ideas on gender seem to be played out in hierarchical interpersonal patterns (IPs) that become stagnant or inflexible, often deteriorating into gendered PIPs (e.g., *dominating coupled with submitting*, or *imposing coupled with conceding*). We view these gendered PIPs as closely associated with Socio-Cultural Interpersonal Patterns (SCIPs)—in this case discourses of entitlement and privilege (see Chapter 6)—in which the general assumption is that some gendered behaviors or practices (more commonly associated with being male and/or heterosexual) are considered better or more apt than others (e.g., compared to female and GLBTT [Gay, lesbian, bisexual, transgender, transsexual] associated behaviors and practices). For us, the rigidity of these gendered IPs perpetuate constraints and limits for the individuals and families engaged in them, while also affecting those who are excluded by them. Furthermore, the inflexibility and persistent repetition of these relational patterns continue to support constraining cultural discourses, upholding and maintaining stereotypical gendered relationships, notably heterosexism. For example, marriage in GLBTT relationships is still considered illegal in many countries (e.g., a PIP of *imposing heterosexual views and practices coupled with disqualifying non-dominant gender views and practices*), and violence related to gender is still quite prevalent today (e.g., *men engaging in controlling, intimidating, or violent practices coupled with women evading and/or submitting as a means of self-protection*).

The inflexible and automatic privileging of one gender, or gendered relationship, over others (and associated privilege-enabling PIPs) tends to overshadow and constrain HIPs and WIPs that would sustain and promote more gender flexibility and/or balance in relationships. A more flexible HIP or WIP might entail *accepting of gender diversity coupled with expressing/living by gender preferences*. We believe that as people engage in relationships, they either sustain or challenge taken-for-granted understandings of what is expected of them as members of a particular gendered group. Gendered identities are co-constructed and lived out in relationships between people. Influenced by repeated messages and demonstrations of certain privileges and entitlements, a person's gender is typically presented as a rigid category that offers identity descriptors, like small "check boxes" into which a person needs to fit, either female or male. Those boxes tend also to be associated with particular rules for those who fit inside them. For example, Almeida, Dolan-Del Vecchio, and Parker (2008) have elucidated what they term *the patriarchal male code*, the set of rules for men that has survived for many decades, if not centuries. These rules continue to influence gender identities and intimate relationships through familiar sayings: "don't act like a girl," "keep your feelings to yourself (showing anger is acceptable)," "solve problems using aggression," "be dominant and in control" (p. 57). It seems to us that individuals and families intuitively understand these fixed gender categories (or check boxes) and their associated rules as narrow and exclusive ways to describe and live their gender identities (e.g., as either female or male, excluding transgendered identities, or other preferred ways of performing gender) and relationships with others (e.g., as heterosexual, excluding bisexual and gay sexual orientations). Further, these categories and rules may "capture" persons in PIPs, by having them commit to ways of relating to others that do not resonate with how they experience themselves as gendered individuals.

The cultural discourses behind these check boxes that restrict gender categories often support a disparity in relationships. For example, the barrage of messages that highlights men's physical strength or superiority in moral or intellectual capacities offers justification for dominating through discourses promoting male entitlement. To complement this idea of male superiority, women are usually portrayed as "nurturing, close to nature, emotional, negatively affected by their hormones, empathic and vulnerable" (Burr, 2003, p. 75). These narrow understandings of gender leave little space for women and men to engage in other types of gendered relationships and can have a pathologizing effect on a person's sense of self-worth when that individual does not conform to these expectations.

We hear both directly and subtly, as we are repeatedly exposed to societal messages and the local and daily reiterations by those close to us, that heterosexual relationships are normative and acceptable and that GLBTT relationships are neither legitimate nor acceptable. These tightly held gendered social expectations influence how partners in non-dominant relationships orient to one another, and inform the kinds of IPs in which they engage. For example, within North American culture, many people equate same sex relationships with their heterosexual counterpart, assuming a "masculine" and "feminine" partner. Vivid illustrations of this kind of equating can be found in derogatory stereotypes for partners in same sex relationships, such as calling a lesbian partner "butch" or a gay man a "flaming queen." In contrast, Knudson-Martin and Laughlin (2005) have suggested that heterosexual couples could learn creativity and flexibility from lesbian and gay relationships.

Performing and Negotiating Gender in Social Interactions

Like the philosopher Taylor (1994), we understand gendered identities as "always in dialogue with, sometimes in struggle against, the things our significant others want to see in us" (p. 33). We believe that we become gendered through the ways we align ourselves with, and participate in, social practices associated with particular gendered groups. Further, we suggest that becoming gendered begins almost instantaneously at the time of or even prior to birth, when the question is posed, "Is it a boy or girl?" By answering that question, parents and others can begin the process of culturally gendering the child and their relationship with that child. As people grow and develop, how one performs being a girl/woman or being a boy/man is contingent on contexts and social relationships. For example, being a woman may be performed quite differently when a woman interacts with her partner at home than when she interacts with her colleagues at work. As she performs the expectations of her situation, those around her will respond to her in accord with their understanding of the social practices expected in each situated encounter.

Our view is that gender and cultural discourses cannot be separated. We agree with Tamasese (2000), who stated,

> Our ways of living as women and as men are always influenced by the symbols, rituals, language and relationship structures of culture ... whenever we are talking about gender, cultural considerations are relevant, as are other considerations of class and sexuality etc. Similarly, wherever we are talking about culture, relations of gender are relevant. (p. 15)

We view gender as the "expectations, characteristics and behaviors that members of a culture consider appropriate for females and males" (Rankin Mahoney & Knudson-Martin, 2009, pp. 17–18). When gender privilege discourses are at play in an interaction (a PIP), it is not uncommon to see peoples' gendered identities performed restrictively, as if corresponding to the previously mentioned check boxes. These limiting gendered identities, represented in gender stereotypes, are continuously available to us in our everyday lives (e.g., through popular media or interactions with others) and can constrain our responses to others based on stereotypical assumptions. For example, Mary may respond to her husband John with "nothing" when he asks her, "What is going on?" John may interpret her response as associated with the generalized stereotype of women's "nothing" meaning that he is in trouble and distance himself. Mary, on the other hand, may see John's response as disinterest and resent him and become further disinclined to share things with him. Or consider another example: A father during family therapy proudly tells of his son's performance in a recent soccer game but does not comment on his daughter's performance in volleyball. When the therapist asks about this, his wife suggests that "sports are more of a guy's thing."

Rather than contributing to the dominance of rigid gendered stereotypes and their associated PIPs, our intent in this chapter is to give meaning to what we observe in ways that loosen the grip of PIPs and provide openings for gendered HIPs and WIPs as alternatives. Rigid essentialist views of gender and gender stereotypes are still widely practiced and promoted in popular media and culture, continuing to generate public cues for how people should coordinate their relationships. An example of such a gendered cue is manifest in the famous Old Spice commercial *The Man Your Man Could Smell Like* (Scruton & Kuntz, 2010). In that commercial, men are portrayed as providers of material goods and women as only interested in those goods (i.e., diamonds and expensive trips). Another illustration comes from the recent movie *He's Just Not That Into You* (Barrymore & Kwapis, 2009), in which male and female characters' relationships are portrayed in accord with heterosexist discourses (e.g., women pursuing men who are not interested in relationships, men fearing relationship commitment, heterosexual couples engaging in PIPs of *pursuing coupled with distancing*). The prevalence of these essentialist stereotypes leaves little room for any gendered identity and relationship that does not fit into these views and as such becomes demeaning for people with non-dominant gender identities and sexual orientations. This caricaturizing becomes part of a disqualifying process in which those who do not fit the culturally defined "check boxes" are portrayed as less than, unworthy, and/or undesirable. These rigid descriptions also become internalized by those who are marginalized and can lead to self-disqualification and, in extreme cases, death through suicide.

Those who live according to stereotypic gendered interpersonal patterns, such as *male dominating coupled with female submitting* (Rankin Mahoney & Knudson-Martin, 2009), or other unacknowledged power differentials (e.g., *controlling finances coupled with financially depending on a partner*), may experience limited satisfaction and creativity in their couple relationships. At times these PIPs can be subtle, such as when a partner is disqualifying or ignoring the contributions of the other, crowding the speaking space, or giving inordinate attention to the achievements of one individual or group, such as White heterosexual males. The ways in which gender gets played out are often invisible to us because they have become so ordinary and familiar. Furthermore, because gender and sexual orientation stereotypes (i.e., heterosexism) are promoted as normal or taken-for-granted in mainstream society, it becomes difficult to reflect upon and enact alternative, more preferred, and meaningful gendered relationships. Many people do not even recognize the possibility of something different.

Moving Toward Balanced Reciprocity

Several decades ago, family therapists regarded families as systemic units unto themselves with little or no acknowledgment of the family's sociocultural context (Falicov, 1983, 1988; McGoldrick, 1998). They viewed families through the "abstract, neutral language of cybernetics" (Avis, 1988, p. 17). The mechanistic notions, once applied to family functioning (e.g., Keeney, 1983), were gradually replaced by new and more complex understandings of family relationships, including the influence of cultural discourses on gender.

This shift was led by feminist theorists who criticized family therapists for their reliance on systems theory (e.g., Avis, 1988; Goldner, 1985; Hare-Mustin, 1978) and circularity, concepts they contend implied equal responsibility and privilege among family members. In particular, Hare-Mustin's (1978) seminal paper criticized family therapists for advocating a theory that implied equality in the interactions of family members, while perpetuating practices that reiterated and reproduced the same gender biases that devalued females as compared to males. In the 1980s and 1990s, feminist theorists and therapists continued to voice their concerns on the direction the profession was taking, opening doors to examine broader social issues such as gender, culture, and race (Akamatsu, 2000; Almeida, 1993; Aronson Fontes & Thomas, 1996; Hare-Mustin, 1978, 1994; Hoffman, 1990; Korin, 1994; Nichols & Schwartz, 2001). Thus, family therapists were challenged theoretically, in their practices, and in their collegial relationships to shift to an understanding of human relationships as unavoidably culturally gendered, contextual, and historical. At the CFTC, dialogue over time has increasingly revolved around these issues related to gender, sexuality, and gendered PIPs, including the following:

- the importance of recognizing power differentials in the relationships between men and women, boys and girls, and those in the therapeutic system;
- the tendency in our culture to blame mothers and to ignore the significance of fathers and fathering in family relationships;
- the pervasive ways in which we (as a cultural group) marginalize and isolate GLBTT people and their relationships.

These ideas were incorporated into our conceptualization and diagramming of PIPs, HIPs, and WIPs as we began to draw the PIP vertically to visually display power dynamics in family life (see Chapter 1). By locating the behavior perceived as more powerful at the top of the diagram, and the behavior perceived as less powerful below, we were able to provide a visual reminder for therapists regarding inequities, helping them to reflect about and imagine ways to talk these observations into the therapy. We illustrate this in Figure 7.1.

We live within hierarchical relationships for most of our lives. At birth, we are "one down" within our families, totally reliant on our parents' care. As we grow and develop into children and young adults, we are

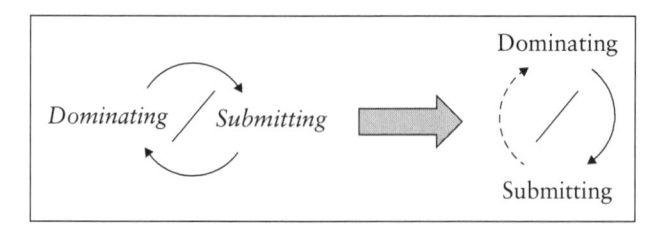

Figure 7.1 A shift from horizontal to vertical drawing to highlight power differential

subject to parental authority within the family and educational authorities at school, and as adults we have bosses, government officials, and courts to whom we are accountable. Thus our world is structured in hierarchical relationships to a very large extent. We would suggest that the greater the degree of rigidity in these relationships, the greater the likelihood of problems. Rigid hierarchies have the potential to do harm not only to those lower on the hierarchy but also to those at the top, as captured in the adage "Absolute power corrupts absolutely." We acknowledge that hierarchical arrangements can also have benefits, especially when it comes to a need for swift decision-making. However, we contend that it is when hierarchical positioning becomes stuck, with little flexibility for the participants, that it becomes most problematic. Since we have relatively few experiences in non-hierarchal relationships during our years growing up, we often find it difficult to engage in non-hierarchical or flexible hierarchical relationships when we form intimate partnerships.

It is important to note that the person who is in a more powerful position usually has less awareness of the inequitable power dynamics than the person who is less powerful. We suspect this is due to the privileged person's automatic and well-practiced actions of saying more, holding a central position, expecting to be taken seriously, using language to constrain choices and maintain the status quo, and remaining blind to the ways he/she draws from the related dominant societal discourses that promote these behaviors. In contrast, we suspect that the person with lesser power experiences the oppressive force of the enacted privileges of the person with more power and often feels silenced, fearful, and continually on the lookout for his/her safety. The latter person's limited opportunity to give voice to her/his experience may further limit the other's awareness of the disparity (for other examples, see Chapter 8). Metaphorically, we might say that the mouse is much more aware of the lion than the lion is aware of the mouse. In our experience, the person in the less powerful or disadvantaged position frequently initiates therapy. This may occur because the task of taking care of the relationship is "delegated" to the person with less power. Alternatively it could occur because the person with less power is striving to recruit some outside support from a therapist.

When it comes to deconstructing PIPs associated with power inequities and discourses of gender entitlement or privilege, we find it useful to first address the person in the dominant position (see Chapter 1), inviting him or her to reflect on the ways in which his or her behavior may have problematic effects in the relationship. By doing so, the unfair arrangements might become more visible with less likelihood of inadvertently offending the dominant partner.

For instance, if a heterosexual couple presented as stuck in the common PIP of *male exercising entitlement coupled with female submitting and doubting her own self-worth*, we might raise questions that we believe could help the male partner (who had engaged in dominating behavior to justify inequality) recognize the ways in which his actions may be associated with discourses of gender privilege (supported as "normal" by his community), and inadvertently invite submitting and self-doubting in his partner. Facilitating such conversation may stimulate his interest in other, more satisfying ways of being a partner and encourage him to consider shifting his behavior. For example, we might ask the following reflexive questions: How might your partner feel when you make decisions without consulting her? To what degree do you think being consulted would be important for her? When you make decisions together, how might your partner perceive whose wishes tend to prevail?[3] What might it mean to your partner if her wishes took priority more frequently? What kinds of benefits to the relationship do you imagine there might be if you were to make it a habit to consult with your partner and honor her wishes more of the time? We might also ask the less powerful partner about successful occasions in which she felt her wishes and feelings were given priority and how each partner felt about and facilitated this. These questions may help partners consider how their behavior is influencing their relationship and the power dynamics within it without being confrontational.

In working toward a healing pattern that might serve as a possible antidote to the PIP, the therapist typically empowers the person in the position of lesser power. However, if a therapist goes too far in this direction and the hierarchy is simply reversed, the therapist might inadvertently foster resentment and protest, perhaps even violence, from the party now in the less powerful position while the PIP is actually maintained (even though the partners exchanged positions in the hierarchy). This points to the need for therapists and clients to think creatively about ways to invite flexibility in sharing or rotating power in gendered relationships. Knudson-Martin and Laughlin (2005) and Knudson-Martin (2013) refer to using *equality* as a guiding frame to address power differences in relationships and have proposed ways this might be facilitated in the therapeutic process. We agree that a goal of equality is admirable and worthy of continued reflection as to how to facilitate this. Therapists could encourage both partners to take equal responsibility for the well-being of the relationship. In

Figure 7.2 we offer a possible WIP to illustrate what symmetrical equality might look like when conceptualized within the IPs framework.

We propose that another way that equality may be achieved is through *balanced reciprocity*. If a relationship is oriented toward reciprocity, it allows for more movement, flexibility, and variation based on the context and the unique needs/desires/talents/gifts of the participants involved. It might mean that one person's desires could be given preference on one occasion, and might be secondary on another, to allow for both parties to have their preferences or needs met, but at different times. Similarly, flexibility can be developed regarding who takes initiative in the caretaking and nurturing of the partner and the relationship. The WIP shown in Figure 7.3 could potentially create balanced reciprocity, in that over time there would be occasions for each participant to have his/her needs, concerns, and hopes expressed and addressed.

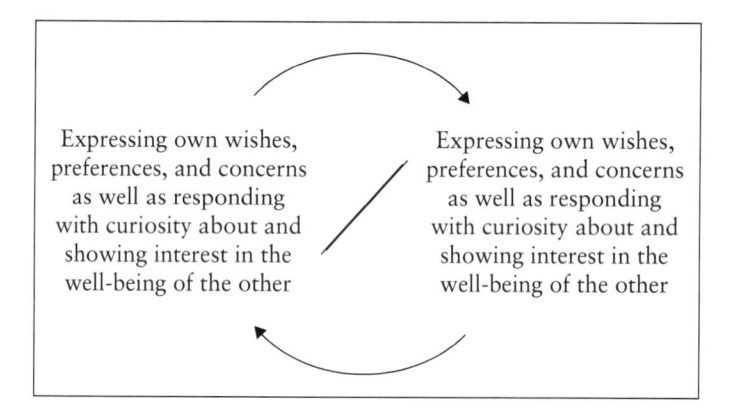

Figure 7.2 Equality through symmetry

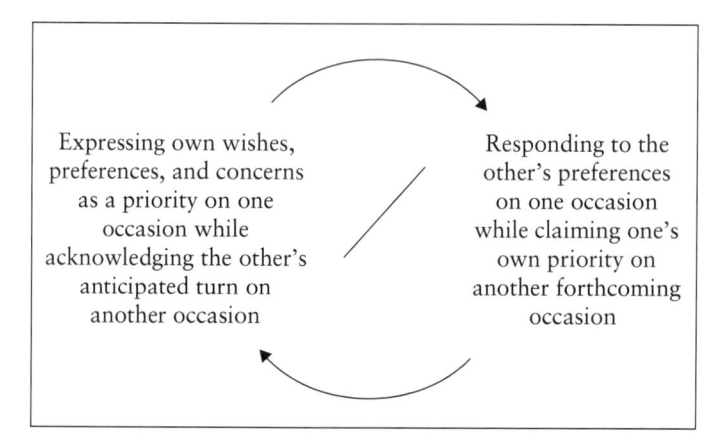

Figure 7.3 Equality through balanced reciprocity

We can also imagine reciprocities that could be established in other domains besides temporal occasions, such as partners sharing and benefiting from each other's unique abilities, interests, and commitments. What is worth bearing in mind when trying to achieve satisfying equity is that a good antidote for too much symmetry is a bit of complementarity, and a good antidote for too much complementarity is a bit of symmetry.

Connecting PIPs and HIPs to Specific Societal Discourses and Stereotypes

As St. George and Wulff indicated in Chapter 6, we have been examining socio-cultural discourses at the CFTC in relation to PIPs and HIPs. We came to realize that it is how family members and therapists interpret gendered Socio-Cultural Interpersonal Patterns (SCIPs) that influence how related pathologizing (PIPs) or healing patterns (HIPs) unfold. For example, we might ask ourselves the following questions: What are the privileges or responsibilities we presume males or females in one's culture should have? How do these privileges and responsibilities influence a couple's relationship, whether heterosexual or homosexual? What kinds of ideas do various cultures have as to the rights and privileges of GLBTT people? How rigidly are these views held? Family members' assumptions about these issues significantly affect their relational dynamics. How we as therapists answer these questions also greatly influences what we pay attention to in the therapy room and what questions we subsequently ask or do not ask. In what follows, we illustrate how certain interpretations of current discourses on gender could contribute to certain PIPs for which we propose contrasting HIPs.

Romantic love as being solely associated with heterosexual relationships (Sanders, 1993). In Western societies, the prevalence of discourses promoting patriarchal and heterosexual practices helps maintain the belief that true love only occurs between males and females. This dominant discourse may sustain a PIP: *considering heterosexual relationships as normal coupled with viewing GLBTT relationships as strange/illegitimate*. A possible HIP might be that of *normalizing and affirming diversity in loving relationships coupled with living freely with a chosen partner based upon experiencing a loving, intimate connection.*

The male sex drive discourse (Hollway, 1984). It is presumed that a male's desires for sex must be satisfied and that the female "is seen as the object that arouses and precipitates men's possessive sexual urges" (Hare-Mustin, 1994, p. 24). Possible PIPs sustained by this discourse might be *demanding sexual fulfillment coupled with acceding to sexual demands,* or *sexually abusing coupled with being sexually abused.* A possible HIP might be that of *females taking sexual initiative when inclined coupled with males taking responsibility to manage their sexual desires and making respectful choices.*

Homophobic language. A phrase like "that is so gay" is used to identify behavior commonly associated with stereotypes of gay and lesbian people as being weak, deviant, or flamboyant. This language can be associated with PIPs that sustain *diminishing the other coupled with lowering one's sense of self-worth*. A possible HIP might be that of *affirming a spectrum of sexual orientations coupled with feeling confident in one's own worthiness.*

Discourses on coupledom. These usually orient to a relationship in which partners have particular roles (e.g., men take out the garbage, women clean the kitchen; men manage finances, women manage the household) that often become fixed. Common PIPs are *females being overly responsible for household chores coupled with males remaining underresponsible for chores* and *males being overly responsible for providing finances coupled with females remaining underresponsible for finances*. A possible HIP might be that of *negotiating preferred contributions coupled with honoring negotiated responsibilities or raising concerns.*

Gender differences in parenting. It is not uncommon to see in commercials and in TV sitcoms (e.g., *According to Jim*) that men and fathers are portrayed as incompetent and bumbling (S. St. George, personal communication, August 26, 2013) and therefore discounted and ignored. A PIP that is sometimes associated with this portrayal is that of *mothers making unilateral decisions coupled with fathers opting out of decision-making and acting like children*. A possible HIP might be that of *mothers creating space for fatherly initiative coupled with fathers taking constructive initiatives.*

Gender differences in participation in therapy. In our work with heterosexual couples, we have noticed the influence of gender discourses in how male and female partners, and we as therapists, participate in therapeutic conversations. For example, men tend to focus on the content and end results of the conversation, while women tend to focus more on emotions. Also, men tend to use "I" discourse and women tend to use "we," and men tend to make more pronouncements and offer solutions, while women are more likely to ask questions and want to talk it out (S. St. George, personal communication, August 26, 2013). This can lead to a PIP of *women focusing on emotional elements to the problem coupled with males focusing on instrumental solutions,* and each becoming frustrated with their partner's lack of understanding or appreciation. A possible HIP might be that of *sharing and clarifying emotional underpinnings of a problem by both parties coupled with mutually exploring possible solutions.*

A second way to present these connections is to visualize the triadic interaction between societal discourses on gender, gender stereotypes, and gendered PIPs and HIPs in the generic diagram in Figure 7.4 and the more specific example in Figure 7.5.

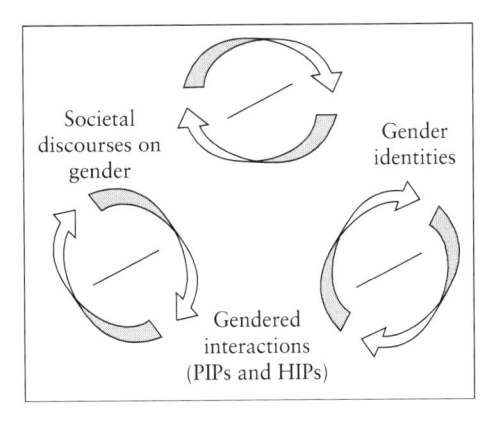

Figure 7.4 Generic triadic interactions

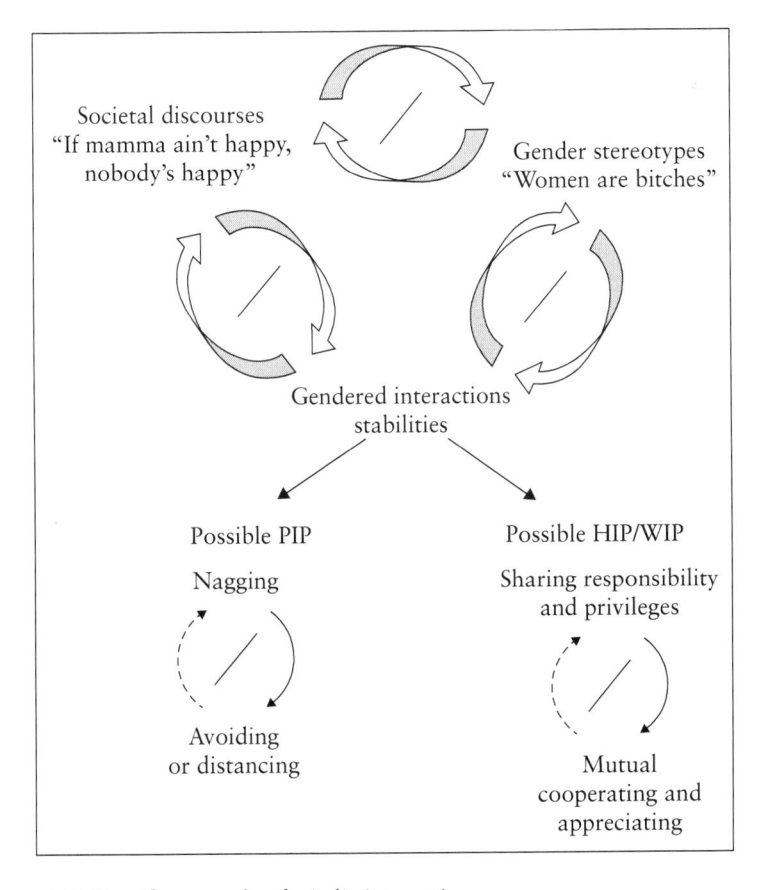

Figure 7.5 Specific example of triadic interaction

A third approach to disclose the relationships among these societal discourses, associated stereotypes, and IPs (including possible TIP initiatives for change) is offered in a table where we provide examples of some common North American discourses in the socialization of boys and girls (see Figure 7.6).

In the next chart (see Figure 7.7), we illustrate how dominant discourses on gender may affect ongoing adult relationships. We identify some common societal discourses and how these may play out in relationships in the form of associated gendered PIPs, which might be replaced by possible HIPs through therapeutic initiatives in possible TIPs.

In juxtaposing these ways of punctuating IPs, we are attempting to highlight alternative couplings in how one might conceive of and alter power dynamics in gendered relationships. In an earlier draft of this chapter, men on our team commented that we were describing gender through a predominantly female interpretive lens. Thus we have included multiple ways of viewing these power dynamics. It remains, however, important to recognize that the overall economic reality of inequitable remuneration for women compared to men in the workplace contributes to unfair dynamics, given that within Western culture, money means power. Furthermore, in relationships where women are homemakers, they are disadvantaged and often do not have the financial wherewithal to leave the injustices, and thus find themselves in a very vulnerable position. In the process of assessing PIPs and hypothesizing possible HIPs, it is very important for therapists to be mindful of which interpretive lenses they are using and how they are assessing power dynamics. What we as therapists notice or pay attention to, and how we interpret power dynamics, will either contribute to maintaining the status quo or challenging it in some way. Exploring and clarifying these dynamics in the therapeutic process usually creates space for both partners to expand possibilities for creative healing directions and greater flexibility in negotiating preferred outcomes.

With respect to the societal discourse related to women bearing responsibility for what happens in family life (noted in Figure 7.7), we might add that we regard the issue of child care and the distribution of related responsibilities (between men and women) as absolutely central in family life. We observe that usually it is the mother who arranges child care, transport, schooling, medical care, and therapy appointments. When we ask a family who we should give the appointment card to, it is almost always the female adult who proffers her hand. In our experience, men in families are gradually moving toward greater engagement in family life and increasingly conveying a desire to have a closer connection with their children. In some situations of separation and divorce, and even in some intact families, men are taking the primary parenting responsibility. These are encouraging developments. However, it appears that females are still assumed to be the adult who will be absent from work if a child is

Common Societal Discourses	Gendered PIPs	Possible HIPs	Possible TIPs
<u>Discourses of Constraint:</u> "Don't be a sissy" "Boys/men don't cry" "Don't be bitchy"	Stifling children's emotional expression, ridiculing vulnerability Boys cutting off emotionally, acting macho or girls turning anger inward	Acknowledging and validating children's emotional experiences and supporting their expression of these Males sharing vulnerabilities and/or females channelling anger proactively	Exploring the origins of these gender ideas as well as the effects of constraints on emotional well-being, and supporting the expression of vulnerability and proactive efforts to address injustice Recognizing and acknowledging effects of constraints and creating space for and supporting flexible gender identities
<u>Discourses of Normalcy:</u> (It's just the way the world works) "Boys will be boys" "Daughters need to be protected" (and controlled)	Adults normalizing inequities and exempting from accountability based on gender Boys acting aggressively or violently or girls accepting male aggression as normative	Adults modeling responsible choices regarding preferred and performed identities Boys managing emotions responsibly and learning to show vulnerability or girls protesting unfair treatment	Inviting and supporting accountability, exploring unique outcomes in which alternative ways of performing gender have been demonstrated (e.g., boys demonstrating courage by showing vulnerability or girls showing strength by standing up for themselves) Taking responsibility and making amends for aggressive behavior and respecting and experimenting with alternative gendered identities
"Our children will be heterosexual and identify as male or female"(see footnote 3)	Describing GLBTT and relationships in negative ways, disqualifying GLBTT denying one's own feelings and experiences (sometimes this can lead to suicide attempts)	Accepting and affirming of difference Accepting self and becoming open about one's own experience	Normalizing diversity in sexual orientation Demonstrating acceptance of self or other
"Daddy's little girl/princess"	Treating daughter like a princess Expecting pampering and being taken care of	Noticing strengths and fostering the development of personal agency Developing competencies and personal agency	Therapist introducing conversation around career goals and aspirations and emerging self-responsibility. Making the distinction between "growing up" and "growing down" Creating a context for optimal development

Figure 7.6 Discourses related to the socialization of boys and girls

Common Societal Discourses	Gendered PIPs	Possible HIPs	Possible TIPs
<u>Discourses of entitlement and privilege:</u> "Men wear the pants in the family"	Men dominating ↓ Women submitting This PIP can escalate to the following:	Men honoring the concerns and ideas of women ↓ Women voicing their ideas and concerns	Therapist opening space for male listening and bringing forth female voices ↓ Both male and female clients accepting therapist initiatives
"A man is the head of his family" "Dad's word is law" "I've (male) earned these rights and privileges"	Threatening, intimidating violating (physically, emotionally, sexually, financially) ↓ Isolating, dismissing own needs, placating and appeasing, blaming self, making excuses for other's behaviors	Ensuring safety of women and children by holding men accountable, and involving third parties (e.g., police) when necessary ↓ Men managing their own intense emotions and holding selves accountable, apologizing and making amends	Initiating conversations around concerns for safety and possible means to ensure it ↓ Family members taking initiative to utilize social and community networks to ensure safety
"A real marriage is only between a man and a woman"	Insisting on heterosexual normality and entitlement ↓ GLBTT accommodating, submitting	Accepting and affirming of diversity in sexual orientation ↓ Privileging one's own needs and priorities	Questioning the validity and fairness of heterosexism ↓ Entertaining alternatives values and beliefs
"Don't you have any balls?" "Don't be a sissy" "Women are bitches"	Female nagging, shaming, complaining ↓ Male avoiding, conceding, striving to please	Woman acknowledging and appreciating male contributions ↓ Man taking initiative and appreciating his own contributions	Therapist noticing and acknowledging woman's acknowledgments ↓ Woman appreciating therapist's selective noticing
<u>Discourses of duty and obligation:</u> "Women are responsible for the children and what happens in the family"	Everyone expecting initiatives by the mother ↓ Mother taking on bulk of child and home care responsibilities	Taking fatherly initiative ↓ Mother creating space for father's initiative	Exploring men's desires as fathers regarding their relationship with their children and bringing forth mother's support for this ↓ Experimenting with greater gender flexibility

Figure 7.7 Gender discourses related to adult relationships

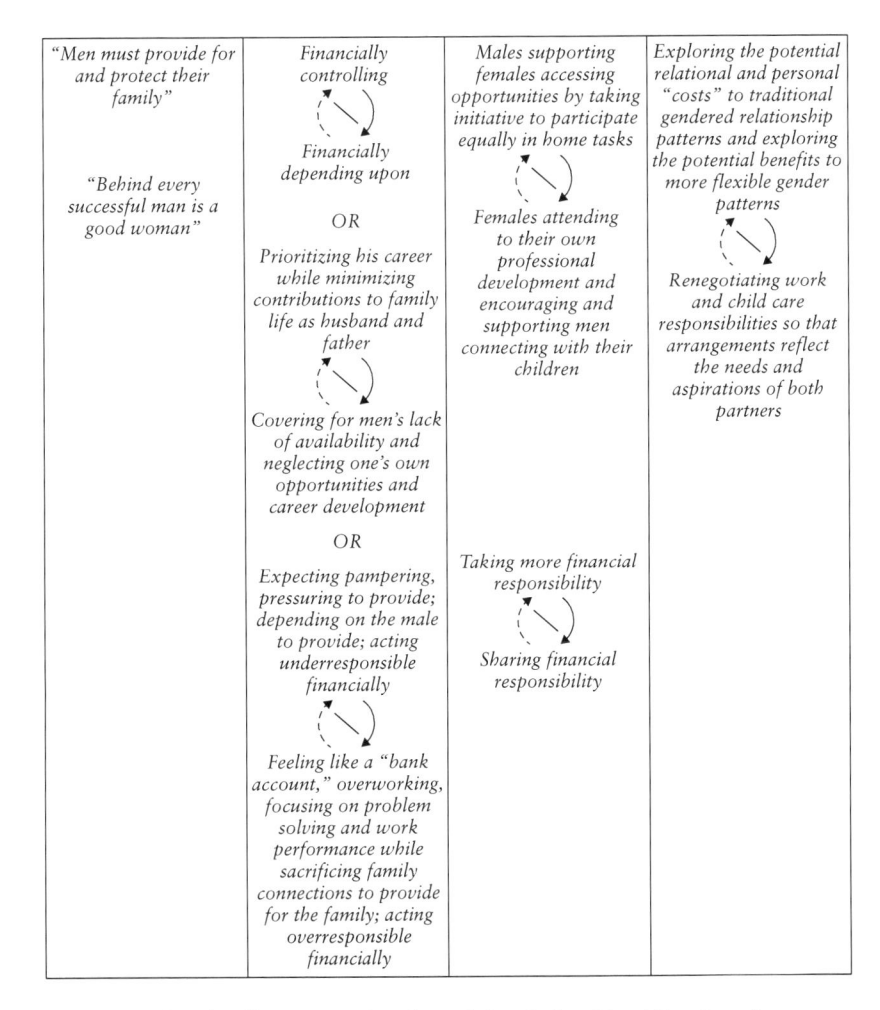

| "Men must provide for and protect their family"

"Behind every successful man is a good woman" | Financially controlling
↓
Financially depending upon

OR

Prioritizing his career while minimizing contributions to family life as husband and father
↓
Covering for men's lack of availability and neglecting one's own opportunities and career development

OR

Expecting pampering, pressuring to provide; depending on the male to provide; acting underresponsible financially
↓
Feeling like a "bank account," overworking, focusing on problem solving and work performance while sacrificing family connections to provide for the family; acting overresponsible financially | Males supporting females accessing opportunities by taking initiative to participate equally in home tasks
↓
Females attending to their own professional development and encouraging and supporting men connecting with their children

Taking more financial responsibility
↓
Sharing financial responsibility | Exploring the potential relational and personal "costs" to traditional gendered relationship patterns and exploring the potential benefits to more flexible gender patterns
↓
Renegotiating work and child care responsibilities so that arrangements reflect the needs and aspirations of both partners |

Figure 7.7 Gender discourses related to adult relationships (Continued)

sick. Often women assume that they know what is in the best interests of their children, which may inadvertently gate out their parenting partner, thus inadvertently contributing to lesser involvement of fathers with their children. Perhaps exploring partners' ideas of what balanced reciprocity might look like for them in their daily lives could become an invitation to consider new and preferred ways of sharing parenting tasks.

While violence in intimate relationships is extremely significant, it is beyond the scope of this chapter to address this issue in any detail. Pease (1997) summarized some of the key models used in the treatment of male violence, including the anger management model, the interactional model, and pro-feminist men's programs. Continued developments in this area include work by Alan Jenkins (1997), who advocates for creating conversations that invite relational responsibility from men who act violently. Almeida and Durkin (1999) utilize the Cultural Context Model to address male violence, stating that their goal is to "raise consciousness about the toxic—and potentially lethal—consequences of the intersectionality of gender, race, class, culture, and sexual orientation" (p. 316). Todd (2010) further examines the potential therapeutic utility of a response-based approach, utilizing an "interpretive repertoire that highlights issues of volition, choice and agency" (p. 74), which allows the therapist to take a collaborative orientation with the client in exploring potential healing directions.

Within the PIPs and HIPs model, the historical shift toward recognizing power differentials became very important, as we drew the PIP vertically to visually emphasize the hierarchy. The generic hierarchical PIP of *dominating coupled with submitting* when applied to a specific situation might be detailed as *bullying, intimidating, or isolating coupled with fearing and withdrawing*. Since such abuse has a better chance of continuing behind closed doors (in privacy and secrecy), we would look for evidence of associated PIPs of *cutting off contact with outsiders coupled with caving in and isolating oneself* from potential supports and *insisting on privacy to avoid shame coupled with privatizing and protecting an abusive partner* as shown in Figure 7.8. These dynamics become particularly malignant when there is also a PIP of *shifting ownership of responsibility coupled with apologizing and appeasing* by the victim, who becomes completely entrapped.

In situations where silencing occurs, a therapist should open conversations to clarify how secrecy creates conditions for abusive practices to persist or recur. TIPish directions for creating conditions of greater accountability, such as potentially involving third parties (e.g., friends, neighbors, mentors, and the law), and for making amends could also be considered.

However, if a therapist expects the disadvantaged partner in the victim position to be the primary person to hold her partner accountable, making

PIP	PIP
Cutting off contact with outsiders ↕ Caving in and isolating self	Insisting on privacy to avoid shame ↕ Privatizing and protecting partner

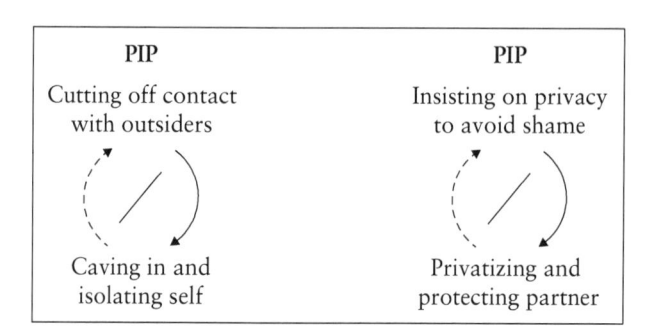

Figure 7.8 Problematic silencing strategies

this *her* responsibility, the therapist can inadvertently perpetuate a societal discourse of women being responsible for what goes on in family relationships, thus reinforcing inequitable patterns within these relationships. Ultimately, it would be far more useful to orient the dominant partner toward holding himself accountable and developing a network of people (extended family, friends, neighbors) who could support him in that process. Almeida and Durkin (1999) describe a version of this within the Cultural Context Model, in which men within the community become sponsors for men who have engaged in violent behavior, providing support and holding them accountable. In addition to facilitating accountability, societal discourses (SCIPs) and gender identities that support unfair male entitlement or legitimize male violence (and a woman's sense of deriving value from being tied to a relationship) need to be examined and deconstructed. For example, in exploring SCIPs promoting male dominance that lead to male violence, we hear comments such as "men like to punch things," "she/he provoked me," "he/she disrespected me," "don't rock the boat," "women are peace keepers," "women have to be loyal," or "women are the relationship's keeper or expert." Exploring these ideas could foster dialogue that serves to deconstruct societal discourses and associated gendered PIPs, while inviting possible HIPs and alternative SCIPs.

More subtle forms of violence (e.g., emotional violence) can occur when a partner exerts his/her will to convince his/her partner of the rightness or correctness of his/her views, thus disqualifying the other and potentially creating escalation. Exploring the underpinnings to this type of disqualification and escalation, often influenced by discourses of expertise, can be useful as a way to invite reflection upon how each may have "a kernel of truth" or some legitimacy that could be acknowledged. Affirming each partner's unique contributions to creating a fuller picture can invite a richer and more flexible "both/and" viewpoint.

Inviting both men and women to explore the cultural ideas and beliefs about what it means to be a man or woman, and the degree to which they have adopted or rejected those notions or societal "directives," can prove fruitful in opening space for a choice about how a particular man or woman chooses to perform gender in relationships. Perhaps one of the primary contributions of the PIPs and HIPs approach, as Dan Wulff suggested (personal communication, August 26, 2013), is that it offers us a device (the IPscope) that can help us to see more clearly how problematic patterns become stabilized and how we could identify flexible alternatives.

Clinical Example

The following transcript, which includes minor edits to foster clarity, is from a consultation interview conducted by Joanne Schultz Hall in the context of a team screening at the CFTC (see Figure 7.9). The therapist

Societal Discourses	Transcript	PIPs/HIPs/TIPs
	Joanne (J): You really care about your brother, and his future. Tom (T): Yeah, I'm really trying to help him learn these things, but he just refuses to even listen. J: Can I ask you, cause you said you come across in a domineering way at times, what do you mean by that? T: I'm very commanding. I don't know if you've had experience with that in your own life. Do you have kids? J: Yeah, I have two sons actually.	PIP Domineering, commanding / ignoring
Men use temper to control the situation	T: You ask one of them to do something and he ignores you. You ask someone to do something and they say "no" and it's important that they do it and you tell them, "do it, do it, do it," and they keep saying "no." Eventually you get pretty angry with them because they are not doing what they are supposed to be doing and I eventually get to the point of yelling and name-calling. J: Can I ask you how you feel about that for yourself as a way of being with your brother? Do you have some feelings about that? T: Well I don't like it. J: You don't like it. What is it that you don't like about you when you are yelling or commanding him? T: I come off as angry and that is the only part of my life that mom sees and I'm always yelling cause Bill never listens to anything. J: I see. T: And that's the big difference between home and the church, is the way Bill responds to me and the kids at church and…	TIP Exploring gender ideas outside of dominant societal discourse / Internalizing personal agency (bringing forth choicefulness)
A family needs a man	J: I suppose you're in a different relationship with the kids at the church than you are with your brother. T: The family we've got, we don't really have a father figure, and whenever he is around he is wrecking things more by being so abusive. These other people that I work with and spend time with got real family situations. They sit down to supper; they've grown up in different surroundings. J: So they have a different life experience. T: (inaudible) so that's kind of the reason Bill…	
Perfect family/not being the perfect family	J: If you could choose the kind of man you want to be in the future, cause you do have a choice, right, about the kind of man you would like to become, what are you hoping for or striving for in terms of how you will relate to other people, both men and women? T: Well a lot better than my dad, I'll tell you that. J: So you are trying to do something different. In what way? If you could describe the kind of man you'd like to be, what would you be doing let's say five years from now, two years from now. T: Eventually I want to be a good father, cause that's way out of my dad's league. Um, he's never been there for any of us. When you think back to your childhood you've got some good memories with your family, throwing a ball around the yard, picnics with your family. Whenever I think back, I can't remember any of that. J: So you're having to create something for yourself. T: Something else, cause I didn't get it. Mary: Their father would come in the back door when Tom was two years old and Tom would run up to the door, "daddy, daddy, daddy" and he would just get screamed at. "Give (inaudible) me the f'ing door before I get my f'ing stuff off."	
Men can be patient and compassionate	J: He hasn't had a model for fathering that he is wanting to duplicate, he's wanting something very different. J: (to Tom) Can you describe the qualities you'd like to sort of be like or emulate? T: Patient.	TIP Constructing desired directions

Figure 7.9 Excerpt of clinical interview

J: You'd like to be patient (writing it down).
T: ...Like I said, I ask Bill to do something and I'd start off nice and everything, keep going using manners and everything 'til it gets to the point where I can't stand it anymore and just yell at him and force him to do it.
J: So you'd like to build your ability to be patient, is that right?
T: Yeah.
J: OK, what would that look like exactly if you could develop that capacity bigger, so that it was bigger in your life?
T: I wouldn't get as demanding. It's pretty much just around the house that I do that in my life, cause everywhere else I go, if I say something once, and they ignore it and I say it twice and they ignore it and I say it a third time with a stern tone in my voice they will listen. But with Bill it keeps on going and going. So hopefully I wouldn't get as angry.
J: So you'd manage your temper and recognize that sometimes people might not go along with you or whatever. That you could accept that people aren't sometimes as cooperative as you would like. OK. What other kinds of qualities would you like to have?
T: I don't know. What do you mean?
J: In terms of becoming a man, cause you are obviously growing into manhood here. What kind of qualities would you like to have, as a person, as a man?
T: I can't think of much else.
J: Being patient.
T: That's pretty much what I can think that is specific.
J: For example, like this patience. It sounds like you experienced impatience from your dad and roughness. (Pause) Do you want to be a person who is nonviolent with other people?
T: Definitely.
J: You do. How have you made that decision for yourself?
T: I have already followed that. In my life I don't fight.
J: How did you make that decision (to not be violent)?
T: I already follow that. In my life, I don't fight. I won't fight. I've been the subject of bullying a lot through my life because I am overweight. (inaudible) And I've gotten into fights before. Um, just recently, the most recent one I was walking kids home on youth group, after youth group one time, and uh some people decided to try and jump me. So I had a big gang of guys there. Only one tried to attack me, and it doesn't matter how many times he tried to hit me I never hit back. I'd defend myself but never hit back.
J: Really! How did you decide that for yourself?
T: Well I don't just understand how other people can inflict pain. It's a sickening kind of thing.
J: You don't want to inflict pain.
T: No. Like it's in a guy's nature to want to hit stuff, so that's why I bought a boxing bag. I don't want to hit people.
J: You'd rather take it out on an object if you're taking your anger out on something.
T: Yes.

Annotations:
- Possible HIPish direction: Choosing to control self versus others
- TIP direction Scaffolding: "Putting meat on the bones of his remark"
- TIP: Offering alternative explanation for Tom to use to help him manage temper
- It's in men's nature to be aggressive

Figure 7.9 Excerpt of clinical interview (Continued)

(an intern at CFTC) who had been working with the family for three interviews invited the family to the screening due to concerns that the elder son was acting in a controlling manner, "much like his father." The son was reported to have been aggressive with his younger sibling in the past. The family members seen in this interview were the mother (Mary), the elder son (Tom) who was in his mid-teens, and his younger brother (Bill) who was in early adolescence.

If one looks at some of the societal discourses identified in this transcript, for example, "A family needs a man" or "the perfect family," and were to frame questions to invite the clients to examine the beliefs associated with those discourses, the therapist might ask, "Where do you think those ideas about the ways families should be, and ideas about the role of fathers, come from?" "Do you think a *real family* has to have a man/father in it, or could a family like yours be a *real family*?" "What would be the qualities of a *real family* that you would value?" "Do you think that a single parent family can be strong and healthy?" Or, to invite reflection on the societal discourse of "It's in a guy's nature to want to hit stuff," possible questions to explore this could include, "Where do you think that idea came from that guys like to hit stuff?" "How strongly do you believe that idea?" "Do you think that idea is true for all men?" "Of the men in your acquaintance, who might have tried to resist that idea?" "Do you think your dad adhered to/was obedient to that idea about manhood?" If he says yes to the latter, one could ask, "What kind of difference do you think it might have made to your experience of him as a dad if he had resisted that idea about how to be a man?"

When I (Joanne) called Tom to ask for permission to use a section of the transcript of the interview for this chapter (a number of years after the session), he offered to come for a follow-up interview. I accepted his offer to see what changes he was making in his life since we ended our sessions (I had accepted the family in a transfer of care after the intern ended her rotation at the CFTC). A few points in our follow-up conversation were notable: Tom reported that he had a responsible job and had, with his employer's sponsorship, taken some college courses. He talked about having a strong work ethic, which he attributed to his father, who had since died. He also reported that he had been able to develop a better understanding of his father since his death and thus seemed to have developed an appreciation of his father's good intentions. He explained that he had invited his brother to live with him, an offer that his brother accepted, and he reported that they were getting along quite well. He shared how, despite his brother making poor choices at times, he was able to ask his brother questions to help him become more reflective about his situation rather than telling him what to do. He relayed that he had worked on his own patience and had made strides in this in a variety of contexts, and that he was no longer violent with his brother.

While we credit the client with his successes in this example, we would suggest that examining gender discourses can create opportunities to take a step back to look at gender issues in less threatening ways, since we are all subject to these ideas at some level, but may become less vulnerable to "obey" these ideas as we reflect upon them.

Conclusions

We believe that conversations on gender identities and gendered IPs provide opportunities for therapists to explore cultural discourses on gender with clients and help us address their influence on our lives. Rather than viewing gender as a rigid or unchangeable individual characteristic, we encourage therapists to consider gendered societal discourses and SCIPs as points-of-entry to revise, change, or create new and more preferred gendered identities and relational patterns. By examining gendered societal discourses, and related pathologizing and healing patterns, therapists may invite clients to reflect consciously upon their preferred identities and ways of being in relationship to others. Therapists and clients may also engage in co-constructing, through Transforming Interpersonal Patterns (TIPs) and HIPs, alternative ways of performing preferred identities in relationships (see Chapter 4). Additionally, we believe that it is crucial for training programs to include in their curricula opportunities for therapists-in-training to examine and explore ideas on gendered identities, related societal discourses, and how these impact relational dynamics. While we all start off as blind to the influence of these ideas and discourses in how we perform gender in relationships, the good news is that we can all come to see more and more of these societal influences on couple and family relationships through clarifying reflective conversation.

Notes

1 We would like to thank Sally St. George and Karl Tomm for their important contributions to this chapter.
2 For a description of what was occurring in home economics departments at many universities in the United States around this time period, the reader can refer to the chapter titled "The Men Move In: Home Economics, 1950–1970" (Rossiter, 1997).
3 Knudson-Martin and Laughlin (2005) highlight the salience of recognizing that it is not only the process of decision-making but also whose wishes tend to prevail that is important (i.e., shared decisions may "regularly support the husband's goals," p. 111).

References

Akamatsu, N. (2000). The talking oppression blues: Including the experience of power/powerlessness in the teaching of cultural sensitivity. In M. Olson (Ed.), *Feminism, community, and communication* (pp. 83–97). New York, NY: Haworth Press.

Almeida, R., Dolan-Del Vecchio, K., & Parker, L. (2008). *Transformative family therapy: Just families in a just society*. Boston, MA: Pearson Education.

Almeida, R. V. (1993). Unexamined assumptions and service delivery systems: Feminist theory and racial exclusions. *Journal of Feminist Family Therapy, 5*(1), 3–23. doi: 10.1300/J086v05n01_02

Almeida, R. V., & Durkin, T. (1999). The cultural context model: Therapy for couples with domestic violence. *Journal of Marital and Family Therapy, 25*(3), 313–324.

Aronson Fontes, L., & Thomas, V. (1996). Cultural issues in family therapy. In F. P. Piercy, D. H. Sprenkle, & J. L. Wetchler (Eds.), *Family therapy sourcebook* (pp. 256–282). New York, NY: Guilford Press.

Avis, J. M. (1988). Deepening awareness: A private study guide to feminism and family therapy. *Journal of Psychotherapy & the Family, 3*(4), 15–46. doi: 10.1300/J287v03n04_03

Barrymore, D. (Producer), & Kwapis, K. (Director). (2009). *He's just not that into you* [Motion picture]. United States: Warner Bros.

Burr, V. (2003). *Social constructionism* (2nd ed.). New York, NY: Routledge.

Falicov, C. J. (1983). Introduction. In J. C. Hansen & C. J. Falicov (Eds.), *Cultural perspectives in family therapy* (pp. xiii–xix). Rockville, MA: Aspen Systems.

Falicov, C. J. (1988). Learning to think culturally. In H. A. Liddle, D. C. Breunlin, & R. C. Schwartz (Eds.), *Handbook of family therapy training and supervision* (pp. 335–357). New York, NY: Guilford Press.

Goldner, V. (1985). Feminism and family therapy. *Family Process, 24*(1), 31–47. doi: 10.1111/j.1545-5300.1985.00031.x

Hare-Mustin, R. (1978). A feminist approach to family therapy. *Family Process, 17*(2), 181–194. doi: 10.1111/j.1545-5300.1978.00181.x

Hare-Mustin, R. (1994). Discourses in the mirrored room: A postmodern analysis of therapy. *Family Process, 33*(1), 19–35. doi: 10.1111/j.1545-5300.1994.00019.x

Hoffman, L. (1990). Constructing realities: An art of lenses. *Family Process, 29*(1), 1–12. doi: 10.1111/j.1545-5300.1990.00001.x

Hollway, W. (1984). Gender difference and the reduction of subjectivity. In J. Henriques, W. Hollway, C. Urwin, C. Venn, & V. Walkerdine (Eds.), *Changing the subject: Psychology, social regulation, and subjectivity* (pp. 227–263). New York, NY: Methuen.

Illouz, E. (2012). *Why love hurts?* Cambridge, UK: Polity Press.

Jenkins, A. (1997, November). *Invitations to responsibility: Working with men who have abused within their families*. Workshop at the Calgary Counselling Centre, Calgary, AB.

Keeney, B. (1983). *Aesthetics of change*. New York, NY: Guilford Press.

Knudson-Martin, C. (2013). Why power matters: Creating a foundation of mutual support in couple relationships. *Family Process, 52*(1), 5–18. doi: 10.1111/famp.12011

Knudson-Martin, C., & Laughlin, M. J. (2005). Gender and sexual orientation in family therapy: Toward a postgender approach. *Family Relations, 54*(1), 101–115. doi: 10.1111/j.0197-6664.2005.00009.x

Korin, E. C. (1994). Social inequalities and therapeutic relationships: Applying Freire's ideas to clinical practice. In R. V. Ameida (Ed.), *Expansions of feminist family theory through diversity* (pp. 75–98). New York, NY: Haworth Press.

McGoldrick, M. (1998). Introduction: Re-visioning family therapy through a cultural lens. In M. McGoldrick (Ed.), *Re-envisioning family therapy: Race, culture, and gender* (pp. 3–19). New York, NY: Guilford.

Nichols, M.P., & Schwartz, R.C. (Eds.). (2001). *Family therapy: Concepts and methods* (3rd ed.). Boston, MA: Allyn & Bacon.

Pease, B. (1997). *Men & sexual politics: Towards a pro-feminist practice*. Adelaide, South Australia: Dulwich Centre.

Rankin Mahoney, A., & Knudson-Martin, C. (2009). Gender equality in intimate relationships. In C. Knudson-Martin & A. Rankin Mahoney (Eds.), *Couples, gender, and power: Creating change in intimate relationships* (pp. 3–40). New York, NY: Springer.

Rossiter, M.W. (1997). The men move in: Home economics, 1950–1970. In S. Stage & V. Branble Vicenti (Eds.), *Rethinking home economics: Women and the history of a profession* (pp. 96–117). Ithaca, NY: Cornell University Press.

Sanders, G. (1993). The love that dares to speak its name: From secrecy to openness in gay and lesbian affiliations. In E. Imber-Black (Ed.), *Secrets in families and family therapy* (pp. 215–242). New York, NY: Norton.

Scruton, J. (Producer), & Kuntz, T. (Director). (2010). *Old Spice—THE man your man could smell like* [TV commercial]. United States: Wieden+Kennedy.

Tamasese, K. (2000). *Talking about culture and gender: An interview with Kiwi Tamasese*. Adelaide, South Australia: Dulwich Centre. Retrieved from www.narrativetherapylibrary.com/media/downloadable/files/links/g/e/gendcult_2.pdf

Taylor, C. (1994). The politics of recognition. In A. Gutmann (Ed.), *Multiculturalism: Examining the politics of recognition* (pp. 25–74). Princeton, NJ: Princeton University Press.

Todd, N. (2010). The invitations of irresponsibility: Utilizing excuses in counselling with men who have been abusive. *Journal of Systemic Therapies, 29*(3), 65–81. doi: 10.1521/jsyt.2010.29.3.65

8
SENSING, UNDERSTANDING, AND MOVING BEYOND INTERCULTURAL PIPS

Inés Sametband, Tamara Wilson, and Chee-Ping Tsai

Introduction

"Culture is the one thing we cannot deliberately aim at."
—T. S. Eliot (1948, p. 19)

As clinicians, our (Inés, Tamara, and Chee-Ping) initial training was influenced by theorists promoting multicultural competence (e.g., Aronson Fontes & Thomas, 1996; Bezanson & James, 2007; Falicov, 1995; McGoldrick & Hardy, 2008). We believe that these guidelines helped in raising awareness of ethnocentric views that historically influenced therapeutic relationships and the mental health professions in general. However, our view now is that more can be done to ensure that cultural differences are not only recognized but also spoken about and negotiated in therapeutic conversations. By doing so, we believe that therapists can identify and move beyond interpersonal patterns that promote and sustain discourses of unfair privilege and social injustice. We describe how practitioners at the Calgary Family Therapy Centre (CFTC) using the IPscope found ways out of rigid, reified cultural interactions (Pathologizing Interpersonal Patterns or PIPs) to engage in culturally negotiated ones (Healing Interpersonal Patterns or HIPs) by bringing forth new therapeutic distinctions to the culturally-laden issues that are often part of their practice.[1] In this chapter, we focus on how therapists may find ways to move forward in conversations with clients beyond seemingly irreconcilable cultural practices.

About the Authors

I (Inés) am a Caucasian woman born in Argentina who comes from a family in which immigration has been a recurring practice. My maternal great-grandparents and grandparents moved from Lithuania and Ukraine to Argentina before World War I, my paternal grandparents and my father from Poland to Argentina before World War II, and part of my extended family moved to Israel and Spain in the 1970s. Growing up, it was not easy to understand or explain my cultural identity: a mix of middle class, European, Argentinian, and non-religious Jewish values. When I moved to Canada, I was faced again with the complexity of explaining my cultural background and often experienced what it feels like to be stereotyped. Many assume that because I am from South America, I am of Spanish descent and Catholic. To make matters more complicated, when I go back to Argentina, many assume that living in Canada means that I am doing very well financially. How we relationally create, maintain, and manage our situated cultural identities is something that I am very interested in and hope to continue researching.

I (Tamara) am a Black woman who was born and raised in a small farming community outside of Edmonton, Alberta, Canada. My parents emigrated from St. Lucia, West Indies, and somehow found their way to Lamont, Alberta. Given that the population of this town was approximately 1,700 people, we were the only Caribbean family to ever set foot in the community. This brought with it a myriad of questions and limited understandings from some members of the community. However, it also presented some wonderful opportunities to educate and enlighten others about being Black. While the majority of my experiences with my peers were very positive, I recall feeling quite oppressed in my early school years by teachers and other school personnel. Although I am Canadian, I felt very different and at times isolated because of my cultural ethnicity. Interestingly, I also noticed some reoccurring stereotypes that emerged from family and friends from St. Lucia who assumed that life abroad meant instant success and riches, again leading to feelings of being misunderstood and isolated. It was these experiences that led to becoming more curious not only about others' experiences but also about how their cultural uniqueness is addressed and utilized in therapeutic settings.

I (Chee-Ping) am an Asian woman who was born and lived with my family in Hong Kong until my early 20s. My journey with culture began at birth, when I was given a traditional male name. Chee-Ping means leading a country and being the world peacekeeper. Also, growing up as the only girl and being the youngest child in my family, I enjoyed many privileges and freedoms, especially considering that, traditionally, Chinese sons are entitled to more privileges than daughters. My cultural experiences have been expanded by living in both Hong Kong and Canada. Social interactions with people from other cultures not only allowed me to learn about cultures different from mine but also opened opportunities for me to reflect on my own culture, my own well-being, and my evolving identity. I appreciate that people were interested in my culture, which made me feel unique, even though I am a visible minority. Moreover, I appreciate and enjoy the similarities and differences across individuals. Among many lessons learned, one that stays close to my heart is that culture permeates through interactions with others every moment as we all are living in it. This first-hand lived experience has sparked my interest, awareness, and sensitivity to cultural issues within a therapeutic context.

Cultures as Degrees of Difference

We understand cultures as ways of living (Monk, Winslade, & Sinclair, 2008)—that is, as peoples' shared practices and ways of relating, including the cultural discourses (see Chapter 6) through which these practices and relatings make sense. These cultural discourses are present in our conversations with each other (e.g., in the words of the language we speak), in how we understand and engage in different social practices (e.g., greetings, rites of passage, parenting activities), in how we perform our memberships in particular cultural groups (e.g., using a burka, or a Mohawk hairstyle), and in how we account for who we are as cultural beings. We usually assume that people around us share the same way of understanding and going about life, but when we encounter differences we are invited into foreign (to us) cultural practices, or when we are exposed to different Socio-Cultural Interpersonal Patterns (SCIPs) than the ones we are accustomed to, tensions over what those differences mean may become more apparent.

How we do things culturally (or locally) can be seen in simple practices such as setting the dinner table: some people use bowls or light candles, and others have specific rules about who sits where. Sitting at a dinner table is not usually a controversial issue, and even if we do not like the dinner setting rules, it is quite easy for most of us to adopt them as a courtesy toward our hosts. However, when the cultural practices are more contentious or hold opposite or varied meanings for different people, engaging in doing things together becomes more difficult. The parties involved are then faced with alternative options for how to go forward; these could include ignoring the differences and keeping the tension inside, acknowledging differences from their own culture, explaining what these differences mean to themselves and to others, negotiating a new meaningful way forward, passing demeaning judgments upon others, protesting in ways that are respectful, protesting in ways that could lead to increasing conflict, or blatantly imposing one's cultural preferences upon others (guaranteed to generate conflict).

It could be said that every encounter is intercultural[2] to some degree. Cultures, as ways of living, may be only slightly different (i.e., how partners set the dinner table, understand parenting, or participate in a classroom) or drastically different (i.e., speaking different languages, holding opposite values, embracing different religious beliefs, or enacting different citizens' rights and obligations within different political systems). When the degree of cultural differences among people is significant, we believe that new, negotiated HIPs and Wellness Interpersonal Patterns (WIPs) may need to be created to develop and maintain meaningful relationships. It may be necessary to push ourselves out of familiar Interpersonal Patterns (IPs) (i.e., influenced by SCIPs we are accustomed to) to unknown or unaccustomed ways of relating with one another. At times however, the degree of difference in how we understand and do things culturally is so important or vital to us that we feel unnerved by the prospect of altering them, sensing that it is too risky to venture into unknown IPs.

In therapeutic conversations, we see ourselves (as therapists) and clients habituating to each other's responses according to what we understand to be culturally appropriate or fitting, consistent with how all of us orient to, and are influenced by, particular socio-cultural discourses. For example, family members may view their relationship with a clinician as one in which advice-giving is coupled with receiving and accepting advice (e.g., influenced by a discourse of expertism). In contrast, a therapist may try to orient his or her interaction with clients from a collaborative and discursive stance (e.g., being curious and inviting openness or sharing). When these differing cultures about therapy meet, family members and therapists may need to work out their understandings of the therapeutic encounter (e.g., collaborative, advice-giving, or something else) to engage effectively. By keeping their interactions acceptably familiar (see Chapter 4) therapists and clients may orient more easily toward more TIPish (from Transforming Interpersonal Patterns) and HIPish conversations.

Developing a Relational Intercultural Sensitivity

In the same way that we recognize our sensitivity to heat, and learn not to put our hands directly into a fire when we want to get warm, as therapists we may need to learn what we call *relational intercultural sensitivity* to avoid getting burned by cultural differences. In our conversations with others, we see ourselves as relationally sensitive in how we sense and make sense of each other's responses when we become curious (e.g., ask questions) or are moved (e.g., become teary) as a response to someone's story that evokes values that are important to us. In contrast, we may respond in a relationally insensitive manner by becoming dismissive or disengaged (e.g., dismissing the other person's account in favor of our own ways of making sense about an experience) when someone's story evokes something that is too strange, or that we see as reproachable. In our work, we use Tomm's (1987) interventive interviewing approach for developing a heightened consciousness while interviewing clients, which involves developing a sensitivity to ongoing cues within the therapeutic system. We feel that developing this sensitivity to actual effects can be particularly useful as a way to orient to, and acknowledge others' and our own, understandings of the tensions between cultural sameness and differences and the influence of those tensions in our interactions.

Developing a relational intercultural sensitivity may help therapists prevent or find ways out of Deteriorating Interpersonal Patterns (DIPs) and PIPs, especially when peoples' cultural ways of being and doing things are seen in absolute terms (e.g., correct/incorrect or true/false). We see these seemingly inescapable traps or objectionable conversations as what is commonly called a "culture clash." We view these culture clashes as maintaining and promoting differences in privileges and entitlements (Tomm, 2011), and associated with discourses of certainty, privilege, and violence (see Chapters 6 and 11). Sadly, at a macro social level, we see many devastating examples of these culture clashes (e.g., slavery, Western colonization, the Holocaust). The magnitude and complexity of these historical examples exceed the scope of this chapter; however, on a more micro level, we believe that in some occasions conflicting socio-cultural discourses operate at the forefront in therapeutic interactions (see Chapters 5 and 6 for an extended discussion and examples of SCIPs associated with PIPs), and we will focus on these occurrences for the remainder of this chapter.

We believe that a useful way to develop or enhance relational intercultural sensitivity is to first recognize and acknowledge that clients' and therapists' interactions are oriented to and influenced by a variety of different cultural discourses. Any particular cultural discourse can effectively explain some behaviors and interactions but may also limit generative dialogue, perhaps unintentionally leading to oppressive practices. For example, people from Western societies are often described as individualistic and as putting their individual interests first, while non-Western groups are often defined as collectivistic and as placing family or community first. While these depictions could resonate as accurate for many, their generalizing and stereotyping effects limit how people from these cultural groups understand and relate to one another (Waldegrave, 2012).

Totalizing cultural assumptions can lure participants into discursively captured systems (see Chapter 2) whereby behaviors are interpreted and responded to as fitting only into rigid categories (e.g., "individualistic" or "collectivistic"). When, in conversations together, our responses to each other are experienced as unacceptable (see Chapter 4)—that is, when our cultural views "clash"—we may find ourselves reacting strongly to other people's attitudes and actions. This may lead us (e.g., therapists and clients) to engage in DIPs (e.g., *misunderstanding and failing to clarify coupled with responding with ambiguity or confusion*), which could deteriorate into PIPs (e.g., *defining the other's beliefs and practices as wrong coupled with rejecting the judgments with indignation and contempt*). Thus, we need to continually orient our intercultural relational sensitivity to the SCIPs that are being sustained, developed, or challenged in our conversations with clients. With a process of turn-by-turn negotiating of objectionable meanings into acceptable meanings (Strong & Tomm, 2007), we can reorient to our conversations in culturally respectful ways. We will focus on such possibilities next.

From Culture Clashes to Acceptable Intercultural IPs

We find that by developing a habit of looking at problematic cultural issues through the lens of the IPscope, we are much less likely to become polarized by cultural differences and are more likely to jointly find ways forward. No matter how experienced or skillful we may be as therapists, it is easy for us to recall times when we felt stuck in our efforts to develop constructive conversations with our clients, times when we needed to turn to further resources (e.g., supervision, consultation, videotape review) in order to find a way forward. It has also been our experience that on some occasions, the tension between clients' and our own cultural ways of being and understanding was quite challenging—to the point that the emotional charge was surprising, sometimes frustrating, and even powerlessness-inducing. We understand these tension-filled conversations or culture clashes as occasions in which SCIPs enacted by clients and therapists in conversations may seem radically unfamiliar, almost invasive, and hence too disagreeable to be negotiated. When the resultant PIPs (and associated SCIPs) are not recognized, the apparent irreconcilability of these differing ways of understanding and being between parties in the therapeutic conversation may draw us further into a DIP or a different PIP, rather than allow movement toward a TIP, a HIP, and eventually a WIP.

We find it useful to differentiate between two types of PIPs (see Chapter 1): those that are mutually and bilaterally destructive, and those that are unbalanced in that one party seems to benefit from occupying a more dominant position in the pattern. We focus in this chapter on the latter kind of PIPs, as we view these more closely related to culture clashes, due to their association with discourses of certainty, privilege, and violence, as discussed earlier. For example, in one of the most malignant PIPs that maintains injustice (i.e., *oppressing coupled with submitting*) we see the person engaged in oppressive practices as benefiting (in terms of maintaining privilege and access to resources) compared to the person who submits to those oppressive practices (with a caveat that the benefits that accrue to the oppressor may also be limiting and harmful to him/her when adopting a larger contextual perspective). An example of this may occur when as therapists, we presume we possess greater knowledge than clients, focus on all their problems and deficits, and initiate a PIP of imposing our "professional truth" upon them. Within this discourse of professionalism, we maintain a position of privilege that contributes to disempowering clients, implying that they need continuing help from us as professionals. By submitting to our "superior" knowledge, they unwittingly diminish their own potential generativity for preferred changes in their own lives. Within this unbalanced PIP, we live the illusion of winning as they lose, when in fact we both lose (in that poor client outcomes imply ineffective therapists).

We believe that becoming more sensitive to practices related to injustice and inequality can be very helpful in our work with clients. In trying to recognize and become more aware of PIPs associated with inequality and injustice, we started using the phrase "pulling the culture card" to refer to a process of claiming a position of entitlement and dominance in certain domains of interaction. Although the action of pulling a card may be seen as individually-oriented at first, we see this move as someone's last-resort power play in an interaction involving a culture clash. For example, when a person experiences his or her cultural values or practices as misunderstood or disrespected, he or she may utter something like "this is the way we do it in my culture" to strongly assert the importance of one's preferred position and values. This seemingly closed remark or conversation stopper (T. Strong, personal communication, May 29, 2013) may be pointing to how some cultural practices or discourses are (mis)understood or disrespected by conversational partners.

It may appear as if the action of pulling a card (by invoking a particular SCIP as the only way to understand a situation) puts an end to a certain conversation. We propose, instead, that pulling the culture card be seen as an invitation to revise and re-orient an interaction, calling the respondent's attention to how totalizing assumptions about him- or herself or others may be influencing his or her interaction (e.g., people from collectivistic cultures defer to authority, or Canadians are distant). That is, rather than responding to pulling the culture card by pulling another card, which would further sustain a PIP or slip into DIP, we see these occurrences as opportunities for therapists to consider how SCIPs invoked in the conversation may be limiting possibilities of understanding. In our work, we found it useful to keep in mind some of the following questions when trying to implement some relational intercultural sensitivity:

- What might I (the therapist) be missing in this situation?
- If someone asked the family I was working with if I was respectful/sensitive to their cultural ways of being and relating, what might they

say? What do I imagine the family might say about how I (therapist) showed them respect?
- What injustices or privileges does this culture card point to?
- If someone asked the family I was working with if I was sensitive to the injustices they face, how might they respond?
- How do I respond when I experience some social injustice?
- What is it about this family's story that frustrates/paralyzes/oppresses me in my relationship with them? How do I respond to this frustration? How do they respond to my response? What does that say about our therapeutic relationship?

In the following section we provide a variety of scenarios illustrating intercultural interactional patterns between therapists and clients that resulted in PIPs or DIPs, and brief discussions on how these situations could have been dealt with differently. Following our examples, we share further reflections on how therapists may respond in helpful ways.

Possible Intercultural Orientations to HIPs and WIPs

Scenario 1. *In my early work with families, I (Tamara) worked at a program facilitating groups for parents whose children were exhibiting behavioral or emotional difficulties. The program's curriculum was grounded in Euro-centric teachings; however, at the time it appeared that most of the families (the majority were North American) who participated shared similar values. This assumption of shared values evaporated quickly when a family of Caribbean descent enrolled in the program. Sandy,[3] a single mother of two girls, was quite vocal about not having her family participate in some of the program practices. For example, we started each group session with a relaxation exercise (deep breathing, progressive relaxation, visualization), but Sandy refused to participate in the activity, indicating it was against her religious and spiritual beliefs. We (the staff involved) labelled Sandy's stance as resisting our views, engaging in a PIP* (condemning judgment coupled with distancing; see Figure 8.1).

On some occasions, pulling the culture card may be seen as an invitation to engage in a PIP or a DIP, such as *totalizing coupled with submitting or resisting*. In this scenario, Sandy's refusal to participate due to religious and spiritual beliefs can be seen as responding to what she may have experienced as oppressive—the imposition of a practice contrary to her beliefs. Although unintentionally, the therapists involved in this interaction presented the program's curriculum and exercises as the right way or the only way to do things, thereby closing down dialogue and reducing opportunities to collaborate. Upon reflection, Sandy's remark could have been seen as an invitation both to acknowledge (and even welcome) a conversation regarding differences.

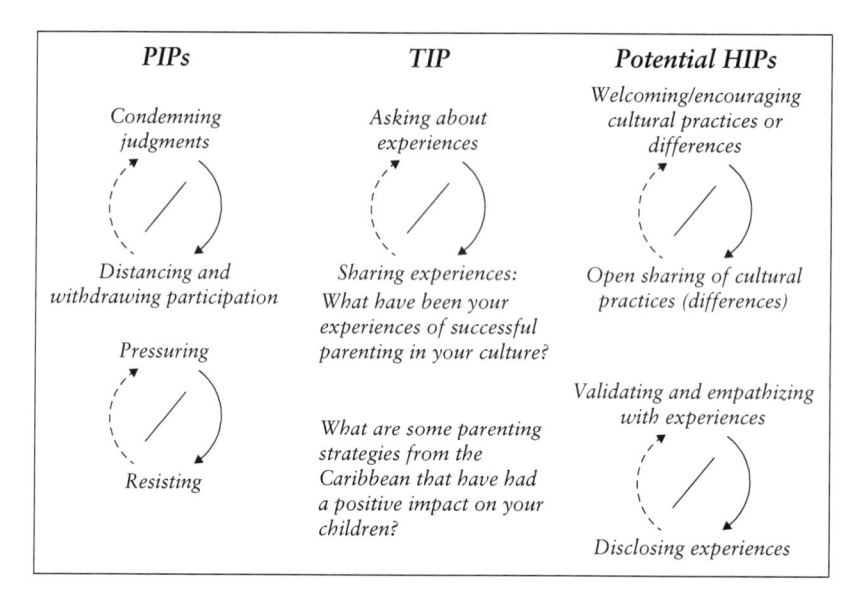

PIPs	*TIP*	*Potential HIPs*
Condemning judgments ↻ Distancing and withdrawing participation	Asking about experiences ↻ Sharing experiences: What have been your experiences of successful parenting in your culture?	Welcoming/encouraging cultural practices or differences ↻ Open sharing of cultural practices (differences)
Pressuring ↻ Resisting	What are some parenting strategies from the Caribbean that have had a positive impact on your children?	Validating and empathizing with experiences ↻ Disclosing experiences

Figure 8.1 Moving from PIPs to a TIP and potential HIPs in Scenario 1

As the weeks passed, we (the staff) failed to understand Sandy's perspective and her distancing from the program in any new ways. Instead, we continued to see the family as unreasonably resistant, thereby sustaining the PIP. On one particular evening, the focus of the parent group session centered on increasing parents' listening skills and opening space for freer expression of feelings and concerns from their child (a potential HIP). During the discussion, Sandy commented that allowing children to speak their minds to their parents was disrespectful. In addition, she stated that parents who would allow such a practice would be considered weak by others in her community and in no way was she willing to be laughed at by her family and friends.

Rather than viewing the program's proposed ideas as constructive, Sandy regarded the ideas as unhelpful and destructive for her family and her community. For her, the parenting skills that were discussed in the group had a different meaning than the one intended by the staff. We see this situation as a culture clash. In retrospect we missed an opportunity to engage in a more generative conversation regarding the SCIPs involved (e.g., becoming curious about the importance of community acceptance for Sandy, exploring other parents' relationships with community and their views on its importance). Exploring these SCIPs would have been a TIP attempt to initiate a HIP of *validating cultural experiences and practices coupled with disclosing cultural experiences*, which could have resulted in a very different outcome.

Interestingly, my West Indian roots had very little impact on my understanding of Sandy's perspective as I still found myself engaged in a PIP of judging Sandy as resistant coupled with Sandy's distancing. *An additional PIP of* pressuring coupled with resisting *also emerged from the frustration I felt toward Sandy. I was working extremely hard to convince her that her stance was wrong and this Western perspective would work better with her family. Upon reflection, my frustration and annoyance were the first of many signs that could have served as a way for me to recognize that I was stuck in a problematic interaction. I found myself attempting to convince Sandy rather than being genuinely curious about her cultural ways; more simply said, because I was emotionally charged and defensive, I could not resist pushing my own agenda. If I had paid closer attention to the atmosphere within the conversation—that is, the oppositional, almost hostile manner in which Sandy and I were responding to one another—I could have seen that a shift in therapeutic posture was required.*

A second indicator that I needed to orient myself to the culture card that was played was the strong physiological reaction I experienced; my heart was racing, my face was hot, and my muscles were tense—most likely a response to the frustration. A third cue that I missed was Sandy's body language. She had initially been vocal and defensive but later became subdued and eventually withdrew completely from the discussion, refusing to even make eye contact. Further, the entire group of parents, who had initially been offering their ideas about the potential HIP (expressing freely coupled with listening actively), became silent during my discussion with Sandy, which again speaks to the atmosphere within the room. I eventually decided to end the discussion because of time constraints, and Sandy and her family pulled out of the program. In retrospect, I realize that I had been unwittingly restricted by an institutional discourse that was associated with a PIP of pressuring coupled with submitting. *And perhaps, it is this pattern* (feeling institutional pressure coupled with submitting to institutional practices) *that is associated with a discourse of privileging professional/institutional authority.*

We (therapists and clients) are influenced by particular institutional discourses (the institution in which the therapy takes place, for example) and SCIPs that we take up such that our interactions become more limited. Cultural discourses are often adopted as the only way to see things, as constituting the right way. Influenced by desperation, tiredness, or frustration, pulling the culture card may be seen by therapists as the only viable option to move forward in their conversations with clients just as it may be seen as the only option for clients to use with their therapists. As therapists, we may believe that we are professionally or ethically obligated to impose certain views in a conversation. However, the consequences of doing so may be that we contribute to practices of oppression and the appropriation of privilege.

After debriefing with my supervisor and staff team, I recognized that my upbringing in Canada had woven Western philosophies into my cultural identity, and these philosophies often guided my point-of-view and subsequent decisions when working with families. At the time, I was not able to make sense of Sandy's position, nor was I able to see that Sandy and I (and my colleagues) were orienting to and influenced by very different SCIPs. I wonder what might have been Sandy's response had I shared with her that "I realize that in my attempts to convince you that allowing your child to have a voice is beneficial, I was actually trying to push a cultural practice on you that does not fit with your views of parenting." And while I intended to be wellness-based, I failed to recognize Sandy's cultural practices as worthy, which could have helped to increase her confidence as a parent. It may have been helpful to ask, "What could our parenting practices here in Canada learn from the parenting practices from the Caribbean?"

This scenario demonstrates that culture clashes may be present (if more subtly) in conversations among people from the same cultural group. In these interactions, an assumption of sameness may overshadow differences in how people view or understand experience, or the kinds of SCIPs to which they orient.

We thought of some possibly helpful questions that might have opened space for a greater understanding of SCIPs in this scenario:

- What are some parenting practices from your community that you think might be useful to bring into our group?
- Who in your family/community would be most impacted if you took a different perspective to parenting?
- Are there certain standards of behavior in your community that you have questioned?
- Who else in the group can appreciate the importance of having extended family/community around you when it comes to parenting?
- What have been your experiences parenting in a culture that promotes a different belief?

In the next scenario we describe how therapists and clients may get stuck in assuming sameness in how they view and understand social practices and reflect on some potential ways to get out of being stuck.

Scenario 2. *I (Chee-Ping) was working with a young father, Arthur, who expressed his concern about his adoptive daughter, Alyssa, who was lacking motivation and effort in her studies. During one of the sessions, Arthur asserted the value of academic excellence in order to be successful in life, especially for someone from a visible minority. Further, Arthur indicated that I would agree with his views because we had emigrated from the same country. While I appreciated Arthur's good intentions of* *caring for his daughter, I felt pressured to align with him, which was very uncomfortable (i.e., experienced as having a big knot in my stomach). Even while I felt coercion, I valued my right to make my own decisions and thus rejected Arthur's expectation of me to join him in lecturing his daughter on the importance of education. My response was to try opening space to invite participation from Alyssa, hoping to understand her position regarding her father's concern and her ideas about education. However, Arthur continued to interrupt and tried harder to tell Alyssa how important education was for her own good. I experienced myself resisting this telling approach, and so did Alyssa. The more Arthur engaged in telling, the more I engaged in resisting, co-creating a PIP. Unfortunately, Arthur and Alyssa discontinued therapy after this conversation.*

On further reflection, I could have been more empathic toward Arthur explicitly. For instance, I could have raised reflexive questions to understand his view of the importance of education based upon his personal experiences and cultural perspectives. Moreover, I could have initiated an open discussion with Arthur about my experience of our cultural values clashing, and the PIP in which we were trapped. By opening space for him to feel heard (and also to listen to other alternatives), hopefully he would have joined me in getting unstuck from the PIP. While I oriented toward discourses promoting individual autonomy in decision-making (a stereotypical Western value), Arthur oriented toward discourses supporting children following parental advice (a stereotypical Chinese value). Furthermore, it appeared that both Arthur and I saw ourselves as authorities (e.g., the therapist having professional knowledge and the father owning parental power).

In this scenario, cultural sameness seemed to make it more difficult to appreciate that the client's and therapist's cultural values were understood differently. It seemed that strong and implicit expectations were brought into the relationship (e.g., "You must agree with me as we both are Chinese immigrants from Hong Kong"), inviting me to align with Arthur, which ran counter to my collaborative stance toward constructive change. Bringing forth, speaking about, or grappling with uncomfortable cultural tensions in conversations may be new ways to initiate TIPish or HIPish conversations with clients. Further, we see these cultural tensions in their extreme form (i.e., culture clashes) as pointing to ways in which inequality may be perpetuated in a relationship, and an opportunity to do something about it.

Our hope in sharing these scenarios is to show how intercultural competence extends far beyond learning about clients' cultural practices or attending to their cultural activities. Maintaining relational intercultural sensitivity requires us to both develop an awareness of cultural differences and orient ourselves to the cues in our immediate context that guide us in responding more respectfully and effectively to clients. As we reflect on these scenarios, it becomes more clear that bringing attention to and negotiating ways in which all cultural practices are recognized can be one possible way of promoting more social justice.

Stepping Beyond PIPs and DIPs Associated With Privilege Discourses

We recognize that in some way or another, most of us, or at least the three of us (Tamara, Chee-Ping, and Inés) are part of non-dominant groups (e.g., according to socio-economic status, gender, race). However, it seems to us that discussions around discourses of racial privilege or racism (e.g., Monk, Winslade, & Sinclair, 2008; Ridley, 2005) are less often originated by therapists. As we reflect on our conversations with clients, we must ask how often differences in understanding race and discourses of race privilege play a leading role in the PIPs and DIPs that emerge from therapeutic conversations.

We view the culture card at play in our conversations with clients, at times overtly, and sometimes covertly. In addition to our sense of this card at times pointing to IPs that interfere with ways forward in conversations, we consider that orienting to the card and bringing it into conversations creates opportunities for us (therapists and clients in conversations) to name injustices (Tamasese & Waldegrave, 1994). By doing so, we recognize and acknowledge how cultural discourses play a role in maintaining relationships of inequality and injustice, such as *silencing cultural practices coupled with rebelling to cultural practices*. In the next scenario, we explore how therapists collaborate with clients in exploring how discourses associated with privilege and injustice may be at play in the problems they are facing.

Scenario 3. *Karl, a therapist and supervisor, was consulted by an intern (Mary) who was working with an Indigenous family consisting of Janine, the mother, and her 8-year-old son, Ted. They were referred to family therapy due to Ted's behavior at school (i.e., fighting, biting, and kicking). Ted's behavior was not problematic at home, and Janine had been protesting the school staff's methods of dealing with Ted's behavior (e.g., questioning her parenting skills and sending her family to therapy) by complaining about the school staff's judgmental attitude toward her family. Karl and Mary connected with the school's resource teacher to gather more information about the situation and inquired if there were any issues of racism at the school. They learned from the resource teacher that these issues had been ruled out by the school staff. Janine described Ted as being very cooperative and helpful at home, but at school he engaged in all kinds of aggressive behaviors. Given that Ted's behavior was problematic only at school, and that Janine protested that things were unfair at the school, Karl and Mary wondered if something in the context in* *which Ted was showing the problematic behavior was contributing to it. They proposed that a meeting of the family and the school staff be held at the school to discuss the situation.*

Once at the meeting with the school authorities and the family, Karl focused on asking clarifying questions tracking the sequence of the problematic situations, trying to understand the context of the unacceptable behavior described by the school staff in which Ted was involved. For example, he asked questions that helped track a problematic situation. When the teacher said, "He bit the girl," Karl asked, "What happened before he bit the girl?" "What were the children doing or saying?" By doing this, he learned from the teachers that there usually had been a demeaning comment from another child to Ted before he would respond with aggression (i.e., kicking, biting). Karl engaged with the staff and the family in a TIP (*asking about details of events coupled with increasing awareness of the sequencing of events*). As sequences of events were clarified by the group, everyone learned that all the problematic situations involved acts of provocation from other children. Karl went on to ask, "To what extent did the other children feel justified in provoking Ted because he was Aboriginal?" and "Which initiatives by the other kids did Ted experience as unfair?" Through this TIPish conversation, it became apparent that Ted was demeaned, criticized, and excluded largely because he was Indigenous, and he responded by kicking and fighting, which perpetuated a PIP of *rejecting/disqualifying/demeaning coupled with further protesting and fighting back*.

The school staff, by evaluating Ted's aggressive behavior out of context and disqualifying it, actually contributed to the same PIP (see Figure 8.2). What is more, their description implicitly conveyed the idea that there was something wrong with Ted, and by default with the boy's mother (i.e., Janine was seen as not able to raise her child, who misbehaved). Further, Janine protesting (e.g., expressing her view of the school staff as being unfair) the school staff's approach to the situation could have initiated a DIP of protesting and blaming if the school staff felt criticized by

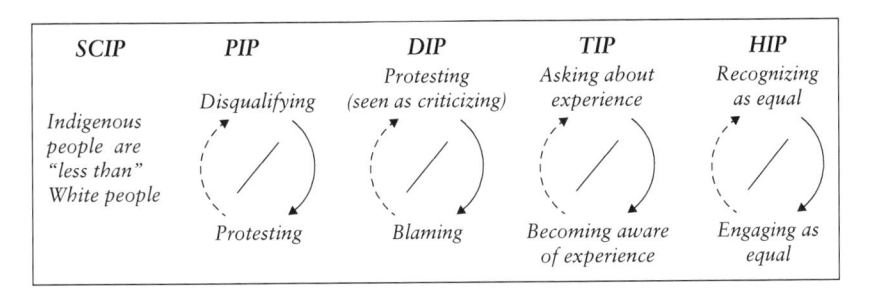

SCIP	PIP	DIP	TIP	HIP
Indigenous people are "less than" White people	Disqualifying ↘ ↖ Protesting	Protesting (seen as criticizing) ↘ ↖ Blaming	Asking about experience ↘ ↖ Becoming aware of experience	Recognizing as equal ↘ ↖ Engaging as equal

Figure 8.2 Moving from injustice to a HIP in Scenario 3

her. Although we cannot be certain, some of the discourses we see associated with these PIPs are those of privilege and racism. After these PIPs were recognized by the school staff, and alternative ways of understanding Ted's behavior were "tried on" by them, Ted's problematic behaviors vanished completely.

By asking questions to explore the possibility that Ted's problematic behavior could be a response to being treated unfairly, Karl invited the school staff to reflect and comment on what Ted was responding to when he protested along with any interactions they might have missed or dismissed. This, in turn, provided relief for Janine and Ted, who could take a break from protesting and rebelling against the injustice and instead focus their efforts toward HIPs or WIPs for further integration in the school community. It also allowed the school staff to change their approach to the situation, and Janine was invited to appreciate their actions. Following the meeting at the school, both the problematic behavior and the unjust and discriminatory patterns dissolved. As previously mentioned, PIPs involving social injustice and inequity can be perpetuated or deconstructed in therapy. We propose disclosing and/or naming the injustice (Tamasese & Waldegrave, 1994) as useful steps to move toward new, creative ways of relating that are more just for everyone involved.

In our conversations with clients, we position ourselves in accord with how we understand racial differences and we perform according to those understandings. By speaking from our familiarity with different SCIPs, we may assume (perhaps erroneously) that our understanding of race is the same as that of our clients. By not checking with others if our assumptions fit with their experience, we could inadvertently contribute to discourses of racial privilege. Many of us have read and perhaps witnessed how racism dehumanizes and marginalizes minorities (Pedersen, 1995); however, how is this issue of differences explored and navigated by the therapist who herself is being oppressed?

Scenario 4. *While I (Tamara) have never been faced with overt racism when working with clients, I can recall situations where I wondered whether racism played a role in a client's overt rudeness or reluctance to continue with therapy. The difficulty in most of these situations was the subtlety of the responses from the client (e.g., a refusal to shake hands, a lack of eye contact, questioning of credentials). And because of this subtlety, I have been left with the question of whether or not to bring this up with clients. Even entertaining this viewpoint could have major implications. Part of my challenge and fear originates from certain beliefs instilled by my parents, who always asserted that acknowledging racial privilege shows weakness toward individuals from the dominant culture and would lead to being discredited in the workplace. I, too, am now* *very much governed by this perspective to remain silent in my noticing, and unless the form of racism is overt, I tend to be cautious when moving forward. If I assume that a particular clash is in fact an issue of privileging one race (i.e., Caucasian) and I am wrong, there is potential for me to slip into a DIP or PIP such as* acting rude/hesitating to participate coupled with stereotyping *("they must be racist"), which could later lead to feeling stereotyped and hence invite a PIP of* withdrawing coupled with giving up. *However, if I am correct in recognizing that there is an issue of racial privileging and remain silent, do I collude in maintaining or supporting the status quo, and subsequently miss an opportunity to question or mount a gentle inquiry or protest that could be the beginnings of a TIP, HIP, or WIP? Or do I risk the potential for a different PIP to emerge if I refrain from speaking up and allow the issue of privileging to be perpetuated* (e.g., remaining silent coupled with oppressing)?

Bringing up issues of injustice and inequality does not need to be awkward, but unfortunately it usually is. This may be partially due to cultural discourses that also inform clinicians' perspectives (e.g., "This isn't racism, I'm simply paranoid," or "I'm worried I will insult someone") and therefore aid in maintaining some of the oppressive practices/behaviors that we as therapists face. But it is in small moves such as raising the issue of racism with colleagues that we might reduce injustice. Forthright and honest discussions among colleagues can open space for therapists to develop increased confidence in addressing racial privileges and injustice within the therapy room. Speaking up about how we see racism affecting our (and others') relationships may help therapists both to recognize SCIPs associated with discourses supporting racism in therapeutic conversations and to respond in ways that invite alternative views (TIPs or HIPs).

When addressing issues of privilege, our goal is to work collectively in understanding and deconstructing the discourses or SCIPs associated with privilege that may constrain us all (therapists and clients). For example, faced with assumptions such as "Blacks are not smart enough," or "Muslims do not understand the rules of this country," we (therapists) may need to take a step back to recognize the ways in which discourses of privilege may be influencing our relationships with clients. Orienting to recognizing the SCIPs that may be at play in our presuppositions, we may be able to invite others in co-creating new and healthier SCIPs. However, this is easier said than done.

In our experience, we find it helpful to slow down the conversation (i.e., by asking clients to give us a moment to collect our thoughts, proposing a break, summarizing the main points of the conversation, checking in with clients to see if we are on the right track). Sometimes, this may be enough for us to re-orient ourselves to our relational intercultural sensitivity. We may ask ourselves or our clients, "What else am I/are you experiencing right now? What is my/your body telling me/you that I/you may have not recognized yet? What would be a word to describe it? What does it tell you/me/us about our relationship? How would you/me/we want to continue now that we have recognized this?"

We encourage therapists to orient to the relational nature of the intercultural sensitivity by operating from a place of commitment and trust. Trust can be mutually beneficial and demonstrated by showing genuine curiosity of other's differing realities, which can invite lowered defensiveness from the client/family. Commitment requires a willingness to "face the storm" when tensions in the relationship run high (Pizana, 2003). Once trust is established, inviting family members to engage in a transforming dialogue (TIPs) of the ways racism and/or privileging has impacted their lives and the lives of others may create openings for greater understanding and subsequent actions. Here is a list of questions that may be used to open up the dialogue surrounding racial privileging. One might state or ask,

- I want to ask a really hard question, but I'm not sure if it will be heard in the way that I intend.
- In what ways does the problem we are facing here in therapy reflect race differences?
- To what degree would you say ethnic differences might have an effect on how we are relating right now?
- What have encounters with others outside of your cultural heritage been like for you/your family?

These questions can be used as ways to address the "elephant in the room" and to decide, together, what to do with the elephant—that is, recognizing cultural discourses that promote privilege and opening space to collaborate in deciding how to approach the influence of these discourses in relationships.

Conclusions

"If it is useful to not be blind, how can we learn to open our eyes and not be overwhelmed by the negative feelings that may rush in when we recognize our own collusion with patterns of injustice?"
—K. Tomm (personal communication, May 10, 2013)

In this chapter, we invited readers into a different view on what are commonly known as culture clashes. Rather than viewing these encounters as dead ends, we propose that culture clashes are poignant and fertile opportunities to re-orient ourselves in our conversations with clients, so that culturally different ways of being and relating are recognized. We used the phrase "pulling the culture card" as one possible way of recognizing occasions when we might shift our relational stance toward a more equal or just way of relating. We propose that developing a relational intercultural sensitivity may inhibit the perpetuation of PIPs or DIPs that reinforce discourses of unfair privilege and social injustice.

We believe that therapists can benefit from recognizing the uncomfortable sensations that are often felt in the body (e.g., a racing heart or knot in one's stomach) in order to initiate a clarifying conversation. Recognizing what else we (clients and therapists) may be experiencing in our conversations together may help us orient to and become curious about the SCIPs that may be involved in our conversations. Rather than feeling overwhelmed, scared, or frustrated by cultural tensions in our conversations, our hope is to find ways to relate to others by recognizing and shifting our stance away from colluding with patterns of injustice. Following from the previous question posed by Tomm, our hope is that orienting to the culture card can become a useful metaphor—a reminder for therapists to attune to their intercultural relational sensitivity and to consider cultural clashes as opportunities to step beyond intercultural PIPs toward new ways of relating culturally.

Notes

1 We would like to acknowledge the valuable contributions from Joanne Schultz Hall and Karl Tomm for this chapter, as well as the rest of the authors of this book.
2 We prefer to use the word "intercultural" rather than "multicultural" or "transcultural," as it conveys a sense of interactive relationship. We believe intercultural therapeutic conversations involve generating new ways of dealing with tensions between cultural sameness and differences (Rober, 2012).
3 All identifying information has been changed to protect clients' privacy.

References

Aronson Fontes, L., & Thomas, V. (1996). Cultural issues in family therapy. In F. P. Piercy, D. H. Sprenkle, & J. L. Wetchler (Eds.), *Family therapy sourcebook* (pp. 256–282). New York, NY: Guilford Press.

Bezanson, B. J., & James, S. (2007). Culture-general and culture-specific approaches to counseling: Complementary stances. *International Journal for the Advancement of Counselling, 29*(3/4), 159–171. doi: 10.1007/s10447-007-9036-7

Eliot, T. S. (1948). *Notes toward a definition of culture*. London, UK: Faber & Faber.

Falicov, C. J. (1995). Training to think culturally: A multidimensional comparative framework. *Family Process, 34*(4), 373–388. Retrieved from: www.familyprocess.org/

McGoldrick, M., & Hardy, K. V. (Eds.). (2008). *Re-visioning family therapy: Race, culture and gender in clinical practice* (2nd ed.). New York, NY: Guilford Press.

Monk, G., Winslade, J., & Sinclair, S. (2008). *New horizons in multicultural counseling*. Thousand Oaks, CA: Sage.

Pedersen, P. (1995). The culture-bound counsellor as an unintentional racist. *Canadian Journal of Counselling, 29*(3), 197–205.

Pizana, D. (2003). *Authenticity in a community setting: A tool for self-reflection and change*. Retrieved from http://alliesforchange.org/documents/Authenticity-in-Community-Setting.pdf

Ridley, C. R. (2005). *Overcoming unintentional racism in counselling and therapy: A practitioner's guide to intentional intervention* (2nd ed.). Thousand Oaks, CA: Sage.

Rober, P. (2012). The challenge of writing about culture and family therapy practice. In I.-B. Krause (Ed.), *Culture and reflexivity in systemic psychotherapy: Mutual perspectives* (pp. xvii–xx). London, UK: Karnac Books.

Strong, T., & Tomm, K. (2007). Family therapy as re-coordinating and moving on together. *Journal of Systemic Therapies, 26*(2), 42–54. doi: 10.1521/jsyt.2007.26.2.42

Tamasese, K., & Waldegrave, C. (1994). Cultural and gender accountability in the Just Therapy approach. *Journal of Feminist Family Therapy, 5*(2), 29–45. doi: 10.1300/J086v05n02_03

Tomm, K. (1987). Interviewing: Part 1. Strategizing as a fourth guideline for the therapist. *Family Process, 26*(1), 3–13. Retrieved from www.familyprocess.org

Tomm, K. (2011, September). *Deconstructing shame and guilt, and opening space for reconciliation through apology and forgiveness*. Lecture and PowerPoint, MdSc 706.01 and SOWK 679.30, University of Calgary, Calgary, AB.

Waldegrave, C. (2012). Developing a "just therapy": Context and ascription of meaning. In A. Lock & T. Strong (Eds.), *Discursive perspectives in therapeutic practice* (pp. 196–211). London, UK: Oxford University Press.

9

IPS SUPERVISION AS RELATIONALLY RESPONSIVE PRACTICE

Jeff Chang and Joaquín Gaete

Clinical supervision has historically been conceptualized in top-down terms that, in our view, underemphasize the interpersonal space between the supervisor and the supervisee (Bernard, 1997; Morgan & Sprenkle, 2007; Norem, Magnuson, Wilcoxon, & Arbel, 2006; Stoltenberg & McNeill, 2010; Watkins, 1997). With rare exceptions (Arthur & Collins, 2008; Chang, 2013a; Holloway, 1995; Winslade, 2003), the relational, institutional, and cultural contexts of supervision have been largely overlooked. In this chapter, we explore the potential of conceptualizing clinical supervision as a relationally responsive practice by reinterpreting extant ideas in supervision in terms of Interpersonal Patterns (IPs).

Typically, supervisors are more experienced than supervisees, have the institutional responsibility to assure quality services to clients, and must evaluate supervisees and make decisions that can significantly affect their careers (Bernard & Goodyear, 2013). These institutional purposes create a power differential. In our view, a relationally responsive approach to clinical supervision can minimize, but not erase, power and hierarchy in supervision. This chapter comes out of our relationship, which has evolved from supervision to *covision* (Rombach, 2000). I (Jeff) have supervised students and licensure interns in agencies and private practice for 25 years. I also serve as the training coordinator of a graduate counsellor education program. Recently, I have described my approach to supervision (Chang, 2013a, 2013b) and was fortunate enough to supervise Joaquín for an 8-month doctoral practicum in counselling psychology at the Calgary Family Therapy Centre (CFTC).

I (Joaquín), in turn, was fortunate to have Jeff as my clinical supervisor. Since then, I have been conducting research on supervision at the CFTC toward my doctoral degree in counselling psychology at the University of Calgary. Taking a relational view of supervision, I am examining how supervisees' professional development is jointly recognized and brought forth in supervision conversations. The conversations we have had coauthoring this chapter have helped us to thicken our respective views of clinical supervision.

In this chapter, we first describe some historical conceptualizations of clinical supervision. Then, we describe some aspects of a relationally responsive approach to supervision with some examples of how supervisors and supervisees might initiate and maintain stable interpersonal patterns that are generative.

Historical Conceptualizations of Supervision

Earlier in this volume (see Chapters 1 and 3), we described the figure that can alternatively be seen as two faces facing each other or as a chalice. Our emphasis on IPs invites us to conceptualize supervision as an interpersonal process—what goes on between people. Conversely, we think the bulk of the current supervision literature focuses on one of the two faces—usually the supervisee's. We are much more interested in the chalice (the interpersonal space). Before we unpack our IPscope-informed approach to supervision, we will briefly review how existing approaches to supervision have largely overlooked the interpersonal space between supervisors and supervisees.

Psychotherapy-Based Approaches

Approaches to supervision solely based on theories of psychotherapy represent a bygone era. Referring to the state of supervision almost 20 years ago, Watkins (1995) stated, "Psychotherapy-based models of supervision have generally shown . . . stability over the last 25–30 years, with . . . limited changes or revision" (p. 570). With rare exceptions (e.g., Winslade, 2003), psychotherapy-based approaches underemphasize the relational and contextual influences in supervision (Bernard & Goodyear, 2013; Falender & Shafranske, 2004; Holloway, 1995; Watkins, 1995).

Developmental Stage Models

Proponents of developmental stages models suggest that supervision should be delivered in accordance with supervisees' level of development (e.g., Stoltenberg & McNeill, 2010). Counsellor development is seen as a linear process of predictable, universal, and qualitatively different stages (Chagnon & Russell, 1995), which explain how the interpersonal space between supervisors and supervisees unfolds. For instance, Stoltenberg and McNeill (2010) state "Level 1" supervisees are typically anxious and focused on themselves; "Level 2" supervisees can focus more on the client and less on themselves and implement basic skills; and "Level 3" supervisees can exhibit empathy for the client, engage in metacognition about their therapeutic work, and apply their knowledge "in the moment." Here, the developmental stage of the supervisee, as assessed by the supervisor, drives the supervisor's relational responses neglecting contextual influences. Thus, despite the intuitive appeal of this approach, the interpersonal space between the supervisor and the supervisee—the chalice—is underemphasized.

Social Role–Based Models

Bernard's Discrimination model (Bernard, 1997) is a prominent example of a social role approach to supervision. It combines the supervisor's role as teacher (instructing, modeling, or providing feedback to a supervisee), counsellor (inviting supervisees to reflect on their thoughts, emotions, or actions), and consultant (acting as a resource) to focus on intervention skills (observable supervisee behaviors), conceptualization skills (making sense of client presentation, treatment planning, and intervention design), and personalization skills (warmth, ability to engage clients, and non-defensiveness).

Conceptualizing clinical supervision as the purposeful use of specific roles can assist supervisors to manage the complexity of supervision but portrays supervision as the supervisor intervening upon the supervisee. As Gaete and Ness (2012) suggested, proponents of social role models treat supervisors' moment-by-moment "positionings" (e.g., monitoring, consulting, teaching) as predetermined roles they are supposed to act out, ignoring how positionings are responsive to supervisees and to actual supervisory situations.

Common Factors and the Supervisory Alliance

Morgan and Sprenkle (2007) have distinguished factors common to effective supervision. Like common factors in therapy (e.g., Wampold & Budge, 2012), the supervisory alliance is assumed to contribute to effective supervision, regardless of theoretical orientation (Ladany, Lehrman-Waterman, Molinaro, & Wolgast, 1999; Patton & Kivlighan, 1997). However, this approach tends to reify the supervisory relationship as monolithic instead of attending to how it presents moment-by-moment during supervision.

Competency Profiles

In keeping with the North American trend toward outcome-and competency-based education (Hoge, Huey, & O'Connell, 2004), professional associations have developed competency profiles in psychology (Canadian Psychological Association, 2004; Rodolfa et al., 2013), marriage and family therapy (Nelson et al., 2007), and counselling (Council for the Accreditation of Counseling and Related Educational Programs, 2009; Task Group for Counsellor Regulation in British Columbia, 2007), which specify desired outcomes of training. While potentially helpful in managing the "whats" or "outcomes" of supervision (i.e., supervisees' performances compared to a competency profile), competency profiles tend to overlook the "hows" or process of supervision. In our view, competency profiles offer little to help us understand how interpersonal dynamics between supervisors and supervisees hinder or facilitate supervisees' competence. In fact, to the extent that competency profiles invite supervisors to approach supervision outcomes as disconnected from process (e.g., supervision Transforming Interpersonal Patterns, TIPs), they may interfere with supervision.

A Relational Approach to Supervision

We were captivated by a series of studies by Magnuson, Wilcoxon, and Norem (Magnuson, Wilcoxon, & Norem, 2000; Norem et al., 2006; Wilcoxon, Norem, & Magnuson, 2005) describing "lousy" and "stellar" supervision outcomes. It is rare for us to describe supervision in such extreme terms; in our experience, most supervision pairings function somewhere in between. However, our reaction to the starkness of the lousy–stellar distinction is to wonder what is going on between supervisor and supervisee rather than just describing lousy or stellar supervisory outcomes in terms of particular behaviors on the part of either the supervisor or supervisee. The IPscope provides a way to focus on interpersonal patterns—the chalice—rather than intrapersonal characteristics or decontextualized behaviors. We believe supervision is a very complex professional activity, with multiple aspects that the IPscope was not designed to consider.[1] We appreciate the IPscope as a framework for supervision, as it helps us to bring forth some interconnected features of supervision that we value. In particular, we value that by looking through the IPscope, we can render supervision as a relational, responsive, participative, reflexive, and transformational practice.

Coupled Invitations

By conceptualizing supervision in terms of IPs, we can see a series of familiar practices inviting or anticipating other familiar practices. For instance, a supervisee engaged in *defending* might be better understood as a response to a supervisor engaged in *criticizing* (i.e., a Pathologizing Interpersonal Pattern, PIP). Alternatively, a supervisee engaged in *enacting professionally valued competencies* might be better understood as responding to a supervisor *selectively noticing* such enactments (i.e., a

IPS SUPERVISION AS RESPONSIVE PRACTICE

Wellness Interpersonal Pattern, WIP). We believe that by conceptualizing supervision as coupled invitations (i.e., IPs) we can actualize more fully a core claim made by proponents of the previous supervision models. An IPscope framework helps us to acknowledge not only that the supervisory relationship is probably the most relevant factor influencing supervision outcome but also *how* the relationship might be specifically facilitating or hindering supervisees' learnings.

At its heart, clinical supervision is a relational practice. We believe there is a temptation of power (Amundson, Stewart, & Valentine, 1993)—a temptation for supervisors to get supervisees to "see things their way," placing canonical ideas, rather than relationships, in the central position. As I (Jeff) reflect on my early supervision efforts, I acknowledge that, as a well-practiced and enthusiastic, solution-focused therapist, I was interested in getting supervisees to think and practice as I did and became frustrated when they did not seem to "get it." I thought supervision was a "one size fits all" endeavor. I did not bother to inquire about what a supervisee already knew, how he/she preferred to work, or his/her particular interests or goals.

Probably, my "lousy" practice invited supervisees to feel ignored, and to share with me neither their interests nor their perceived strengths/challenges. We think that by using the IPscope, we can conceptualize this type of supervisee experience as a "relational chalice," opening potential for more generative pathways. We could describe such a supervisee experience as a Deteriorating Interpersonal Pattern (DIP, shown on the left of Figure 9.1), which if not interrupted could develop into a stable PIP (on the right of Figure 9.1).

Using the IPscope as an interpretive framework, we believe a more productive pattern could be initiated with a TIP, which could stabilize into a WIP, as shown in Figure 9.2.

In my (Jeff) role as training coordinator for a graduate counsellor education program, I recently encountered a more problematic example.

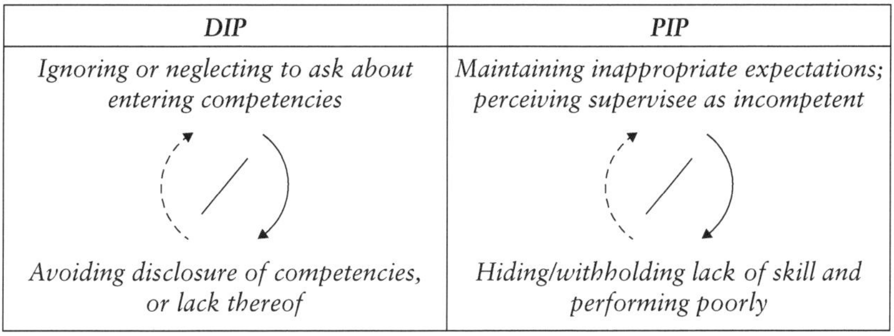

DIP	PIP
Ignoring or neglecting to ask about entering competencies	*Maintaining inappropriate expectations; perceiving supervisee as incompetent*
Avoiding disclosure of competencies, or lack thereof	*Hiding/withholding lack of skill and performing poorly*

Figure 9.1 Describing supervisee's experience as an interpersonal response

191

A practicum student and his supervisor developed a conflictual relationship in which I was asked to intervene. I asked the student and the supervisor for a written list of the changes needed to create a context for the student to succeed. Among other things, the supervisor wrote, "Robert (pseudonym) must stop fighting with me about whether narrative therapy is appropriate for certain problems." All the supervisor's comments reflected that she had punctuated the issue individually—as the student's shortcoming in not honoring her expertise or authority. Thus, two possible ways to conceptualize this situation in terms of PIPs are shown in Figure 9.3.

In this situation, had I been asked to consult with the supervisor, I might have asked questions to invite her to reflect on how IPs, supported by individualistic thinking, enabled the conflict (i.e., a deconstructive TIP; see Chapter 5). Alternatively, I could have attempted a constructive TIP by asking the supervisor to simply notice what was occurring when the supervisee "did not fight as much" or was less defensive.[2] The reader might see this as a solution-focused question. Whatever the origin, the question invites the supervisor to notice possible WIPs. If the supervisor

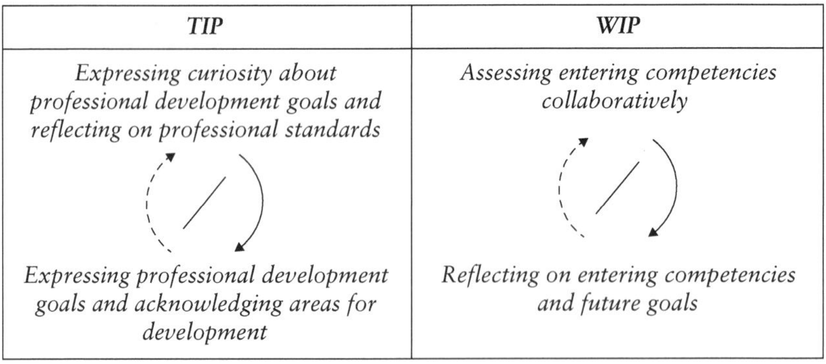

TIP	WIP
Expressing curiosity about professional development goals and reflecting on professional standards	*Assessing entering competencies collaboratively*
Expressing professional development goals and acknowledging areas for development	*Reflecting on entering competencies and future goals*

Figure 9.2 Inviting a preferred supervisory pattern

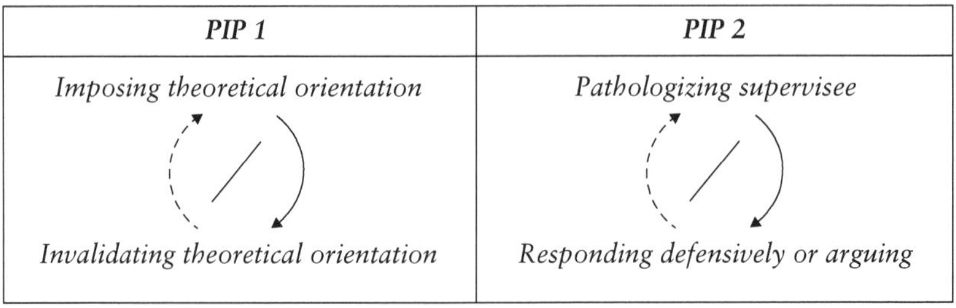

PIP 1	PIP 2
Imposing theoretical orientation	*Pathologizing supervisee*
Invalidating theoretical orientation	*Responding defensively or arguing*

Figure 9.3 Conceptualizing problematic interaction patterns

noticed she was contributing to these WIPs, I would invite her to reflect upon the benefits of continuing in this direction. The supervisor could ask questions about the supervisee's theoretical ideas. These attempts to initiate TIPs have the potential to be useful if asked out of genuine curiosity, not to cross-examine the supervisee or colonize the supervisee to the supervisor's way of thinking. I might have suggested that the supervisor explore options for re-engaging with the student with TIPish questions:

- What is it that is so appealing to you about narrative ideas?
- What other ways of handling X do you know?
- How are these ways similar or different to a narrative approach?
- If these approaches could be seen as complementary, in what ways could you make sense of this?
- What kinds of difficulties do you find when handling X?
- Would you be willing to explore other ways to handle X?
- What is it about narrative ideas that tell you that they are not robust enough to handle difficult problems like X?
- How does narrative therapy help you orient yourself with families who are in a great deal of distress?

As we illustrate next, we think asking these types of questions might have been helpful to invite the emergence of TIPs between the supervisor and the supervisee, focused on the issue of theoretical exploration and development, possibly enabling the emergence of a Healing Interpersonal Pattern (HIP, an "antidote" to the PIP), and perhaps even propelling the supervisory relationship more broadly into a WIP (see Figure 9.4).

Responsiveness

By using the IPscope as a framework for supervision practice, supervisors do not act out any particular decontextualized predefined practices, fixed roles, stage-relative interventions, or even relational patterns. Supervisors using the IPscope acknowledge that what they do with supervisees depends on what a particular supervisory situation "calls for" (cf. Shotter, 2011). Thus, IPscope-informed supervision does not involve following a pre-established recipe for developing and delivering certain ingredients, traits, skills, roles, or behaviors to accomplish certain supervision outcomes (cf. Stiles, Honos-Webb, & Surko, 1998). Rather, in an IPscope-informed approach, supervisors respond to supervisees in the moment, based on the situation.

Surprising directions. In my (Jeff) first meeting with a new supervisee, I usually ask about what theories and models guide his/her work, how he/she has been supervised in the past, and what he/she would like to learn. Sarah (pseudonym) surprised me by explaining with great energy

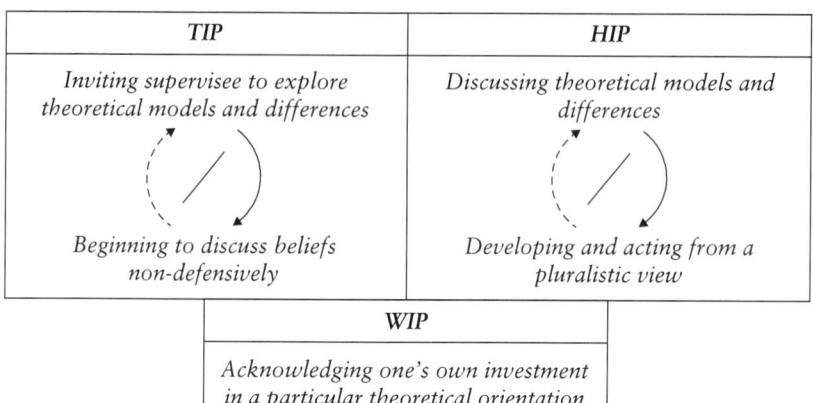

TIP	HIP
Inviting supervisee to explore theoretical models and differences ↕ *Beginning to discuss beliefs non-defensively*	*Discussing theoretical models and differences* ↕ *Developing and acting from a pluralistic view*

WIP
Acknowledging one's own investment in a particular theoretical orientation ↕ *Appreciating the acknowledgment and feeling enabled to explore and reflect*

Figure 9.4 Inviting a HIP and a WIP

and many tears that this was the first full day she had spent apart from her 11-month-old son, inviting her to doubt whether she ought to be doing this practicum, or doctoral studies at all. Working to be responsive, I shared how my stepdaughter was experiencing a similar dilemma. Throughout the 8-month practicum, I tried to position myself as a catalyst and professional mentor (Chang, 2013a) to acknowledge Sarah's concern about not spending as much time with her son as she would have preferred, and clarify her motivation for doing a PhD. In our initial meeting, we initiated a TIP (see Figure 9.5, left), which led to a stable WIP (see Figure 9.5, right).

Convergent conversations. In my (Joaquín) research on supervision at the CFTC, I have also focused on supervisory dyads' situational responsiveness. In doing so, I have noticed how supervisory dyads develop their own idiosyncratic language to identify and track the particular challenges of a given supervisee's professional development. The dyads may start by describing supervision goals or tasks in a general way. However, as they customize the supervision relationship to their unique situation, they jointly develop a common language to monitor and reflect upon recurrent issues.

For instance, one dyad developed the capacity to recognize that the supervisee struggled when clients shared strong emotions. In discussing these struggles, she shared feeling uncomfortable and fretting about not knowing where to go next. Together, supervisor and supervisee started

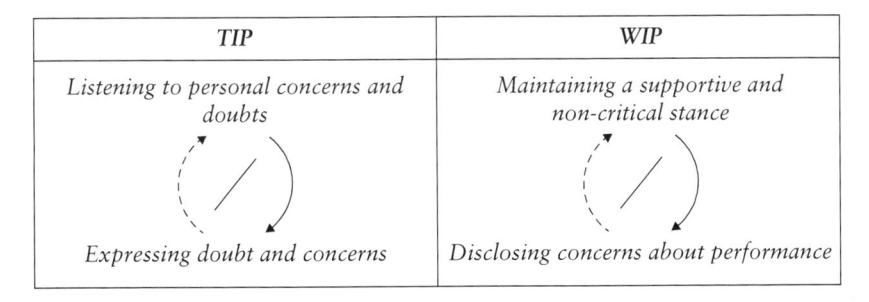

TIP	WIP
Listening to personal concerns and doubts ↻ *Expressing doubt and concerns*	*Maintaining a supportive and non-critical stance* ↻ *Disclosing concerns about performance*

Figure 9.5 Initiating a WIP

to refer to the supervisee's task in a particular, jointly acceptable way, which they called "staying there." In jointly monitoring and reflecting on "staying there," they noticed more ways to recognize when "it" (the supervisee's discomfort with strong client emotion) was present. When discussing clients, the supervisee started referring to "it" nonverbally. She would simply make a facial gesture, which her supervisor recognized and responded to. Sometimes the supervisor responded simply by gently smiling, showing that she understood the supervisee's challenge. At other times, the supervisor responded by spontaneously asking TIPish questions, which invited the supervisee to explore the issue (e.g., "So when that happened, what did you notice?") or comments (e.g., "Oh really! So you did something different this time!").

Participation

By conceptualizing supervision with the IPscope, we assume supervisors and supervisees are jointly involved in forming their perceptions and judgments about supervision. What supervisors and supervisees notice is not neutral but a function of the distinctions they select and enact. Supervisors' and supervisees' observations are shaped by their expectations, interests, and theoretical and interpretive frameworks (the IPscope included). Conceptualizing supervision as a relational recursive process invites both supervisors and supervisees into a stance of participation. As participants, supervisors and supervisees can never step out of their histories, trainings, and particular circumstances to make objective judgments—think of the previous supervisor stating, "Robert is fighting with me."

Imagine a situation in which Josefina, a supervisor, judges that Lana, her supervisee, "has important theoretical gaps in understanding her clients. Accordingly, I need to instruct her on her theoretical development." Far from being a detached, objective judge, we believe Josefina is actively participating in what she observes, judges, and reports. If Josefina sees her job as delivering content or "training" to Lana, this may already create a context to view Lana as deficient in how she conceptualizes her clients' situations. Without noticing it, Josefina might be inviting Lana into a PIP (e.g., *prescribing how to act as a therapist coupled with feeling dismissed and inadequate*). Participating as a more appreciative type of observer, Josefina could initiate constructive TIPs (see Chapter 5), to bring forth areas of potential growth for Lana. Josefina could ask the following questions:

- How would you make sense of [client's] situation?
- Would you agree it has been challenging for you to make sense of [client's] situation?
- Do you have any ideas about how you may get better at . . . ?
- Would you be open to discuss some theoretical ideas that might be helpful?

In the long run, and informed by co-developed learning goals, Josefina and Lana could participate in a WIP such as *noticing enactments of a particular goal for development coupled with strengthening skills related to that particular goal*.

In a similar vein, Wilcoxon et al. (2005) described how some supervisors view supervisees considered deficient in therapeutic skills and theoretical fluency: "Either [supervisees] come in with pretty good innate, mechanical skills or they don't" (p. 44). By emphasizing a supervisee's shortcomings, a supervisor might inadvertently initiate a less than optimal relational context. We would see such participation as inviting a possible DIP shown on the left in Figure 9.6. If the supervisor persists in focusing on the supervisee's deficits without distinguishing potential positive developments, the supervisee would be gradually less inclined to take

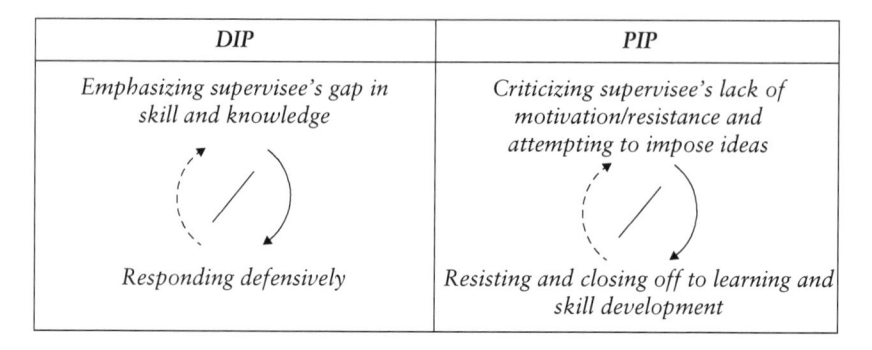

DIP	PIP
Emphasizing supervisee's gap in skill and knowledge	*Criticizing supervisee's lack of motivation/resistance and attempting to impose ideas*
Responding defensively	*Resisting and closing off to learning and skill development*

Figure 9.6 Participating in a DIP and drifting into a PIP

up the supervisor's suggestions. This might be interpreted by the supervisor as "lack of motivation," or perhaps as the student actively "resisting." This could stabilize into a PIP, as shown on the right in Figure 9.6.

On the other hand, because participants' observations are not neutral, we choose to orient to supervisees' skills and competencies. We must keep supervisees' needs for development (both what they wish to learn and their disciplinary requirements) in mind. And because supervisors are gatekeepers to our professions, we are required to identify and help remediate areas in which a supervisee's performance does not meet institutionally-produced requirements for competence. Our preferred way to operate is to hold essential professional competencies in mind, while intentionally noticing skills and competencies that can be utilized as a foundation for further development (see Figure 9.7).

When a supervisee's performance falls below institutionally defined standards, the supervisor is responsible to deliver feedback to remediate the supervisee's performance. Our preferred ethical posture (Tomm, 2010) is *empowerment*, which would be characterized primarily by asking reflexive questions from a posture of mutual reflection. However, in cases where we judge the supervisee's performance as inadequate in relation to institutionally defined standards, we may take a different ethical posture. We may move to a more *strategic* posture, or even to direct *confrontation*. In any case, that would speak more about our own incapacity as supervisors to take our preferred ethical posture (i.e., an empowerment posture that resulted in TIPish interactions). We believe part of our role as supervisors is to reflect on our thinking and actions, acknowledging that sometimes our preferred ways of working may not match with what we judge the situation requires from us professionally and ethically. Using alternative ethical postures as a framework for decision-making supports supervisors to be intentional, responsive, and ethical in their relational positioning.

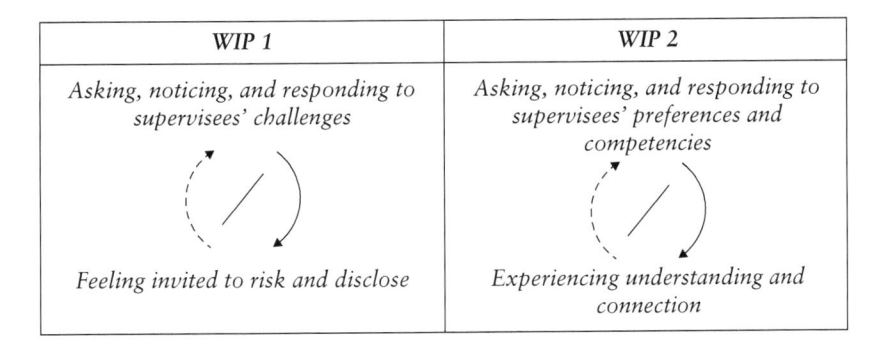

WIP 1	WIP 2
Asking, noticing, and responding to supervisees' challenges	*Asking, noticing, and responding to supervisees' preferences and competencies*
Feeling invited to risk and disclose	*Experiencing understanding and connection*

Figure 9.7 Two WIPs for "gatekeeping"

Inviting Reflection

Researchers of counsellors' professional development (Carroll, 2009, 2010; Jennings, Goh, Skovholt, Hanson, & Banerjee-Stevens, 2003; Jennings & Skovholt, 1999; Orlinsky & Rønnestad, 2005; Skovholt & Ronnestad, 1992) suggest that supervisors can best facilitate supervisees' professional development by fostering reflection. Starting from the maxim that supervisees know more than they can tell, some authors have developed strategies for supervisors to invite supervisees to reflect on their own practices (Carroll, 2009, 2010; Neufeldt, 2007; Orchowski, Evangelista, & Probst, 2010). In alignment with these endeavors, we see the IPscope framework as an invitation for supervisors and supervisees to engage in inner and outer dialogue fostering reflexive (Andersen, 1991) and reflective practice (Schön, 1983). Striving to conceptualize supervisory interactions through the IPscope does not provide certainty but provides a useful heuristic for supervisory dialogue, conceptualizing, and *learning* from the moment-by-moment interaction in supervisory conversations.

At times, I (Jeff) have noticed myself becoming impatient with a supervisee as I observed from behind the mirror. Perhaps the supervisee permitted family members to be blameful of one another in what I considered a destructive way, or missed openings to inquire about potential TIPs that I noticed, or I may have noticed the supervisee regress and have difficulty with a situation that I had seen him/her previously manage well. This might be punctuated this way (see Figure 9.8, left) but, if permitted to deteriorate, could stabilize into a PIP something like the one on the right (see Figure 9.8).

We believe that one of the most relevant benefits supervisory dyads can get from participating in supervisory TIPs is reflective dialogue. First, we suggest that supervisors and supervisees engage in outer dialogue or

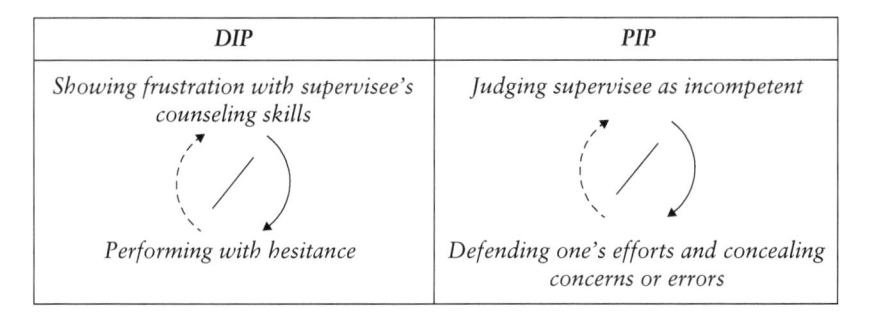

DIP	PIP
Showing frustration with supervisee's counseling skills	*Judging supervisee as incompetent*
Performing with hesitation	*Defending one's efforts and concealing concerns or errors*

Figure 9.8 A possible DIP slipping into a PIP

in conversations in which they reflect about how to better understand the oftentimes challenging situations supervisees have to deal with and ways in which to frame their work with clients. Furthermore, they could also talk about their own supervision relationship. Second, we suggest attending to the inner dialogues that are occurring about the interpersonal dynamics of human problems.

As we suggested previously, from an IPscope-informed approach we can, as supervisors, position ourselves as active participants, even in our seemingly most neutral judgments. We believe that from this participatory stance we can further *reflect*, within ourselves (i.e., inner dialogue) and with supervisees and colleagues (i.e., outer dialogue) about our participation. In our inner dialogues, the IPscope may help us, as supervisors, in *noticing our noticing, reflecting on our thinking*, and if we feel frustrated (e.g., behind the mirror), *articulating our bodily responses/emoting* as we observe supervisees.

Additionally, we believe supervisors' internalized TIPs in their inner dialogues may be fruitfully interconnected with outer dialogue with supervisees (Andersen, 1991). Imagine an (outer) post-session supervision dialogue, following a supervisor's attempt to initiate a TIP: "I noticed what the husband said about his wife—would you see that as a type of blaming or did you see it differently? How comfortable do you feel with how you responded? If you could go back to that situation, how would you like to have responded differently?" I (Joaquín) believe this TIPish path is similar to one of the supervisory conversations I witnessed as a researcher at the CFTC. The supervisee had shared she wanted to be more "in the position of a facilitator" rather than teaching people strategies to solve "family problems." The supervisor noticed the supervisee asked clients questions starting with "Have you tried . . .?" which was usually construed as making suggestions. In the supervision session, the supervisor invited the supervisee to reflect:

> *Supervisee*: . . . and I'd rather be in the position of a facilitator.
> *Supervisor*: (*nods*) OK, so like the other day with the other couple? You know, I forgot what you asked them, but you said, "Well, *have you tried?*"
> *Supervisee*: Mm hm.
> *Supervisor*: "Have you tried?" So, do you see that more as facilitating? Or . . .

We believe this type of supervision conversation could be framed as enacting the following TIP (see Figure 9.9, left), leading to potential WIPs (see Figure 9.9, center and right).[3]

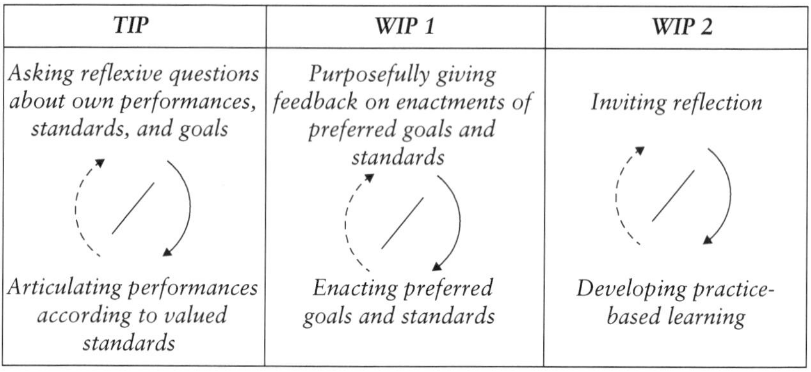

TIP	WIP 1	WIP 2
Asking reflexive questions about own performances, standards, and goals	Purposefully giving feedback on enactments of preferred goals and standards	Inviting reflection
Articulating performances according to valued standards	Enacting preferred goals and standards	Developing practice-based learning

Figure 9.9 Conceptualizing empowering supervisory conversations

Transformational and Wellness Potential

Conceptualizing supervisory interactions through the IPscope provides a useful heuristic for supervision that is more focused on moment-by-moment supervisory interactions than "set piece" supervisory interventions. We hope that, by attending to the TIPish and WIPish possibilities presented previously, the reader can already envision the transformational and wellness potential that an IPscope-informed supervision practice invites. We believe the IPscope can help supervisors and supervisees to engage and develop preferable relationship patterns (i.e., TIPs and WIPs) that help accomplish the goals of supervision. We conceptualize "stellar supervision" residing in the relationship—the capacity of supervisors and supervisees together to create TIPs and WIPs, forming a sustainable context for the supervisee to develop professionally.

We think supervisors have the main (but not only) responsibility and power to create stellar supervision. As we mentioned earlier, we believe the institutional contexts in which supervision is typically embedded structures the supervision relationship as a hierarchical one, which can be quite limiting. Supervision has multiple aims (e.g., developmental, gatekeeping, assuring quality of services) which may conflict (Gaete & Ness, 2012). Collaborative supervisors are expected to be more responsive practitioners while respecting the knowledge of supervisees and clients (e.g., Anderson, 2005; Bernard & Goodyear, 2013; Sinclair & Pettifor, 2001).

To invite supervisors to acknowledge and navigate through some of these tensions, we would like to conceptualize supervision practice or *spirit* with a dialectic attitude. By dialectic attitude we mean that, given the power differential, supervisors can take the lead in acknowledging that the supervision relationship is not a monolithic, hierarchical entity but is always "becoming." The supervisory relationship has a history, but it is also shaped by the future anticipated by the supervisee and supervisor. Through time, a "spirit" of covision (Rombach, 2000) develops, so to speak. Supervisors can open space to bring the future into the present and facilitate a process of dialectic contradiction (Taylor, 1975), a contradiction between "what the [relationship] concerned is aiming at or is meant to be, on one hand, and what it effectively is on the other" (p. 130). We invite supervisors to use their power to minimize their power, opening space for the supervisory relationship to evolve, into a relationship of equals—"covision," as opposed to "super-vision." Here, we would like to share how some seeds of covision grew in our supervisory relationship.

A Dialogue: From Supervision to Covision

Jeff: Do you remember a seed of covision that you would like to share in this chapter?

Joaquín: The first one that pops up is that I remember, at the beginning of my practicum, wanting to divorce from my "strategic self" as a therapist.[4] I think I was expecting you to help me with that from the beginning.

Jeff: I actually remember you talked about that in our very first meeting. I asked about what you were expecting and anticipating from this practicum.

Joaquín: Yes. So I thought you would join me by taking the same negative attitude toward being strategic—which you didn't! (*Smiles*). I'd say it wasn't just that you were respectful of that strategic way of being, but you were pretty appreciative about that. I think this might be an example of covision, not because you took exactly my view, but because I learned from your more appreciative view to be more appreciative myself with all that practical knowledge that I had.

Jeff: Well that's interesting, because I actually think that I was intending that (*laughs*). I normally try to do that—try to meet students where they are at; use what they already know . . . I wonder though if we got "PIPish" at some point about that, like, if it was frustrating for you, or if you thought things like, "What's with this guy insisting on me about being strategic?" or . . .

Joaquín: Well, at the beginning it felt a bit like that. Maybe we did get DIPish at some point, but I think we didn't go all the way to a more stabilized PIP. At the very beginning, and because I noticed you noticed my strategic stuff in session with clients, I remember wondering if I was going to be put in a box, like "You are the strategic guy," but it didn't get to the point of being frustrating (see Figure 9.10).

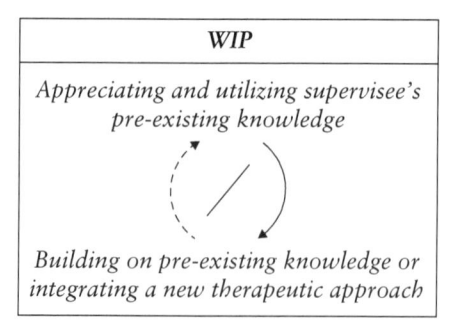

```
┌─────────────────────────────────────┐
│              WIP                     │
│                                      │
│  Appreciating and utilizing supervisee's │
│       pre-existing knowledge         │
│                                      │
│              ( / )                   │
│                                      │
│  Building on pre-existing knowledge or │
│  integrating a new therapeutic approach │
└─────────────────────────────────────┘
```

Figure 9.10 Theoretical integration as a WIP

Jeff: OK that's interesting. Do you remember a particular time when I noticed what you would call strategic stuff in session with a family, and we were able to reflect on that?

Joaquín: I actually do. I was working with a family with a teenager, a mom, and a dad, and dad really wanted to spend more time with his son, but the son just wanted to hang out with his peers. This was consistent with my feeling during the first session that the adolescent wasn't as motivated as dad about coming to therapy.

Jeff: I remember that family.

Joaquín: Well, by the end of the session, the son was willing to do a little "noticing homework," about how dad was able to hear his concerns and needs, and how we was trying to be more respectful of his space. The son was pretty excited about the homework (and I myself was too!). However, dad wanted to "add a little piece" to it (something like "OK, and maybe if he sees I'm pulling my weight he could spend some more time with me."). Influenced by my strategic framework, my inner dialogue was probably something like "Dad is getting ambitious. Be paradoxical; prescribe not changing, so it's a win-win situation next session. Try to stop him right now!" I remember coming back to the back room after the end of a session and you gave me a high five because of that move at the end.

Jeff: Oh! Did I? (*Laughs*). So did we talk about that? Or what did you, or do you, make of that?

Joaquín: Yes, we did. We talked about the main PIP being *pursuing coupled with avoiding*, and how my "gently stopping dad" at the end was a good way to stop that PIP and continue in the HIPish direction of the homework (i.e., dad's ... dad's empathizing with the son may invite the son's noticing and acknowledging dad's effort, and maybe empathizing with dad). So I think your selective noticing and our joint reflection actually helped me in interpreting my own practice from a richer and preferred perspective.

Jeff: Well, that's cool because I want to invite supervisees not to replace what they know and are coming with, but rather, start from there, and be able to reflect on their own practice. They can start to see their own practice from whatever perspective they want to learn more about—being more collaborative, in your case—so that they can feel more oriented and intentional in their future practice and learnings.

Joaquín: Absolutely. I think that reflective space gave me room to learn the other more collaborative ways of working that I was looking for. It felt like I could do both, strategic and collaborative, even when they seemed to be contradictory in my head (see Figure 9.11).

Jeff: Normally I try to utilize whatever the supervisee already knows and build upon it. This wasn't necessarily your situation, but more generally, students often say that they experience feeling "de-skilled" at the beginning (at the CFTC), because they see family therapy as completely different from individual counselling, so I try to help them realize how what they know can be integrated with family therapy skills.

Joaquín: Oh! And there is another experience I remember that might be relevant in terms of covision. It is related to what I have been noticing from my research on supervision here at the CFTC; I would call it covision in evaluation. I remember both of us reflecting on my practicum experience when we were filling out that evaluation form sent by the director of training of my PhD program at that time, remember?

Jeff: Oh yes, that form based on the [Canadian Psychological Association] accreditation standards. It can be quite annoying sometimes having to fill that form with standards that, I believe, are not the most relevant sometimes to evaluate trainees at the CFTC, and that just doesn't fit with how I see the world.

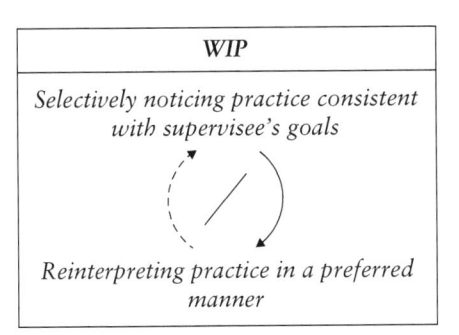

WIP
Selectively noticing practice consistent with supervisee's goals
Reinterpreting practice in a preferred manner

Figure 9.11 Co-constructing preferred ways of practice through a WIP

Joaquín: Yes! So I remember precisely that feeling of both of us trying to make sense of the form, lending some of our own preferred way of talking about practice to interpret the neutral language of the form. So I remember us doing a bit of discursive work later on, when meeting with my director of training in trying to translate our shared view, with our shared language, to a more standard type of language, one that she could relate to from her position.

Jeff: That's interesting because I usually have a rather negative view of those forms, because I see evaluative criteria in those forms as being driven by the dominant discourse—ideas about what psychologists need to know, which is not a fit for how, I think, we both see therapy, and how we prefer to view things at the CFTC. What are your thoughts on this?

Joaquín: This reminds me of a common remark in the Christian tradition in which I was raised: "Give Caesar what is due Caesar, and give God what is due God" (Mark 12:17). That is to say, every language is developed to be responsive to different kinds of phenomena. The important thing is to be aware of the goodness that each discourse makes available to us, and not trying to colonize one with the other. As long as practicum experiences are not *reduced* to the neutral language of microskills and macrocompetencies, I think those evaluative forms are a good resource (these more sharable languages make more available for us a sense of a professional community that cares about similar standards for the sake of the public). But my research on professional development in supervision has made me more aware that there is no such thing as neutral language. What do you think?

Jeff: I like your idea of making our languages responsive to particular situations of practice, serving different, yet equally important ends. I think it is easier for supervisors not fully "submitting to imposed discourse" to respond in a PIPish way, like "rebelling," which would only invite more "imposing" practices. For example, it is easier for supervisors to either submit to neutral language at the expense of their students' particular learning needs and what they bring as they enter supervision, or to rebel, like, "I'm going to just rate you excellent in everything, because I don't believe in this discourse." Personally I think there is another way. I think it is a good idea to take these forms as an opportunity for joint reflection.

Joaquín: More like in a "TIPish" way.

Jeff: Right! Supervisors and supervisees can jointly craft their responses to those forms, and in doing so create TIPish space for bringing forth supervisees' learning. And I do think that supervisors, in their more powerful position, should take the leadership in that process (see Figure 9.12).

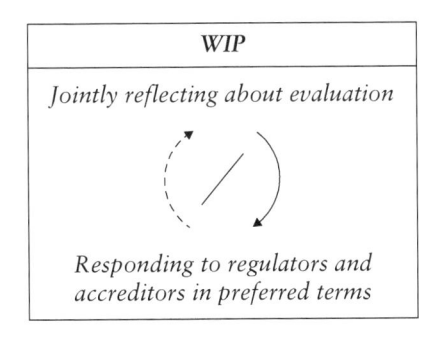

```
┌─────────────────────────────────┐
│            WIP                  │
│                                 │
│  Jointly reflecting about evaluation │
│                                 │
│         ⟲                       │
│                                 │
│  Responding to regulators and   │
│  accreditors in preferred terms │
└─────────────────────────────────┘
```

Figure 9.12 Incorporating evaluation in a WIP

Joaquín: That makes sense. Well you know, I think we should talk about this in our chapter.
Jeff: We definitely should!

Which is exactly what we did!

A Final Reflection: From Parallel Process to Isomorphism to Relational Responsiveness

Perhaps a word about isomorphism is in order here. It is necessary for supervisors to consider the interactional patterns inherent in a therapeutic system—that is, the supervisor-supervisee-client system. Parallel process, originating from psychodynamic theory (Bernard & Goodyear, 2013; Giordano, Clarke, & Borders, 2013), is an intrapsychic phenomenon in which the relationship in one context (i.e., therapy) is unconsciously replicated by the supervisee in another context (i.e., in supervision), occurring when the supervisee unconsciously identifies with the client, and re-enacts the client's defensive behavior in supervision. On the other hand, isomorphism is a systemic concept signifying how the supervisee's interactional patterns with the client system are replicated in supervision. Breunlin, Liddle, and Schwartz (1988) suggest that a supervisor can use isomorphism to intervene with the supervisee by the supervisor shifting the pattern of his/her responses to the supervisee, which in turn alters the pattern of the supervisee's in-session behavior. Supervisors tend to notice isomorphic interactions when supervisees get into relational tangles with clients.

In our view, a relationally responsive approach both brings isomorphism alive and deemphasizes it as a specific phenomenon. Relational responsiveness opens space for unique and novel interactions to also arise. We view all interactions between the supervisor and the supervisee as influencing their relationship, as well as the relationship between the supervisee and the family. Accordingly, both isomorphism and novelty are everywhere. Approaching supervision as a relational practice invites supervisors to be aware of interpersonal patterns in an ongoing way, not just when supervisees slip into troublesome interactions with their clients.

Conclusion

In this chapter, we presented some ways that the IPscope can help supervisors orient themselves and conceptualize the endeavor of clinical supervision. We presented the IPscope as a framework that supervisors and supervisees can use to enhance their capacity to distinguish supervision as a relational, responsive, participative, reflexive, and transformational practice. Using the IPscope toolkit, supervisors can practice as involved reflective practitioners. We think supervisors can use the IPscope to make useful distinctions that help them become more responsive (as opposed to merely reactive) to supervisees' relational invitations.

This is not to say that individual differences or behaviors are irrelevant. In situations when supervisors intend to exercise "power over," abusing their supervisees to accomplish their objectives, we would not be tempted to account for such behavior as *responding* to supervisees. Fortunately, these instances are rare. In most supervisory situations, supervisors care very much about what supervisees do—and vice versa. Our main interest here is to invite readers to consider the benefits of accounting for "good" and "bad" supervision using the IPscope framework. Rather than seeing supervision outcomes in terms of reified characteristics of supervisors and supervisees (the "faces" in the figure), we built upon the IPscope to sustain our preferred view that, in relationally responsive practice of supervision, it is more important to attend to the shape of the chalice.

Notes

1 This is why we do not consider the IP-supervision a supervision model. For a broader and compatible conceptualization of supervision, see Chang (2013a).
2 I would try to ask these questions in non-prescriptive ways; otherwise, I might risk inviting, isomorphically, a similar PIP (*imposing coupled with rejecting*) to this new interpersonal space between myself as a training coordinator and the supervisor.
3 Note that WIP 1 in the middle could also be framed as a HIP to counter a PIP like the one mentioned right above it (i.e., *assuming supervisee's incompetence coupled with responding defensively and concealing concerns or errors*).
4 During my masters in Chile, I (Joaquín) was trained in a strategic model of family therapy first developed at the Mental Research Institute in Palo Alto, California.

References

Amundson, J., Stewart, K., & Valentine, L. (1993). Temptations of power and certainty. *Journal of Marital and Family Therapy, 9*(2), 111–123. doi: 10.1111/j.1752-0606.1993.tb00971.x

Andersen, T. (Ed.). (1991). *The reflecting team: Dialogues and dialogues about the dialogues*. New York, NY: Norton.

Anderson, H. (2005). Myths about "not-knowing." *Family Process, 44*(4), 497–504.

Arthur, N., & Collins, S. (2008). Culture-infused counselling supervision. In N. Pelling, J. Barletta, & P. Armstrong (Eds.), *The practice of supervision* (pp. 267–295). Samford Valley, QLD: Australian Academic Press.

Bernard, J. M. (1997). The discrimination model. In C. E. Watkins Jr. (Ed.), *Handbook of psychotherapy supervision* (pp. 310–327). New York, NY: John Wiley & Sons.

Bernard, J. M., & Goodyear, R. K. (2013). *Fundamentals of clinical supervision* (5th ed.). Upper Saddle River, NJ: Pearson.

Breunlin, D. C., Liddle, H. A., & Schwartz, R. C. (1988). Concurrent training of supervisors and therapists. In H. A. Liddle, D. C. Breunlin, & R. C. Schwartz (Eds.), *Handbook of family therapy training and supervision* (pp. 207–224). New York, NY: Guilford Press.

Canadian Psychological Association (2004). *Mutual recognition agreement of the regulatory bodies for professional psychologists in Canada—As amended June 2004*. Retrieved from www.cpa.ca/docs/file/MRA2004.pdf

Carroll, M. (2009). From mindless to mindful practice: On learning reflection in supervision. *Psychotherapy in Australia, 15*(4), 38.

Carroll, M. (2010). Supervision: Part II. Critical reflection for transformational learning. *Clinical Supervisor, 29*(1), 1–19. doi: 10.1080/07325221003730301

Chagnon, J., & Russell, R. K. (1995). Assessment of supervisee developmental level and supervision environment across supervisor experience. *Journal of Counseling & Development, 73*(5), 553–558.

Chang, J. (2013a). A contextual-functional meta-framework for counselling supervision. *International Journal for the Advancement of Counselling, 35*(2), 71–87. doi: 10.1007/s10447-0129168-2

Chang, J. (2013b). On being solution-focused in adversarial places: Supervising parenting evaluations for family court. In F. N. Thomas (Ed.), *Solution-focused supervision: A resource-oriented approach to developing clinical expertise* (pp. 187–196). New York, NY: Springer Science and Business.

Council for Accreditation of Counseling and Related Educational Programs (2009). *2009 standards*. Alexandria, VA: Author.

Falender, C. A., & Shafranske, E. P. (2004). *Clinical supervision: A competency-based approach*. Washington, DC: American Psychological Association.

Gaete, J., & Ness, O. (2012, November). *Preferred positionings in supervision: Reflective practices for conflict transformation*. Paper presented at the TAOS conference, San Diego, CA.

Giordano, A., Clarke, P., & Borders, L. D. (2013). Using motivational interviewing techniques to address parallel process in supervision. *Counselor Education and Supervision, 52*(1), 15–29. doi: 10.1002/j.1556-6978.2013.00025.x

Hoge, M. A., Huey, L. Y., & O'Connell, M. J. (2004). Best practices in behavioral health workforce education and training. *Administration and Policy in Mental Health, 32*(2), 91–106. doi: 10.1023/B:APIH.0000042742.45076.66

Holloway, E. L. (1995). *Clinical supervision: A systems approach.* Thousand Oaks, CA: Sage.

Jennings, L., Goh, M., Skovholt, T. M., Hanson, M., & Banerjee-Stevens, D. (2003). Multiple factors in the development of the expert counselor and therapist. *Journal of Career Development, 30*(1), 59–72. doi: 10.1177/089484530303000104

Jennings, L., & Skovholt, T. M. (1999). The cognitive, emotional, and relational characteristics of master therapists. *Journal of Counseling Psychology, 46*(1), 3–11. doi: 10.1037/0022-0167.46.1.3

Ladany, N., Lehrman-Waterman, D., Molinaro, M., & Wolgast, B. (1999). Psychotherapy supervisor ethical practices: Adherence to guidelines, the supervisory working alliance, and supervisee satisfaction. *Counseling Psychologist, 27*(3), 443–475. doi: 10.1177/0011000099273008

Magnuson, S., Wilcoxon, S. A., & Norem, K. (2000). A profile of lousy supervision: Experienced counselors' perspectives. *Counselor Education and Supervision, 39*(3), 189–202.

Morgan, M. M., & Sprenkle, D. H. (2007). Toward a common-factors approach to supervision. *Journal of Marital & Family Therapy, 33*(1), 1–17. doi: 10.1111/j.1752-0606.2007.00001.x

Nelson, T. S., Chenail, R. J., Alexander, J. F., Crane, D. R., Johnson, S. M., & Schwallie, L. (2007). The development of core competencies for the practice of marriage and family therapy. *Journal of Marital and Family Therapy, 33*(4), 417–438. doi: 10.1111/j.1752-0606.2007.00042.x

Neufeldt, S. A. (2007). *Supervision strategies for the first practicum.* Alexandria, VA: American Counseling Association.

Norem, K., Magnuson, S., & Wilcoxon, S. A., & Arbel, O. (2006). Supervisees' contributions to stellar supervision outcomes. *Journal of Professional Counseling: Practice, Theory, & Research, 34*(1–2), 33–48.

Orchowski, L., Evangelista, N. M., & Probst, D. R. (2010). Enhancing supervisee reflectivity in clinical supervision: A case study illustration. *Psychotherapy, 47*(1), 51. doi: 10.1037/a0018844

Orlinsky, D. E., & Rønnestad, M. H. (2005). *How psychotherapists develop: A study of therapeutic work and professional growth.* Washington, DC: American Psychological Association.

Patton, M. J., & Kivlighan, D. M. (1997). Relevance of the supervisory alliance to the counseling alliance and to treatment adherence in counselor training. *Journal of Counseling Psychology, 44*(1), 108–115. doi: 10.1037/0022-0167.44.1.108

Rodolfa, E., Greenberg, S., Hunsley, J., Smith-Zoeller, M., Cox, D., Sammons, M., . . . Spivak, H. (2013). A competency model for the practice of psychology. *Training and Education in Professional Psychology, 7*(2), 71–83. doi: 10.1037/a0032415

Rombach, M.-A. (2000). *Covision: A quest for inner expertise* (Unpublished doctoral dissertation, Purdue University, Lafayette, IN).

Schön, D. A. (1983). *The reflective practitioner: How professionals think in action.* New York, NY: Basic Books.

Shotter, J. (2011). *Getting it: Withness-thinking and the dialogical . . . in practice.* Cresswell, NJ: Hampton Press.

Sinclair, C., & Pettifor, J. (2001). *Companion manual to the Canadian Code of Ethics for Psychologists* (3rd ed.). Ottawa, ON: Canadian Psychological Association.

Skovholt, T. M., & Ronnestad, M. H. (1992). Themes in therapist and counselor development. *Journal of Counseling & Development, 70*(4), 505–515.

Stiles, W. B., Honos-Webb, L., & Surko, M. (1998). Responsiveness in psychotherapy. *Clinical Psychology: Science and Practice, 5*(4), 439–458. doi: 10.1111/j.1468-2850.1998.tb00166.x

Stoltenberg, C. D., & McNeill, B. W. (2010). *IDM supervision: An integrative developmental model for supervising counselors and therapists* (3rd ed.). New York, NY: Routledge.

Task Group for Counsellor Regulation in British Columbia. (2007). *National entry-to-practice competency profile for counselling therapists.* Victoria, BC: Author.

Taylor, C. (1975). *Hegel.* New York, NY: Cambridge University Press.

Tomm, K. (2010, October). *Alternative ethical postures that therapists can adopt in clinical decision-making.* Presentation at 1er Congreso Internacional Terapia Breve y Familiar, Puebla, Mexico.

Wampold, B. E., & Budge, S. L. (2012). The relationship—and its relationship to the common and specific factors of psychotherapy. *Counseling Psychologist, 40*, 601–623. doi: 10.1177/0011000011432709

Watkins, C. E., Jr. (1995). Psychotherapy supervision in the 1990s: Some observations and reflections. *American Journal of Psychotherapy, 49*, 568–581. Retrieved from www.ajp.org/

Watkins, C. E., Jr. (Ed.). (1997). *Handbook of psychotherapy supervision.* New York, NY: John Wiley & Sons.

Wilcoxon, S. A., Norem, K., & Magnuson, S. (2005). Supervisees' contributions to lousy supervision outcomes. *Journal of Professional Counseling: Practice, Theory, & Research, 33*(2), 31–49.

Winslade, J. (2003). Storying professional identity. *International Journal of Narrative Therapy and Community Work, 4.* Retrieved from www.dulwichcentre.com.au/johnwinsladearticle.htm

10

RESEARCHING INTERPERSONAL PATTERNS

Sally St. George, Dan Wulff, and Tom Strong

Interpersonal Pattern (IPs) were originally constructed and adopted as an alternative to the individualistic diagnostic system of the *Diagnostic and Statistical Manual* (DSM), in part to enable research and evaluation of therapeutic practice with families. The Calgary Family Therapy Centre (CFTC), a publicly funded service, needed a clinical and administrative way to assess the severity of family concerns and to evaluate the progress and outcomes of families participating in therapy (see Introduction). However, the recent push for a psychotherapy evidence-base, extended to family therapy, has almost exclusively required use of the individual psychiatric diagnoses of the DSM-IV-TR (Strong & Busch, 2013). Tying the diagnostic/assessment and treatment focus of family therapy to symptoms/behaviors, or pathology *in* individuals obscures the relational features that we can see when conceptualizing from an IPs view (assessment of *family* concerns). Using the IPs system, we can differentiate family difficulties and the level of distress involved to assure funders that funded therapy is apportioned in helpful and efficient ways.

As in the case of diagnosing mental disorders, the individualistic predilection extends into the conducting of research in the field of social science. Research in the Western tradition requires standards of rigor that are built upon objectivity, a fixed reality, and generalizability (Crotty, 1998). Traditional research stands on the modernist platform of individuality and universal truth. If we approach research from the standardized and traditional ways of science, we would be discouraged from seeing complexities as wholes because the methods of scientific discovery themselves are located outside of any interactional patterning in society. Working within an IPs framework, we are encouraged to see patterned interactions in all human endeavors, including research.

As Researchers

All three of us locate ourselves in the postmodern realm of thought and work from a social constructionist stance (McNamee & Hosking, 2012).

I (Sally) have been a practitioner my entire professional life and have used practice-based evidence as my guide toward making professional decisions whether in my junior high school or graduate school classrooms. After hearing so many complaints from students and fellow practitioners that research was irrelevant, unintelligible, and overly complicated, I have made it a priority that research and inquiry are well-used, meaningful, and readily available to all. In addition to building these ideas into my classroom curricula and activities, I have spent the last 20 years working on *The Qualitative Report,* learning how to more effectively help researchers and extend the potential of various methods.

I (Dan) have always been good at mathematics and the definitiveness that comes along with calculating. Studying quantitative and qualitative research methods in graduate school revealed how each methodology brings utility along with some gaps. I also believe that no single methodology can encompass everything. Maturana and Varela (1992) remind us that when something gets foregrounded, something else is backgrounded. So it is also with research approaches. My interest in research started with the preciseness of quantitative, moved into the valuing of personal accounts of qualitative, and now my choice has been to privilege research that maximizes participation, particularly by those persons who may be considered by some researchers to only be the *subjects* of the research. This choice fits most closely with my social work disciplinary background and experience, opening up the possibility of engaging with quantitative *and* qualitative approaches in concert.

My (Tom) interests in research shifted upon taking up academic life after 9 years of full-time practice as a therapist. What mattered most to me was finding ways to research the postmodern therapies that had animated my work with clients. Most research I had read (or done in graduate school) seemed quite irrelevant to practice, and a new frontier was opening up regarding qualitative and process-oriented research of therapy. My initial research interests upon my return to academia related to the conversational practice of therapy (what people said, did, and accomplished through therapeutic dialogue), and the new forms of research—particularly narrative and action research—that increasingly seemed related to therapeutic practice as I had come to understand it. I have become enthused with what I see as blurring boundaries between research and practice.

Purpose

For many therapists, particularly those who self-identify as social constructionist or postmodern, the word *research* can evoke uneasiness or suspicion. Until recently, most researchers have used methods that have focused on measuring change in discrete variables and have discredited ways of practicing that contribute to change but do not readily adhere to the discrete quantification of variables (Strong & Gale, 2013). We are practitioner-researchers who believe that research or inquiries into practice are necessary and can be generative means to develop and refine clinical understandings and practices (cf. Green & Latchford, 2012).

In this chapter, we will discuss some of the possibilities of conducting research on IPs from a social constructionist position and, in particular, ways to employ the IPscope framework as a template for research itself. We will provide illustrations of research projects we have conducted at the CFTC on IPs that have extended current forms of practice-based research in ways that increase the relevance and availability of research for front-line practitioners and simultaneously foster an examination of the inherent limitations of research as traditionally taken up by researchers.

Moving Into Research as Daily Practice

Let us briefly deconstruct contemporary understandings of research to illustrate the distinctions we make and positions we hold. An Enlightenment view of science was that research was the way to make experience and what we do within it understood and controllable. Extended to the social sciences (e.g., Gergen, 1994; Manicas, 1987), this view did not translate as well as it did in the so-called hard sciences. Humans can not be understood as "trivial machines" (von Foerster, 1981), nor can social science knowledge be applied to human problems with the same certainty as the knowledge of physics applied to mechanical engineering problems. Humans do not react in fully predictable ways as understood and managed according to consistent measurable reactions to specific variables/influences. Billiard balls could be exposed to forces in carefully prescribed and managed ways and could react in measurable and calculable ways that humans simply could not.

As social constructionists, we approach research in more variegated ways than traditional scientific approaches. We prefer processes that help us inquire into the practices that clinicians and clients consider mutually helpful or effective rather than seeking to locate universal truths (Gergen, 1994, 2009). Effective or useful understandings differ from purportedly correct or foundational understandings (from which therapeutic prescriptions are scientifically warranted). Accordingly, through looking for processes of research/inquiry that better serve therapists and clients we have developed diverse ways to invite critical reflection and generativity into aspects of family life and therapy.

We remind readers that IPs are not observer-*independent* structures or phenomena. Therapists, clinical administrators, and researchers at the CFTC are always working from therapists' IPs-constructions of family interactions and therapist-family interactions. When family members find these constructions interesting, engaging, and helpful, they work within the possibilities that these constructions provide. By contrast, a substantial amount of clinical wisdom and research evidence remains under-utilized or not utilized at all because it is not available to the practitioner or client family in a listenable or embraceable form. It remains decontextualized and consequently sits quietly on the shelf.

As conversationally-oriented therapists, we believe that our inquiry practices should be coordinated and consonant with what we do in everyday practice and within the structures of our work context. Therefore, we have developed what we call "research as daily practice," an approach in which research and daily practice are integrated. From this position or location, clinicians are able to reflect upon their own clinical practices collectively, purposively, and deliberately. The purpose is to both improve those practices and evolve research methods that are appropriate and feasible for busy clinicians (Alvesson & Kärreman, 2011).

Filled with the excitement of studying, using, and developing the IPs framework, we have been conceptualizing the research endeavor itself as a patterned interaction with practice, a generative way of thinking that has implications for how we specifically design the research projects we conduct. Viewing our practices through the IPscope relational lens, we find that interpersonal relationships in families are noteworthy and relationships between research and practice are similarly valued. If seen as separate endeavors, it is possible for research and practice to become disjointed and perhaps conflictual. Given our Pathologizing Interpersonal Patterns (PIPs) schematic, research and practice enterprises can develop a PIP-like relationship whereby research knowledge attempts to supplant practitioners' wisdom, which then engages practitioner pushback asserting that such research knowledge lacks the specificity and contextual grasp necessary to help particular families. Figure 10.1 illustrates how the patterning between research and practice could be imagined as a PIP. Unfortunately, this PIP-like relationship is all too common. However, it is also possible for the research and practice relationship to be enacted as a Wellness Interpersonal Pattern (WIP; see Figure 10.2). This

> Researchers promoting decontextualized data as superior
>
> Practitioners dismissing research as a useful way to develop practice

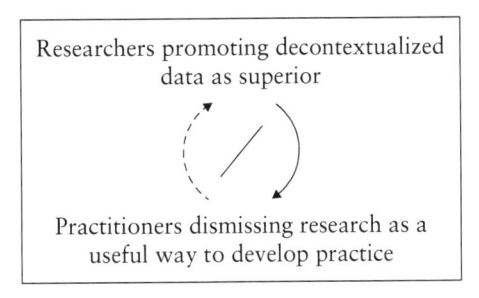

Figure 10.1 PIP between research and practice

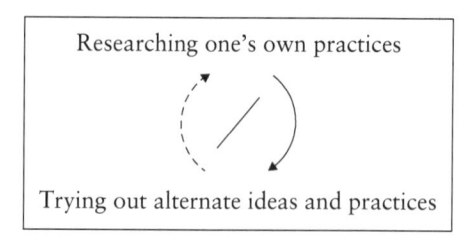

Figure 10.2 WIP between research and practice

WIP-like version has been the prototype for how research has been primarily approached at the CFTC from its inception. The family therapists routinely have collectively conceptualized, and reconceptualized, their work. One of the primary innovations was the IPscope framework itself (see Introduction).

Many forms of research (qualitative, quantitative, mixed methods) can be useful to practice provided that the research is available, understandable, and relevant enough to the practice context. These criteria are difficult for most researchers to meet given the present-day conditions regarding how research is supported (e.g., grants) and disseminated (e.g., peer-reviewed publications for academic audiences). Both of these aspects of modern-day research take the researcher and the research away from the practice context and practitioners, increasing the difficulty for the research to be applicable and useable. Formalized research that is detached from practice uses language that is specifically designed for communicating with other researchers, which adds another layer of mystification for the practitioner. Similarly, practitioners who do not occasionally interact with researchers in meaningful ways become insulated from them and also develop preferred language practices that further distance them from researchers. The clear separation of functions of researchers and practitioners fails to provide conditions that might lead to a common language and purpose that could, in turn, create conditions for integrated efforts to stimulate needed societal changes.

Consequently, in this chapter we will not detail the research that subscribes to the traditional form and delivery, even though some of it has been very useful. Specifically there have already been some very generative research projects that focused on Karl Tomm's work (Couture, 2004; Eeson, 2012; Godard, 2006; Sutherland, 2008). However, we will focus on particular ways of approaching research that engage practice and research in a WIP-like relationship.

Researching PIPs and Societal Discourses

Soon after joining the CFTC in 2007, we (Sally and Dan) began noticing very similar problems in different families. We were seeing patterns of escalating aggression between parents and children that seemed to have behavioral and interactional similarities across families (e.g., daughters engaging in self-violence, sons and daughters threatening family members leading to an atmosphere of fear and dread, parents demanding compliance through escalating words and deeds). We wondered if there were aspects of the community surrounding these families such as societal discourses that could be involved in supporting and justifying each family's interpersonal practices that were so distressing (PIPs) (Wulff, St. George, & Tomm, 2013b). We posed the following questions to ourselves in a research meeting:

- What practices, if any, seem to be justified by societal discourses that guide parents in how to interact with their children, especially when trying to respond to problems presented by their children?
- In family therapy practice, how might we conversationally address these societal discourses in order to better help families deal more effectively with the stress and conflict within their families?

The CFTC clinical team considered these questions by devoting our regularly scheduled 1-hour monthly research meetings to this project. We created a list of common societal discourses we sensed were relevant to families today and a collection of the PIPs that had been generated in recent therapy sessions with our client families. Societal discourses are those largely unspoken, unacknowledged, and unchallenged community beliefs and expectations that we uphold in our lives and social interactions (see Chapter 6). It is because of this possible invisibility or lack of examination that we wanted to see if certain societal discourses identified in therapy mapped onto certain PIPs.

We used situational analysis (SA; Clarke, 2005) as our methodological guide to help us conceptualize and visualize any connections between PIPs and the larger societal discourses. SA is a flexible methodology that we hoped would allow us to see existing connections as well as places where connections *could* occur (but were not obvious or present).

We brainstormed a list of the societal discourses that we, as clinicians, thought were commonly embraced by the families we were seeing in therapy. Two teams of clinicians then sorted and categorized all these sayings into six overarching societal discourses: responsibility, hierarchy, expertism, individualism, acceptability, and tradition (Wulff et al., 2013b). We had anticipated that certain societal discourses would map onto specific PIPs (e.g., the societal discourse of tradition might map onto a PIP of *dominating coupled with submitting*), imagining that the societal discourses would be negative influences, thereby leading to trouble for families who took up those discourses. We were surprised after our analysis to notice the discourses to be rather flexible, lacking any inherent singular negative quality.

We developed a second data set that included the PIPs identified by the clinicians from the first four sessions for families who came to therapy identifying parent-child conflict as their main issue. It is worth noting here that the clinicians engaged in a reflective process to create the PIPs and rated them on a severity scale (see Appendix B) that they wrote about in their clinical notes. This process is itself a form of reflective practice (Schön, 1983) with the opportunity to focus more attention on the clinical interview, the actions that were noticed in those sessions, and the therapist's tacit knowledge.

The clinician group sorted and thematically categorized this large set of PIPs into six generic PIPs that were inclusive enough to represent the original set. When we tried to map these PIPs and the societal discourses neatly and discretely onto each other, we were unsuccessful. Our expectation that PIPs would be wedded in some specific and unique ways to specified societal discourses was not supported.

Moving to our second question of inquiry, we were successful in creating questions based upon these two sets of categories (societal discourses and PIPs) that we could use to talk about the societal discourses in conversations with families about the PIPs we were noticing. While this research project did not connect specific societal discourses to specific PIPs in consistent, discrete ways, this analysis provided a platform from which these influences could be explored in our therapeutic conversations. While we did not find consistencies across all the families we were studying, we could see some coherent use of societal discourses within a given family or at a given point in time. For example, if we detected that the importance of responsibility was an active societal discourse within a particular family, we could ask the following questions:

1. How does [PIP] show/reflect your senses of responsibility? How does your enactment of "responsibility" inadvertently feed the [PIP]?
2. How does [PIP] fail to show your senses of responsibility?

If hierarchy was evident as an active societal discourse (Smith, 2005) and the PIP focused on decision-making, we might ask the following questions:

1. How are decisions made within your family?
2. Which decisions should be made collectively and which by individuals?
3. Who is the best person to make this particular decision?

In addition to the generative questions we created, we were intrigued by the changes that conducting this research together had produced in our clinical work at the CFTC. Our interns came to supervision with "confessional tales" of beginning to ask about societal discourses they were noticing with their clients long before the project was completed. They even began to record societal discourses in their session notes next to the PIPs schematic. This research-into-action initiative was influential in prompting us to continue to examine Socio-Cultural Interpersonal Patterns (SCIPs; see Chapter 6).

By using this form of research design, we privileged developing local knowledge, which also happens to be immediately useful. The students and the staff would use the reflective research group meetings as a stimulus to pursue the questions of societal discourses and PIPs within their subsequent family sessions, and what was learned from those sessions found its way back into the next research group meeting and conversation. The goal of clinical research is to help inform practice, and this way of conducting research helps practice in the moment. There is no need for knowledge translation or transport—the knowledge is developed in practice and therefore can be immediately implemented for further experimentation.

In order to evaluate this research, we needed to find appropriate criteria to use. Rather than reliability and validity (established through objectivity and systematic replication of variables), we looked toward a criterion of *the degree to which research opens space for practitioners to change their clinical practice, creating something that was not there before*. The traditional scientific approach is focused on finding something that exists and to be able to predict its re-occurrence. In contrast, our approach to research/inquiry is to stimulate newness and potentials for constructive change; therefore, we needed to privilege criteria that we could use to sense movement in those stated directions. We could use criteria based in actions that are generative, imaginative, playful, or creative, which leads us to imagine arts-based methods and other ideas that come from outside the confines of the customarily scientific. To measure stability of a variable, researchers and practitioners would utilize criteria that capture stability. To understand change, researchers and practitioners would need criteria that would help them see change potential and movement.

Researching HIPs and Societal Discourses

As a follow-up to the PIPs–societal discourses project, our team of practitioner-researchers decided in our research follow-up group conversations that it might be helpful to understand the relationships between HIPs and societal discourses (Wulff, St. George, & Tomm, 2013a). We asked: What influences do clients attribute to societal discourses for the ways they respond to their presenting problems and that may initiate, support, and maintain Healing Interpersonal Patterns (HIPs) within their families and communities? Once again we used SA (Clarke, 2005) as our methodological guide, and this time we were successful in generating maps to help us in the analysis. Reflecting on our previous project on PIPs and societal discourses, instead of focusing on specific societal discourses that mapped onto HIPs, we were looking for ways to refine our abilities to usefully talk societal discourses into the therapeutic conversation, specifically as they might relate to HIPs. The societal discourses we noticed in the earlier research project allowed us to see societal discourses as sets of ideas that families put into practice in a variety of ways, some that create better relating and some that block desired relationships.

In a qualitative metasynthesis (Chenail et al., 2012), we learned that families tend to progress in, and maintain, their healing patterns (HIPs) when they believe in their ability to change and when the change process is enjoined collectively. Although in that study we did not label the "family's belief in their ability to change" as a societal discourse per se, it could be described that way. Their perceived ability to change themselves and their interactions and the inclusion of these beliefs in the therapy seemed to provide sustainable support for families to embrace various HIPs (and WIPs).

We not only learned more about what helps families to emphasize and sustain HIPs but also became more efficient and generative in doing research collaboratively as therapists. Like the outcome of the previous project (developing therapeutic questions to bring forth possible connections between the societal discourses and PIPs *into* the therapeutic conversations), our clinical team began emphasizing societal discourses associated with HIPs and talking those into therapeutic conversations even before the end of the project (thus fulfilling our criterion of good clinical research). Because of the multiple ways that societal discourses can be part of the therapeutic conversation, we began experimenting with various ways to incorporate this talk both in the service of deconstructing PIPs but now also co-constructing HIPs.

From PIPs to HIPs

The CFTC is a clinical training site for about 10 interns each year from the disciplines of psychiatry, psychology, social work, nursing, and family therapy. Our students quickly develop their abilities to use the IPscope framework both in specific coursework and agency orientation (see Chapter 3). In using the PIPs and HIPs system as our clinical recording device (see Appendix A), the CFTC supervisors were curious to know more about how students learn to create PIPs and HIPs in their clinical notes. In their coursework, our interns learned about PIPs and the "antidote" (see Chapter 3), HIPs, in the abstract sense, but we wondered what processes they used in actually constructing *their* PIPs and HIPs for the families they were seeing. Supervisors also began wondering how experienced clinicians created IPs as well. So we simply asked the question, "How do beginning and experienced clinicians use the IPscope to create PIPs and HIPs with a given family?"

In order to conduct this study within the agency and to not over-tax the agency work being done, we again wanted our method of inquiry to be consistent with our methods of practice. Our question was grounded within the educational and supervisory functions of the agency, thereby making the inquiry relevant and valuable to both supervisors (who wanted to improve their supervisory skills of which the IPscope framework was an integral part) and interns (who were eagerly attempting to learn how to see and utilize PIPs and HIPs).

We organized three focus group conversations within our agency. In the first group conversation, we asked the interns to discuss how they conceptualized PIPs and HIPs and how they would describe helping families move from PIPs to HIPs. Behind the two-way mirror, the more senior and experienced clinicians took notes on what they heard and reflected on what they were hearing and noticing—this became a portion of our data. In the next group conversation, the two groups reversed positions and activity with the experienced clinicians conversing and the interns listening behind the mirror, taking notes. For the third meeting, our research group decided that the students should have one more conversation because they had learned things from the previous two focus groups and they wanted to talk more.

In this research, we used a narrative analysis (Frank, 2010). We found that the experienced clinician would move from PIPs to HIPs by listening for the ways in which the family spoke of their attempts and successes at altering and interrupting PIPs by instituting the family's own healing patterns. The inexperienced therapists, for the most part, wrote HIPs as the opposite behaviors identified in the PIP, referring back to their understanding of the notion of antidotes they had learned in their lectures. Listening to the more experienced clinicians articulate their ideas about building HIPs from family initiated attempts to heal themselves led to the students incorporating that idea into their clinical work. Again, the act of inquiring into our own practices invited changes in practice and teaching in a formative way, even before the project was officially completed and we produced summative statements.

This project was particularly suitable for the agency's efforts in teaching students in the use of the IPscope. They reported that they were developing more ways to see and understand the PIPs, HIPs, WIPs, and Transforming Interpersonal Patterns (TIPS) as a result of participating in this inquiry. It allowed us to experiment with some other formats by which students could learn about IPs that could then be incorporated with subsequent practicum cohorts. We focused our attention on a piece of our teaching and supervising that had been ongoing for years, but with attention to how the students translated the coursework and readings into actionable practices. Because this was done in a group setting, we co-created more insights and surprising ideas than would be the case if these issues were discussed in one-on-one supervision meetings.

Researching PIPs and Financial Discourses

This project was designed slightly differently from the projects previously described in this chapter, as this was a funded project, and a select team that consisted of clinicians and interns organized the data collection and conducted the analysis (Strong, Wulff, Mudry, St. George, & Sametband, 2013). We continued to use our regular agency meeting to report progress on the project and to get clinicians' impressions by reviewing taped segments or talking about the societal financial discourses they noticed in their sessions. Using SA as our guide, our primary finding was that financial or money talk can be thought of as relational talk. That is, the problem is not usually the material dollars-and-cents aspect of the talk—money talk seemed to provide the time and space for "unsatisfying interactions that tend to draw family members into increasingly emphatic defenses of their conflicting discourse positions, which in turn reinforce the pattern leading to clear costs for their relationship" (Strong et al., 2013, p. 20). The topic of money oftentimes provided the avenue to talk about individual differences that became DIPish (from Deteriorating Interpersonal Patterns) and/or PIPish.

Thus, we learned that family therapists need not be avoidant of financial conversations, but that we should consider those conversations as germane to understanding how family members were relating to one another and a relevant grounding from which to engage family members' differences. Again, because we kept a research focus on financial matters as related to therapy and societal discourse, we began to "see it everywhere," whereas before it had been rather invisible to us.

Seeing financial issues as relevant to families' troubles that bring them to therapy was an important finding. It highlighted that a family's material issues are legitimate elements of therapeutic conversations. Too often, such topics are considered "out of bounds" for therapists, and they take steps to avoid such topics. Indeed, by avoiding such talk we might actually be colluding with, and participating in, a covert PIP of *avoiding financial talk coupled with maintaining conflictual positions regarding finances*. We need to have the ability to engage in these conversations as readily as we would issues of parenting, communication, or other typical mental health topics or themes.

Reiterations and Emphases

Through our *research practices* at the CFTC, we try to turn overt and covert PIP relationships between researchers and practitioners into HIPs or WIPs. Karl Tomm has mentioned that our attention to research has opened space that we did not recognize was there, and that within such spaces we have generated new ideas and practices. In changing potential PIPs into HIPs, we have constructed and employed a system of doing practice-based research that supports studying one's own ways of working or one's agency's ways of working. In developing research as daily practice, we have created a fertile space for research and practice to co-evolve. The following points highlight the specific features of using research as daily practice:

- Conducting inquiry was time efficient, respectful of practitioners' time, and involved an entire cohort of agency practitioners.
- Existing research methodologies were chosen that were practice compatible (Wulff, 2008) and fit nicely within our already established clinical patterns of working relationally and collaboratively.
- Immediate experimental use of still-evolving knowledge in the practice context created richer feedback for the research process and significantly reduced the application time for new ideas and practices.
- Our inquiries demonstrated an honoring of the work of practitioners who can effectively plan studies of their own practices that produce genuine innovations.
- Inquiries can be conducted with or without external funding.
- Our projects were at times planned in advance and at other times somewhat improvised in order to fit our situation. We were willing to adjust our processes as we went along in the service of better understanding the focus of our inquiry.

Further Possibilities for IPs Research

Practitioner-researchers at the CFTC are creating unique ways of making sense of how the societal conversations that shape families are linked to the dialogues families have with us in family therapy. The projects mentioned highlight the role that research can play in understanding the linkages; we also use this knowledge and understanding in teaching and supervising students and new therapists (see Chapters 3 and 9). Research as daily practice in this regard reflexively connects our practice as therapists back to what we can learn from our practice in the service of more effective therapeutic work. An idea that extends our research-as-daily-practice approach would be to place our client families directly in the research project with us. Some years ago Karl conducted such a study collaboratively with a family to determine which therapeutic distinctions were experienced by family members as most useful (Karl, Cynthia, Andrew, & Vanessa, 1992)—a study which appeared to enhance the therapeutic outcome. Family members could become full-fledged co-researchers on an element of therapy that directly impacts them or their situation could become the entire research focus. Other families might also be involved in their research project looking into their patterns. The theme of inclusiveness in research is rich with possibilities. Because we have experienced success with research on PIPs and HIPs, we are spurred to imagine other projects that study IPs, some of which we will now share.

Seen as a teaching and learning resource, the IPscope links how we conceptualize family concerns to how we conceptualize therapeutic progress and well-being. One project being conducted by a doctoral student in counselling psychology has just begun at the CFTC in which the researcher is exploring identity construction in terms of the transitory stories and descriptions family members make evident in PIPs, HIPs, and WIPs. This "small story" approach (e.g., DeFina, Schiffrin, & Bamberg, 2006) helps us focus on how families do "identity work" around spoken understandings pertaining to particular members, and how family life together is "storied" (e.g., Tannen, Kendall, & Gordon, 2007). While the notion that identity is constructed in storied ways of talking is central to narrative therapy, how such story-making occurs over the course of family therapy—from PIPs through HIPs and WIPs—has only been theoretically mapped (e.g., White, 2007). We are interested in how such stories, and the forms of identity-talk in which they take their form, are invited through therapist questions, but equally importantly, we are interested in how clients respond to these story-making invitations (and how therapists respond to clients' responses). The specific steps or activities involved in a study of this nature could take many forms—in a "research as daily practice" approach, decisions about the hows and whats of the study would be constructed by the co-researchers, taking into account the parameters of their curiosity and the pragmatics of their work situation.

Many CFTC therapists involve families in explicating the family's own PIPs or HIPs, and it would be interesting and instructive to learn about the specific ways families are involved in such co-construction processes. For example, the IPscope is used as a pedagogic resource for families when therapists draw a PIP or HIP on a blackboard for families to discuss a relational formulation of their concerns. We are curious about client responses to this practice. Similarly, we have only anecdotal understandings of therapists' (interns' and experienced therapists') experiences in using the IPscope (see Eeson, 2012).

We acknowledge that the clinicians at the CFTC are using an IPs discourse in unique institutional and administrative ways. While most family therapy is administered as a form of health service, we recognize that many other family therapy services are administered according to their use of psychiatric diagnoses—a different, non-systemic, discourse of practice. Our use of the IPscope has administratively provided a means to assess the severity and transformation of family concerns in ways that are meaningful to our funders (Alberta Health Services). As is common elsewhere, here in Calgary there is a need to justify how public funds are being allocated responsibly to address family concerns (see Introduction). However, we assess and monitor family concerns in terms and metrics related to our postmodern practice of family therapy, not individually-focused therapy. The scales associated with our use of PIPs, HIPs, and WIPS (see Appendices B and C) are similar to the co-constructed, client-preferred, and circumstance-specific scales used to monitor therapeutic progress for relational and other concerns in publicly funded mental health services such as that in Norway (e.g., Anker, Duncan, & Sparks, 2009). The scales of the IPscope provide contextualized and co-constructed ways to assess therapeutic progress and can be used by clinicians to modify the course of therapy (cf. Sundet, 2012). Quantitatively tracking the numeric severity scales could provide some intensity dimensions to the situationally specific PIPs and HIPs, which could then reveal new aspects of the work with IPs that might lead to additional research projects.

We have noticed many researchable questions and ideas emerging from our discussions about writing this book: What are the conditions out of which DIPs and PIPs arise? What keeps different PIPs going? Within what kinds of PIPs are we, as therapists, most liable to become captured? How can we become aware of our PIPish collusion? Are particular TIPs more successful in displacing particular PIPs? How can HIPs be strengthened and stabilized in vulnerable systems? What therapist and client initiatives enable TIPs and HIPs to evolve into stable WIPs? How do SCIPs get taken up by families? When do specific SCIPs have PIPish, HIPish, or WIPish effects? What are the various ways that we could deconstruct SCIPs when they appear to dominate relationships and become problematic? The original group that created the IPscope (see Introduction) began looking at how particular kinds of PIPs might relate to diagnoses found in the DSM-5 (American Psychiatric Association, 2013), but much more exploratory research needs to be carried out in this area. For example, are there particular kinds of PIPs that family members enact when there is an eating disorder? Another curiosity has related to the role of particular genres of questioning (see Tomm, 1988) that might be helpful in inviting family members' movements away from PIPs and toward HIPs.

Where much of the evidence base for family therapy is based on individualistic DSM diagnoses and interventions to address such diagnosed conditions, we are concerned that family therapy is not evaluated on its own systemic terms. Therefore, we also seek ways that family therapy research could use more systemic formulations such as those enabled by the IPscope. For example, what PIPs and societal discourses might be associated with communications around a family member's DSM-diagnosed condition, such as depression, anxiety, an eating disorder, post-traumatic stress disorder, or disorders of sexual desire?

We have talked about specific questions we have with regard to our utilization of the IPs system. Within the overall design of research as daily practice, we could also explore utilizing a variety of other methodologies or ways in which we could approach our questions. There have been many recent social constructionist developments in qualitative research (e.g., Denzin & Lincoln, 2012; McNamee & Hosking, 2012), as well as developments in mixed methods research (i.e., quantitative and qualitative; cf. Creswell & Plano Clark, 2010), and these developments enable further possibilities for research into IPs.

Our preference is to use methods or create methods that are closely related to our practice, thus reducing the need for translation from research to practice. Cognizant of our need to institutionally justify the helpfulness of our work with families (e.g., Larner, 2004), we are advocates for stretching methods, modifying them to meet contextual circumstances (Alvesson & Kärreman, 2011; Pascale, 2011). While we have centered our talk in this research chapter on the notion of research as daily practice to benefit the frontline practice context, we can also see the benefits of writing about research to and for professional audiences as well. Not only are our results of interest to other researchers, the research design component may be even more interesting. The design of doing research in situ can provide the impetus for other practitioner groups to undertake their own research in their unique settings. At the center of all our inquiries we see the possibilities for paying attention, noticing our curiosities, examining relationships, making sense of information, reflecting-in-action (Wulff & St. George, 2011), and what we can generate when we engage in these activities.

Summary and Discussion

> "When the investigator starts to probe the unknown areas of the universe, the back end of the probe is always driven into his own vital parts."
> —Gregory Bateson (as cited in Keeney, 1983, p. 129)

Recently, research has acquired a somewhat tarnished reputation, particularly among postmodern family therapists. Modern research was typically done in controlled circumstances and in ways that bore no resemblance to the frontline practice familiar to family therapists. If anything, for many therapists, such research was suspected of being used to legislate how they were to practice (e.g., Bohart, 2005). We approach our research of the IPscope and its possible uses with a range of approaches to inquiry, and with varied questions and research aims (e.g., Crotty, 1998). While most of our projects have been qualitative in nature, we share

Pascale's (2011) view that the range of possible inquiries, and knowledge gained from them, is only starting to be appreciated.

We recognize that we are not alone in our efforts to conceptualize and research family therapy in relational terms (e.g., Kaslow, 1996). Perhaps a unique focus we bring to our IPs-related inquiries is a way of inquiring about what one does within the rigors of one's own practice processes (Wulff et al., 2013a, 2013b). Rather than see research as distinct from the practice, we see research or reflexive inquiring as an element of competent practice itself.

Gregory Bateson, shortly before he died, shared the following view on science and research: "Rigor alone is paralytic death, but imagination alone is insanity" (as cited in Keeney, 1983, p. 94). Good research, as we see it, is both imaginative and rigorous, but most important is that it is helpful to our ways of helping families. Our research into aspects and applications of the IPscope has included many conversations about what we believe needs to be understood about the IPscope and its usefulness to families and the therapists helping them. We think there is much to be learned from families in the course of our work with them, and this informs our critically reflective approach to talking about and transforming our practice (Fook & Gardner, 2007; Schön, 1983). Our researching and talking together is sometimes a source of new and possibly generative metaphors (cf. Rosenblatt, 1994) and at the same time we recognize that our methods and ideas are our ways of making sense (Law, 2004) on the social realities of family therapy.

Like it or not, research informs much of what gets decided in corporate and publicly funded institutions involved in the mental health field (Johnson, 1995). Arguably, the questions we invite and join families in answering can also be seen as genuine forms of inquiry as well—not just questions useful for mapping what clients tell us onto our own professional accountabilities. There is a healthy tension currently in play regarding what role prior research should have in informing how we practice (i.e., evidence-based practice; e.g., Sexton, 2010), and what role practice-based evidence should play in informing how we proceed with families (Green & Latchford, 2012) regardless of what the prior research says. The IPs-related research we have been describing and fore-telling is intended to encompass both aspects of this tension: prior IPs research informing our practice while regarding families' feedback as integral to how we proceed in our work with them. Research, in our view, is inseparable from practice, but then come the questions: What kinds of research? Who will be served? Might our research get some part of Bateson's balance between rigor and imagination wrong and turn into methodolatry or results that have no recognizable grounding in the social realities of clients' and therapists' lives?

We believe the tensions present in the relationships between practice and research provide the space and energy to innovate. Practitioners and researchers (seen as separate persons) have much to gain by continuing the dialogue that they appropriately share. Practitioners-as-researchers (in one body) have much to gain in reflecting upon how one activity enhances and enables the other activity. The challenge of relational work is to stay in contact with the inherent movement of relationships. Therefore our practices (therapy and inquiry) must resist the temptation to see relationships as static or fixed. Chenail (2012) highlights this in his "evidence-supported practice" notion from which we underscore the importance of our therapeutic interest in the movements *in and out* of PIPs, HIPs, and WIPs. This resembles the challenge that scientists faced when they wanted to study subatomic particles that they could not freeze or stop in order to study (Barad, 2008).

We hope that you see that the spirit of research lies in making sure our research and practice activities are in sync with each other (WIPish) and that clinicians can be the researchers of their own practices, which in turn influences their practice, thereby blurring the distinction between researchers and clinicians. This has become the gold standard for us. We see research and practice as aiming for somewhat different objectives but practitioners of research and practitioners of practice need not be separate persons.

References

Alvesson, M., & Kärreman, D. (2011). *Qualitative research and theory development: Mystery as method.* Thousand Oaks, CA: Sage.

American Psychiatric Association. (2013*). Diagnostic and statistical manual of mental disorders* (5th ed.). Washington, DC: American Psychiatric Association.

Anker, M. G., Duncan, B. L., & Sparks, J. A. (2009). Using client feedback to improve couple therapy outcomes: A randomized clinical trial in a naturalistic setting. *Journal of Consulting and Clinical Psychology, 77*(4), 693–704.

Barad, K. (2008). *Meeting the universe halfway: Quantum physics and the entanglement of matter and meaning.* Durham, NC: Duke University Press.

Bohart, A. C. (2005). Evidence-based psychotherapy means evidence-informed, not evidence-driven. *Journal of Contemporary Psychotherapy, 35*(1), 39–53.

Chenail, R. (2012, September). *Qualitative research adventures in the pyramids of evidence.* Workshop presented at the American Association for Marriage and Family Therapy (AAMFT) 2012 Annual Conference, Charlotte, NC.

Chenail, R. J., St. George, S., Wulff, D., Duffy, M., Wilson Scott, K., & Tomm, K. (2012). Clients' relational conceptions of conjoint couple and family therapy quality: A grounded formal theory [Special Issue]. *Journal of Marital and Family Therapy, 38*(1), 241–264.

Clarke, A. E. (2005). *Situational analysis: Grounded theory after the postmodern turn.* Thousand Oaks, CA: Sage.

Couture, S. (2004). *Moving forward: Therapy with an adolescent and his family* (Unpublished doctoral dissertation, University of Calgary, AB).

Creswell, J. W., & Plano Clark, V. L. (2010). *Designing and conducting mixed methods research* (2nd ed.). Thousand Oaks, CA: Sage.

Crotty, M. (1998). *The foundations of social research: Meaning and perspective in the research process.* Thousand Oaks, CA: Sage.

DeFina, A., Schiffrin, D., & Bamberg, M. (Eds.). (2006). *Discourse and identity.* Cambridge, UK: Cambridge University Press.

Denzin, N. K., & Lincoln, Y. S. (2012). *The handbook of qualitative research* (4th ed.). Thousand Oaks, CA: Sage.

Eeson, J. (2012). *The Calgary Family Therapy Centre's HIPs and PIPs diagnostic system: A case study* (Unpublished master's thesis, University of Calgary, AB).

Fook, J., & Gardner, F. (2007). *Practicing critical reflection: A resource handbook.* New York, NY: Open University Press/McGraw-Hill Education.

Frank, A. W. (2010). *Letting stories breathe: A socio-narratology.* Chicago, IL: University of Chicago Press.

Gergen, K. (1994). *Toward transformation in social knowledge* (2nd ed.). Thousand Oaks, CA: Sage.

Gergen, K. J. (2009). *An invitation to social construction* (2nd ed.). Thousand Oaks, CA: Sage.

Godard, G. (2006). *Karl Tomm's ethical postures and positioning in counseling* (Unpublished master's project, University of Calgary, AB).

Green, D., & Latchford, G. (2012). *Maximising the benefits of psychotherapy: A practice-based evidence approach.* Malden, MA: Wiley-Blackwell.

Johnson, L. (1995). *Psychotherapy in the age of accountability.* New York, NY: Norton.

Karl, Cynthia, Andrew, & Vanessa. (1992). Therapeutic distinctions in an ongoing therapy. In S. McNamee & K. Gergen (Eds.), *Therapy as social construction* (pp. 116–135). London, UK: Sage.

Kaslow, F. (Ed.). (1996). *The handbook of relational diagnosis and dysfunctional family patterns.* New York, NY: John Wiley and Sons.

Keeney, B. (1983). *The aesthetics of change.* New York, NY: Basic Books.

Larner, G. (2004). Family therapy and the politics of evidence. *Journal of Family Therapy,* 26(1), 17–39.

Law, J. (2004). *After method: Mess in social science research.* New York, NY: Routledge.

Manicas, P. T. (1987). *A history and philosophy of the social sciences.* Oxford, UK: Blackwell.

Maturana, H., & Varela, F. (1992). *The tree of knowledge.* Boston, MA: Shambhala.

McNamee, S., & Hosking, D. M. (2012). *Research and social change: A relational constructionist approach.* New York, NY: Routledge.

Pascale, C.-M. (2011). *Cartographies of knowledge: Exploring qualitative epistemologies.* Thousand Oaks, CA: Sage.

Rosenblatt, P. (1994). *Metaphors of family therapy: Toward new constructions.* New York, NY: Guilford.

Schön, D. A. (1983). *The reflective practitioner: How professionals think in action.* New York, NY: Basic Books.

Sexton, T. (2010). *Functional family therapy in clinical practice: An evidence-based treatment model for working with troubled adolescents.* New York, NY: Routledge.

Smith, D. E. (2005). *Institutional ethnography: A sociology for the people.* Lanham, MD: Rowman & Littlefield.

Strong, T., & Busch, R. (2013). DSM-V, family therapy, and evidence-based practice: Coupling incompatible formulations with incongruent interventions? *Australian and New Zealand Journal of Family Therapy, 34*(2), 90–103.

Strong, T., & Gale, J. (2013). Postmodern clinical research: In and out of the margins. *Journal of Systemic Therapies, 32*(2), 46–57.

Strong, T., Wulff, D., Mudry, T., St. George, S., & Sametband, I. (2013). *Financial discourses in family therapy*. Manuscript submitted for publication

Sundet, R. (2012). Therapist perspectives on the use of feedback on process and outcome: Patient-focused research in practice. *Canadian Psychology, 53*(2), 122–130.

Sutherland, O. (2008). *Collaboration in family therapy: Conversation analysis of a family therapy session by Dr. Karl Tomm* (Unpublished doctoral dissertation, University of Calgary, AB).

Tannen, D., Kendall, S., & Gordon, C. (Eds.). (2007). *Family talk: Discourse and identity in four American families*. New York, NY: Oxford University Press.

Tomm, K. (1988). Interventive interviewing: Part III. Intending to ask lineal, circular, strategic, or reflexive questions? *Family Process, 27*(1), 1–15.

von Foerster, H. (1981). *Observing systems*. Seaside, CA: Intersystems.

White, M. (2007). *Maps of narrative practice*. New York, NY: Norton.

Wulff, D. (2008). "Research/therapy": A review of Adele Clarke's *Situational analysis: Grounded theory after the postmodern turn*. *Weekly Qualitative Report, 1*(6), 31–34. Retrieved from www.nova.edu/ssss/QR/WQR/clarke.pdf

Wulff, D., & St. George, S. (2011). Family therapy with a larger aim. In S. Witkin (Ed.), *Social construction and social work practice: Interpretations and innovations* (pp. 211–239). New York, NY: Columbia University Press.

Wulff, D., St. George, S., & Tomm, K. (2013a). *Interpersonal patterns in family therapy: A modified situational analysis of the relationships between societal expectations and healing interpersonal patterns*. Manuscript in progress.

Wulff, D., St. George, S., & Tomm, K. (2013b). *Talking societal discourses into family therapy: A modified situational analysis of the relationships between societal expectations and parent-child conflict*. Manuscript in progress.

11

CONTINUING THE JOURNEY

Karl Tomm

> "We find ourselves here in the happening of living; talking and drawing distinctions in our experiences."
> —H. Maturana (workshop in Calgary, September 1, 1987)

Upon rereading my colleagues' chapters in this book, I found myself becoming energized by the possibilities that arise when we look at the world through the lens of the IPscope (see Chapter 1). Whenever we contextualize and deconstruct individual phenomena into relational phenomena, we gain access to the interpersonal dynamics that activate specific individual behaviors. With this enhanced access we can mobilize a wider range of therapeutic initiatives to facilitate the changes that our clients prefer. I find this increase in therapeutic possibilities very exciting. However, much more has been implied in the earlier chapters. Beyond simply shifting from an individual to a relational focus, there have been suggestions of micro and macro extensions of the IPscope perspective. For instance, we can adjust the level of focus and zoom in to understand individual persons differently and also zoom out to understand larger social phenomena differently. As we make such adjustments in the level of exploration and find other coupled stabilities, we open additional possibilities and enlarge the field of potential initiatives even more! In this chapter, I will describe a few examples of these further developments by zooming in and zooming out. But first, let us pause for some reflection.

Some Reservations About the IPscope

As my enthusiasm for the generativity of the IPscope grew, I began to wonder: Could it be that my colleagues and I are getting a bit too enthusiastic about the applicability of this conceptual tool? Are we expecting too much from the relational perspective? In what ways could our disposition toward distinguishing Pathologizing Interpersonal Patterns (PIPs) and Healing Interpersonal Patterns (HIPs) become a liability rather than an asset? Could it be that you as a reader are beginning to wonder about these questions as well?

When something works particularly well in one situation we are often tempted to generalize and to use the same tool or procedure in other situations as well. This phenomenon has come to be known as "The Law of the Instrument" (Kaplan, 1964, p. 28) and refers to an over-reliance on a familiar tool. In other words, there is a risk that we or any therapists who buy into the IPscope perspective could inadvertently limit possibilities rather than expand them by overusing the IPscope and abandoning other useful ideas and metaphors in our work with clients. We certainly do not want our excitement about interpersonal patterns (IPs) to create conditions for a form of discursive capture (see Chapter 2) and sincerely hope that such a constraint does not descend upon our readers. And if it does, we hope it remains very transient (e.g., feeling de-skilled, see Chapter 3). At the Calgary Family Therapy Centre (CFTC) we explicitly encourage the exploration of a wide range of clinical ideas and practices, while maintaining a bias toward systemic ways of thinking and practicing.

In my opinion, the potential dangers of an over-reliance on the IPscope are restrained by two major phenomena: (a) the difficult stretch entailed in expanding our minds to actually think systemically and (b) the power and pervasiveness of individualistic habits of thought and practice.

With respect to the first restraint, it takes a lot of mental energy to rise above the fray and search among a multiplicity of candidate behaviors and meanings to find coupled invitations that appear to cohere and resonate within an actual clinical situation. The complexities of systemic formulation are often quite daunting. Given the elusive and transient nature of these relational stabilities, one might wonder whether it is even worth the effort. However, it only takes a moment of reflection to realize how a whole vista of new possibilities opens up to us when we persist in the search and climb up (in our awareness) to a relational perspective. On occasion, the new relational view provides dramatic relief to individualistic judgments and strivings that can be quite liberating. Coming into a broader relational awareness of their mutual entanglement in a PIP usually provides the persons involved with both relief and new options. They come to recognize how their separate strivings to achieve something with the other person may actually be pushing the hoped-for-outcome further away, because of an unintended interpersonal process that is larger than either one of them. So yes, it definitely is worth the effort, especially when we have the mental energy to work toward greater clarity in the domain of interpersonal interaction.

With respect to the second major restraint against overuse of the IPscope, we almost always live and act as if we are separate individuals, even though such separateness may be an illusion (more on this illusion later). To be sure, in our activities of daily living we intuitively notice natural cleavages in reality whereby skin-bounded persons emerge non-consciously as separate in our seeing and doing. As noted in Chapter 3, our perceptual systems of vision and hearing bias us toward seeing ourselves, and others, as separate persons. Furthermore, our linguistic habits of describing people as having individual qualities and characteristics amplify this. Seeing the shape of a relationship is far more difficult than seeing the separate faces of the persons who are interacting. From this vantage point, the IPscopic perspective is far from a liability; rather, it is a valuable asset. It serves as a refreshing antidote to the taken-for-granted power of pervasive habits of seeing persons as individuals and helps limit the subterranean exuberance of rampant individualism in our Western culture.

We acknowledge, however, that there are some real limits, and even dangers, in the use of the IPscope. When we adopt a relational systemic perspective, we implicitly assume that all of the parties involved have a functional nervous system that enables them to participate in the unfolding interaction. Indeed, we assume that the nervous systems of all the parties involved are plastic enough to actually change during the course of interacting and as the nature of the relationships change. This assumption is probably not valid in many situations, such as intoxication with alcohol or drugs, neurotransmitter imbalances, brain diseases, or senility. An adequate discussion of the biological/neurological limits for entering into, modifying, and maintaining relationships would be a major undertaking and is far beyond the scope of this book. Suffice it to say, we assume that when people are able to engage in ordinary human communication, even if it is quite limited, they are also capable of becoming coupled in recurrent patterns of interaction.

One danger in applying the IPscope is to do so in a formulaic, non-reflective manner, by using taught, familiar, or initially apparent patterns, without discernment about their local applicability. When we employ IPs in such a rote manner, we actually risk initiating a Deteriorating Interpersonal Pattern (DIP) when the pattern does not fit, thus undermining our therapeutic alliance. Such rote application is different from an over-reliance on the tool—it smacks of insufficient enthusiasm rather than too much enthusiasm. This difficulty can readily be overcome by becoming more attentive to the specifics of the situation and always looking for goodness-of-fit—or even by asking clients directly about their intuitive impressions of the applicability of a particular IP in their situation. When we search carefully for the unique coupled invitations that seem to be taking place within this particular family at this particular time, we are much more likely to strengthen the therapeutic alliance and succeed in initiating Transforming Interpersonal Patterns (TIPs) rather than DIPs.

Another more significant danger arises when we apply the IPscope with too much objectivity (i.e., with certainty and/or rigidity). Whenever we do so, we run the risk of actively creating a PIP in our relationships with clients and/or colleagues who see clinical situations differently. The more we believe that we are objectively right in describing a particular PIP with accuracy and precision, the more justified we feel in imposing our correct view upon our clients and colleagues, who inevitably feel compelled to resist when they hold a different view. The resultant emergence of a PIP of *imposing the IPscope coupled with resisting the IPscope* (see Figure 11.1b) then becomes a seriously problematic side effect of employing this tool as a hard objective instrument. Given that the whole purpose of the tool is to produce healing and wellness, such an outcome is clearly unintended and counterproductive.

To elaborate on this danger further, I personally oscillate between proposing the IPscope as an alternative to the *Diagnostic and Statistical Manual* (DSM) of the American Psychiatric Association (2013), as opposed to a healing complement to the DSM. As described in the Introduction, the concept was originally developed as I was resisting the imposition of the DSM (see Figure 11.1a), and I still believe there is significant merit to that stance. However, I have too often slipped into counterproductive ideological struggles with my psychiatric colleagues when I persist in the *alternative* stance and find that if I offer descriptions of PIPs as *complementary* to individual mental disorders, our conversations about possible pragmatic initiatives usually move forward more easily (see Figure 11.1c). Another reason that I am leaning further toward a complementary *both/and* view is that as lived events unfold over time, pervasive relational patterns can be seen to *transform* into individual phenomena, as end results or distillates. Ongoing PIPs can end up presenting as individual problems, and likewise longstanding WIPs can end up becoming positive individual traits. This transformational process deserves further explication.

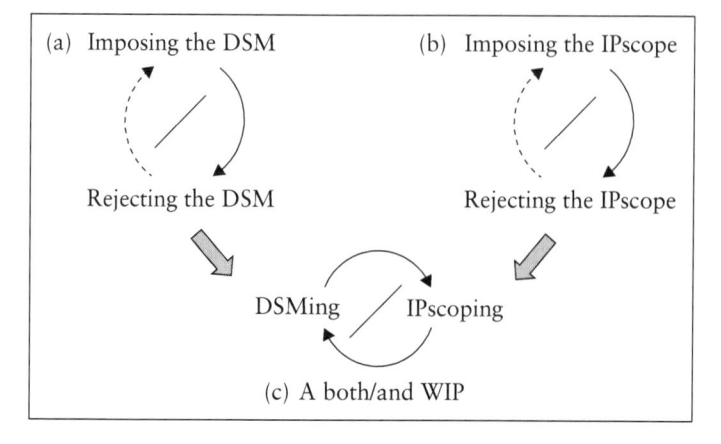

Figure 11.1 Problematic versus complementary diagnosing

From IPs Into Individual Characteristics

The transformation from interpersonal interaction pattern into individual distillate is captured artistically in the famous marble sculpture of Apollo and Daphne created by Bernini in the 17th century (see Figure 11.2). The sculpture shows Apollo lusting after and pursuing Daphne, who is refusing his advances and fleeing, an interaction that could easily be distinguished as a common PIP of *pursuing coupled with distancing*. What is incredibly insightful about this sculpture is that it portrays how, as the PIPish relational stability persists, Daphne begins turning into a laurel tree; her skin transforms into bark, her feet into roots, her arms into

Figure 11.2 Bernini sculpture suggesting transformation of interpersonal pattern into individual distillate
Credit: Alinari/Art Resource, NY.

branches, and her hair into leaves. Her ongoing fear of his pursuit ultimately transforms her into a wooden tree. In other words, living in a pervasive and ongoing PIP can transform one or other of the interactants into manifesting a relatively static individual characteristic, trait, or disorder.

Indeed, sex therapists are quite familiar with the phenomenon of how differences in sexual desire between partners in a committed relationship, when enacted recurrently as *pressuring for sex coupled with refusing sex*, can eventually result in one partner losing sexual desire altogether and becoming unresponsive, non-orgasmic, and even wooden. Similarly, living in a pervasive pattern of *oppressing coupled with submitting* can eventually become transformed into individual depression. Conversely, living in a pervasive wellness pattern of *attentive listening coupled with responsive sharing* can, over time, become transformed into an individual characteristic of competence in empathy. These transformative dynamics in mental health, from interpersonal patterns into individual characteristics, are extremely significant, yet they are easily overlooked.

It might be useful to digress for a moment and reflect upon an existential question: How is it that we, as human beings, come into existence, become conscious, develop qualities, and become aware of ourselves as persons in the first place? Philosophers have been exploring this issue for millennia, and there have been many highlights in the debates along the way. For instance, the famous statement by Rene Descartes, "Cogito ergo sum" (I think, therefore I am), has been a focus for a great deal of discussion for more than three centuries (Cottingham, Stoothoff, Murdoch, & Kenny, 1991). Our IPscopic perspective could be nicely encapsulated by a modification in Descartes' statement to read, "I respond, therefore I am," or "I interact and relate, therefore I exist." In other words, we place the emergence of relationships as prior to, and more fundamental than, the emergence of individuals. Indeed, individual human beings as persons may be seen to arise only through a long series of concatenated patterns of interactions with other human beings. Consequently, our individual separateness may be regarded as an end point or illusion.

The most comprehensive and satisfying explanation for human existence and awareness that I have come across (to date) has been Maturana's theory of cognition (Maturana & Varela, 1980, 1992). In his lectures, Maturana often began with the statement cited at the beginning of this chapter: "We find ourselves here in the happening of living; talking and drawing distinctions in our experiences." He used this statement of realization as an active starting point to explain how each one of us as an individual human being arises at a unique intersection of two gigantic processes of drift in structure determined interaction. Although his theory is too complex to explain adequately here, I would like to point out that one of these gigantic processes has to do with millennia of phylogenetic drifting (with preservation of adaptation and autopoiesis) through a series of species and generations up to the present moment, culminating in each person's unique genetic heritage and biological make-up in the molecular space. The other gigantic process has to do with the increasingly coordinated conduct among plastic living systems to generate complex ecologies and ultimately a huge socio-cultural drift in the interpersonal space. It is within the latter drift that we, as cognizing living systems, are structure determined to become aware, conscious, and free to talk, draw distinctions, and make choices in our daily living.

One crucial aspect of the socio-cultural drift has been the emergence of language, which Maturana and Varela (1980) define recursively as "the consensual coordination, of the consensual coordination, of conduct" (H. Maturana, personal communication, January 21, 1987). These coordinations reflect relational stabilities that arise in the interpersonal (social) space. While language depends on an incredible amount of plasticity in a large brain to enable such complex coordinations of conduct, language is not in the brain. Language is among us as languaging living systems. For instance, English as a language exists as an evolving constellation of specific coordinations of certain sounds, signs, gestures, and movements among English speakers. The reason I speak English is that I was born, raised, and live in a Canadian context where English is spoken. If I had been born in Poland like my parents, I would probably be speaking and writing in Polish. Language is first and foremost social and secondarily internalized through memory to become psychological, where it supports intrapersonal reflection and thinking. Similarly, most phenomena of mind are first social and secondarily psychological. In this respect, seeing through the IPscope and focusing on social interaction takes us a step closer to the interpersonal origins of individual mental phenomena.

Upon our physical birth we arrive in a particular cultural niche, where we begin interacting and continue to do so for as long as we are alive. We become progressively more coupled with caregivers and others, gradually becoming coordinated to enter into the ambient language, and learn to give meaning through repetitive, recurrent, and recursive social interaction. Usually our parents provide the outer social structure in recurrent patterns of interaction, which over time becomes internalized as part of the inner psychological structure of our selves. The meaning of *I* as an individual person arises entirely in this social domain, yet it remains totally contingent upon the intersection with *my* physical body and nervous system in the biological domain, which provides the infrastructure for *me* to become sufficiently coordinated (coupled) in the social domain for language, meaning-making, and consciousness to arise. If we accept Maturana's explanation, it is easier to become skeptical about the reality of our experience as separate individual selves. Our separateness can then more readily be recognized and acknowledged as a functional illusion—a realization that allows us to embrace relational understandings more fully. Our individual characteristics, whether they are positive or negative, may then be understood as concatenated end points of a huge process of interactive drifting, including long histories of dynamic patterns of interpersonal interaction.

Extending the IPscope by "Zooming In"

One pragmatic application of this insight of how our psychological selves arise through social interaction is a unique pattern of therapeutic interviewing referred to as "Internalized Other Interviewing" (Burnham, 2000; Emmerson-Whyte, 2010; Epston, 1993; Hurley, 2006; Lysack, 2002; Nylund & Corsiglia, 1993; Paré, 2001; Tomm, Hoyt, & Madigan, 1998). It depends heavily on the phenomenon of memory that is contingent on the plasticity of the nervous system to retain prior patterns of interaction. As we interact recurrently with other persons, we automatically create impressions of them (and of their experiences) within ourselves, which eventually coalesce or become distilled into a composite *internalized other* within our memory and imagination. This internalized other and our ongoing internal relationships with it, are of course part of us. When we greet a familiar person, like a close friend, we are already always listening to our internalized constellation of that friend before we materially engage with and interact with the outer actual other. This anticipatory listening prepares us to re-engage coherently with the actual other, where we left off in our prior interaction. The presumed qualities and characteristics of the internalized other and the actual other are usually quite similar, but never identical. There is typically significant overlap or congruence in lived experiences and meanings between my internalized friend and my actual friend, especially after my friend and I have drifted side by side in our living for substantial periods of time and have become mutually coordinated.

To take this metaphor further, the self, as a whole person, can be deconstructed conceptually into a whole internalized community. Included in this community are all those real and imaginary persons we have interacted with, in our actual living and in our imagination, plus all the interactions and relationships among them. Thinking this way opens space for us to see our way clear to speak to and interact with any member of that internalized community and work systemically on relevant patterns of interaction. In doing so, we, as therapists, can obtain access to previously internalized PIPs that could be externalized to become available for deconstructive TIPs and could potentially be replaced by HIPs and WIPs and re-internalized within the individual self of a client.

Perhaps a clinical example could help illustrate this application. Some years ago, I met with a middle-aged man in the context of a workshop during which I had offered to demonstrate my interviewing style. The client had struggled with serious alcohol and substance misuse for most of his life but had managed to turn his life around after several years of support in Alcoholics Anonymous (AA) and individual psychotherapy and was now "doing well." His therapist had invited him to volunteer for our interview and he agreed. It just so happened that a few days prior to our meeting, he had been struggling with a head cold that spread into his chest. His coughing at night had made it difficult for him to sleep, so the day before the meeting he asked his physician to prescribe some cough syrup with codeine. When he got ready for bed that night he took some of the cough medicine, then a bit more, and a bit more until he realized that he was taking the medication for the "codeine kick," and not just the cough suppressant. He became extremely upset with himself, assumed that he had fallen "back to square one," and that all his years of effort and treatment to recover from multiple addictions had been "for naught." Hopelessness descended upon him and he began to seriously contemplate suicide. Fortunately he phoned his AA sponsor who advised him to "sleep on it" and suggested they meet the next day. When he woke up the next morning, he remembered his commitment with the therapist and came for the demonstration interview.

Up to that point in time, no one knew that he had taken the codeine for its chemical effects, yet he was so consumed with shame and guilt about it that the impulse to seek relief through suicide seemed overwhelming. I asked him, "If everyone who does know you had known you had taken the codeine in this way, who do you imagine would have been the most upset?" After a long pause, he answered, "My mother." He had not actually had contact with his mother in several years, largely because they had had such a tumultuous relationship in the past. Nevertheless, I inquired whether I could speak to his mother as an internalized other within him, and after a brief explanation he accepted my request. Following a few orienting questions I proceeded to ask his internalized mother (addressing her with her actual name) how she had raised him when he was a child. She claimed that he had been extremely difficult as a child and adolescent (hyperactive, acting out, rebellious, defiant, destroying things), and that she had had to use a great deal of discipline to correct him, including a lot of criticism and punishment. I went on to ask her, "If you were aware that your son had internalized the criticizing habit to the extent that he was now criticizing himself so strongly for taking the codeine that he was contemplating suicide, would you have any regrets for having relied so much on criticism as a way to raise him?" He hesitated and responded slowly in her voice, "Yeah, maybe." I continued on, "Say you (addressing the internalized mother further by name) did convey some regret, and perhaps even apologized to him for criticizing him so much, do you think he could forgive you?" and the man began sobbing. It became a very tender moment as a shift took place within him. Thereafter he was able to re-engage with his positive self-worth and his impulse to suicide fell away.

Through these questions to the internalized mother, it was possible to bring forth a previously internalized PIP of *internal criticizing and punishing coupled with internal acting out and destroying*, deconstruct

```
┌─────────────────────────────────────────────┐
│  Internal criticizing        Internal        │
│  and punishing               apologizing     │
│         ⤹                         ⤹          │
│                                              │
│  Internal acting out with    Internal        │
│  self-harming impulse        forgiving       │
└─────────────────────────────────────────────┘
```

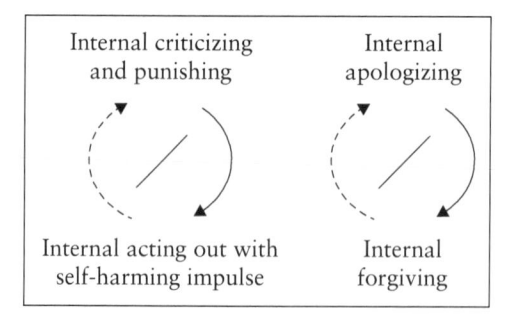

Figure 11.3 Possible internalized PIP and HIP

it, and invite him into a healing pattern of *internal apologizing coupled with internal forgiving* (see Figure 11.3). My questions were, of course, highly selective. I initially brought forth only one specific aspect of his internalized mother that resonated with his current state of mind (i.e., his immersion in self-criticism and thoughts of self-punishment). Once these connections were made, I could initiate TIP attempts (see Chapter 5) by asking about apology and forgiveness, bringing forth another aspect of his internalized mother that was potentially available for healing. In other words, by zooming in with the IPscope we can see opportunities to engage in TIPish reflexive questioning, to potentially reverse the process of drift from outer and inner PIPs into problematic individual distillates, and create conditions for a reconfiguration of a "separate" self that is better grounded in internal HIPs and WIPs in our ongoing living as individuals.

To go even further, when this kind of internalized other interviewing takes place in the presence of the actual other, the actual other (by watching and listening) comes to meet an aspect of himself or herself that exists in the client being so interviewed. In other words, if the actual mother were present to witness the interviewing process, she would meet her *distributed self* as the interview unfolds and would be invited to consider, and perhaps enter into, selective aspects of her self, that could be more HIPish or WIPish in relation to her son. This kind of interviewing obviously could become extremely complex when applied in clinical work and calls for another full-length book for an adequate exploration. My hope here is simply to point toward this micro application of the IPscope perspective as one domain for potential future extension.

Extending the IPscope by "Zooming Out"

I have commented elsewhere about an ethical imperative for therapists to adopt a proactive stance of contributing toward greater social justice in our communities and culture (Tomm, 2003). Many family therapy centers have taken significant initiatives in this area, most notably the Dulwich Centre in Adelaide, Australia (www.dulwichcentre.com.au), and the Family Centre in Wellington, New Zealand (Waldegrave, Tamasese, Tuhaka, & Campbell, 2003). Much of the mental suffering that we are called upon to address in our clinical work has to do with the consequences of local and societal injustices. It seems unethical to simply stand by and do nothing about social injustices that produce problems from which we and/or our professional colleagues later profit through providing clinical services for financial compensation. What seems far more ethical to me is that we, as therapists, try to live congruently and prevent or reduce injustice whenever we can, both inside and outside of therapy. Thus, when we anticipate a social injustice, we need to act in some way to try to prevent the injustice from being enacted to preclude unnecessary injury and a need for future therapy. When we identify an injustice already underway, we need to act in some way to try to interrupt the injustice to minimize pain and suffering. These are initiatives we should be prepared to take, not only as responsible citizens, but also as ethical professionals who strive to live with personal and professional consistency in our commitment to reduce mental pain and suffering. Whenever a significant injustice or crime occurs, the traumatic ramifications usually spread and ripple through many individuals and families, through various communities, and sometimes through several generations. As a result, the need for therapeutic resources to enable healing expands, which potentially serves our pocketbooks well.

Most of us probably would not hesitate to act to interrupt a blatant injustice, like a sexual assault or a terrorist attack, if we saw the opportunity to do so. However, there are many, much more subtle, social domains where we could help reduce and/or avert unnecessary injustice and trauma on an almost daily basis. In what follows, I would like to clarify several such areas where possible initiatives toward greater justice could become more visible by looking through the lens of the IPscope.

In exploring this macro level, I would like to build on the work of a philosopher, Trudy Govier (2002), who in her book on *Forgiveness and Revenge* differentiates between primary, secondary, and tertiary victimization. The primary victim is the person who has been directly wounded and personally suffered physical, psychological, and/or spiritual injuries. Secondary victims are those persons, such as family members and friends, who know the primary victim personally, care about him/her, and are deeply hurt when someone they love has been injured or traumatized. Tertiary victims are much less obvious, yet they constitute an extremely important group. They are persons who do not know the primary or secondary victims personally but who are also hurt and offended because they identify with the primary and/or secondary victims in some way. It is this tertiary group that Govier singles out for closer study.

She describes how the psychological need for vindication after being victimized typically results in an impulse to seek retaliation or revenge. Indeed, our whole justice system in the West is based on seeking retribution. Whenever we are hurt or wounded, we feel diminished, "knocked down," or demeaned in some way, and the impulse toward recovery is to strike back, retaliate, and "knock the perpetrator down" as well. This impulse to vindicate oneself is as generic for the healing of a psychological wound as the generalized physiological response of inflammation of body tissues is for the healing of a physical wound. However, when such an impulse to vindicate moves into action, further aggression often occurs, leading to escalation and/or recurrent cycles of violence, which produces more victimization and more injustice (see Figure 11.4). What is helpful to recognize is that the impulse to vindicate operates at all three levels of victimization and that initiatives to seek tertiary vindication sometimes occur remotely in time. Govier gives the example of how the ethnic cleansing of Islamic Bosnians during the 1990s war in Yugoslavia could be explained, in part, by the impulse of the Serbs to vindicate themselves as tertiary victims in relation to the atrocities committed by the Turks who invaded Serbia in the 14th century to establish the Islamic Ottoman Empire. The recent Serbs, who internalized their history and identify with their own people, experienced themselves as tertiary victims and took advantage of the social upheaval during the war to vindicate themselves of injustices from centuries past by seeking revenge against the Muslims who they associated with the historical Turks.

This phenomenon of tertiary vindication is a plausible explanation that helps account for an enormous amount of violence and injustice in the world. When we bring the IPscope to bear on these kinds of social dynamics, we can more readily recognize the pervasive societal PIPs of *collective perpetratorship coupled with collective victimization* (see Figure 11.4a) and *seeking justice and perpetrating retribution coupled with suffering injustice and seeking vindication* (see Figure 11.4b). These PIPs predict future violence perpetrated through the impulse to vindicate prior

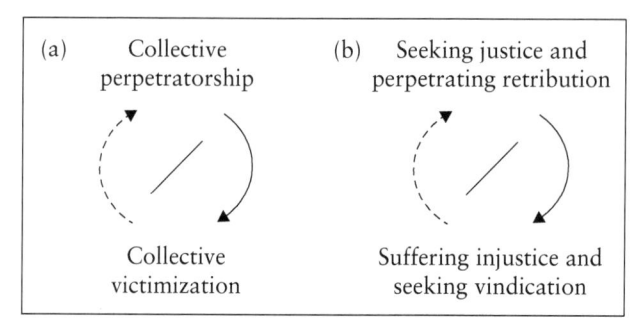

Figure 11.4 Societal PIPs producing cycles of violence

victimization and suffering. When we collapse time in our imagination, the circularity in these recurrent cycles of violence becomes more apparent. One of the main points Govier (2002) makes in her book is that in order to reduce recurrent cycles of aggression and violence, we need to find other ways to vindicate ourselves, and she proposes individual and collective forgiveness as a preferred alternative. The IPscope is also helpful here as we look for the kinds of couplings that might serve as candidate HIPs that we could seek to bring forth, such as *collective apologizing coupled with collective forgiving, acknowledging the worth of the other (individual and/or group) coupled with appreciating and acknowledging the acknowledgments publicly,* and/or *expressing regret and taking restorative action coupled with expressing appreciation and showing gratitude* (see Figure 11.5). These healing patterns would be extremely difficult to achieve yet potentially could be realized at all three levels of victimization, contributing to a broader base of overall wellness, all the way from a specific interpersonal relationship, to relationships between kinship groups, to relationships between communities, and relationships between whole nations.

In an extension of Govier's (2002) victim-focused analysis, I would like to propose differentiating primary, secondary, and tertiary levels of perpetratorship as well. The primary perpetrator is the person who directly inflicts the injury or commits the crime. The secondary perpetrators may be seen as those who participate in the planning and/or decision-making that contribute to implementing the harmful actions of a primary perpetrator. For instance, Slobodan Milosevic, the former Yugoslav leader, could be seen as a secondary perpetrator for his role in masterminding the ethnic cleansing of over 200,000 Muslims. Similarly, Osama bin Laden could be regarded as a secondary perpetrator in the 9/11 terrorist attacks on the United States. However, it is the tertiary group that is again much less obvious but very significant nonetheless. Tertiary perpetrators may be defined as those persons who collude in the injustice (knowingly or unknowingly) by espousing the same values and beliefs that support the

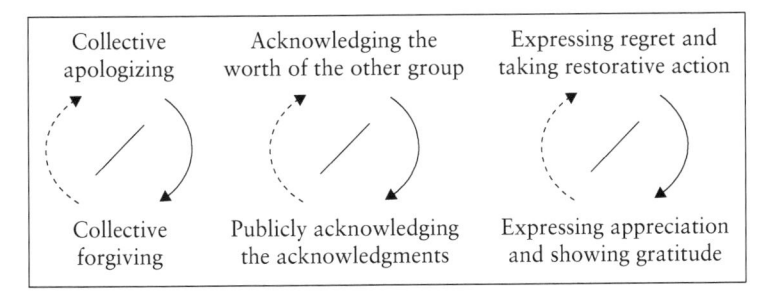

Figure 11.5 Societal HIPs promoting reconciliation

decisions and actions of the primary and secondary perpetrators. For instance, the TV news clips of crowds in the streets of Palestine immediately following the 9/11 attacks chanting "Down with America! Down with America!" demonstrate the kind of values and beliefs that would support the decisions of bin Laden and the actions of the terrorists on board the airliners. These are extreme examples to illustrate the point and I acknowledge that my explanation is a huge oversimplification of incredibly complex situations.

However, the relational dynamics of tertiary perpetration are far more common and pervasive than we like to admit. For instance, in our own backyard, the demeaning attitudes of the predominantly White Canadian population toward the Indigenous Peoples as primitive and inferior supported the decisions of our government in developing the assimilation policies of the residential school system, which when implemented wrested children away from their parents, confined them in residential schools, punished them for speaking their own language, and much worse. These actions have resulted in widespread tragic consequences that are still rippling through our communities.

Interestingly, the direction of influence regarding the three levels of perpetration appears to be the reverse of that with the three levels of victimization. Whereas primary victimization leads to secondary and tertiary victimization, it is tertiary perpetration that leads to secondary and primary perpetration of both minor and major injustices. These directions of influence can be combined and connected to clarify the dynamics of recurrent cycles of violence in our communities and cultures as illustrated in Figure 11.6. One major implication from this process is that if we carefully examine our individual and collective values and beliefs, we might be able to take some significant preventive action to reduce such recurrent cycles of injustice and violence.

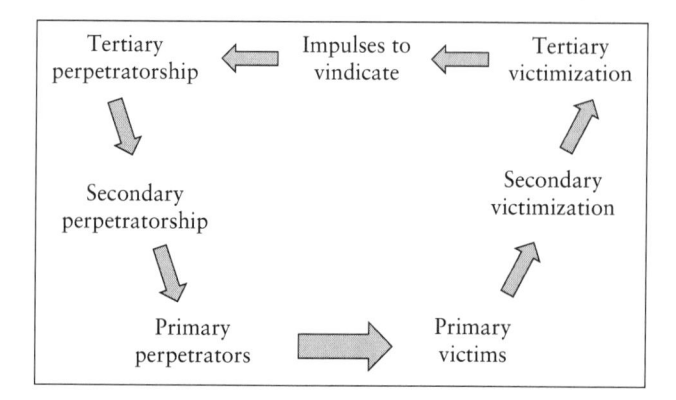

Figure 11.6 Recurrent cycles of injustice and violence

The collective values, beliefs, and practices of a group, a community, a society, or a culture become distilled into the kinds of Socio-Cultural Interpersonal Patterns (SCIPs) discussed in Chapters 6, 7, and 8 of this book. Some of these SCIPs support PIPs in certain domains at certain times, and HIPs or WIPs in other domains at other times. When we apply the IPscope lens we can better differentiate these effects and clarify the couplings that generate the stabilities that support tertiary perpetration and eventually lead all the way through to actual crimes and back to tertiary victimization (see Figure 11.6). Healing initiatives in the interaction between perpetrators and victims can sometimes be taken at the primary level, usually at the secondary level, and almost always at the tertiary level.

For instance, as we were reminded in Chapter 7, patriarchal sexism remains alive and well within families and in our culture at large. I would submit that holding sexist values and beliefs is a form of tertiary perpetration. If a major incident of male to female spousal violence is reported in our local media, and I, as a man, do not take an explicit position against such sexist injustice, I end up colluding with my violent brother by implicitly supporting the prevailing attitudes, values, beliefs, and practices that contribute to such sexist aggression. Not taking a position is taking *the position of not taking a position*, which is to support the status quo. While I may try to deny it (to myself and others), my stance of silence would then position me as a tertiary perpetrator of sexist aggression. Furthermore, insofar as the females in my life hear about the reported violence and identify with the woman who was abused, they become tertiary victims and are left feeling vulnerable. Their vulnerability and fear may lead to increased deference in relation to me as a male (in which case, I benefit from the violence of my brother) or they may enact an impulse to vindicate themselves and seek some form of overt or covert retribution, perhaps in relation to me as well. In either case, my female associates and I could also end up participating in a covert ongoing sexist PIP.

If I were to explore this situation through the lens of the IPscope, I would be more liable to search for constructive initiatives toward a HIP or WIP instead. For instance, I could explicitly acknowledge the sexist injustice, express regret that my brother engaged in such abuse, and recommit myself to respectful egalitarian values, which could lead to my female associates feeling safer, more valued as women, and appreciating me for my stance. Similar patterns of tertiary perpetration operate in relation to racism and ethnocentrism as suggested in Chapter 8. Indeed, the same is true for any form of social injustice. Thus, it is incumbent upon us, as therapists and citizens, to reflect and try to become more aware of our possible collusion in tertiary perpetration if we wish to avoid contributing to more injustices, when we could be contributing to better worlds instead.

One personal dilemma that I struggled with for many years had to do with my guilt feelings about the Holocaust. I tried to resolve this guilt in various ways, even by visiting Dachau in Germany, Auschwitz in Poland, and Yad Vashem in Israel, all to no avail. I discussed my dilemma with one of my close Jewish friends early on in our relationship and tried to apologize to him for what had happened during World War II. However, he rejected my apology on the basis of the fact that I was a very young child at the time and was not even in Europe where the atrocities took place. It was only when I understood and acknowledged my tertiary perpetratorship through my German ethnic origins that I was able to make some progress. When I subsequently expressed deep regret that it was my people that had perpetrated horrendous crimes against his people and declared a clear position against anti-Semitism, my friend was able to accept my apology, which contributed to enormous personal relief.

Ideally, patterns of healing for the dynamics of tertiary perpetratorship and tertiary victimization should be worked out and resolved at the level of collectives (i.e., by groups of people, by communities, and by nations). According to some contemporary philosophers, our global culture may be entering an "Age of Apology" (Brooks, 1999; Gibney, Howard-Hassmann, Coicaud, & Steiner, 2008), which gives me some hope that we might be beginning to create more respectful ways to address unresolved needs for vindication for those who continue to suffer victimization, not only at the primary and secondary levels, but also at the tertiary level. For instance, in 1997 on the 150th anniversary of the Irish potato famine, Tony Blair, who was prime minister of the United Kingdom at the time, read a statement expressing regret for British policies that contributed to the starvation of 1,000,000 Irish people. In 1996, F. W. De Klerk, the last South African leader of the apartheid era, apologized before the Truth and Reconciliation Commission for 40 years of "deeply mistaken" racist policies of the White supremacist government. In 2008, Kevin Rudd as prime minister of Australia made the famous "Sorry Speech" to apologize for laws and policies that led to mistreatment of Australian Indigenous Peoples. In Canada in 1998, Indian Affairs Minister Jane Stewart (under Jean Chretien) apologized to the Indigenous Peoples for decades of systematic assimilation, theft of lands, and suppression of cultures. And in 2008, Stephen Harper apologized to the Canadian First Nations for the residential school policies of the federal government.

These apologies may be seen as significant tertiary TIP attempts. By apologizing, the offending group clearly acknowledges that the offended group deserved to be treated better. This could provide some tertiary vindication that could in turn reduce the amount of victimization experienced by the offended group. An IPscopic question could then arise: What kinds of responses from tertiary victims might help transform these TIP attempts into TIP accomplishments that could enable a further move toward stabilizing HIPs? To be sure, these public apologies have been very controversial, and so far the initiatives to live the apology by taking restorative action and by adopting more respectful collective values and beliefs seem rather thin. The skeptic in me might wonder if some of these TIP attempts reflect covert PIPs masquerading as HIPs. However, such skepticism itself might contribute to a DIP of *questioning the sincerity of the apology coupled with backing away from accountability* that might deteriorate into a PIP of *criticizing the lack of sincerity coupled with exaggerating and defending thin redemptive efforts.*

I prefer to remain encouraged by these public initiatives to seek new ways to move toward some healing in larger social domains. Hopefully, within a few decades an "Age of Forgiveness" will also begin to emerge, to begin coupling with more substantive public apologies to stabilize a healing pattern of *deeper apologizing coupled with circumscribed forgiving* among us as human beings on our common planet. Enacting this HIP at many different levels in our relationships and communities could help provide a basis for more of the joyful moments alluded to by William Blake's (1793) poem, "Mutual Forgiveness of each vice, Such are the Gates of Paradise." It is not my intention to minimize or trivialize the profound challenges that would be involved in moving in this direction. For instance, I believe that placing pressure on any individual or group of victims to forgive perpetrators, when they are not yet emotionally willing or able to do so, would be tantamount to perpetrating further injustice upon those victims. Despite these complexities, my colleagues and I suspect that the IPscope holds significant potential in usefully elucidating various stabilizing (PIPs, HIPs, and WIPs) and destabilizing (TIPs and DIPs) interactional dynamics in a wide range of human relationships, including within and between organizations, institutions, neighborhoods, communities, and even nations.

In the meantime, these zooming out distinctions can already be applied within the therapy room. Proxy expressions of tertiary regret and of tertiary forgiveness can be cautiously proffered by therapists during the course of therapy and sometimes lead to powerful healing effects. When a primary perpetrator is not available or has deceased, a therapist could express tertiary apologetic regret to the victims on his or her behalf. Similarly, when the primary and secondary victims are not available or are unwilling to be involved, a therapist might be able to help ameliorate some excruciating self-loathing in a former perpetrator by extending some circumscribed tertiary forgiveness.

A macho manner of *being a man* that tyrannizes his female partner could potentially be deconstructed and reconstructed at all three levels to yield broader-based and more stable therapeutic change. For instance, conversations about alternative ways of living an identity of being a man by exploring problematic and helpful SCIPs related to gender in the culture at the tertiary level, conversations about male members of one's social network who could serve as mentors for preferred ways of behaving as a man at the secondary level, and conversations about specific encounters with one's actual partner at the primary level could all contribute synergistically toward stabilizing preferred interactions in a couple's relationship. Indeed, a whole kaleidoscope of possibilities arise when we examine difficult therapeutic situations through the lens of the IPscope.

Would it be reasonable at this point to leave it to you as a reader to exercise your own creative imagination to generate further applications?

Conclusion

If, as human beings, we could learn to live in ways that are more grounded in our social origins and become more aware of the interpersonal patterns in which we participate, chances are greater that we would spontaneously opt for more time and energy in wellness patterns rather than pathologizing ones. Living systems inherently tend to move away from pain and suffering and toward healing and wellness. Obviously, living with greater awareness of the interpersonal origins of suffering makes it easier for us to orient ourselves to move away from those origins. Is it possible that adopting IPscopic habits, and perhaps even an IPscopic lifestyle, could enable this? It seems to me that the more we look into the interpersonal space, the more likely it is that we will step into that space and take appropriate action to invite each other into preferred patterns of interaction and relationship. And when such constructive initiatives become coupled with constructive responses to become mutual invitations, our wellness becomes stabilized more regularly and for longer periods of time.

As we continue interacting in our living together, conflict and associated suffering is inevitable. This inevitability arises simply because resources are finite and because we are all so unique and different. When our differences come up against each other, we are always at risk of imposing our views/desires upon the other, who then typically feels compelled to resist, which leads to a problematic interaction and often escalation. In the end, it is usually the case that all parties involved in any major conflict become both victims and perpetrators, even though the magnitude of the injuries inflicted usually differ, and often significantly. Thus, we will always be vulnerable to slipping back into DIPs and PIPs. Hopefully, however, such slips will become increasingly transient as we learn greater competencies to initiate TIPs to recover and to resume preferred ways of living together in HIPs and WIPs. I remain cautiously optimistic that over time, as more and more people in families, communities, and cultures co-construct greater collective awareness of our interactional origins, we will become stronger and stronger in generating more mutual invitations for wellness as we journey forward in our living together.

My colleagues and I invite you as a reader to consider these possibilities seriously, discuss them in your social networks, and experiment with them in your own relationships and work. While these constructs were developed in a clinical context, they are readily generalizable, and can be applied to many domains, including our day-to-day living. We wish you well in using and extending these ideas and look forward to the possibility of you joining this conversation to add your own unique perspectives.

References

American Psychiatric Association. (2013). *Diagnostic and statistical manual of mental disorders* (5th ed.). Washington, DC: American Psychiatric Association.

Blake, W. (1793). *For the sexes: The gates of paradise.* London, UK: William Blake.

Brooks, R. (Ed.). (1999). *When sorry isn't enough: The controversy over apologies and reparations for injustice.* New York, NY: University Press.

Burnham, J. (2000). "Internalized Other" interviewing: Evaluating and enhancing empathy. *Clinical Psychology Forum, 140* (Special Edition—Working with Adults and Children), 16–20.

Cottingham, J., Stoothoff, R., Murdoch, D., & Kenny, A. (Trans.). (1991). *The philosophical writings of Descartes* (Vol. 3). Cambridge, MA: Cambridge University Press.

Emmerson-Whyte, B. (2010). Learning the craft: An "Internalised Other" interview with a couple. *International Journal of Narrative Therapy & Community Work, 8*(2), 3–21.

Epston, D. (1993). "Internalized Other" questioning with couples: The New Zealand version. In S. Gilligan & R. Price (Eds.), *Therapeutic conversations* (pp. 183–196). New York, NY: Norton.

Gibney, M., Howard-Hassmann, R., Coicaud, J., & Steiner, N. (2008). *The age of apology: Facing up to the past.* Philadelphia, PA: University of Pennsylvania Press.

Govier, T. (2002). *Forgiveness and revenge.* London, UK: Routledge Press.

Hurley, D. (2006). "Internalized Other" interviewing of children exposed to violence. *Journal of Systemic Therapies, 25*(2), 50–63.

Kaplan, A. (1964). *The conduct of inquiry: Methodology for behavioral science.* San Francisco, CA: Chandler.

Lysack, M. (2002). From monologue to dialogue in families: "Internalized Other" interviewing and Mikhail Bakhtin. *Sciences Pastorales/Pastoral Sciences, 21*(2), 219–244.

Maturana, H., & Varela, F. (1980). *Autopoiesis and cognition: The realization of the living.* Boston, MA: Reidel.

Maturana, H., & Varela, F. (1992). *The tree of knowledge.* Boston, MA: Shambhala.

Nylund, D., & Corsiglia, V. (1993). "Internalized Other" questioning with men who are violent. *Dulwich Centre Newsletter, 2,* 29–34.

Paré, D. (2001). Crossing the divide: The therapeutic use of "Internalized Other" interviewing. *Journal of Activities in Psychotherapy Practice, 1*(4), 21–28.

Tomm, K. (2003, January/February). Promoting social justice as an ethical imperative. *Family Therapy Magazine,* 30–31.

Tomm, K., Hoyt, M., & Madigan, S. (1998). Honoring our "Internalized Others" and the ethics of caring: A conversation with Karl Tomm. In M. Hoyt (Ed.), *The handbook of constructive therapies* (pp. 198–218). San Francisco, CA: Jossey Bass.

Waldegrave, C., Tamasese, K., Tuhaka, F., & Campbell, W. (2003). *Just Therapy—a journey: A collection of papers from the Just Therapy Team, New Zealand.* Adelaide, Australia: Dulwich Centre.

Appendix A
IPS COMPONENT OF THE BRIEF INTERVIEW RECORD (BIR)

1. Brief verbal description of primary current issue/concern/problem:
   ----

2. Diagram and rating of major PIP and a corresponding HIP antidote in the family:

   Coupling in the PIP   Coupling in a HIP

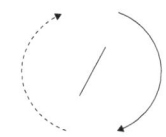

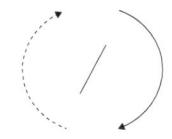

   Experienced severity of   Experienced strength of
   PIP −5 −4 −3 −2 −1 0   HIP +5 +4 +3 +2 +1 0

   Reported severity of   Reported strength of
   PIP: −5 −4 −3 −2 −1 0 X   HIP: +5 +4 +3 +2 +1 0 X
   ----

3. Diagram of a possible TIP for the therapeutic system and WIP for the family system:

   Coupling in a TIP   Coupling in a WIP

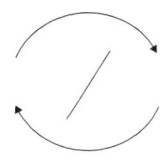

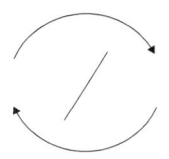

   ----

4. Use other side for additional patterns (PIPs, HIPs, DIPs, TIPs, or WIPs).

   Copyright: Calgary Family Therapy Centre

Appendix B
SEVERITY SCALES FOR PATHOLOGIZING INTERPERSONAL PATTERNS (PIPS)

EXPERIENCED SEVERITY (ES) - refers to the *therapist's experience and distinction of a PIP occurring during the interview, either between family members, or between the therapist and one or more clients.* This rating depends partly on the therapist's intervention skills.

  0. No Pathologizing Interpersonal Pattern (PIP) is distinguished in the session.
 -1. The therapist is able to interrupt the PIP with ease, and there is no recurrence in the session.
 -2. The therapist is able to interrupt the PIP with ease, but spontaneous reemergence of the pattern occurs.
 -3. The therapist is able to interrupt the PIP with vigorous effort, and there is little, if any, reemergence in session.
 -4. The therapist is able to interrupt the PIP with vigorous effort, but the PIP reemerges repeatedly.
 -5. The therapist is not able to interrupt the PIP to any significant degree during the session.

REPORTED SEVERITY (RS) - refers to the *therapist's distinction of a PIP occurring prior to the first session or between sessions based on the reports of family members and/or on reports from other sources (e.g., referral source, professionals, friends).* This rating depends partly on the therapist's listening skills.

  0. No reports that suggest the presence of the PIP.
 -1. Reports suggest occasional manifestation of the PIP without problematic consequences.
 -2. Reports suggest the intermittent manifestation of the PIP with some problematic consequences.

Copyright: Calgary Family Therapy Centre

APPENDIX B

-3. Reports suggest the frequent manifestation of the PIP with chronic stress (for at least one person).
-4. Reports indicate an escalation of the PIP resulting in significant deterioration of one or more meaningful relationships.
-5. Reports indicate an escalation of the PIP resulting in unwanted physical separation and/or physical violence toward self or others (or serious threats thereof).
X   Unable to estimate due to lack of information.

Note. Multiple PIPs may, of course, be apparent with a particular client or family. Rate the pattern(s) of greatest severity (at the end of each interview) using an abbreviated code (e.g., ES −3, RS −4).

Appendix C
STRENGTH SCALES FOR HEALING INTERPERSONAL PATTERNS (HIPS)

EXPERIENCED STRENGTH (ES) - refers to the *therapist's experience and observation of a HIP occurring during the interview, either between family members, or between the therapist and one or more clients.* This rating depends partly on the therapist's intervention skills.

0. There is no client awareness or behavioral evidence of client contributions to the Healing Interpersonal Pattern (HIP).
+1. There is prompted awareness of the possibility of a HIP but no enactment of the pattern.
+2. There is occasional spontaneous enactment of at least one component of the HIP (1–2 times).
+3. There are intermittent efforts to initiate the HIP with or without prompting (3–5 times).
+4. There are frequent efforts to initiate the HIP with or without prompting (6–10 times).
+5. There are sustained efforts to initiate and maintain the HIP with or without prompting (11 or more).

REPORTED STRENGTH (RS) - refers to the *therapist's distinction of a HIP having occurred prior to the first session or between sessions based on the reports of family members or on reports from other sources (e.g., referral source, professionals, friends).* This rating depends partly on the therapist's listening skills.

0. There are no reports of, or recollection of components of, the HIP having occurred.
+1. There is prompted awareness that some aspect of the HIP had occurred at least once.

Copyright: Calgary Family Therapy Centre

+2. There is prior awareness that some aspect of the HIP had occurred occasionally (1–2 times).
+3. Intermittent deliberate efforts were made to initiate the HIP (3–5 times).
+4. Frequent deliberate efforts were made to initiate the HIP (6–10 times).
+5. The family reports sustained awareness and enactment of the HIP (11 or more initiatives).
X   Unable to estimate due to lack of information.

Note. Multiple HIPs may, of course, be apparent with a particular client or family. Rate the pattern(s) of greatest strength (at the end of each interview) using an abbreviated code (e.g., ES +3, RS +4).

INDEX

acceptably/unacceptably familiar 84–6, 88–9, 98–9, 121, 171
Age of Apology 244
Age of Forgiveness 245
Akamatsu, N. 149
Almeida, R. 145, 149, 160–1
Alvesson, M. 213, 224
American Psychiatric Association (APA) 6, 40, 41, 44, 223, 232
Amundson, J. 43, 191
Andersen, T. 39, 70, 198–9
Anderson, H. 39, 42, 75, 200
Anker, M. 223
antidote 21, 23–4, 30–2, 68–9, 87, 119, 218–19
Aronson Fontes, L. 149, 168
Arthur, N. 187
Avis, J. 149

balanced reciprocity 148, 152, 159
Bamberg, M. 222
Barad, K. 44, 226
Barrymore, D. 148
Bateson, G. 5, 13, 36, 38, 45, 60, 122, 126, 128, 224–5
Bavelas, J. 1, 13, 45, 66, 86
Beavers, R. 1
Becvar, D. 126
Becvar, R. 126
Bernard, J. 187–9, 200, 205
Bernstein, R. J. 41
Bertalanffy, L. von 4, 13, 43
Bezanson, B. 168
Billig, M. 91
Bishop, D. 13
Blake, W. 13, 28, 245
Bohart, A. 224
Boscolo, L. 13, 91

Bowen, M. 1, 13
braiding 127, 129
Breunlin, D. 205
Brief Interview Record (BIR) 76–7, Appendix A
bringforthism 13, 78
Bronfenbrenner, U. 43, 83
Brooks, R. 244
Budge, S. 189
Burnham, J. 236
Burr, V. 146
Busch, R. 210

Campbell, W. 126, 239
Canadian Psychological Association 189, 203
Cecchin, G. 13, 91, 109
Chagnon, J. 188
Chang, J. 65, 84, 187, 194, 206
Chenail, R. 218, 226
Circular Pattern Diagramming 7, 14, 60
clarifying conversations 105, 115
Clarke, A. 215, 217
Clarke, P. 205
Coates, L. 66
Coicaud, J. 244
collaborative 75, 100, 103, 114, 121–3, 160, 171, 192, 200, 218, 221
Collins, S. 187
"complementarity marker" 19
complementary 16–17, 19, 24, 34, 46, 59–60, 67, 69, 134, 193, 232
Conrad, P. 39
Corsiglia, V. 236
Cottingham, J. 234
coupled interaction 24, 75

255

INDEX

coupled invitations 16–17, 33, 190–1, 230–1
Couture, S. 74, 79, 80, 214
covision 65, 187, 201, 203
Creswell, J. 224
Cronen, V. 50, 127
Crotty, M. 210, 224
"culture card" 174–5, 177, 180, 185
"culture clash" 172–4, 176, 178–9, 184
Cushman, P. 40, 43
cybernetics 38, 149

deconstruct 20, 25, 27, 92, 103, 105–8, 111, 114–15, 121–2, 151, 182–3, 229
DeFina, A. 222
Deleuze, J. 41, 50, 85
Denzin, N. 224
Derrida, J. 86
deShazer, S. 13, 23, 63, 84
de-skilled 62, 77, 203, 230
Deteriorating Interpersonal Patterns (DIPs) 20–1, 26, 44, 84, 89, 99, 109, 173, 175, 231, 245, 249; diagram of: 18, 27–8, 90, 92, 181, 191, 196, 198
diagnosing 6, 11, 29–30, 38–40, 42, 44, 48–9, 75, 79, 210, 222
Diagnostic and Statistical Manual (DSM) 6, 41, 44, 52, 210, 223, 232
discourses 39, 40, 50, 87, 124–8, 131, 155, 157–9, 170, 172, 215; discourses, examples of: acceptability 136, 139; certainty 135; constraint 157; duty and obligation 158; entitlement 158; expertism 139–40; financial 220; justifiable violence 136; normalcy 157; privilege 135; professionalism 174; tradition 139
discursive capture 40, 50–1, 77, 85–7, 134, 172, 230
distinctions (distinction-making) xx, xxi, 16, 22, 30, 33, 40, 44–5, 77, 226
Dolan-Del Vecchio, K. 145
Dolnick, E. 41
Dreier, O. 46–7, 49
Dulwich Centre (Australia) 239
Duncan, B. 223
Durkin, T. 160, 161

Edwards, D. 47
Eeson, J. 214, 222
Eliot, T. 168
Emmerson-Whyte, B. 236
Engel, G. 43
Engstrom, D. 46
Epstein, N. 13
Epston, D. 13, 49, 50, 63, 78, 84, 124, 236
Esposito, R. 85
ethical posture 74, 197
ethnomethodology 46–7
Evangelista, N. 198
evidence-based (practice) 39, 76, 225
"evidence-supported practice" 226
externalize 17, 30, 236

Fairclough, N. 39, 134
Falender, C. 188
Falicov, C. 148, 168
Fisch, R. 86
Fishman, H. 84
Foerster, H. von 212
Fook, J. 225
Foucault, M. xxi, 40
Frances, A. 40
Frank, A. 131, 219

Gadamer, H. 41, 121
Gaete, J. 65, 189, 200
Gale, J. 212
Gardner, F. 225
Garfinkel, H. 45, 46
general systems theory 4, 13
Gergen, K. 13, 38–41, 131, 212
Gergen, M. 13, 131
gerund 19, 67, 69
gestalt shift 9, 18, 58–9
Gibney, M. 244
Giordano, A. 205
Godard, G. 74, 214
Goffman, E. 51
Goldner, V. 38, 149
Goodyear, R. 187–8, 200, 205
Goolishian, H. 39, 42, 75
Gordon, C. 222
Govier, T. 239–41
Green, D. 212, 225
Grob, G. 40
Guattari, F. 41, 50, 85
Gubrium, J. 49

INDEX

Haley, J. 38, 84
Hampson, R. 1
Hardy, K. 168
Hare-Mustin, R. 124–5, 149, 153
Harré, R. 51, 52
Healing Interpersonal Patterns (HIPs) 7, 20–1, 30, 32, 49–50, 61, 68, 87, 145, 168, 217–19; diagram of: 28, 31, 69, 95, 98, 117, 120, 157–9, 176, 181, 194, 238, 241
Heidegger, M. 85
Heritage, J. 131, 132
Hoffman, L. 38–9, 75, 91, 149
Hoge, M. 189
Holloway, E. 187, 188
Hollway, W. 153
Holstein, J. 49
Holzman, L. 42
Honos-Webb, L. 193
Hope, T. 74
Hosking, D. 211, 224
House, R. 41
Howard-Hassmann, R. 244
Hoyt, M. 236
Huey, L. 189
Hulgus, Y. 1
Hurley, D. 236
Husserl, E. 43

Illouz, E. 144
inner and outer dialogues 199
"internalized other" 236–8
interpersonal space 7–8, 14, 17, 34, 58, 100, 134, 187–8, 206
interventive interviewing 91, 123
intuition 22, 66
IPscope 7, 18–19, 20, 44, 51, 57, 60–1, 76, 79, 190, 210, 232, 238–9

Jackson, D. 1, 13, 38, 45, 86
James, S. 168
Jenkins, A. 160
Jennings, L. 198
Johnson, L. 225
Johnson, T. 66

Kaplan, A. 230
Kärreman, D. 213, 224
Kaslow, F. 39, 225
Katz, A. 51
Keeney, B. 86, 149, 224–5
Kelso, J. 46

Kendall, S. 222
Kershaw, C. 87
Kivlighan, D. 189
Knudson-Martin, C. 144, 146–8, 151, 165
Koffka, K. 58
Korin, E. 149

Ladany, N. 189
Laing, R. 36
Lane, G. 109
Langenhove, L. van 51–2
larger social systems 32, 50, 126–8, 240–7
Larner, G. 42, 224
Latchford, G. 212, 225
Laughlin, M. 146, 151, 165
Law, J. 225
Lawrence, E. 50, 87
Lehrman-Waterman, D. 189
Levin, S. 13
Liddle, H. 205
Lincoln, Y. 224
Lock, A. 36, 43
Lyman, S. 46
Lysack, M. 236

McGoldrick, M. 148, 168
McNamee, S. 211, 224
McNeill, B. 187–8
Madigan, S. 236
Madsen, W. 42, 44, 94
Magnuson, S. 187, 190
Manicas, P. 212
Massumi, B. 40–1, 50–1, 85–6
Maturana, H. 5, 13, 17, 22, 34, 45, 57, 66, 78, 211, 229, 234–5
Merleau-Ponty, M. 44
Minuchin, S. 1, 13, 39, 84
Molinaro, M. 189
Moncrieff, J. 39
Monk, G. 170, 180
Morgan, M. 187, 189
Mudry, T. 87, 220
Murdoch, D. 234
mutual invitations 17, 246–7

Nelson, T. 190
Ness, O. 46, 189, 200
Neufeldt, S. 198
Newman, F. 42
Nichols, M. 38, 149

257

INDEX

Nicolini, D. 46, 52
Norem, K. 187, 190
Nyland, D. 236

Olson, D. 1
Orchowski, L. 198
Orlinsky, D. 198

Pantzar, M. 85
Paré, D. 57, 76, 236
Parker, L. 145
Parsons, T. 45
Pascale, C. 224–5
Pathologizing Interpersonal Patterns (PIPs) 7, 20–4, 29–30, 32, 44, 48, 51–2, 61, 66–8, 86, 99, 115–16, 124, 127–8, 143, 149, 153, 168, 174, 190, 206, 213, 232, 234, 236, 251; diagram of: 18, 20, 28, 31, 33, 69, 89–90, 95, 98, 117, 120, 155, 157–60, 176, 181, 191–2, 196, 198, 238, 240
Patton, M. 189
Pearce, B. 50, 127
Pease, B. 159
Pedersen, P. 182
Penn, P. 91
Percy, W. xix
perpetratorship 240–4
Pettifor, J. 200
phronesis 41–2, 76
Pizana, D. 184
Plano Clark, V. 224
Pollner, M. 47
postmodernism/poststructuralism 37, 39, 41–2, 52, 211
Potter, J. 47
power 5, 20, 38, 148–51, 156, 160, 187, 200, 231
practice-based evidence/research xx, 79, 125, 130, 212, 221
practitioner researcher 212, 217, 221, 226
Prata, G. 13
preferred/non-preferred interactions 48, 52, 99

qualitative research 211, 224
questions, types of: behavioral effects 68, 91; circular 61, 67–9, 86, 91, 94, 99; distinction-clarifying 91, 97; interpersonal perception 93–4; reflexive 25, 95, 120, 200, 238

Rankin Mahoney, A. 144, 147–8
Rapley, M. 39
Ray, W. 109
reflecting team 70–2
relational intercultural sensitivity 171–4, 179, 183–5
relational stabilities 1, 10, 16, 34, 44, 77, 229–30, 233, 235
research as daily practice 10, 78, 130, 213, 221–2, 224
Reusch, J. 38
Ricoeur, P. 42
Ridley, C. 180
Rober, P. 185
Rodolfa, E. 189
Rombach, M. 187, 201
Rønnestad, M. 198
Rose, N. 41
Rosenblatt, P. 43, 225
Rossiter, M. 165
Rushdie, S. 130
Russell, C. 1
Russell, R. 188

Sametband, I. 87, 107, 220
Sanders, G. 153
Santa-Barbara, J. 1
scales 77, 223, Appendices A, B, and C; severity 8, 216; strengths 8
Schatzki, T. 46–7, 49, 85–7
Scheflen, A. 44
Schiffrin, D. 222
Schön, D. 41, 76, 198, 216, 225
Schultz, S. 126
Schwartz, R. 38, 149, 205
Scott, M. 46
Scruton, J. 148
second-order perspective 33–4, 38, 75
Selvini Palazzoli, M. 13
sense making 36, 40, 43, 45–6, 51–2, 74, 89, 125, 221, 225
Sexton, T. 225
Shafranske, E. 188
Sharfstein, S. 39
Shawver, L. 75
shift from the personal to the interpersonal 29–30, 57, 63
Shotter, J. 46–7, 51, 66, 115, 123, 131, 193
Shove, E. 85, 87
Sinclair, C. 200
Sinclair, S. 170, 180
Situational Analysis (SA) 215, 220

skin-bounded individuals 14, 57, 60–1, 230
Skinner, H. 1
Skovholt, T. 198
Smith, D. 216
social construction 13, 38–9, 43–4, 131, 212, 224
social justice xxi, 2, 156–7, 168, 173–5, 180–5, 238–45
social practice(s) 46–9, 51–2, 85, 87, 147, 170
Socio-cultural Interpersonal Patterns (SCIPs) 21, 27, 29, 145, 153, 161, 165, 170, 172, 174, 178, 182–3, 223, 243; diagram of: 18, 181
Sparks, J. 223
Spencer-Brown, G. xx, 19
Sprenkle, D. 1, 187, 189
Steinhauer, P. 1
Stewart, K. 43, 191
St. George, S. 87, 215, 217, 220, 224
Stiles, W. 193
Stoltenberg, C. 187–8
Stoothoff, R. 234
stories 37, 39, 44, 128, 130–1
Strong, T. 36, 39, 43–8, 51, 74, 83–4, 87, 107, 173, 210, 212, 220
Sundet, R. 223
Sutherland, O. 43, 51, 74, 214
Szasz, T. 40

tacit interacting/understanding 47, 50, 85, 87, 216
Tamasese, K. 126, 147, 180, 182, 239
Tannen, D. 222
Tarragona, M. 57, 76
Taylor, C. 111, 146, 201
techne 41–2, 76
Teo, T. 43
The Family Centre (New Zealand) 239
"The Law of the Instrument" 230
The Qualitative Report 211
Thomas, V. 149, 168
Todd, N. 160

Tomm, K. 6–7, 14, 20, 30, 32, 36, 39, 45, 48, 60, 68, 84, 91, 95, 104, 106–7, 119–20, 123–4, 172–3, 197, 215, 217, 223, 236, 238
Toulmin, S. 41
Transforming Interpersonal Patterns (TIPs) 20–1, 24, 44, 49, 86, 121–3, 135, 161–2; diagram of: 18, 25, 28, 95, 117, 120, 157–8, 176, 181, 192, 194–5, 200; attempt versus accomplishment 103, 107; constructive 104–7; deconstructive 104–7
Tuhaka, F. 126, 239

Urban Walker, M. 87

Valentine, L. 43, 191
Varela, F. 5, 13, 17, 22, 45, 78, 211, 234–5
victimization levels 239–45
Vygotsky, L. 51

Waldegrave, C. 126, 172, 180, 182, 239
Wampold, B. 189
Waters, D. 50, 87
Watkins, C. 187–8
Watzlawick, P. 1, 13, 45–6, 86, 94
Weakland, J. 38, 86
Wellness Interpersonal Patterns (WIPs) 20–2, 29, 44, 48–50, 58, 84, 86, 214, 232; diagram of: 18, 26, 28, 95, 100, 152, 155, 192, 194–5, 197, 200, 202–3, 205
Wetherell, M. 132
Whitaker, C. 14
White, M. 13, 23, 49–50, 63, 78, 84, 87, 94, 124, 138, 222
Wilcoxon, S. 187, 190, 196
Winch, P. 41
Winslade, J. 170, 180, 187–8
Wittgenstein, L. 48, 83
Wooffitt, R. 47
Wulff, D. 87, 215, 217, 220–1, 224–5
Wylie, M. 39